Classics and Contemporaries

THE HIPPOCAMPUS PRESS LIBRARY OF CRITICISM

S. T. Joshi, *Primal Sources: Essays on H. P. Lovecraft* (2003)
S. T. Joshi, *The Evolution of the Weird Tale* (2004)
Robert W. Waugh, *The Monster in the Mirror: Looking for H. P. Lovecraft* (2006)
Scott Connors, ed., *The Freedom of Fantastic Things: Selected Criticism on Clark Ashton Smith* (2006)
Ben Szumskyj, ed., *Two-Gun Bob: A Centennial Study of Robert E. Howard* (2006)
S. T. Joshi and Rosemary Pardoe, ed., *Warnings to the Curious: A Sheaf of Criticism on M. R. James*
Kenneth W. Faig, *The Unknown Lovecraft* (2009)
Lovecraft Annual (2007–)
Dead Reckonings (2007–)

Classics and Contemporaries
Some Notes on Horror Fiction

S. T. Joshi

Hippocampus Press

New York

Copyright © 2009 by S. T. Joshi

Published by Hippocampus Press
P.O. Box 641, New York, NY 10156.
http://www.hippocampuspress.com

All rights reserved.
No part of this work may be reproduced in any form or by any means
without the written permission of the publisher.

Cover art by Allen Koszowski.
Cover design by Barbara Briggs Silbert.
Hippocampus Press logo designed by Anastasia Damianakos.

First Edition
1 3 5 7 9 8 6 4 2

ISBN13: 978-0-9814888-3-7

To
Stefan Dziemianowicz

Contents

Preface 9

I. Some Overviews 13
    Arkham House and Its Legacy 15
    The Haunted House 27
    Professionals and Amateurs 30
    Some Thoughts on Weird Poetry 36
    Bram and Bela and Mary and Boris 45
    What the Hell Is Dark Suspense? 49
    The Small Press 56

II. Classics 63
    Algernon Blackwood: The Starlight Man 65
    Arthur Machen: A Minor Classic 70
    William Hope Hodgson: Writer on the Borderland 74
    E. F. Benson: Spooks and More Spooks 76
    A. M. Burrage: The Ghost Man 80
    Herbert S. Gorman: Where Is the Place Called Dagon? 83
    Andrew Caldecott: The Well-Crafted Ghost 87
    Rescuing Shirley Jackson 89

III. Contemporaries 93
    Les Daniels: The Sardonic Vampire 95
    Dennis Etchison and His Masters 98
    Thomas Tryon: The Return of the Posthumous Collaboration 103
    Stephen King and God 106
    Peter Straub and the Blue Pencil 107
    Ramsey Campbell: Alone with a Master 109
    Clive Barker: Weird Fiction as Subversion 131
    David J. Schow: Zombies, Tapeworms, and Kamikaze Butterflies 137
    Donald R. Burleson: Enmeshed in the Bizarre 142
    Norman Partridge: Here to Stay 149

Thomas Harris: Lecter as Albatross 152
Thomas Ligotti: The Long and the Short of It 156
Michael Cisco: Ligotti Redivivus? 162
Sherry Austin: The Southern Ghost Story 165
Shades of Edgar and Ambrose 166

IV. Scholarship **171**
The Charting of Horror Literature 173
Classics and Contemporaries 183

V. H. P. Lovecraft **199**
Some Lovecraft Editions 201
The Cthulhu Mythos 207
Lovecraft as a Character in Fiction 226
Some Lovecraft Scholarship 236
    Barton L. St Armand *237*
    Donald R. Burleson *241*
    Peter Cannon *249*
    Robert M. Price *256*
    Kenneth W. Faig, Jr *259*
    Edward W. O'Brien, Jr *261*
    Robert H. Waugh *262*

Index 267

Acknowledgements 293

Preface

This volume is a selection of my reviews of horror fiction from, approximately, 1980 to 2007. The reviews have been edited slightly to eliminate repetition, and some have been combined or melded into a single "article" when they are linked by subject-matter, theme, or some other element of continuity.

I do not know how one learns the art of book reviewing except by the act of reviewing. My first review—not counting some hilariously pompous and self-important reviews of Lovecraft, Shirley Jackson, and Thomas Tryon that I wrote in the early 1970s for my high school newspaper and literary magazine—was published in the first issue of *Lovecraft Studies* (Fall 1979), and is distressingly crude and opinionated; it is not included here. As more and more critical and scholarly work on Lovecraft began to appear in the 1980s, I felt the need to evaluate it in *Lovecraft Studies*, *Crypt of Cthulhu*, and other journals. Then, as I began work on the "classic" horror writers (chiefly Arthur Machen, Lord Dunsany, Algernon Blackwood, and Ambrose Bierce) whom I would discuss in *The Weird Tale* (1990), the scope of my reviewing expanded.

It expanded still more exponentially—and unexpectedly—as a result of two fortuitously conjoined circumstances: my work on a sequel to *The Weird Tale*, entitled *The Modern Weird Tale*, begun as early as 1990 but not published until 2001; and the founding, with Stefan Dziemianowicz and Michael A. Morrison, of the review journal *Necrofile* in 1991. The need for the journal grew out of the fact that I could not accommodate very many reviews of contemporary horror writing in the review section of my journal *Studies in Weird Fiction* (1986f.), so that a separate journal was deemed necessary. The relative critical success of *Necrofile* over the eight years of its run was gratifying, and it also gave me the opportunity to review a far greater number of works—both by "classics" and by contemporaries—than I ever expected to do. Moreover, from 1995 to 2002, Darrell Schweitzer provided me the opportunity to write a substantial review column ("The Den") for *Weird Tales*. I hope that I gained some skill in the art of reviewing by this process; in particular, I like to think that I learned how to address broader literary, philosophical, social, and cultural issues in the course of a review, especially the task of linking the work under review to the previous history of supernatural fiction. The significant length we allowed for some reviews in *Necrofile* (up to 3000 words) allowed us to come at least within striking distance of our rather arrogant ambition of making the journal a kind of *New York Review of Books* of the field.

The demise of *Necrofile*—and the coincident demise of *Studies in Weird Fiction* and the near-demise of *Lovecraft Studies* (now resurrected as the *Lovecraft Annual*)—curtailed my reviewing activity significantly, although June M. Pulliam's online venture *Necropsy* allowed me to indulge in assessing some authors and titles from time to time. By this point I believe I had mellowed somewhat: my initial reviews in *Necrofile* were such that Ellen Datlow deemed me "the *nastiest* reviewer in the field" (her emphasis); probably some of the Lovecraft scholars whose work I evaluated during this period may have felt the same way. I have indeed amended some of my harsher reviews to eliminate what I now see were cheap shots, needless insults, and blundering attempts at humour; but I still feel that some of the shots I have taken at certain eminent (but, in my estimation, aesthetically barren) figures in the field were by no means cheap, and in any case they can hardly be bothered by what I have to say about them; their bank accounts are safe for the foreseeable future.

Although it appears that I have gained a reputation as a student of "classic" horror literature, I am struck by the fact that the largest section in this book is that on "Contemporaries." For many years I resisted reading the work of modern horror writers, thinking them not worthy of my attention. I still feel that a large proportion of this work is not worthy of my or anyone's attention, but I also feel that it is important that someone say so, bluntly but with intellectual cogency. The new review journal I have begun with Jack M. Haringa, *Dead Reckonings* (2007f.), will perhaps allow me to assess the work of contemporaries with whom I have sympathy—or not, as the case may be.

I have come to enjoy the task of reviewing because it allows for an intimate engagement with the text, to the point that in some of my reviews I even make note of errors of spelling and grammar. Far too much criticism—especially of the academic variety—has the disadvantage of becoming highly theoretical, so that the actual text fades to insignificance, or, worse, becomes merely a prop to "prove" the theory. Some of my reviews, of course, in their plain speaking have not been uncontroversial, and a few of them elicited interesting exchanges of correspondence that I would like to have included here; I have, in fact, revised some of my reviews in light of the rebuttals expressed by some authors or their friends and colleagues.

The notion that anyone's book reviews are "literature" in any meaningful sense of the term is laughable; indeed, I have never made the case that any of my work—monographs, articles, or reviews—enters or even approaches that lofty realm. What I do hope is that this volume might take its place with my other studies of horror literature as one person's considered judgments on the overall state of the field, on individual writers both old and new, and on the directions this untidy but distinctive literary mode has taken in the last two or three decades and may take in the decades to come. All that criticism can ever be is the exercise of critical judgment, and the validity of that judgment will rest upon the critic's sensibility, knowledge of the field, and understanding of the aims and directions of the authors being evaluated. No one critic's judgment can ever be definitive, but unless that judgment is expressed vigorously and exhaustively, it can never make a valid contribution to the broader conversation as to the scope and nature of the subject it is addressing.

—S. T. JOSHI

Moravia, New York
30 September 2007

I. Some Overviews

Arkham House and Its Legacy

To contemporary readers, all too many of whom are unaware that horror fiction did indeed flourish before the advent of Stephen King, the mystique that Arkham House continues to hold may perhaps be puzzling. Certainly, the fact that this publishing firm was founded by August Derleth and Donald Wandrei initially for the sole purpose of preserving H. P Lovecraft's work in hardcover made Arkham House a monument to the devotion that friendship can inspire. The uniformity of design that Arkham House preserved under Derleth's editorship (with the celebrated "Holliston Black Novelex" covers and their gold spine stamping) lent an added distinctiveness to its publications. But Arkham House gained its devotees chiefly by being the principal hardcover publisher of such pulp legends as Lovecraft, Clark Ashton Smith, Robert E. Howard, and Seabury Quinn, along with such of their disciples as Robert Bloch, Ramsey Campbell, and Brian Lumley. Let it pass that much of what Arkham House published would probably never have been published by other hardcover firms on the basis of its actual quality: its succession of volumes nurtured a nostalgia for the pulp magazines even among those who had never lived during the pulp era. Arkham House itself, of course, is by no means passé, although it was quiescent for much of 1996 and 1997. But over the last decade a number of other small presses have emerged to take up the slack in the wake of Arkham House's relative paucity of publications and its shift to "cutting edge" science fiction under the editorial leadership of the capable and professional James Turner.

That shift—a significant point of criticism on the part of Arkham House loyalists and devotees of weird fiction in general—was in fact never as complete as many have believed. To be sure, books by Michael Bishop, Greg Bear, Lucius Shepard, Bruce Sterling, and other young science fiction writers constituted an increasing number of the two or three books that Arkham House annually published; some of these volumes did indeed have a significant horror content, but by and large they belonged in the realm of science fiction. We tend to forget, however, that Turner also arranged for the republication of Clark Ashton Smith's best work (*A Rendezvous in Averoigne* [1988]) and issued landmark collections of the fantasy tales of Tanith Lee (*Dreams of Dark and Light* [1986]) and the horror fiction of Ramsey Campbell (*Alone with the Horrors* [1993]). And, of course, there were the textually corrected editions of H. P. Lovecraft's work produced under my editorship, along with such Lovecraftian anthologies as the revised *Tales of the Cthulhu Mythos* (1990) and *Cthulhu 2000* (1995). Even if some of Turner's other selections in the horror/fantasy field were suspect (David Case's *The Third Grave* [1981], David Kesterton's *The Darkling* [1982]), his continued nurturing of Russell Kirk and Basil Copper was noteworthy.

And yet, the gradual but inexorable shift from horror and fantasy to science fiction, under Turner's aegis, had some interesting and perhaps unexpected consequences. While each of the Arkham House publications remained impeccable both in design and in intrinsic literary quality, it is somewhat ironic that Arkham House had almost no impact upon the horror "boom" of the late 1970s and 1980s. Perhaps, indeed, it could not have; for with horror becoming a spectacularly commercial phenomenon with such best-selling writers as Stephen King, Peter Straub, Clive Barker, and Anne Rice, a small press could not possibly compete with the million-dollar advances offered by major publishers.

There is perhaps a still further irony: that "boom," which died of inanition in the early 1990s, produced relatively little work of lasting literary merit; and now that the horror market is contracting in the commercial arena, perhaps it is once again time that small-press publishers in the field take their rightful position as both the preservers of the heritage of weird fiction and the vanguards of new and pioneering work.

Have any such publishers emerged? Several candidates are certainly putting themselves forward. Ash-Tree Press has in the last few years published a substantial number of reprints of classic ghost stories, and deserves the admiration of weird fiction devotees for its resurrection of the work of A. M. Burrage, H. R. Wakefield, E. G. Swain, and others. These reprints might be seen as analogous to Arkham House's reprints of the best work from the pulp magazines; however, Arkham House was not content merely to revive older work, but actively fostered newer writing, something Ash-Tree is only now beginning to do. Moreover, the Ash-Tree Press books have extremely small print runs and are very expensive (something that does not seem to have changed even with the proprietors' move from England to Canada).

These same virtues and drawbacks also affect R. B. Russell's Tartarus Press, which—similar to August Derleth's founding of Arkham House initially for the purpose of publishing Lovecraft's work in hardcover—began life devoted to the salvaging of Arthur Machen's fugitive writings. Russell has done outstanding work in gathering Machen's uncollected or unreprinted fiction (*Ritual and Other Stories* [1992; rev. ed. 1997]; *Ornaments in Jade* [1997]), issuing some of his immense body of essays and journalism (*The Secret of the Sangraal and Other Writings* [1995]), and even promoting criticism of Machen's life and work (*Machenalia* [1990]). Lately Russell has ventured into other realms, publishing the work of the modern Welsh writer Rhys Hughes (*Worming the Harpy and Other Bitter Pills*) and editing a volume of previously unpublished stories, *Tales from Tartarus* (1995). He has also published my edition of the selected writings of the obscure nineteenth-century Irish writer Henry Ferris

(*A Night with Mephistopheles* [1997]). But, as with Ash-Tree, the extremely limited print runs of Tartarus Press books (sometimes as few as 200 copies) make Russell's enterprise virtually invisible.

There are many other worthy small presses in our field, including Kenneth Abner's Terminal Fright Publications, which should be remembered if it issues nothing other than Brian McNaughton's scintillating collection of fantasy tales, *The Throne of Bones* (1997). But perhaps the most notable small press of recent years is Fedogan & Bremer.

This company began existence in the late 1980s on a somewhat curious premise: it was consciously designed to succeed Arkham House by publishing those works that August Derleth or Donald Wandrei had, as early as the 1960s, announced for publication but never in fact issued. And yet, F&B's first "publication" was not a book but a tape recording of Lovecraft's sonnet cycle *Fungi from Yuggoth* (1986), capably read by John Arthur, although the musical background by Michael Olson is a little too obtrusive and "New Age" for my taste. Another three years passed before F&B actually issued a volume: Donald Wandrei's *Colossus* (1989). This book had indeed been announced for publication in various Arkham House catalogues, but the finished book does not duplicate Wandrei's conception for it. He had envisioned it as containing nothing more than the long story "Colossus" (1934), its even longer sequel "Colossus Eternal" (1934), and a lengthy introduction. (Wandrei had told Richard L. Tierney that there was to be a third, unpublished story as well, but whether this story was ever written is in doubt; if it was, it was not found among Wandrei's effects after his death on October 15, 1987.) Evidently the editors of the F&B *Colossus*, Philip J. Rahman and Dennis E. Weiler, found this idea too constricting, so they chose to issue a large volume containing the entirety of Wandrei's science fiction tales, gathered from his previous Arkham House volumes (*The Eye and the Finger* [1944] and *Strange Harvest* [1965]) and containing several uncollected stories as well. It was not until eight years later that F&B got around to issuing the tales of horror and fantasy for which Wandrei is best known, but that volume finally emerged under the title *Don't Dream* (1997).

These two volumes allow, for perhaps the first time, a comprehensive study of Wandrei's work as a writer of imaginative fiction. While I do not have the space here to conduct such a study, I can at least suggest some avenues for exploration. In the first place, the distinction between "horror" and "science fiction" is pretty tenuous in Wandrei's work; like his mentor Lovecraft, Wandrei was a pioneer in the fusion of these two realms. The editors of these two volumes acknowledge that in some cases the distinction is merely a matter of emphasis.

Wandrei's earliest fictional works were sketches or prose poems in the *Minnesota Quarterly*, the student magazine at the University of Minnesota.

Several of these (mostly gathered in a separate section of "Prose Poems, Essays, and Marginalia" in *Don't Dream*) are uncommonly fine, revealing a verbal witchery that would endure throughout Wandrei's literary career. But as early as 1927, when he was nineteen, Wandrei had broken into *Weird Tales* with "The Red Brain," and for the next half-dozen years that magazine would be his chief market. But when *Astounding Stories* revived under Street & Smith's ownership in 1933, Wandrei quickly switched gears and wrote a substantial number of science fiction tales that made him one of the luminaries of the pre–John W. Campbell era. These latter stories are, of course, chiefly gathered in *Colossus*, although a fair number appear in *Don't Dream*. Along the way Wandrei also broke into such rarefied markets as *Esquire* and *Argosy*.

Lovecraft believed that Wandrei possessed one of the most genuinely cosmic imaginations of any writer he knew, and certainly this is his chief distinguishing characteristic. "The Red Brain" (originally titled "The Twilight of Time") is perhaps a somewhat juvenile expression of the idea, but the tale still works for me. Even now I get a kick in reading the story's conclusion, where the only hope of halting the spread of the "Cosmic Dust" that is overwhelming all entity seems to reside in the brain of the title: "The hope of the universe had lain with the Red Brain. And the Red Brain was mad."

Then there is "Colossus," recognised as a landmark of science fiction even though it seems to raise more chuckles than thrills today. But I remain capable of suspending my disbelief at the thought of a spaceship that can "reach a maximum velocity of thousands of light-years, *per second!*" and thereby break through the known space-time continuum into another realm in which our own universe is itself but an atom. (At the same time, of course, the inhabitants of the spacecraft become as large as our universe, rendering it impossible for them ever to return to it.) "Colossus" is a story whose breadth of scope is such that it could not be encompassed within a single story, and its sequel—although no doubt inspired also by commercial considerations—thereby became a necessity.

In both his science fiction and his horror tales, Wandrei is capable of achieving certain moments of utterly unnerving terror or awe that go far in redeeming his several deficiencies—occasionally slipshod writing, clumsiness in the handling of plot sequences, wooden or unconvincing characters, and poor dialogue. Perhaps his best weird tale is "The Eye and the Finger" (*Esquire*, December 1936), a madly irrational tale in which an ordinary man returns to his cheerless apartment to find a disembodied eye on the top of his bureau and, later, a hand hanging in midair with its finger pointed directly at him. No explanation is made to account for these bizarre events; they simply occur, and the diction is so matter-of-fact that we are compelled to believe it. "The Tree-Men of M'bwa" (*Weird Tales*, February 1932) is not far behind in its depiction of individuals who have become living trees.

Wandrei's literary career was largely over by 1940. Why this is the case has never been satisfactorily explained. Richard L. Tierney's long and detailed introduction to *Colossus* offers some hints, but no more. Certainly, Wandrei's induction into the army in 1942 would not have allowed much time for creative work; but even upon his discharge in 1945 he made no effort to renew his literary career with the exception of preparing his novel *The Web of Easter Island* for publication in 1948. Of course, Wandrei was spending a great deal of time editing Lovecraft's letters (and it should be noted that the final two volumes of *Selected Letters*, appearing in 1976, seem largely to be based upon compilations by Wandrei even though they do not bear his name as coeditor), and Tierney asserts that it was Wandrei who did the bulk of the selection and editing of Derleth's fine anthology of macabre poetry, *Dark of the Moon* (1947). Over the next several years he engaged in brief stints at comic-book writing and songwriting, but only a few stories were produced.

By the 1950s, however, fortunes took a marked turn for the worse for Wandrei's family, and he was forced to spend more and more time taking care of his ailing mother and sister. The death of his brother Howard in 1956 did not help matters. In letters to Derleth, Wandrei frequently announced that he was at work on a variety of massive philosophical or aesthetic treatises, none of which were published and may not have been completed or even begun. His last work of fiction appears to have been the poignant end-of-the-world story, "Requiem for Mankind," published in Derleth's final anthology, *Dark Things* (1971).

I may note here that in 1932 and 1933 Wandrei wrote two novels in quick succession. One of them—whose original title is *Dead Titans, Waken!*—is what we know as *The Web of Easter Island*. The other—long thought to be lost—survives in manuscript as *Invisible Sun*. This latter is a mainstream novel, although with occasional fantastic elements, and contains some of Wandrei's finest and most daring writing. The manuscript for *Dead Titans, Waken!* also survives, and is markedly different from its later revision; a case could be made that it is somewhat more effective in its original form. These two novels will someday be published by F&B in one volume under my editorship.

F&B's most significant contribution to weird fiction to date is the publication of two volumes of Howard Wandrei's fiction, *Time Burial* (1995) and *The Last Pin* (1997); the first contains his horror and fantasy fiction, the second some of his detective tales. I had previously known next to nothing of Howard Wandrei aside from the fact that he was a superlatively brilliant artist and illustrator; as for his fiction, I could recall nothing save for Lovecraft's quip when he heard the title of Wandrei's "The Hand of the O'Mecca": "It sounds like an Irish Arab." Later, when Lovecraft actually read that story, he remarked in a letter to R. H. Barlow (April 20, 1935): "I'm hang'd if I don't think the kid is, all apart from his pictorial genius, getting to be a better *writer* than big bwuvver!" There is good reason to believe that Lovecraft was right.

I actually wish to consider Wandrei's detective stories first, even though they are obviously outside the purview of the weird tale. Although Wandrei initially attempted to duplicate his brother Donald's success in horror fiction and had a few items published in *Weird Tales*, by the 1930s he seemed to sense that hard-boiled mystery was where his strengths lay.

He quickly gained a foothold in both the "spicy" pulps issued by Culture Publications and the various magazines of the Trojan Publishing Corporation chain. These latter, like the spicies, wanted a lacing of sex and nudity—which also seems to have come naturally to Howard, as it rarely did to his more strait-laced brother—but, unlike the spicies, wanted no incursion of the supernatural. The result was a really admirable series of substantial novelettes written under a variety of pseudonyms. Perhaps they are not quite up to the Raymond Chandler standard—but then, whose are?

Two of the most piquant are "The Man with the Molten Face" and "League of Bald Men," which both feature a unique detective—Ferris Gerard, the mayor of the small town of Niles Park, who has suffered a horrible accident in which much of his face is mutilated. A remarkable surgical operation, using some sort of resin to take the place of his destroyed jaw, allows Gerard literally to remould his face at will and thereby conceal his identity. Implausible as this may be, Wandrei manages to pull it off. "League of Bald Men" is to my mind one of the most enthralling tales ever to come out of the detective pulps; with little alteration it could be adapted today into an exciting action film. Many of the other tales in *The Last Pin* are not far behind.

Wandrei was apparently forced by magazine requirements to throw in a certain amount of sex or sexual situations beyond the requirements of the narrative; but it is interesting to note that, according to a note by D. H. Olson, editor of the two Howard Wandrei books, "the versions of [some of the] stories reprinted here . . . are appreciably more risqué than those which were actually printed" in the magazines. Wandrei had a particular flair for describing women's costumes and overall appearance; he displays far more knowledge than most male writers do in points of clothing, makeup, and the like.

The interesting thing is that many of the stories in *Time Burial* are also of the hard-boiled type, but of course they cross the line into the supernatural. Perhaps this would not have been a surprise to the original readers of the magazines (notably *Spicy Mystery Stories*), since this mingling of detection and the weird was the premise on which these magazines were based. But reading these stories now, we gain an added thrill when we find some crime scenario veering off insidiously into the supernatural.

I do not find any moments of that clutching fear that distinguishes a few of Donald Wandrei's tales; but on the whole there can be no question that

Howard Wandrei was a notably more polished and skilful writer than his brother.

D. H. Olson's lengthy introductions to both *Time Burial* and *The Last Pin* should be singled out for praise. Although they in part cover the same ground (understandably so, since the books are designed for different audiences), they tell a compelling story of Howard Wandrei's strange life—a life that included an arrest for burglary at the age of seventeen and several years spent in a reformatory, a turbulent marriage, suspicion of wrongdoing in the later 1940s when some members of Trojan Publications were indicted for embezzlement, and an early death of cirrhosis of the liver.

I have not left myself much space to discuss F&B's several other publications, even though these other titles are somewhat uneven. There are several volumes of "Cthulhu Mythos" barrel-scrapings edited by Robert M. Price—*Tales of the Lovecraft Mythos* (1992), *The New Lovecraft Circle* (1996), and *Acolytes of Cthulhu* (2000)—not to mention Stephen Jones's anthologies *Shadows over Innsmouth* (1994) and *Weird Shadows over Innsmouth* (2005); and F&B has made another error in publishing Richard L. Tierney's disappointing Mythos novel, *The House of the Toad* (1993). But it is to be commended for issuing Karl Edward Wagner's last story collection, *Exorcisms and Ecstasies*, two collections of Hugh B. Cave's work, *The Door Below* and *Death Stalks the Night*, and books by Robert Bloch, Basil Copper, Carl Jacobi, and other standbys. On the whole, the F&B line shows careful judgment in the publication of old-time pulp material as well as newer work. It and other small presses may well be leaving commercial firms behind in perpetuating the best that our field has to offer.

After a considerable hiatus, Arkham House resumed the publication of books in late 1997. The departure of James Turner (who died suddenly and unexpectedly in 1999 just as he was developing his own imprint, the Golden Gryphon Press) appears for a time to have produced a state of confusion at Arkham House; but now, with Peter Ruber—a friend of Derleth's during the latter's last decade of life—as editorial adviser, the publishing company that August Derleth founded—and which he did not expect to survive him—is attempting to renew its claim as the preeminent small press in our field.

During the past three years Arkham House has issued (or reissued) seven books. Three of these can be dealt with briefly. The reprint of Lovecraft's *Selected Letters III* (1997), which had inexplicably been out of print for a decade and a half, was very welcome. *New Horizons: Yesterday's Portraits of Tomorrow* (1999) is an insubstantial but entertaining science fiction anthology that August Derleth had conceived, apparently in the early 1960s, but never issued; it has been capably assembled, with introduction and biographical notes, by Joseph Wrzos. My own *Sixty Years of Arkham House* (1999) is an exhaustive updating of Derleth's *Thirty Years of Arkham House* (1970), with a complete author and title index to every Arkham House, Mycroft & Moran, and Stanton & Lee publication. *Lovecraft Remembered* (1998) is Peter Cannon's superlative compilation of memoirs of Lovecraft, ingeniously arranged and intelligently annotated. The three other books require more extended commentary.

Robert Bloch's *Flowers from the Moon and Other Lunacies* (1998) is a volume of uncollected stories (mostly dating from the 1930s and 1940s) edited by Robert M. Price. This is, decidedly, a very mixed bag—there are good reasons why Bloch himself did not reprint some of these tales in his own collections when he was alive. But Price has found some gems that deserve our attention: the title story, a bizarre horror/SF amalgam, with even a little hard-boiled mystery mixed in; "Be Yourself," a typically Blochian mixture of humor and horror; the early tale "The Dark Isle" (1939), almost an echo of a Robert E. Howard sword-and-sorcery tales, albeit with Romans rather than barbarians; and "Black Bargain" (1942), perhaps Bloch's finest Cthulhu Mythos tale, fusing a clipped, hard-boiled prose with ruminations on the baleful effects of a spell from *De Vermis Mysteriis*. Price's brisk and scintillating introduction, full of a wordplay that Bloch himself would have enjoyed, is itself almost worth the price of admission.

Perhaps the most interesting volume published by Arkham House during this period is *Dragonfly* (1999), a first novel by Frederic S. Durbin. At a minimum, it is a testimonial that slushpile submissions do, on rare occasions, make it into print. We are here introduced to a ten-year-old girl, nicknamed Dragonfly, who, in falling down the laundry chute of her home, stumbles into a huge and complex fantasy world called Harvest Moon beyond or underneath the basement. The premise sounds rather like C. S. Lewis's *The Lion, the Witch and the Wardrobe*, but Durbin's Harvest Moon is a much darker place, presided over by the evil Samuel Hain who, with numerous scoundrelly cohorts, literally feeds off other people's pain and is seeking to force himself into our world. Dragonfly gathers her own set of offbeat sidekicks to foil their efforts. As a horror-fantasy amalgam, *Dragonfly* is a marked success. Durbin is gifted with a prodigious fantastic imagination—indeed, perhaps a bit too gifted: after a time the endless succession of bizarre events begins to weary the reader through sheer surfeit. Durbin will need to be a bit more disciplined in the use of fantastic imagery; sometimes less really is more. But the verve, panache, and assurance with which *Dragonfly* is written make us marvel that it could be a first novel; Durbin is a "find" in whom Arkham House can rightly be proud.

I have one further reservation on *Dragonfly*, however, and that concerns the increasing frequency of its mentions of God, prayer, and the like toward the end. At one point a character blithely affirms, in regard to some relatively minor event: "That was the hand of God." This is, I think, an aesthetic and philosophical mistake. It is too easy for the fantasy writer—who is, after all, himself a kind of god of his imagined universe—to attribute some event or incident to God; it makes the reader suspect that the author didn't have the cleverness to account for the incident in any other way. It also makes the reader wonder where God was during the several more central episodes of the novel where Dragonfly and her mates could have used His assistance. Later we are soberly asked to accept the myth of the Tower of Babel as a literal explanation for the proliferation of human languages throughout the world. Durbin is at perfect liberty to believe whatever religion he wishes, but he would be well advised to keep it out of his writing. The last thing one would wish to see is a writer of Durbin's undoubted talents restricting his imagination to the narrow confines of some religious dogma.

Arkham's Masters of Horror (2000) is the most challenging and provocative volume published by Arkham House in many years. Edited by Peter Ruber, it gathers stories or other works by twenty-two of the leading Arkham House authors over the first thirty years of its existence, along with lengthy biographical/critical notes on the authors. Ruber's prose is, I fear, somewhat slipshod, and much of this book appears to have been written and compiled in considerable haste. More than any other volume published recently by Arkham House, it could have benefited from a good copy editor. But it suffers greater problems than this.

Ruber's manifest intention is to defend August Derleth on many fronts. There is something charming in this endeavour—it is always good to see friends stand up for each other, especially when one of them isn't around to defend himself; but Ruber's defence—as embodied in a lengthy introduction, "The 'Un-Demonizing' of August Derleth"—seems curiously off the mark. No one in his right mind would deny that Derleth spent a considerable portion of his own money in keeping Arkham House afloat for its first three decades. As to the actual success—either aesthetic or commercial—of the books that Derleth chose to publish, the record is much more mixed: a good many literarily outstanding books appeared, but Arkham House also published a number of books (usually by pulp writers with whom Derleth was acquainted) that do not speak well of Derleth's critical judgment; other books (some of them quite respectable on an aesthetic level) remained in print for many years, although that merely indicates the radical divergence of genuine literary merit and popular appeal.

But Ruber fails to come to grips with the true sources for many critics' complaints about Derleth, most of them focusing around his handling of the Lovecraft material. These complaints centre around four points: (1) his careless editing of Lovecraft's texts, resulting in thousands of textual or typographical errors in the editions of the 1960s; (2) his ruthless (and possibly illegal) control of the Lovecraft literary rights; (3) his dissemination (by way of books, articles, and introductions) of highly misleading views of Lovecraft the man and writer, specifically relating to the "Cthulhu Mythos," which was largely Derleth's own invention; (4) his grinding out of those truly awful "Cthulhu Mythos" pastiches (including the deceitful "posthumous collaborations" with Lovecraft), which may well have "kept Lovecraft's name alive" during the 1940s and 1950s but also ended up casting disrepute upon Lovecraft's own work. Ruber never discusses any of these points—although some of them are alluded to in a long letter by Stefan Dziemianowicz quoted by Ruber—and therefore his attempt to "undemonise" Derleth is incomplete. Some defence could possibly be made on these issues (and, indeed, has been made recently by John D. Haefele), but the fact that Ruber does not even address them reveals a strange oversight as to the true sources of Derleth's current unpopularity in certain circles.

Ruber states repeatedly that Derleth was forced to publish Lovecraft's works himself when mainstream publishers like Scribner's refused to do so. Since Ruber has paid no attention to my discussion of this point in *H. P Lovecraft: A Life* (1996), and since it gets to the very heart of Derleth's founding of Arkham House, it may be worth summarising my arguments. Let us consider the precise wording of Derleth's own comment on the submission of the immense *Outsider and Others* to Scribner's: "Since Charles Scribner's Sons were then my publishers, I sent the manuscript to them. They were sympathetic to the project and recognized the literary value of Lovecraft's fiction; but in the end they were forced to reject the manuscript because the cost of producing so bulky a book, combined with the public's then sturdy resistance to buying short story collections and the comparative obscurity of H. P. Lovecraft as a writer, made the project financially prohibitive" (*Thirty Years of Arkham House*). Is it not clear from this that, had Derleth submitted a smaller book of Lovecraft's best stories, Scribner's would have been much more receptive? Only six years after publication of *The Outsider and Others*, Derleth did exactly that in assembling Lovecraft's *Best Supernatural Stories* (1945) for the World Publishing Company—an edition that sold *more than 67,000 copies in hardcover in a year and a half*, an incredible figure for the time. It is safe to say that a volume of this kind published by Scribner's—a far more prestigious firm than World—would have made a huge difference in Lovecraft's recognition, and perhaps in the course of weird fiction as a whole. But Derleth was so fixated on publishing *The Outsider and Others* as he had originally compiled it that he was unable to compromise on this vital point.

The overriding problem with Ruber's whole account is its parochialism—not merely focusing entirely on Derleth, but failing to contextualise the history of weird fiction within the general literary trends of the period. Ruber speaks blithely of the "legitimization of genre fiction" engendered by the pulp magazines in the 1920s, when the very opposite occurred: the existence of the pulps led to the ghettoising of the genres of mystery, fantasy, horror, and science fiction, as these genres disappeared almost entirely from mainstream magazines. It is telling that no writer except Lovecraft and Ray Bradbury has emerged from the weird fiction pulps to gain a genuine foothold in American literature; Clark Ashton Smith and Robert E. Howard are considerably to the rear, and Seabury Quinn, E. Hoffmann Price, and other hacks are not even on the map, nor do they deserve to be. (Derleth has a small niche for his mainstream work, but not for his weird work.) It is a plain but depressing fact that the overwhelming majority of the material published in the pulps—weird, detective, science fiction, mystery, or what have you—was subliterate rubbish that deserves the oblivion that has overtaken it. Arkham House contributed, in its small way, to this ghettoisation: after his first several publications garnered hostile or condescending reviews in the mainstream press, Derleth refused to send out review copies of Arkham House books to standard newspapers and magazines (except to sympathetic reviewers such as Vincent Starrett), making these books virtually invisible in the general literary community.

Ruber's biographical notes on the authors he covers tend to be harsh, dogmatic, and intolerant—compounded, in some cases, by an inadequacy of research that results in numerous errors large and small. Ruber chides the Derleth-haters for failing to conduct "serious research" on their subject; but Ruber's own work is subject to much the same criticism, especially in regard to Lovecraft, Smith, and other figures, and his comments are on occasion scarcely above the level of the fan criticism he excoriates. Their only worthy feature is the abundance of quotations from Derleth's unpublished letters, which are unfailingly crisp, lively, and pungent ("The trouble with —————— is that he's a dumb bastard"). Arkham House or some other enterprising publisher should certainly consider a volume of Derleth's selected letters.

The worst of the biographical notes is the one on Lovecraft, which is crude to the point of caricature. Ruber (as did L. Sprague de Camp) continually calls Lovecraft a "schizoid personality"; but given that Ruber is not a psychiatrist and that, even if he were one, he never had the chance to psychoanalyse Lovecraft, the remark is only indicative of Ruber's profound failure to understand Lovecraft's mentality. Also like de Camp, Ruber seems to regard Lovecraft's unprofessional stance as an inherent failing. To be sure, it was a very different stance from that of the resolutely professional August Derleth, but (aside from Lovecraft's immense superiority as a weird writer, and as a thinker, to Derleth) it is very largely Lovecraft's aesthetic integrity—his refusal to sell himself out to commercial or pulp markets—that has ensured the literary recognition of his work. No one is writing dissertations on E. Hoffmann Price or Seabury Quinn.

Ruber speaks derisively of the large quantity of criticism, both biographical and critical, devoted to Lovecraft in the past two or three decades; certainly, he seems to have read little of it himself, if the errors peppering his account are any indication. One example among many: "'The Dunwich Horror' was reportedly so gruesome for its time that readers [of *Weird Tales*] and censorship groups filed complaints with the magazine." In fact, this incident pertains to the publication of C. M. Eddy's "The Loved Dead" (revised by Lovecraft) in the May–June–July 1924 issue. Ruber also claims that when, in New York, Lovecraft lacked money he "simply sold some of his furniture and books." This never happened. Ruber then makes the outrageous claim that Lovecraft, in his final years, was "perfectly at ease letting his aunt, Mrs. Gamwell, pay for the roof over his head out of the small income she had." This is a pure fantasy. Lovecraft had his own portion of the inheritance from his grandfather, as well as a small mortgage in the western part of the state, not to mention his work as a revisionist and ghostwriter; these, rather than his sparse sales of professional fiction, were the sources of Lovecraft's income—he never borrowed any money from his aunt, who herself was unemployed and living off her meagre inheritance.

Ruber admits that he has not even read Lovecraft's complete fiction, so it is hardly surprising to find him making the astounding claim that "since so much of [Lovecraft's] work was derivative of the past and firmly rooted in the tradition of Edgar Allan Poe, it cannot be said that his stories were experimental—or that he brought any true innovation to the genre." Can Ruber really be unaware of Lovecraft's pioneering amalgamation of horror and science fiction in his later work—an innovation that influenced generations of writers in both genres, from John W. Campbell to Arthur C. Clarke to Stephen King to Ramsey Campbell? It would appear that Ruber is intent on demoting Lovecraft as an indirect means of vaunting Derleth; but to do so by uttering falsehoods about Lovecraft does not seem a very effective means to accomplish this end.

Ruber seems to have a particular problem with authors who didn't exhibit the maniacal dynamism of Derleth. Hence, Lovecraft "was virtually without ambition and pathetically idled away most of his waking hours writing letters"; Clark Ashton Smith was "a lazy and unambitious person"; Donald Wandrei led an "unfulfilled" life—presumably because he didn't write more stories. Who is Ruber to cast these imperial judgments on the personal lives of authors he does not understand or sympathise with? If Lovecraft "idled away" his time writing letters, that was his prerogative: maybe he *liked* writing letters. All that the lazybones Smith accomplished was to produce about a thousand poems (including some of the finest poetry written in his century), 130 or so short stories or novelettes, hundreds of paintings and sculptures, and sundry other things. Ruber, for his part, can't help tallying up the appalling amounts of subliterate trash produced by his favored pulpsmiths. ("Arthur J. Burks was the consummate professional pulp story writer; he could write any type of story to order at a moment's notice.") Quantity production is not, in itself, admirable. Smith's *The Hashish-Eater* or Lovecraft's "The Shadow out of Time" is, aesthetically, in itself worth more than the collected charlatanries of Seabury Quinn. You would never know it from Ruber, but there are higher literary values than merely the ability to write an "entertaining" story.

As for the actual contents of the anthology, Ruber is hampered by his need to find contributions by his "masters" not previously included in Arkham House books. As a result, many trivial and ephemeral items are included. Clark Ashton Smith's two-page Arabian Nights tale, "Prince Alcouz and the Magician," is so slight that it is immediately forgotten after it is read. Among the British authors published by Arkham House, Ruber made the error of choosing the mediocre H. Russell Wakefield (largely because Ruber himself discovered a mass of unpublished Wakefield stories at Arkham House) rather than such superior writers as Algernon Blackwood or Lord Dunsany. There are unpublished stories by David H. Keller and by Derleth and Mark Schorer, but they don't amount to much. The stories by E. Hoffmann Price, Arthur J. Burks, Seabury Quinn, Carl Jacobi, and many others are pure hokum. Ramsey Campbell's "Property of the Ring" is far from being his best story; but, alone in the volume (with, of course, the exception of Bradbury's classic "The Small Assassin"), it actually deals with the genuine emotions of real human beings, rather than the conventionalised emotions of stick figures. If one did not have independent knowledge of the genuinely meritorious work of most of these writers, one would never know from the contents of this book that they were "masters" of anything but hackwork and mediocrity.

If Peter Ruber plans to continue being Arkham House's editorial adviser, he had better give up his devotion to pulp rubbish—or, at any rate, cease to recommend its republication—and focus on truly sound weird literature, whether of the past or of the present. Only in that way will Arkham House recapture its position as the flagship small press in our field.

The Haunted House

It is difficult to believe that Peter Haining's *The Mammoth Book of Haunted House Stories* (Carroll & Graf, 2000) is "the first major anthology of the best tales about haunted houses," as is announced on the back cover; but as a matter of fact I cannot think of any significant predecessor on this exact theme. There may, however, be a reason for this: it is possible that canny anthologists have realised that a book—especially a book of this size—entirely about haunted houses presents daunting problems of monotony and tedium that are not easily overcome. Veteran anthologist Peter Haining has stepped in where others have feared to tread; but the job he has done can at most be called adequate.

If a haunted house story is one in which something odd happens in a spooky house or building, then the difficulty of coming up with enough interesting variants of this root conception does indeed seem formidable. Although Haining has divided his volume into six apparently discrete subsections, the distinctions between them seem nebulous at best. Haining has also chosen to spread his net over a wide chronological range, and here his results are more satisfactory: we are treated to tales as early as Bulwer-Lytton's classic "The Haunted and the Haunters" (1859) as well as to stories published only a few years ago. One supposes, however, that Haining could have done even a bit better in this regard. He is certainly well aware that the Gothic novels of the late eighteenth and early nineteenth centuries focused far more on the "haunted castle" than on any other topos; and it could legitimately be maintained that all three of the early classics of Gothic fiction—Radcliffe's *The Mysteries of Udolpho* (1794), Lewis's *The Monk* (1796), and Maturin's *Melmoth the Wanderer* (1820)—are haunted house stories in essence. Possibly Haining decided not to include that potent horrific fragment, "Sir Bertrand" (1773) by Anna Letitia Barbauld, because it was already in his fine *Gothic Tales of Terror* (1972); but it would certainly have lent an even greater chronological range to his volume. And did he exclude such of Poe's masterworks as "Metzengerstein" and "The Fall of the House of Usher" because they are too well known? If so, what about the inclusion of "The Haunted and the Haunters," certainly as hoary an anthology chestnut as any one can think of? (That story, I should mention, holds up surprisingly well on rereading.)

Haining faces another problem in the assembly of his book: the inclusion of enough stories that can actually be termed "haunted house" stories. In all honesty, a good many of the tales in this book cannot be so classified. Many of them are "ghost stories" (using that term in its narrow sense—a story involving, or suggesting the involvement of, a ghost) and nothing else. The mere fact that a ghost happens to manifest itself in some dwelling or other does not make a story a "haunted house" tale; after all, the ghost has to go *somewhere*, and in many cases a house is the most logical place.

And yet, whether they actually belong in a volume of this kind, many of the tales are good reads. I have mentioned "The Haunted and the Haunters" (although one wishes that Haining had included the important subtitle, "or, The House and the Brain"), a tale that fuses intellectual substance with a clutching horrific atmosphere. Other old specimens are similarly rewarding. Charlotte Riddell's "The Old House in Vauxhall Walk" and Ralph Adams Cram's "No. 252 Rue M. le Prince" offer richly textured prose and that leisurely but gradually intensifying narration typical of Victorian writers, both British and American. (A much later story, Basil Copper's "The Grey House," offers these same virtues, and shows what a charming throwback to an older tradition its author is.) Of stories from the early to mid-twentieth century, L. P. Hartley's "Feet Foremost" may be worth singling out, although Robert Bloch's little-known "House of the Hatchet" offers an aggressively American tough-guy cynicism in sharp contrast to the elegance and refinement offered up by the British writers who predominate in this volume. M. R. James's "Lost Hearts" is, to my mind, not at all a haunted house story, but it one of his more delightfully nasty ventures. In a few cases, however, it appears that Haining has included a tale merely for its illustrious author, as with Virginia Woolf's brief and inconclusive prose-poem "A Haunted House." A later specimen, Fay Weldon's intolerably precious "Watching Me, Watching You," is of this same sort. Weldon has made herself a laughing-stock by writing a novel commissioned by Bulgari, the jewellery firm; and this tale emphatically underscores her sour-grapes remark that she wrote the novel because she knew she would never win the Booker Prize anyway. On the basis of this story, she certainly does not deserve to.

The contemporary selections are on the whole well chosen. Far the best of the lot is Ramsey Campbell's magnificently evocative "Napier Court," in which his nightmarish, hallucinatory prose is used both for establishing the horrific scenario and for laying bare the character of the hapless woman who serves as the narrative's focus. Ian Watson's "Happy Hour" is a grim, gratingly modern tale that manages to fuse ancient horror with modern technology. Haining has, however, horned in James Herbert under false pretences, as "The Ghost Hunter" is nothing more than an ineptly edited excerpt from Herbert's novel *Haunted* (1988).

Haining has done well to unearth relatively rare specimens as well as authors who are either little-known or not known for their contributions to weird fiction. I would, for example, never have guessed that romance writer Norah Lofts had written any horror tales, and her "Mr Edward" is an able piece of work. Richard Dehan is, to me, entirely unknown. In fact, this is the pseudonym of a woman writer from Ireland, Clotilde Mary Graves, who published several novels in the early twentieth century, described by Haining as "humorous novels and stories of witchcraft and pagan religions." Similarly, Louisa Baldwin (1845–1925) is a Victorian writer who produced at least one collection of weird tales, *The Shadow on the Blind* (1895); and, on the basis of the story from this collection included herein, "The Real and the Counterfeit," the entire volume would appear to be worth reprinting by one of our diligent small-press publishers of "classic" ghost fiction.

In other ways, however, Haining's editorial skills are not quite up to standard. Even if we omit his brief and frivolous introduction—in which we are asked to believe that he himself lives in a haunted house—his biographical notes on the authors he has included contain numerous sins of omission and commission. The American writer Mary Eleanor Wilkins Freeman is referred to as Mary Eleanor Freeman. Ralph Adams Cram's classic collection of weird tales, *Black Spirits and White* (1895), is dated to 1885. Hugh Walpole's most notable contribution to the weird—*Portrait of a Man with Red Hair* (1925)—is omitted from his biographical note. Ramsey Campbell's *The House on Nazareth Hill* (1996)—in my estimation the best haunted house novel ever written, surpassing even Shirley Jackson's *The Haunting of Hill House*—is mentioned neither in his biographical note nor in the appendix, "Haunted House Novels: A Listing." In most of the notes, no information is supplied on the original publications of the stories in question; sometimes this information can be clawed out of the acknowledgements for copyrighted works, but for works in the public domain we are left helpless.

But perhaps these are mere cavils. No one expects scholarly rigour from Haining (although, as a matter of fact, *Gothic Tales of Terror* contained much ampler and more accurate biographical notes than are presented here) or from this "Mammoth Book of . . ." series, and we should perhaps be content that an ample supply of entertaining weird work has been resurrected from the books and periodicals of the past century and a half. I again maintain that a certain element of monotony and repetition is inherent in a collection of this kind, so that it is best not to read this volume all in one go; but as a book to dip into from time to time, especially in front of a cosy fireplace when a chill rain is descending, one could hardly ask for more.

Professionals and Amateurs

There are, perhaps, three ways of evaluating a book like Brad Leithauser's *The Norton Book of Ghost Stories* (W. W. Norton, 1994): 1) on the basis of what is included; 2) on the basis of what is *not* included; and 3) on the basis of the editor's introduction. For various reasons I will use all three methods.

I have no idea why Mr Leithauser was asked to edit this anthology. I have not read a word of his fiction or poetry, but have it on good authority that relatively little of it is weird or supernatural. He tells us in his introduction that he has "long found it [the ghost story] a particularly lush and verdant site" and, later, that he has "immersed [himself] for some time in the literature of the supernatural"; this may lead the innocent reader to fancy that Leithauser is some sort of authority in the field, but I think it will become abundantly evident that he is anything but that. First of all, I am not even sure that Leithauser understands the whole purpose of weird fiction. Toward the end of his introduction he orates:

I've occasionally been asked, by someone who has heard that I was assembling this anthology, whether I myself believe in ghosts—to which I've replied, less facetiously than might first appear, "Everybody does." I can't believe any of us, if we dig deep enough in our psyches, is utterly free of a suspicion that the dead continually attend the living.

Well, this may make a nice back-cover blurb, but that's about all. It is true that 60% of the people in this country believe in angels, but I don't imagine that very many of them are going to read this upscale volume. Lovecraft settled this matter of "belief" long ago:

> The real *raison d'être* of [weird] art is to give one a temporary illusion of emancipation from the galling and intolerable tyranny of time, space, change, and natural law. If we can give ourselves even for rather a brief moment the illusory sense that some law of the ruthless cosmos has been—or could be—invalidated or defeated, we acquire a certain flush of triumphant emancipation comparable in its comforting power to the opiate dreams of religion. Indeed, religion itself is merely a pompous formalisation of fantastic art. Its disadvantage is that it demands an intellectual belief in the impossible, whereas fantastic art does not. (Letter to Helen Sully, 28 June 1934.)

That contrast between fantastic art and religion is critical, for it shows that Lovecraft had independently arrived at I. A. Richards's distinction between intellectual and aesthetic belief, a distinction on which this entire literary mode rests. Very few writers of supernatural fiction believe in the supernatural, and relatively few readers do as well. In most work of this sort—work, that is, that goes beyond mere shudder-mongering—the supernatural is symbol, metaphor, allegory, or (as Lovecraft would say) imaginative liberation from the mundanely real.

Most of Leithauser's introduction is a sort of termpaperish comparison and contrast of Henry James and M. R. James—the latter of whom Leithauser rather egregiously refers to as "Montie." (He defends this usage by saying that all James's friends called him that—but I fear that you're no friend of his, Brad.) The chief distinction Leithauser sees in the two writers is that M. R. wrote "plot ghost stories" while Henry wrote psychological ones. This is a singularly infelicitous way of saying that, in M. R., the weird phenomena have preeminence and are generally supernatural, whereas in Henry's work the supernatural, if it comes into play at all, is chiefly a means for the exploration of character. Leithauser tries not to be prejudicial in his formulation of this distinction, but his later admission of his pronounced preference for the psychological form may account for many of the anomalies in this book.

The two Jameses are the only ones who are represented by four stories each. The M. R. selections are unexceptionable: "Casting the Runes," "'Oh, Whistle, and I'll Come to You, My Lad,'" and "Count Magnus" are certainly three of James's best tales, although I think Leithauser has erred in including the windy and tedious "Mr. Humphreys and His Inheritance," which James himself admitted was written to "fill up" his second volume of ghost stories. I will be charitable enough to assume that Leithauser has actually read through *The Collected Ghost Stories of M. R. James,* even though all four stories are taken from his first two of James's collections; but James's work reveals a rapid drop in quality and substance even after *Ghost-Stories of an Antiquary* (1904), so perhaps this is not an anomaly.

As for the four stories by Henry—"The Romance of Certain Old Clothes," "The Friends of the Friends," "Maud-Evelyn," and "Sir Edmund Orme"—I find it difficult to speak kindly. It has been a long time since I read the collection first published in 1949 as *The Ghostly Tales of Henry James* and reissued in 1980 as James's *Stories of the Supernatural*; but I cannot recall ever being so disappointed by a big name before. "The Romance of Certain Old Clothes"—an early story published when James was twenty-five—is curiously wooden and stiff, and every plot development (including the supernatural denouement) is utterly predictable. "The Friends of the Friends" is, by contrast, a late work; this intolerably verbose and mincing tale confirms that old witticism about James's three styles—James the First, James the Second, and the Old Pretender. In my humble opinion the other two tales don't amount to much either.

It is now time to make some forays into the omissions from this book and their possible motivations. Leithauser proclaims with lofty disdain that there is considerable rubbish in the genre of the ghost story (he cannot bring himself to say that there is just as much rubbish, proportionately, in mainstream fiction), and that he has failed to include certain hallowed names because their actual work is not commensurate with their reputations. "Many an illustrious writer, justly renowned for accomplishments in mainstream genres, has stumbled when attempting a ghost story; not surprisingly, it calls for talents that are exacting, narrow, and quirky." Leithauser will not be pleased to note that this was exactly my view after reading *The Norton Book of Ghost Stories,* which indeed is largely made up of "mainstream" writers who dallied (quite unsuccessfully, to my mind) in the weird; and, of course, Leithauser's formulation evades the whole question (which he never addresses anywhere in his introduction) of what to do with those writers who did in fact specialise in the weird, a group about whom he seems to know next to nothing. Leithauser doesn't name very many names of those of whom he disapproves, but he does rattle off Sir Walter Scott, the Brontës (?), Dickens, Gaskell, Cather (??), Bierce, Hardy, Wells, and Walter de la Mare.

Pardon my saying so, Mr Leithauser, but you haven't the faintest idea what you're talking about. The Henry James stories are the only representatives of nineteenth-century material we have. This does not disturb me overly: one assumes that Poe was excluded because he really did not write any ghost stories;

I am sad that there is nothing of Le Fanu's (ever heard of Joseph Sheridan Le Fanu, Mr Leithauser?), whose "Green Tea" is as psychological and disturbing as one could have wanted. Scott's excursions into the weird still give me a kick and are not nearly as antiquated as Leithauser believes, but this is a small point. As for the Brontës, I don't know what short work Leithauser could have in mind; surely he cannot possibly think *Wuthering Heights* is not a masterwork of both weird and mainstream fiction. As for Bierce, if Leithauser cannot perceive both the literary artistry and the shudders to be found in "The Death of Halpin Frayser," then he stands self-convicted of inferior taste and judgment. (Whether the supernatural entity in the story is a ghost as such or a zombie or something else altogether—or, indeed, whether there is anything supernatural in the story at all—is immaterial; as I shall examine below, Leithauser feels no obligation to include only "ghost stories" in the strictest sense of the term.) Perhaps Bierce's style is not quite as suave and highbrow as that of the other writers in this book (Leithauser shows a marked preference for slickness of a rather effete British variety), but I think his dark, chilling work lingers in the mind far longer than much of what Leithauser has amassed.

The omission of Walter de la Mare is cavernous. Leithauser must be simply deficient in sensibility if he cannot find in "A Recluse," "The Tree," or half a dozen other tales in *The Riddle* and *The Connoisseur* as sensitive an approach to the psychological ghost story as could be imagined. De la Mare was, along with L. P. Hartley, Oliver Onions, and Robert Aickman, instrumental in the transmutation of the (M. R.) Jamesian supernatural ghost story into the psychological ghost story, and his use of this mode for the delicate portrayal of character is unexcelled by any, Henry James not excepted.

Leithauser's evident attempt to avoid anthology chestnuts is a curiously mixed affair. He has gone ahead and included Oliver Onions's very familiar "Beckoning Fair One," a magnificent tale to whose reprinting no one could object; but he also includes Saki's "Open Window," a cheap trick story that has already appeared too many times. If Leithauser had wanted a sardonic ghost story of this kind, he would have been better off reprinting John Collier's "Back for Christmas" or "De Mortuis." (Ever heard of John Collier, Mr Leithauser?) In seeking to avoid using W. F. Harvey's well-known "Beast with Five Fingers," Leithauser presents us with "The Clock," an insubstantial tease of a story. Most curious of all, Leithauser includes Shirley Jackson's "The Tooth," which is not by any stretch of the imagination a ghost story, although it is "psychological." My admiration for Jackson (and this story) is high, but it is a pity that Leithauser did not evidently take the trouble to look beyond *The Lottery* and consult Jackson's posthumous collection, *Come Along with Me* (1968), which has the haunting tale "The Lovely House" (also titled "A Visit"), a story that is at least closer to the ghost story in atmosphere.

Many other items in this volume prove, to my mind, that mainstream writers are on the whole quite ill-equipped to handle the weird. "Pool Girl" by the British writer Elizabeth Taylor is a poignant tale of a young governess beleaguered both by her fractious pupil and the man of the house, who clearly seeks carnal knowledge of her; but the incursion of the supernatural (in the form of a mysterious perfume that seems to waft from the governess) is entirely adventitious, and the tale would have been the better without it. Elizabeth Bowen spoils the fine atmosphere of horror in "Hand in Glove" by smart-aleck wit at the end. V. S. Pritchett's "A Story of Don Juan" is nothing more than a flippant joke, with the supernatural used as a prop for humour. Elizabeth Jane Howard's "Three Miles Up" and Marghanita Laski's "The Tower" are marred by a lack of clarity as to the nature and source of the supernatural phenomena. Many writers not accustomed to this realm seem to feel that the supernatural is irrational and that it can therefore be introduced entirely at random in a tale; but in fact the weird must be even more rigidly accounted for (and by this I don't mean "explained") than the mundane, lest it seem unmotivated and contrived. As Hartley says in the introduction to Cynthia Asquith's *Third Ghost Book:* "Chaos is not enough. Even ghosts must have rules and obey them." (Ever heard of L. P. Hartley, Mr Leithauser?)

Toward the end of the volume Leithauser includes two stories by, of all people, John Cheever. I freely admit that I have not read anything of Cheever's before (and, now, am not much inclined to do so), but I can say categorically that neither "Torch Song" nor "The Music Teacher" is a ghost story. They don't strike me as very good stories either, but they are, if anything, tales of witchcraft. Leithauser has left himself an escape hatch on this point by saying that this volume does not in fact contain exclusively ghost stories, and that he would have preferred to use the title "The Norton Book of Modern Supernatural Fiction in English, with an Emphasis on the Two Main Branches of the Ghost Story, as Epitomized by M. R. James and Henry James." This is a fatal equivocation. If Leithauser had really wanted to include the best supernatural fiction generally, there is no earthly reason for the exclusion of Poe, Le Fanu, Bierce, Machen, Blackwood, Lovecraft, Dunsany, Aickman, Ramsey Campbell, and a dozen other writers. Some of these authors even wrote actual "ghost stories" that are, by and large, better than most of the stories in this book. How about Dunsany's early tale "The Ghosts" (in *A Dreamer's Tales*) or his late works "Autumn Cricket" and "The Ghost of the Valley," in Asquith's second and third *Ghost Books,* respectively? How about Blackwood's poignant "Woman's Ghost Story"? Anything of Aickman's? Campbell's "The Previous Tenant"? I mention this story in particular because it actually bears some thematic resemblance to Henry James's "The Romance of Certain Old Clothes" (the ghost as a metaphor for jealousy); but I frankly think Campbell has made a much more evocative, emotionally engaging, and—yes—frightening story than his illustrious predecessor. But there is no evidence, alas, that Leithauser has ever heard of Lord Dunsany, Algernon Blackwood, Robert Aickman, or Ramsey Campbell, or—if he had—that he took the effort to examine their work.

One of the many things I found missing in this volume is any genuine sensation of fear. Leithauser addresses this issue in an unusually fatuous passage in his introduction (almost as fatuous as his cringe-inducing disquisition on the purportedly homosexual overtones of M. R. James's "'Oh, Whistle'"), saying that "I can't help thinking that if the virtue of any artwork that deals with the supernatural is to be directly correlated to adrenaline production . . . one would be better off looking to film rather than typescript." I scarcely know how to respond to this piece of unrelieved idiocy. Fear, terror, and unease are not equivalent to the production of adrenaline, Mr Leithauser; and this genre would have no *raison d'être* if it was merely designed to probe psychological states or portray character. This deemphasis on fear seems to be part of a calculated attempt to sanitise this unruly literary mode—to banish, in other words, those writers who find the chief purpose in weird fiction to be something so reprehensible as to disturb us from our complacency. Leithauser soberly intones that few works of literature can make us jump out of our seats as some films can; but does he really imagine that this was the actual purpose behind the writing of "The Fall of the House of Usher" or "The Colour out of Space"? Does he think that any film ever made can come close to matching the complex network of sensations we feel when reading these masterworks? Leithauser has a "good deal of patience with ghosts that are other than malign," but he is relatively alone in this preference; M. R. James himself stated definitively (in the preface to *More Ghost Stories of an Antiquary*) that "the ghost should be malevolent or odious: amiable and helpful apparitions are all very well in fairy tales or in local legends, but I have no place for them in a fictitious ghost story."

On the whole, my chief response to this volume was rather similar to what I might feel after successively watching a college and a professional football game. Both sports and weird fiction should be left to professionals, not amateurs. Admirable as Henry James and Edith Wharton and Elizabeth Bowen and V. S. Pritchett and Muriel Spark and John Cheever and A. S. Byatt may be as mainstream writers, they are amateurs in this field as compared to Poe and Le Fanu and Machen and Blackwood and Lovecraft and Aickman and Campbell. Only the latter know how to write profoundly about life while at the same time sending an effective shiver up one's spine; indeed, only they know how to make that shiver itself speak volumes about life and our tenuous hold on it. It is they who ought to fill a book like *The Norton Book of Ghost Stories*, but they won't until amateurs like Brad Leithauser step aside and let a professional take over.

Some Thoughts on Weird Poetry

The subject of weird poetry appears today to be little discussed, and the poetry itself little read, for a variety of reasons having much to do with the overall status of poetry in our society. We need hardly be told that poetry has been, for long periods in Western history, not merely the dominant but in some cases the only mode of literary expression; so how has it come about that poetry is now so little a part of even the literate person's cultural baggage? Modern poetry seems utterly irrelevant to our present-day concerns, and most of us would be at a loss to name even a single contemporary poet who could authentically be called great. Is it that we have become insensitive to poetry, or that the poets themselves (as Lord Dunsany, unremittingly hostile to the tendencies of modern poetry, famously put it) have "failed in their duty" to express their age in a way that readers can understand? My own view is strongly on the side of Dunsany, as I will hope to explain as this article progresses.

But the domain of poetry offers much that can satisfy the devotee of the weird. Certainly, the pedigree of the fantastic in poetry is as old as poetry itself, if we consider such instances in classical verse as Odysseus' descent into the underworld (*Odyssey*, Book 9), the various grisly or horrific scenes in ancient tragedy (Oedipus' self-blinding in Sophocles' *Oedipus Rex*, the deaths of Creon and his daughter in Euripides' *Medea*, and many scenes in the Roman playwright Seneca's tragedies), and Catullus' mad "Attis poem" (in which that hapless demigod castrates himself out of frustrated love for his own mother, Cybele). Moving several centuries forward, we find the Romantic poets revelling in the weird—Coleridge's imperishable *Rime of the Ancient Mariner*, Keats's *Lamia*, the spectral ballads of Thomas Moore and James Hogg, and so many others, culminating in the small but immensely influential body of Poe's verse, which was nearly as great a landmark in our field as his short fiction. Much of the best of this work can be found, of course, in August Derleth's compilation *Dark of the Moon* (Arkham House, 1947), although recent research has revealed that many of the selections were in fact made by Donald Wandrei, who was much more knowledgeable in the history of English poetry than Derleth was. I had once thought that, aside from the omission of *Lamia* and some other items I will mention presently, *Dark of the Moon* was well-nigh definitive; but there is reason to believe that a fresh anthology of seventeenth-, eighteenth-, nineteenth-, and twentieth-century weird poetry, whose selections will differ significantly from Derleth's, could be assembled, including much meritorious work from such writers as Emily Dickinson, Thomas Hardy, and others not included in *Dark of the Moon*.

Two of the most noted omissions from the Derleth anthology were the weird poems of Ambrose Bierce (1842–1914?) and his pupil, George Sterling (1869–1926). Bierce, of course, was primarily a satirist, both in prose and verse; and the two large volumes of his *Collected Works* (1909–12) devoted to his poetry contain only a relatively small number of items that could be labelled weird. But among them are several distinctive dream-fantasies, several futuristic poems, and a number of cosmic verses that dimly anticipate the work of some of his successors. (Donald Sidney-Fryer collected many of these in the distinctive volume *A Vision of Doom* [1980].) It was probably these last items that led Bierce to embrace the work of Sterling, whom he had known since the 1890s. Sterling's long "star poem," *The Testimony of the Suns*, is indeed a riot of cosmic imagery, and Bierce was so taken with Sterling that he deemed another long (and more purely horrific) poem, "A Wine of Wizardry," a greater work than *Hamlet!* This is of course a bit of an exaggeration, but Bierce was not far wrong in saying that Sterling had added something unique to literature. Sterling became a master of the sonnet, and some of his finest weird effects are embodied in that form, as in "The Black Vulture":

> Aloof upon the day's unmeasured dome,
>> He holds unshared the silence of the sky.
>> Far down his bleak, relentless eyes descry
> The eagle's empire and the falcon's home—
> Far down, the galleons of sunset roam;
>> His hazards on the sea of morning lie;
>> Serene, he hears the broken tempest sigh
> Where cold sierras gleam like scattered foam.
>
> And least of all he holds the human swarm—
>> Unwitting now that envious men prepare
>>> To make their dream and its fulfilment one,
> When, poised above the caldrons of the storm,
>> Their hearts, contemptuous of death, shall dare
>>> His roads between the thunder and the sun.

Is it any wonder that Sterling himself served as the mentor of the young Clark Ashton Smith (1893–1961) when the latter hesitantly showed his early poems to "the poet laureate of San Francisco" in 1911? It was Sterling who, as Bierce had done before him, tutored Smith in the niceties of metre, diction, imagery, and symbolism; Sterling who shepherded Smith's early volumes of poetry, from *The Star-Treader* (1912) to *Sandalwood* (1925), into print; Sterling whose suicide in 1926 was so traumatic to Smith that it was perhaps a significant factor in his shift away from poetry to prose fiction in the later 1920s. Clark Ashton Smith should be acknowledged as not merely the finest weird poet of all time, but, if there is any justice in the world, as one of the finest American poets of his century, and his *Selected Poems* (Arkham House, 1971) would be regarded as a landmark if literary history had not taken a very different direction at the very time that Sterling and Smith were producing their best work.

The decade of the 1920s is currently remembered as the era of Modernism; one would like to think that in the distant future it will be judged as the period when literature and perhaps other arts took a wrong turn that has condemned entire branches of aesthetics to irrelevance. Poetry is one of these. Whereas Sterling, Smith, and other conservative poets of their day still found strength and inspiration (as all artists up to their time had done) in the great work of the past—specifically, the poetry of Keats, Shelley, and Swinburne—the Modernists were so overwhelmed by the cultural heritage of prior ages that they felt that only a complete break from the past could cause their work to be "original" and vital. They failed to observe Ambrose Bierce's dictum: "The best innovation is superior excellence. The great men are those who excel in their art as they find it; the revolutionaries are commonly second and third rate men—and they do not revolutionize anything." We all know the result. Poetry fundamentally split into two types: one type, headed by William Carlos Williams (with posthumous support from Walt Whitman), regarded conventional metrical poetry as too restrictive, and so poetry became more like prose, and in many instances indistinguishable from it; another type was embodied by T. S. Eliot, Ezra Pound, Hart Crane, and their followers, who, while also abandoning formal metre, felt that poetry must be "difficult" to express a complex and difficult age, and as a result their work became esoteric, obscure, and well-nigh incomprehensible even to the majority of literate readers.

To my mind, however, if poetry is not kept distinct from prose—not merely in terms of rhythm and metre, but also in terms of imagery, metaphor, and symbolism—then it is nothing. It is simply bad prose.

If the Modernists had paid some attention to their humble fellow-poets in the weird tradition, they might not have brought poetry to the dire state it is in. Many members of what has been called the "Lovecraft circle" produced outstanding verse, and did so very largely because they adhered to traditional metrical forms; but they also filled their poetry with the pungent metaphors and images that create an unbridgeable gap between verse and prose and render poetry one of the highest expressions of the human aesthetic sense.

Lovecraft himself was by no means the leading poet of his own literary circle, and he knew it. Setting Clark Ashton Smith's work aside as an unapproachable pinnacle, Lovecraft's verse cannot even be judged comparable to that of some of his younger colleagues, whom he far outstripped in prose fiction. My edition of Lovecraft's *Fantastic Poetry* (Necronomicon Press, 1990, 1993) does contain a modicum of good work; but my edition of Lovecraft's *The Ancient Track: Complete Poetical Works* (Night Shade, 2001)—which includes even scraps of verse buried in published and unpublished letters—is of interest only because we long ago reached the stage where every word of Lovecraft's, good or bad, is of some interest.

Donald Wandrei (1908-1987) perhaps ranks second only to Smith as a weird poet. He himself was thrilled by Smith's *Ebony and Crystal* when he read it in 1923, and he began corresponding with Smith the next year—two years before he became acquainted with Lovecraft. Wandrei's two early volumes of poetry, *Ecstasy* (1928) and *Dark Odyssey* (1931), are choice items for the collector; scarcely less so is his *Poems for Midnight* (Arkham House, 1964), with its 750-copy print run. That volume, however, failed to include several poems from his earlier collections, as well as a number of uncollected poems, necessitating my edition of his *Collected Poems* (Necronomicon Press, 1988) and a still further augmented edition, titled *Sanctity and Sin* (Hippocampus Press, 2008).

Frank Belknap Long (1901-1994) was also an able poet, although his output was slimmer and more uneven than Wandrei's. He too produced two early collections of poetry much sought after by the collector, *A Man from Genoa* (1926) and *The Goblin Tower* (1935; typeset by Lovecraft and R. H. Barlow), as well as a later gathering of his best work, *In Mayan Splendor* (Arkham House, 1977). But like Wandrei, Long omitted a number of his poems from this volume, and the remainder have now been gathered up in Perry M. Grayson's 1995 compilation, *The Darkling Tide* (Tsathoggua Press, 1995).

The verse of Robert E. Howard (1906-1936) also deserves mention, and the slim Arkham House collection *Always Comes Evening* (1957) gathers only a small proportion of it. Howard's verse may be as voluminous as Lovecraft's, and it deserves to be assembled.

The members of the Lovecraft circle did their best poetic work in the 1920s and 1930s. Smith, of course (although in this context it is unfair to consider him in any sense a satellite of Lovecraft), went on to great work well into the 1950s. It is a shame that Derleth (himself a noted poet, although not primarily in the weird vein) delayed publication of Smith's *Selected Poems* for so long: Smith had completed assembling the volume by 1949, but Arkham House's financial difficulties of the 1950s, along with the general difficulty of selling large volumes of poetry, delayed publication until 1971, eight years after Smith's death and just prior to Derleth's own. Hundreds of Smith's poems long remained uncollected and unpublished, requiring two or three large volumes to gather them all. David E. Schultz and I have long been at work on such a project, and one volume (containing his translations from Baudelaire and other French and Spanish poets) appeared from Hippocampus Press in 2007; two further volumes, containing all his original verse, appeared in 2008.

Since Smith's heyday, no one has attained to his eminence as a weird poet. Joseph Payne Brennan (1918-1990) did creditable work, and his *Sixty Selected Poems* (New Establishment Press, 1985) is an admirable volume. Arkham House continued to issue limited editions of various poets, among them Stanley McNail and Donald Sidney-Fryer. McNail's *Something Breathing* (1965) was reissued in an expanded edition in 1987 by Embassy Hall Editions, while

Sidney-Fryer's *Songs and Sonnets Atlantean* (1972) is already two and a half decades old, and the author has done much good work in the interim; an omnibus of his collected Atlantean verse is scheduled to appear in 2008 from Hippocampus Press. G. Sutton Breiding, Bruce Boston, and many others in the small press have produced fine work, but their poetry is little read outside of a small band of devotees.

Now, however, several poets young and old have stepped forward to claim the mantle of Sterling, Smith, and Wandrei. Their work in many ways reflects the dichotomy we find in modern poetry in general.

As novelist, short fictionist, and essayist Richard L. Tierney has made a multifaceted impress upon the Lovecraftian world. His exquisitely wrought poetry, however, has hitherto appeared only in such journals as *Nyctalops*, *Macabre*, and the like, and their collection in a handsome volume, *Collected Poems: Nightmares and Visions* (Arkham House, 1981), is an event of which every enthusiast of fantasy should take note. Since the death of Clark Ashton Smith we have had few poets who could claim mastery at fantastic verse; but—although the fantasy world knows of such other craftsmen as Sutton Breiding, David E. Schultz, and Lin Carter—with this volume Tierney has put himself close to the forefront of macabre poets, his only rival being perhaps the very Donald Sidney-Fryer to whom this volume is dedicated.

Strange to say, the influence of Smith is not paramount here as it is in the work of many other modern fantasy poets; rather, it is the Lovecraft of *Fungi from Yuggoth* whom we find lurking behind nearly every page of these flawlessly chiselled verses. Of the sixty-seven poems included herein, no fewer than forty-six are of the Italian sonnet form used by Lovecraft in his sonnet sequence (this overabundance being, perhaps, the only drawback of the volume); many of Tierney's, indeed, contain so many faint and subtle phraseological echoes of the *Fungi* that they could easily pass for additional sonnets of Lovecraft's cycle. The Smith influence is, of course, not absent, and manifests itself in Tierney's skilful handling of the most diverse rhythms and metres—iambs, anapaests, alexandrines, and the like.

The bleak cosmic vision found in many of the more philosophical poems is again reminiscent of Lovecraft; but here there is a sharper scorn for the human race than we are accustomed to find in Lovecraft's poetry. Note "The Vengeance of Earth":

> Above, the human vermin that infest
> The crust, and with dull smoke pollute the sky,
> Live out their trivial lives and tritely die,
> Blind to the forces rising to a crest. . . .

Or an unforgettably poignant couplet in "Hate":

> But hate is hate, and I am but a man
> Trapped on a line of history's hackneyed page. . . .

Other poems reveal that mingling of the erotic with fantasy which also recalls Clark Ashton Smith (especially "Fulfillment," "A Vision on a Midsummer Night," and others). Further, we have poetic tributes specifically to Lovecraft, Poe, E. R. Eddison, Bierce, and others; some of these are not as inspired as other specimens in this volume, but all are noble and sensitive acknowledgements of Tierney's literary influences.

A quintet of poems translated from the *Fleurs du mal* of Baudelaire invites comparison with Smith; and from the one poem ("Giantess") which I was able to compare both with the original and Smith's rendition, it is evident that Tierney's version, though no less poetic, eschews the exotic vocabulary (in Smith's version we find such terms as "anigh," "matutine," "rondures," and "thighward") that is also lacking in the delicate and straightforward French of Baudelaire.

The late Keith Allen Daniels's *Satan Is a Mathematician: Poems of the Weird, Surreal and Fantastic* was issued by his Anamnesis Press in 1998, while Brett Rutherford brought out a second edition of his *Whippoorwill Road* (first published in 1985) in 1998 through Grim Reaper Books, a subdivision of his The Poet's Press. These are neither poet's first book by any means: Daniels made his debut with the exceptional volume *What Rough Book* (Anamnesis Press, 1992), while *Whippoorwill Road* gathers together the weird verse from Rutherford's many previous volumes. They are comparable in many ways, contrasting in others, and perhaps most interesting in exhibiting both the virtues and the failings of the modern poetic muse.

In his somewhat aggressive introduction Daniels resurrects the argument from C. P. Snow's lecture *The Two Cultures*—lamenting the intellectual cleavage between the humanities and the sciences—and hopes that his work can do its small part to bridge the gap. Daniels himself had a "daylight career in polymer science and engineering," and his back cover boasts a blurb from Roald Hoffmann, a Nobel laureate in chemistry. It is all very good to attempt to infuse the findings of science with poetic feeling, but I am not sure that Daniels has found the proper way of doing it. Consider the opening lines of "Bight of Sonic Blasters":

> In benthic valleys where cetaceans wail,
> half hidden by the veils of filtered sight,
> with gonyaulax polluting every scale
> and veiscle inherent in the bight
> of sonic blasters . . .

I suppose Daniels would simply call me ignorant for not knowing the meanings of several of the scientific words used here, but I think there is a greater underlying problem that he fails to see: the plain fact that many scientific terms do not have sufficient poetic resonance to generate a poetic response. Much of Daniels's work in this volume is opaque (thereby embodying the second type of Modernism I outlined above), not merely because of the abundance of unexplained scientific terms, but because Daniels has chosen a tortured and contrived manner of utterance that defies comprehension by even the most alert reader.

I hope I am not revealing my prejudices when I say that almost all the memorable and notable poems in *Satan Is a Mathematician* (and there are many) are those that follow strict metrical schemes. In this book there are some uncommonly fine sonnets, as well as poems written in pentameter blank verse, regular quatrains, and the like. And Daniels has learned the all-important secret of verse: that the message must be conveyed by means of imagery, metaphor, and symbolism rather than by plain statement. Consider a few simple lines from one of the finest of the poems, a series called "Sciomancy Nights." One section, "An Evening with Aldous Huxley," has the following:

> [he] knew . . . that dying's just a glitch,
> a transitory bummer in the now
> of being.

The range of tone in the book—from pensive reflection to tart satire to cosmic fantasy to outrageous humour and grotesquerie—is notable. If Daniels could have been prevailed upon to be a trifle less esoteric, then one might have confidently predicted that he was on the way to becoming a not unworthy successor to his idol, Clark Ashton Smith. Unfortunately, his early death cut off a vital poetic voice in midstream.

The first thing that strikes us about *Whippoorwill Road* is that it is a superlative job of book production, in the finest tradition of Thomas Bird Mosher and Roy A. Squires. Rutherford himself notes: "The binding is done by hand, employing gluing, side sewing, and a cloth-reinforced spine. The outer wrap-around covers are made from hand-made or artists' papers." And much of the contents fully equals the meticulous quality of the physical product.

Rutherford embodies the first type of Modernism I enunciated above, in which the rhythmical distinction between prose and verse is muted, and sometimes disappears altogether. Many of the poems are, I regret to say, nothing but prose. But there are enough genuine poems to redeem the volume. In the remarkable "Fête" (Rutherford's own favorite poem) we find not only the striking expression "I am Love's Antichrist" but the following flawless stanza:

> I cough a cloud and let it blot the moon
> so that no distant star may hear and mock
> the oath that is sworn in the hidden copse.
> Here! now even fireflies are dimming out,
> now ravens avert their ebony orbs,
> now sputter and die, ye will o' the wisp!
> Not even a random thought can penetrate
> this furry arbor of my wretchedness.

Or this from "He's Going to Kill Me Tonight":

> Midnight. The Reaper's shift begins.
> The minute hand tips past Reason,
> careens into Murder's tithe of night.

The division of the poems into loosely thematic groupings is singularly felicitous, with the result that each poem strengthens or adds colour to the others, and all gain a cumulative power by adroit juxtaposition. Perhaps the only drawback in the book is an unwarrantedly lengthy section at the back in which Rutherford, telling of the genesis of the poems, leaves himself open to charges of self-praise by the tenor of some of his remarks. Poets should resist the temptation to comment on their own work—at least in the manner that Rutherford does. But this is a small flaw in an otherwise highly creditable volume.

The work of two California poets deserves some attention. One of them is our old friend Donald Sidney-Fryer, who embodies, in his long and distinguished career, a line of continuity between the Californians of the early twentieth century and those of the present day. A friend and colleague of Clark Ashton Smith who, even before Smith's death, was at work on a bibliography of that writer's work (culminating in *Emperor of Dreams: A Clark Ashton Smith Bibliography*, 1980), Sidney-Fryer burst into celebrity with *Songs and Sonnets Atlantean* (1971), one of the last volumes published by Arkham House under its founder August Derleth's direct supervision. This remarkable collection of poems and prose-poems displayed Sidney-Fryer as an assured master of many poetic forms—the quatrain, the sonnet, the ode, and especially the alexandrine, which has become his signature metre—as well as a fantastic imagination that, to be sure, draws upon the work of Smith, Bierce, and the Elizabethans but remains distinctively his own.

Sidney-Fryer at long last issued *Songs and Sonnets Atlantean: The Second Series* (Wildside Press, 2003), and it is a welcome addition to the still slim array of meritorious fantasy verse. (The back cover blurb seriously errs in stating that the book is merely a "new and expanded edition" of *Songs and Sonnets Atlantean*; in fact, there is no duplication of contents, and this new volume contains works that have never been gathered in book form.) It displays all the virtues we have come to expect from Sidney-Fryer: felicitous word-choice, precision in metre, and especially a vibrant, exotic imagination that vivifies realms of fantasy into living realities.

There is, indeed, a touch of melancholy to the volume—a melancholy resulting from its frequent dedication of individual poems to notable weird authors who have passed on. Fritz Leiber, H. Warner Munn, Stanley McNail, and others are recipients of eloquent poems and elegies; the one on Leiber concludes as follows:

> Attended then by a vast rush of wings unseen but without number,
> He summons yet those further shadows—from beyond the cosmic stream—
> More dark than dark, more deep than deep, ineffable as dreams in slumber:
>
> Endued with all the appanage of dreams, and loves, and fears;
> The Mage stands firm upon that peak, the dominus of strange spheres.

Neither Sterling nor Smith could have done better than this.

The crown jewel of *Songs and Sonnets Atlantean: Second Series* is *A Vision of a Castle Deep in Averonne*, a sixty-page narrative poem with all the richness of incident, depth of character portrayal, and fantastic imagination of a novel, yet written in smoothly flowing alexandrines that leave the reader hoping that the poem will never end. To be sure, there is a somewhat more prosaic quality to this work, a product both of its setting in the present day ("If he were free, then they would go to that old realm— / She would arrange it all with her own travel agent") and of the need to carry the narrative forward briskly. But Sidney-Fryer deftly lures the reader both from the present to the past and from the real to the imaginary, in this cumulatively potent account of an elderly couple who seek to probe their ancestral ties to a family that occupied a castle in Clark Ashton Smith's mythical French realm of Averoigne. Sidney-Fryer has successfully recited this poem at many poetry readings in California, and it is gratifying to see it in print.

Alan Gullette's *Acts of Love* (Elephant Printing, 2003) is not to be compared with Sidney-Fryer's volume, for it is a small chapbook chiefly meant to accompany some elegant line-drawings of two models, posing in various positions simulating sexual union, by Norm Rosenberger. And yet, Gullette, a young poet who, as a teenager, achieved celebrity with two superlative issues of the fanzine *Ambrosia* (1972–73), is himself worthy to carry the torch of Californian imaginative poetry. Consider, for example, the delicate lyric "Trees" from Gullette's earlier volume, *Another Eucharist* (Elephant Printing, 1995):

> Trees stand naked—
> Winter trees.
> Autumn trees have shed their wear
> Of colored leaves

> Revealing smooth black limbs
> Rain-wet and bare.
>
> Mists of passioned breath
> Rise from the earth
> Through me.

This seemingly slight poem perfectly fulfils the true function of poetry—the exquisite etching of the symbolic ramifications of a single, simple image. Much other good work by Gullette can be found in *From a Safe Distance* (Anamnesis Press, 2000), *49 Pieces* (Corelli Press, 2005), and *Twenty-seven Liqueurs* (Corelli Press, 2006), as well as in a volume of prose-poems, *A Book of Dreams* (Corelli Press, 2006). Gullette, who runs one of the most notable websites devoted to supernatural literature (http://alangullette.com/lit/horror.htm), has also written an SF/fantasy novella, *The Green Transfer* (Corelli Press, 1995). His writing is far too little-known, and one can only hope that a publisher like Wildside or Hippocampus Press sees the wisdom of gathering it into an accessible volume. In the meantime, copies may be obtained from the author himself (alang@alangullette.com).

Why is it that poetry is no longer read? Why is it that there are, quite literally, more poets than readers of poetry? Some of it has to do with education: the schools do not teach the appreciation of poetry anymore. A large part of it has to do with the tendencies of modern poetry, which have alienated many potential readers with obscurity or prosiness. But weird verse has been inherently conservative, and appears to draw its greatest strengths from that circumstance. It is perhaps too early to state that poetry is a dying art; but we can at least maintain with confidence that, with poets like Donald Sidney-Fryer, Brett Rutherford, and Alan Gullette, weird verse will continue to flourish for some time.

Bram and Bela and Mary and Boris

Three anthologies compiled by Byron Preiss and his colleagues—*The Ultimate Dracula, The Ultimate Frankenstein,* and *The Ultimate Werewolf* (all Dell, 1991)—were designed to commemorate the sixtieth anniversary of the film versions of *Dracula* and *Frankenstein* (1931) and the fiftieth anniversary of *The Wolf Man* (1941). They are for the most part original: Anne Rice's tale in *Dracula* is a restored version of her only short story, from a 1984 issue of *Redbook; Frankenstein* has a reprint of a Kurt Vonnegut story; and *Werewolf* contains previously published stories by Harlan Ellison and Robert Silverberg. I will confess that I have only seen *The Wolf Man* once and have no especially clear or fond recollections of *Dracula* and *Frankenstein*; my attitude to all these "classic" films being roughly similar to Lovecraft's, who remarked in 1933: "Last year an alleged *Frankenstein* on the screen would have made me drowse had not a posthumous sympathy for poor Mrs. Shelley made me see red instead. Ugh! And the screen *Dracula* in 1931—I saw the beginning of that in Miami, Fla.— but couldn't bear to watch it drag to its full term of dreariness, hence walked out into the fragrant tropic moonlight!"

I have never understood the nostalgic fascination for these very crude early films, which have always struck me as pitiable travesties on the literary works (Stoker's *Dracula*, Shelley's *Frankenstein*; there seems no transcendently famous literary treatment of the werewolf theme, and *The Wolf Man* was not based upon any) they were purporting to adapt. Accordingly, I was pleased to note that a number of writers in all three of these volumes chose to hark back not to the films but to the literature, and that in some cases the result is not simply a tepid evocation of the film but the production of a distinguished literary product in its own right.

But there are, I fear, problems in the very conception of these volumes, problems that must surely plague most "theme" anthologies: boredom and sameness. Consider *The Ultimate Dracula*. When one opens this volume, one is already aware that every story in it will deal with vampires in some fashion or other. Half the surprise of any given story is, accordingly, robbed at the very outset. This problem is exacerbated in this book because it was an invitational anthology in which every author was asked specifically to write a vampire tale. (It is all the more unfortunate, therefore, that Byron Preiss and his associates have failed to provide even the least information about how they went about compiling these anthologies, especially in light of the fact that a number of authors in the volumes are very little known and could not have been invited merely for name recognition. Instead, all we have are simple-minded introductions to the books by Leonard Wolf, Isaac Asimov, and Harlan Ellison, respectively, along with select filmographies in all three volumes by Wolf.)

The boredom factor is particularly evident in *Dracula*. The vampire theme is, on the whole, so stale and so exhausted of freshness that it now seems very difficult to do anything original with it; and few of these writers have done so. In terms of the surprise factor, many of them renounce it at the start. Consider the following first lines: "The vampire was real" ("The Vampire in His Closet" by Heather Graham); "Rudolph Redeemer had just finished sucking my blood" ("Nobody's Perfect" by Philip José Farmer); "Mr. Lucrada [anagrams, anyone?] tried hard to be young" ("Mr. Lucrada" by John Lutz); "Cammie pounded the stake into his heart" ("Children of the Night" by Kristine Kathryn Rusch). Many other stories make it very obvious very quickly that we are dealing with a more or less conventional vampire, with all the conventional trappings (crosses, garlic, sleeping by day, etc.); in those that don't, the reader is simply waiting around for the vampire to appear, and the least little sign—as when, in Edward D. Hoch's "Dracula 1944," a prison guard dies from loss of blood—provides a telltale giveaway.

Accordingly, many writers resort to various forms of humour. Perhaps it is some flaw in my temperament that I do not respond to this sort of thing very well, but to my mind the only truly successful comic story in *Dracula* is Karen Robards's "Sugar and Spice and . . .," which is effective not merely for its perfect capturing of the sentiments and language of a six-year-old boy but for its unexpectedly grim conclusion. Some writers attempt to produce novel settings (Dan Simmons's "All Dracula's Children," set in post-Ceausescu Romania; Hoch's tale, set in Nazi Germany) or time periods (Anne Rice's "The Master of Rampling Gate," set in England in the 1880s; Janet Asimov's "The Contagion" and Kristine Kathryn Rusch's story, both set in the future). Not many of these are very successful, either. But Simmons's spectacularly powerful tale, weaving together the horrors of the Ceausescu regime, AIDS, and vampirism, may be worth all the rest of the stories in the volume combined. Rusch's tale is poignant and sensitive, even if marred by a repeated misuse of "like" for "as" ("Her hands trembled, like they had before" is, I fear, illiterate). Rice's story is trumpeted as a great feature of the volume, but my own feeling is that it ought to have been called "The Master of Rambling Gate," for it is mightily confused and meandering; and, like many of her other works, it merely cannibalises some of the ideas and themes in her admittedly brilliant *Interview with the Vampire*.

The Ultimate Frankenstein would seem to provide more variation, since the idea of an artificial human or quasi-human being can be handled in a number of different ways and for a number of different purposes; but, sadly enough, this turns out not to be the case. Instead, writer after writer—among them Brian Aldiss, F. Paul Wilson, Philip José Farmer, Chelsea Quinn Yarbro, Benjamin M. Schutz, Loren D. Estleman, and Karen Haber—does little more than rewrite Mary Shelley's novel, using the same characters and occasionally transferring events into the present. There are some notable failures here. Farmer provides much merriment at his own expense by a disastrous attempt at imitating eighteenth-century diction; Estleman, while producing a fairly able pastiche of Shelley's style, concludes with a grotesque and ridiculous comic ending. All this reminds me of some of Lovecraft's poorer imitators, chief among them Brian Lumley, who seem to fancy that the highest tribute they can pay to their model is not to conceive some imaginative elaboration of Lovecraft's ideas but to churn out a half-baked pseudo-plagiarism of one of his stories. It is all very puzzling.

This volume too has the expected comic treatments, including such things as "Monsters of the Midway" by Mike Resnick, in which (yuk yuk) huge artificial humans play for the Chicago Bears (didn't Rod Serling do something like this already?); "Near-Flesh" by Katherine Dunn, which at least is original in conception as it depicts the widespread use of sex-robots in the future; and Esther M. Freisner's wholly fatuous "Mad at the Academy," which opens: "It was, as it had to be, a dark and stormy night. Somewhere, anyhow. But the California skies over Forest Lawn Cemetery were clear . . ." I regret to inform Ms Freisner that this is NOT FUNNY. Considerably more amusing is Schutz's "The State versus Adam Shelley," which takes delightful potshots at right-wing pro-lifers (after a botched illegal abortion, Mary Shelley "was committed to the Jesse Helms Memorial Reproduction Center"). As an emphatic pro-deather, I found all this very piquant, if a little obvious; those on the other side of the issue might not be so amused. In this category of humorous tales I suppose we are forced to include David J. Schow's "Last Call for the Sons of Shock." This is probably the most daring *tour de force* in the entire three volumes, especially as it features Frankenstein's monster, Dracula, and the Wolfman all in one story. I do not, I confess, have any clear idea what this story is actually about, but Schow's brashly scintillating style is a reward in itself.

There are some notable failures in some of the more serious tales also. Michael Bishop's "The Creature on the Couch" is one of the most windy and vacuous things I have read in recent years; it conveys absolutely nothing. Much better is "This Icy Region My Heart Encircles," a sensitive tale by Steve Rasnic Tem and Melanie Tem dealing with the life of Mary Shelley. But the prize in this book, which stands out as triumphantly as does Dan Simmons's in *Dracula*, is S. P. Somtow's "Chui Chai," a noxiously powerful and moving tale of love and death in Thailand. The throbbing vitality of Somtow's prose, along with the extraordinarily bizarre conception and execution of this tale, make it the one authentic literary contribution in the volume.

The Ultimate Werewolf is easily the poorest of the three anthologies. This may be both because of the very lack of a dominant literary treatment that could be used as a springboard and because the werewolf theme does not in fact seem to have very many interesting thematic or symbolic ramifications. A man (or, more rarely, a woman) turns into a wolf at the full moon—but what of it? As a result, the boredom and sameness factor figures very largely here: on the whole this volume consists of very flat and prosy retellings of the werewolf myth (Philip José Farmer, Kim Antieau, Bill Pronzini), lame excursions into humour (Jerome Charyn, Mel Gilden, Kevin J. Anderson, Brad Linaweaver, Robert Silverberg), failed attempts at novel settings (Nancy A. Collins, Pat Murphy, Stuart A. Kaminsky), lacklustre science fiction tales (Larry Niven, Brad Strickland), and one ridiculous and badly written pulp story (Robert E. Weinberg). The nadir is reached with "Partners" by Robert J. Randisi, a subprofessional piece of writing that has no place in an anthology of this sort. As with the *Dracula* volume, those stories that do not announce at the outset that a werewolf is involved lose much of their suspense because every reader knows that a werewolf will be involved at some point or other.

But there are a few glimmers of hope. Kathe Koja's "Angels' Moon" is, like Simmons's and Somtow's tales in the other anthologies, worth all the rest of the stories in the volume put together; it is a magnificent and heart-rending prose poem that shows that Koja is one of the more accomplished stylists in the field. "Claws on the sidewalk, hard against his hard pads. Shiver of hair about his ears, pointed to the moon, cacophony of smells inside his wise nostrils. He had just ripped a small mongrel cat to rags, for no reason, all reasons. Nothing spoken, in this world, and everything understood." That, my friends, is prose. Everything else in the book is a distant second, but Nina Kiriki Hoffman's "Unleashed" ingeniously uses the werewolf myth to explore the theme of sexual liberation, and "Pure Silver" by A. C. Crispin and Kathleen O'Malley is a tough, gritty tale of werewolves in the big city.

I do not know what one can say about these volumes as literature: only three or four stories in each anthology deserve to escape the oblivion that I fervently hope overtakes all the others, and these stories gain their strength not by playing off the respective films but by producing some innovative, imaginative treatment of the basic supernatural theme to lend it freshness after the countless reworkings of the idea in literature and film alike. I really do think it is a disservice for the editors not to have told either how they picked their selections or, more important, what guidelines they gave to their prospective authors. Were writers told specifically to allude to or elaborate upon the films? And did the best writers simply ignore these constraining instructions and write their tales using only the nucleus of the conception? We will, evidently, never know. What we do know is that one must sort laboriously through the dross of these volumes to find the few nuggets of gold therein.

What the Hell Is Dark Suspense?

Non-supernatural horror has always been with us. We can start as early as the Gothic novel as exemplified by Ann Radcliffe and Charles Brockden Brown, which I would term *pseudo-supernatural* in that it hints at the supernatural but then explains it away at the end by natural means. This form has been the object of much scorn from readers and critics, perhaps justifiably, for its suggestions of authorial trickery; it may, ironically, have its closest modern analogue in the "weird menace" brand of pulp writing, in which seemingly supernatural events were accounted for by elaborate (and implausible) contrivances by fiendish villains. Otherwise, this particular type of non-supernatural work does not appear to have exercised much influence either upon the later Gothic novel—in spite of at least one triumphant example in the work of

J. Sheridan Le Fanu, "The Inn of the Flying Dragon" (1872)—or upon modern weird writing.

Far superior as an art form, but more problematical in terms of its relation to the weird tale, is the *conte cruel,* which had already reached its apogee in the later nineteenth century in the work of Philippe-Auguste Villiers de l'Isle Adam ("The Torture by Hope"), Ambrose Bierce ("The Coup de Grâce" and several others), and Villiers's French successor Maurice Level. In "Supernatural Horror in Literature" Lovecraft defined the *conte cruel* ably as a work "in which the wrenching of the emotions is accomplished through dramatic tantalisations, frustrations, and gruesome physical horrors"; he disapproved of the form—or, rather, did not feel it to be genuinely a part of the weird tale—precisely because he thought the weird tale to be something more than "gruesome physical horrors." Lovecraft, indeed, seems to have had a prejudice against the non-supernatural horror tale, precisely because it did not seem to him to embody those "subversions of basic natural law" (letter to August Derleth, 6 November 1931) which he felt to be essential to the weird tale. I think Lovecraft is on the whole correct in this preference; but I think his bias toward external, cosmic horror and his general lack of interest in human beings (I do not say this pejoratively: I see nothing especially wrong in not being interested in human beings) caused him to underrate the degree to which the mysteries of the mind could be nearly as powerful and bizarre as the mysteries of the universe.

"Psychological horror," which may be considered a third type of non-supernatural horror (although its distinction from the *conte cruel* is not always clear), is having a great vogue today, although it too can be traced back at least to Brockden Brown's *Wieland* (1798). Psychological horror can itself be divided into two forms, one of which is somewhat akin to the pseudo-supernatural in that events that appear to be supernatural turn out to be the delusions of a twisted psyche, and the other a mere exhibition of the horrors of a mentally aberrant individual. The first form is fully within the spectrum of the weird, and one can point to some magnificent and classic instances of it; in some cases (most notably in Henry James's *The Turn of the Screw,* but also in the work of Walter de la Mare, Oliver Onions, and Shirley Jackson) doubt is maintained to the end as to whether we are dealing with the supernatural, a twisted psyche, or both. The second form is the dominant mode of today, and its supporters and practitioners are making grandiose claims as to its preeminence in the current range of weird fiction.

If anyone is a pioneer in this field, it is Robert Bloch, whose *The Scarf* (1947; rev. 1966) and *Psycho* (1959) are among the pinnacles of the form. It seems to me very clear that Bloch's example has led the way for many later writers—writers as different as Thomas Harris and Bret Easton Ellis, whose brilliant satire *American Psycho* makes a nod at least to the Hitchcock film, if not to the novel on which it was based. But I am not certain that the practitioners of psychological horror—especially those recent writers who are playing off the current fascination with serial killers—have genuinely come to terms with the status of this type of work. What, exactly, are its aims? Where (if anywhere) ought it to be placed within the realm of weird fiction? How is it different from the suspense or mystery story? How can weird fiction continue to be a distinct mode of writing if it is constantly borrowing themes and devices from neighbouring modes, whether it be the mystery story on the one hand or the science fiction tale on the other? Is there not a real sense in which psychological horror of the "crazed criminal" type is fundamentally different from, and perhaps subordinate to, supernatural horror? No matter how extreme the mental aberration, it is difficult to see how this embodies Lovecraft's "violation of natural law." The question is whether the actions of a deranged individual, however loathsome they may be, in themselves occasion fear or horror when there is not even the remotest suggestion that they may be supernatural. How frightening, really, are serial killers unless one happens to be the potential victim of one?

Robert Bloch attempts to deal with these issues in his thoughtful introduction to *Psycho-Paths* (Tor, 1991). Bloch sees a need to "forsake literary voyages through outer space in favor of exploring 'inner space'" by entering the mind of a criminal and, presumably, discovering the horror that lies therein. "The credible," says Bloch, "is a greater menace than the incredible." This is an exact reversal of Lovecraft's notion of the defining quality of the weird tale ("something which could not possibly happen" [letter to August Derleth, 20 November 1931]), and it proclaims that this anthology will present "horror stor[ies] dealing with the psychopathological rather than the supernatural." But this is exactly my difficulty: is "menace" genuinely equivalent to "fear" or "horror"? Is the mundane menace of being killed or brutalised by a madman somehow equivalent, as an emotional state, to the perception of some entity (e.g., Cthulhu) which defies all our metaphysical conceptions of the laws of nature?

Bloch himself deals with the psychopathological ably in his best work, but I fear that almost none of the stories in *Psycho-Paths* do so, or even attempt to do so. This is one of the most mediocre original anthologies I have ever had the misfortune to read, and I am comforted only by the fact (and I believe it is a fact) that Bloch himself did not actually commission the stories. The copyright to the volume is jointly shared by Bloch and Martin H. Greenberg, and it is only one more black mark against the latter that he has selected such uniformly wretched tales for publication here. It is clear that Greenberg merely wanted a handful of "name" authors to fill out an anthology, even if several of these authors have produced consistently subprofessional work.

Bloch, interestingly enough, is attempting to present his anthology as a counterweight to the splatterpunks, whom he skewers effectively and wittily ("More is not a synonym for better"); but several of the tales in his own volume are distressingly close to the sort of gratuitous and aesthetically purposeless display of gruesome physical horror that he so takes to task. Steve Rasnic Tem's "Jesse" is a moderately effective story of a boy who is so traumatised at the sight of some corpses that he begins to see tokens of death and decay everywhere; but the whole effect is really not very far from splatterpunk. A number of much poorer tales do no more than inspire revulsion and disgust.

The only things I can recommend in this volume are the stories by Dennis Etchison ("Call Home," a clever tale about a manipulative child psychopath) and David J. Schow ("Pick Me Up," about a murderous hitchhiker). Everything else in here is a disgrace: Gahan Wilson's "Them Bleaks," a cryingly stupid attempt at macabre humour; David Morrell's "Remains to Be Seen," a bombastic shoot-'em-up story; J. N. Williamson's "No Love Lost," a crude and superficial account of a paranoid schizophrenic; lame historical tales by Chelsea Quinn Yarbro and Edward D. Hoch . . . but there is no need for a catalogue. As I mentioned, many of the tales do not even attempt any psychological analysis of the disturbed characters, which makes one believe that Bloch wrote his introduction without actually having read any of the contents.

Then there is *Dark at Heart: All New Tales of Dark Suspense* (Dark Harvest, 1992), which seems to be proclaiming an entirely new genre or subgenre of "dark suspense." The editors, Karen and Joe R. Lansdale, define this as "stories [that] incorporate horror, mystery, detective, hardboiled, you name it," and go on to claim: "Stories of that nature will be for the nineties what horror was for the eighties. Except they'll be scarier, and less restrictive." This is complete rubbish. How on earth can one call horror—even contemporary horror—restrictive, when it includes everything from Ramsey Campbell's impressionistic portrayals of urban decay to T. E. D. Klein's supernatural realism to the unclassifiably *outré* prose-poetry of Thomas Ligotti? These three writers surely stand at the forefront of modern weird writing, and nothing in any of the volumes under review can even remotely measure up to their best work. The Lansdales' throwaway phrase "you name it" betrays the serious problems of focus that beset *Dark at Heart*: it is as if anything goes nowadays—anything that has some blood or some tough language or some perversity can now be called "dark suspense." Rather than defining a new mode of writing, the term becomes a catch-all for an indiscriminate hodge-podge of tales that have no commonality of theme, purpose, or mood.

There are two fundamental problems with *Dark at Heart*, the one a direct outgrowth of the other. First, there is not a single story that to my mind can be classified as "horror"—not one that is even remotely akin to the work of Poe or Bierce or Lovecraft or Machen or Blackwood or Shirley Jackson. They are all stories of crime or death, and presumably we are meant to be horrified either by the particularly gruesome nature of the crimes or by the psychological aberration of the perpetrators. But because (and this is the second problem) nearly all the stories are thoroughly undistinguished, the gruesomeness seems merely tedious and the psychological motivations of the characters not probed in any depth or subtlety. Once again I am struggling to recommend anything in this volume. F. Paul Wilson's "The Long Way Home" and Lewis Shiner's "Dirty Work" are perfectly good stories of crime (Wilson's is troubling only because of a suspicion of racism: the criminals are all black, the police are all white), although they are not horror stories by any stretch of the imagination, and David J. Schow's "Action" is genuinely chilling in its suggestion of an evil conspiracy between law enforcement and the media; but they are just about all that is worth reading here.

On the down side there are too many to mention; but my duty as a critic forces me to single out Joe R. Lansdale's windy, superficial, and implausible novelette that opens the volume, "The Events Concerning a Nude Fold-Out Found in a Harlequin Romance," which presents the novel picture of a woman who has been struck in the head and the back with a hatchet but who somehow manages to revive to avenge her attacker; and David Morrell's wretched novelette that concludes the book, "The Shrine," a story that is, anomalously, *supernatural* but which is as maudlin, pompous, and just plain bad as any story I have read in recent years. It is, I suppose, what one would have expected from a purveyor of cheap popular hokum whose great contribution to world civilisation is the creation of Rambo. The nadir is reached with Neal Barrett, Jr's "Hit," a spectacularly moronic tale whose plot is so dopy that it cannot be described with a straight face. (The Lansdales, by the way, think Barrett is "original, whacky [sic], and there's not a writer in any of the genres, category, mainstream, literary, [sic] that can hold a candle to him," thereby destroying for all time what little reputation for critical acumen they may have had.)

Another thing that puzzles me about nearly all the writers in *Dark at Heart* is their addiction to a slangy, colloquial, profanity-ridden style to tell their tales. I must say that this sort of lower-class prose becomes very wearisome after a while: don't these people realise what a narrow range of expression this idiom yields? This is something that afflicts the splatterpunks also, and it is one of the many reasons why most of them will never amount to anything. The effect is rather uncannily similar to being bombarded by rap music for hours on end. As an antidote, I again point to the Campbell-Klein-Ligotti triumvirate, whose fine feeling for language and style will cause their work to survive long after that of their hip contemporaries has become fodder for future sociologists.

Now Richard Chizmar comes along and, in *Cold Blood: New Tales of Mystery and Horror* (Mark V. Ziesing, 1991), trumpets yet another subgenre, which he calls "dark mystery" and defines as "a powerful blend of horror, mystery, and/or suspense fiction." Chizmar does not ban the supernatural, although Douglas E. Winter—who has added a meandering and unhelpful introduction—claims that the volume will contain stories "in which supernatural elements are downplayed and often dispensed with entirely, in favor of the more personal horrors of which Poe spoke so profoundly." The idea of comparing anything in this volume to Poe is a little nauseating, but I can at least announce with some relief that this anthology is not wholly worthless. There are, of course, the usual run of stories ranging from the lacklustre (F. Paul Wilson, Bentley Little, Ardath Mayhar, Rex Miller, Roman A. Ranieri, James Kisner, Nancy A. Collins, Ed Gorman) to the exceptionally stupid (Ronald Kelly, Joe R. Lansdale, Barry Hoffman, J. N. Williamson, William F. Nolan, Richard Laymon, William Relling, Jr.). At least there is nothing by David Morrell. Like the Lansdales in *Dark at Heart*, however, Chizmar can't resist adding fatuously effusive biographical notes that vaunt the contributors far beyond their actual merits. This sort of mutual backpatting is getting very common in the horror field, and seems to have two prime motivations: (1) the need to stay on good terms with authors, editors, and publishers for the sake of monetary gain; and (2) a simple lack of critical judgment, whereby people think that the bulk of material written today is actually meritorious. I think the latter is in the end more dangerous and insidious than the former; it will, I think, seem particularly ridiculous to future generations when nearly all this work is swept into the dustbin of oblivion. One feels a certain objective pity for writers like Williamson and Laymon, whose careers have been and will continue to be one long excursion into mediocrity.

The tales in *Cold Blood* are split rather evenly into supernatural and non-supernatural; it is no accident that there are more lacklustre and stupid instances of the latter than the former. Some of the most interesting stories, however, effect a clever reversal on the pseudo-supernatural trope: they seem initially to be merely grim tales of crime or murder, but swerve startlingly into the supernatural at the end. The best thing in the book, Brian Hodge's "Cancer Causes Rats," is of this type; it is a tale that ingeniously links serial killing with the supernatural, and is written with such verve and piquancy that we do not immediately notice the utter implausibility of the final supernatural phenomenon. Thomas F. Monteleone's "Love Letters" is somewhat similar but less striking. Rick Hautala dredges up the hackneyed device of the psychic detective and manages to make something fresh and ingenious out of it, while Paul F. Olson writes a respectable story that deliberately fails to resolve into either the supernatural or the non-supernatural.

The crime stories in *Cold Blood* tend on the whole to be both undistinguished and indistinguishable; they all blur together after a while. The only one of any substance is John Shirley's "Jody and Annie on TV," a grim portrayal of mindless violence. I should note that a number of the crime tales in this and the other anthologies seem to look with insouciance, and even with favour, upon the idea that it's okay to exact a sort of vicious vigilante justice upon the ever-burgeoning ranks of criminals and psychos in our society; the idea being that crime is so rampant, and the justice system so feeble in dealing with it, that taking matters into our own hands is the only way to survive—or at least to gain some satisfying revenge. This strikes me as genuinely frightening, although it does not appear as if the authors intended it to be so.

On the whole, I see neither anything very new about "dark suspense" nor any signs that it is about to cause the supernatural tale to fall by the wayside. The problem with all this writing about crime and death and murder, aside from revealing a dismal poverty of imagination, is that it will be—or, indeed, has already been—overtaken by what we read in the daily paper. The tale of Jeffrey Dahmer is far more loathsome than anything conceived by any splatterpunk or "dark suspense" or "dark mystery" writer. Weird fiction will lose its *raison d'être* if it is reduced merely to reiterating the mundane horrors of daily life. Lovecraft long ago delivered, to my mind, the definitive word on this subject when he responded to a reader's complaint that the trauma of war has exhausted our capacity for such things: "The physical horrors of war, no matter how extreme and unprecedented, hardly have a bearing on the entirely different realm of supernatural terror. Ghosts are still ghosts—the mind can get more thrills from unrealities than from realities!" ("The Defence Reopens!," 1921). By using the supernatural as a metaphor for profound human concerns, the weird tale can serve both as a commentary on our society and as an imaginative liberation from the mundane or narrowly realistic. This is what the best supernatural fiction has always done, and continues to do.

And yet, let me not be taken as condemning this entire "dark suspense" movement—or, at least, the idea behind it. There is very good work to be done in this mode; but I fear that, by and large, the people represented in these anthologies are not the ones to do it. (I want to go on record as excluding David J. Schow, Chet Williamson, F. Paul Wilson, and perhaps one or two others from this judgment.) As I have suggested, "dark suspense" isn't even a very new movement: Patricia Highsmith and Margaret Millar, in their very different ways, had done brilliant work of this sort over the course of decades, and their novels and tales ought to be read by everyone who has an interest in psychological horror. Ramsey Campbell's several novel-length forays in this venue, including *The Face That Must Die*, *The Count of Eleven*, and *Secret Stories*, are also magnificent triumphs. We will need more writing of this kind if "dark suspense" is ever to be anything more than a marketing gimmick.

The Small Press

[The following article was written in early 1995.]

Is the horror boom over? It is, certainly, difficult to speak conclusively on the subject, but certain signs are unmistakable.

As I write, there is not a single book by Stephen King, Anne Rice, Clive Barker, Dean R. Koontz, or Peter Straub on the *New York Times* bestseller list; several major publishers have either entirely eliminated or severely reduced the number of horror titles they issue; horror magazines even in the small press are dying like flies. Of course, each new work by King or Rice or Koontz does reach the best-seller list, sometimes the top of it (if Danielle Steel happens to be having a slow year), but even these books are staying on the bestseller list for shorter and shorter periods of time.

But if major publishers are shying away from horror, the small press is stepping in to fill the void. At a time when desktop publishing is becoming increasingly affordable, the enterprising small-press publisher need be able to dispose of only 500 or 1000 copies—sometimes even less—to make a modest profit, and not by producing artificially inflated "signed limited" editions. Whether the field in general will return to its pre-King state, where writers worked in obscurity, had day jobs, or wrote horror under the guise of suspense or science fiction, it is too early to say; but it is difficult to deny that, amidst the predictable masses of mediocrity and outright rubbish, some of the most distinctive and innovative work in the field is emerging from the small press.

TAL Publications seems to be attempting to make a name for itself as the publisher of "erotic horror." To date it has issued several chapbooks, including books by Elizabeth Massie, Wayne Allen Sallee, and D. F. Lewis, none of which I have read. What I *have* read is Edward Lee's *Quest for Sex, Truth and Reality* (1992), and I wish I hadn't. This is about the most contemptible little book I have come upon in a long time: it reminds me of nothing so much as the stories high school students write to see who can gross each other out the most. Marginally better—but only marginally—is Lucy Taylor's *Unnatural Acts* (1992). The three stories in this collection—as in Taylor's work generally—could only pass for horror in an age when anything with a little sex, blood, and violence can pass for horror.

Taylor has now issued two larger collections of stories with Silver Salamander Press, *Close to the Bone* (1993) and *The Flesh Artist* (1994). I hardly know what to say about these tales. Most of them are merely wild stories of bizarre sex with some bloodletting thrown in. Any "message" they may contain is of the most fatuously obvious sort. Consider the title story of the second collection. Here we have a mad plastic surgeon who becomes obsessed with the women—or, more specifically, certain parts of them—he has operated on and takes to killing them out of a crazy sense of personal ownership. No one needs to be told what the underlying themes are—the possessiveness of men, the objectification of women, our society's emphasis on physical appearance, etc., etc. This is all old stuff—we've heard it before, and Taylor's treatment is simply too undistinguished to be interesting. Those comparatively few tales where she ventures into fantasy, science fiction, or the supernatural would make good parodies if they were so intended. And repeated doses of Taylor's work lead not to revulsion or horror, but to boredom. It all starts sounding the same.

Norman Partridge's silly introduction to *The Flesh Artist*, where he compares Taylor's emergence to that of Clive Barker, unwittingly gets to the heart of the matter: Taylor, like Barker, is severely hampered by her chosen subject matter. She utterly fails to realise that this monotonous emphasis on aberrant sex and mindless violence—with its implication that the apex of horror is the harm that can be done to the physical body—only testifies to a staggering poverty of imagination. All she can do to jolt the jaded reader is to increase the dosage of violence—but the end result is still tedium. Writers like Edward Lee and Lucy Taylor have, of course, a built-in defence against negative criticism: they, like the splatterpunks, can take a weird sort of moral high ground and claim that objections to their work rest upon mere squeamishness or prudery. They can say that their stories are bold, confrontational, in-your-face, etc., etc. It never occurs to them to think that they may simply be bad writers.

Silver Salamander has done slightly better with Michael Shea's *I, Said the Fly* (1993), a horror/SF novella that was itself an expansion of an earlier short story. Here we are plunged into a world in which a strange alien invasion has resulted in "holes" in "electromagnetic informational flow-systems" around the world, the cause or purpose of which is not immediately evident. Engagingly written as it is, this story could have benefited in being turned into a full-fledged novel, for its provocative conceptions require still more elaboration for proper development. Shea is a veteran writer of science fiction, fantasy, and horror, one whose charmingly warped view of the world is peculiarly captivating.

Roadkill Press has apparently gained some sort of reputation as the publisher of cutting-edge horror; but on the evidence of the three booklets I have read, I can't see how. Unlike the TAL booklets, the Roadkill Press pamphlets are not actually bad but merely mediocre and undistinguished. Edward Bryant's *Darker Passions* (1992) contains three stories of mundane violence and menace, all written in a flat, toneless idiom that lulls one to sleep instead of producing unease. Dan Simmons, who has written a long-winded introduction to the book, makes a perfect clown of himself by comparing one of the stories to Hemingway's—as if writing one-sentence paragraphs and being sparing with the adjectives makes one a Hemingway. *Not Broken, Not Belonging* is a story written by Randy Fox from a "concept" by Alan M. Clark. What this really means is that Clark drew some (quite striking) illustrations and wanted Fox to write a story around them; but the result is confused, fragmentary, and insubstantial. The story ends where it should begin, leaving a myriad of plot threads unresolved. Of the third Roadkill Press book—Norman Partridge's *Mr. Fox and Other Feral Tales* (1992)—I shall have more to say elsewhere.

Necronomicon Press began its life in 1976 with the sole purpose of publishing the obscure writings of H. P. Lovecraft. Its founder, Marc A. Michaud, was for a long time content to fill this humble niche, but lately he has been branching out by publishing the obscure writings of other classic writers (William Hope Hodgson, Robert E. Howard, Clark Ashton Smith) and, most recently (under the editorship of Stefan Dziemianowicz), a series of small booklets of original fiction. The results are, in most cases, very pleasing to behold. Three of the titles, to date, were—at least in part—initially designed as contributions to an anthology of sequels to or elaborations on Lovecraft's "The Shadow over Innsmouth," edited by Stephen Jones and scheduled for publication in 1990, the year of Lovecraft's centennial. The plans were put on hold, although the volume was finally brought out in 1994 by Fedogan & Bremer; but in the interim, several of the tales appeared elsewhere.

Brian Stableford's *The Innsmouth Heritage* (1992), the first in the Necronomicon Press Fiction series, makes its indebtedness to Lovecraft's tale explicit in its very title. And yet, Stableford's tale avoids the pitfalls of most pastiches by being a genuine extension of the idea contained in the original. Stableford takes the basic premise of Lovecraft's story—the mating of human beings and amphibians and the loathsome hybrids that result—and refashions it: the physical abnormalities of the town's denizens ("the Innsmouth look") are now interpreted as a genetic mutation. This is familiar ground for Stableford, whose *Sexual Chemistry: Sardonic Tales of the Genetic Revolution* (1991) also broached this theme; but here, I fear, the exposition is a trifle too clinical to carry much punch. Lovecraft, for all the pseudo-science of his later tales, never failed to tell a rousing story—a narrative that achieved an almost unbearable cumulative effect by the steady augmenting of tension and suspense. Stableford's story appeals exclusively to the intellect, and what emotional resonances it has derive largely from its allusions to Lovecraft's tale.

The next offering in the Necronomicon Press Fiction line, Steve Rasnic Tem's *Decoded Mirrors: 3 Tales After Lovecraft* (1992), also contains, in its first story, a contribution to Stephen Jones's abortive anthology. This tale, "Decodings," is a masterwork of suggestion that justifies the entire booklet; the other two tales are less distinguished. Like Stableford's, these stories attempt to fuse Lovecraft's cosmic horror with the intimate, domestic horror that has dominated the field in the last several decades; the union of such antipodal approaches will always be uneasy and rarely successful, but in at least one instance Tem has turned the trick.

The third spinoff of "The Shadow over Innsmouth" is "Deepnet," the first of three tales in David Langford's *Irrational Numbers* (1994). Langford is primarily a science fiction writer and, like Stableford, ingeniously takes the "Innsmouth heritage" of disease and decay into the disturbingly near future: what would happen if the Innsmouth folk entered the computer age and began marketing video games and computer programs? Although, like Stableford's story, this tale lacks any overt climax or any real action to speak of, it manages to create a really unnerving effect in its quiet way. The other two tales in the booklet are narrated a little too fragmentarily to carry a very potent effect, although there are points of merit in both.

As if to reassure readers that the Necronomicon Press Fiction series would not be merely a forum for Lovecraft pastiches, the next booklet, Scott Edelman's *Suicide Art* (1992), takes us into a very different world—our own world of serial killers, child molesters, transsexuals, and other phenomena that Lovecraft could not even have imagined. The two tales in this booklet are certainly confrontational—the first one, "The Suicide Artist," quite literally so in its berating the reader for enjoying its account of child abuse, the second in its uncompromising tale of a transsexual haunted by the penis he has had cut off—but would be more successful if Edelman could remedy the clumsinesses, awkwardnesses, and occasional illiteracies in his prose style. I am not even sure the second tale is a horror story at all; its culminating scene presents what a Roman Catholic would no doubt find outrageously blasphemous, but to this hardened old unbeliever it seemed merely comical.

One can speak only with reverence of Ramsey Campbell, surely the leading horror writer of our time, and perhaps of all time. His *Two Obscure Tales* (1993) ought to be considered a sort of pendant to his landmark story collection *Demons by Daylight* (1973), for they were written shortly after most of the tales in that collection were set down. They are, to be sure, mighty obscure, and Campbell's brief afterword doesn't help matters much. Campbell himself sums up the matter by saying: "All one's fiction is to some extent about how one was at the age of writing it, and I can only be relieved I'm growing old."

If it were not enough that Necronomicon Press has convinced such luminaries in our field as Stableford, Tem, and Campbell to issue booklets, one of its latest offerings is by no less prestigious a mainstream writer as Fred Chappell. Chappell, of course, has had a long, if intermittent, love affair with Lovecraft and with horror fiction in general: his *Dagon* (1968) ranks with Colin Wilson's *The Mind Parasites* (1967) as one of the most successful novellength elaboration of Lovecraft's conceptions, and several stories in his collection *More Shapes Than One* (1991) also feature takeoffs of Lovecraft. *The Lodger*, a novelette published by Necronomicon Press in 1993, is a partial sequel to the short story "Weird Tales," a sort of historical fantasy in which the brief encounters between Lovecraft and Hart Crane are used as a springboard. In *The Lodger* we are introduced to a little-known member of this Crane-Lovecraft circle, a poet named Lyman Scoresby, who by means of his poetry collection takes possession of a man of our time, much to the latter's irritation. *The Lodger* is not a horror story, nor even a fantasy in any meaningful sense: it is a comedy and a satire, and an exquisite and hilarious one. As a poet and an academician, Chappell is both well qualified and well equipped to skewer the absurdities of modern poetry and modern academic scholarship. His tale is wholly delightful.

It must flatly be declared that the production standards of most of these books are not of professional calibre. TAL is the worst of the lot: its title page features the author, title, copyright notice, author's signature, and publisher's address all crammed together in a plain sans-serif type—apparently to save paper. Almost all these publishers are in desperate need of a copy editor and some basic instruction in layout and design. Most of the authors (established professionals like Chappell, Stableford, Tem, Campbell, and others of course excluded) can't write grammatically to save their lives. Lucy Taylor is the worst of the lot: to choose some examples purely at random, it seems that she does not know how to spell the verb *breathe*, how to spell *Coney Island* or *Euripides*, does not know the difference between *effect* and *affect*, and is unsure how to spell the possessive case of *men* and *women*.

In terms of design, we have awful things like page numbers on the inside margins, type too large for the page dimensions, typos by the bushel, and the use of many different display fonts in a single book. ("Well, I paid for 'em when I bought PageMaker, so why shouldn't I use 'em?") Only the Necronomicon Press line consistently features a design, typeface, and artwork that come up to professional standards.

It is interesting to note how many of these publications (the Necronomicon Press pamphlets excluded) feature effusive introductions by writers' friends—as if the authors (or publishers) could not risk allowing the works to stand on their own. Ed Bryant must be ranked as one of the prime offenders: in introductions and reviews alike he so egregiously exaggerates the merits of mediocre writers as to make one lament the near-total lack of critical standards in the current horror market. (The real horror is the very distinct possibility that Bryant *actually likes* the stuff he praises.)

The small presses I have surveyed here are by no means the only ones in this field; indeed, I have by design ignored some of the more prestigious imprints such as Arkham House or Mark V. Ziesing, whose products both in literary merit and in physical appearance need fear no comparison with commercial publishers. Arkham House's editor James Turner consistently produces products of exquisite design, although most of his recent volumes are in the science fiction field. Ziesing has just issued David J. Schow's *Black Leather Required* (1994), a landmark story collection by one of our leading writers.

I also do not wish to convey the impression that all work from commercial presses is distinguished while all, or nearly all, work from the small press is amateurish. The fact is that most of what the commercial presses publish is also pretty amateurish, and it now seems purely a matter of luck whether a given writer is published by the one or by the other.

Small press magazines are gamely making a go of it, even though a vast amount of what they contain is perfect rubbish. And yet, it certainly does seem as if quality eventually rises to the surface. Ramsey Campbell, T. E. D. Klein, Thomas Ligotti, Dennis Etchison, and many of the other leading writers in the horror field gained their start in the small press; Norman Partridge seems ready to join their company. As for the others, they will remain where they are, and some of them may perhaps develop a twisted pride in being unacceptable to the mainstream; but all they will accomplish is to perpetuate the half-truth that the small press is the home of the has-been and the never-was.

II. Classics

Algernon Blackwood: The Starlight Man

Algernon Blackwood. Mark that name well, my friends, for it may denote the greatest all writers of weird fiction. Only Edgar Allan Poe, H. P. Lovecraft, Lord Dunsany, and Ramsey Campbell are even within striking distance of Blackwood's towering achievement—an achievement that includes not only such anthology chestnuts as "The Willows" and "The Wendigo" but such little-known novels as *The Education of Uncle Paul* (1909), *The Human Chord* (1910), and *The Centaur* (1911).

And yet, both the life and work of Algernon Blackwood (1869-1951) remain irksomely little-known. The image of the ageing Blackwood—bald, gaunt, leather-skinned, with deep-set eyes that seem simultaneously grave and impish—is perhaps not as ubiquitous as H. P. Lovecraft's similarly gaunt profile, but it must have fascinated those lucky viewers of the BBC who witnessed it on various television shows on which Blackwood appeared in the last fifteen years of his life. Unfortunately, his work—hundreds of short stories, more than a dozen novels, several plays, scores of essays and reviews, and a number of works for children—has now, in large part, fallen out of print, with only intermittent attempts to bring it to the attention of new readers.

But all that could be changing. And if there is a revival of interest in Blackwood the man and Blackwood the writer, the overwhelming bulk of the credit for it will fall upon a single man—Mike Ashley.

Algernon Blackwood: An Extraordinary Life (Carroll & Graf, 2001; first published by Constable as *Starlight Man: The Extraordinary Life of Algernon Blackwood*) is the result of nearly a quarter-century's research by Ashley into every possible nook and cranny that could shed any light on this British colossus whose life extended into eight decades and whose literary work spanned more than six. As one who has toiled for an approximately similar period in the research and writing of a biography, I can attest that Ashley's achievement in this book is titanic, monumental, and almost beyond cavil. Criticism becomes almost an impertinence when faced with a book that displays such massive research, such skilled organisation of that research, and, most significant of all, such a remarkable revivification of its subject. Blackwood *lives* in this book as few other subjects of biographies have ever lived in theirs.

I trust readers will pardon a brief comparison of this work with my biography of Lovecraft—a comparison, I hasten to add, that will only make Ashley's accomplishment stand out in greater relief. The differences in writing a biography of Lovecraft and a biography of Blackwood are stark and telling. Most important is the matter of the existing documentary record. Whereas Lovecraft overwhelms us with his thousands upon thousands of surviving letters (totalling more than four million words), Blackwood by design left a paucity of correspondence: if there are even as much as 100,000 words of letters extant, I would be surprised. Matters were, of course, not helped by the fact that Blackwood's home in London was destroyed in the Blitz in 1940, with the resultant destruction of many of his papers and effects. The end result is that Ashley has had to undertake an enormously tedious and time-consuming paper-chase for any existing scraps of letters by or to Blackwood that might shed light on his life, work, and thought.

Another difference between Blackwood and Lovecraft is the sheer length of the former's life as compared to the latter's. Lovecraft, to be sure, witnessed a significant amount of cultural change from the age of Grover Cleveland to the Depression; but Blackwood, born in the height of Queen Victoria's reign, did not die until well after World War II, a period of eight decades that, in Bertrand Russell's view, saw more historical changes than the preceding two millennia combined. If any criticism of Ashley's biography can be made, it is that we are occasionally rushed through the years with little attempt to paint the historical background. Perhaps the paucity of the documentary record is in part to blame for this; it also appears that Ashley's British publisher enforced a rather Procrustean word-limit, compelling him to cut a substantial portion of text to bring it down to size. The end result is that Ashley is obliged to focus largely on Blackwood's own life and does not have the room to portray that life against the backdrop of his time.

One would suppose that Blackwood's own autobiography, *Episodes Before Thirty* (1923), obviated the need for any detailed treatment of the first three decades of his life. (I gain the impression that biographers of Arthur Machen have been more than a little intimidated by the panache and poignancy of his three autobiographies. We still have no satisfactory life of the great Welsh mystic.) But Ashley shows that that volume both conceals and omits vital information: many of the names of his friends and colleagues during his years in New York and Canada in the last decade of the nineteenth century were deliberately changed, and even Ashley's exhaustive researches have not always succeeded in unearthing their real identities. In any event, Blackwood's biography ends just as his literary career is about to begin, so that, at a minimum, we need a detailed treatment of the final five decades of his life. Blackwood himself occasionally made efforts to write an *Episodes After Thirty*, but never brought the book to completion.

The image of Blackwood that emerges from Ashley's biography is undeniably appealing. He remained for the whole of his life a child at heart, and it is this—the ability to view the bewildering events of the modern world with the innocent, wonder-filled eyes of childhood—that lends to his work (even his weird fiction) its utterly refreshing quality. As heedless of money and incompetent at the task of gathering shekels as Lovecraft, Blackwood was luckier in that much of his life was spent in relative economic comfort, if by no means luxury. As with Lord Dunsany, this comfort allowed Blackwood to write whatever he wished to write, without concern for markets or audience.

Blackwood put nearly all the events of his life to good use in fiction, even if in some cases it took decades for him to digest those events and transmute them into literary creation. The wilds of Canada, which he experienced in the late 1880s and which helped to nurture a lifelong sense of the overwhelming power and vitality of Nature, finds its way into "The Wendigo" and other works. The grinding poverty he experienced as a cub reporter in New York in the 1890s is perhaps most strikingly etched in *Episodes Before Thirty*, but also led to such works as "The Strange Adventures of a Private Secretary in New York." A trip to the Danube in 1900 is echoed with surprising faithfulness in "The Willows," as is a trip to the Caucasus in *The Centaur*. The great majority of Blackwood's work is autobiographical, and in a sense far more profound than merely the use of known locales; every one of his works reflects the Nature-mysticism and the desire to expand the bounds of consciousness that are at the source of his view of life, and which led him fleetingly to look for answers—or, perhaps, to seek an escape from the grinding materialism of modern life—in occultism, theosophy, the Golden Dawn, and, later, the philosophy of Gurdjieff.

I have no intention of retelling Blackwood's life in small compass here; all readers owe it to themselves to see how skilfully Ashley has marshalled a bewildering mass of fragmentary data into a seamless narrative of a life rich with friends, family (although Blackwood remained a lifelong bachelor), and literary accomplishment. The unexpected success of the best-selling *John Silence—Physician Extraordinary* (1908) allowed Blackwood to spend the next half-decade in Switzerland, and Ashley is right to remark that "The next five years would see Blackwood produce the most remarkable body of supernatural fiction ever written." The story collections *The Lost Valley* (1910), *Pan's Garden* (1912), and *Incredible Adventures* (1914; my own choice as the greatest collection of weird tales ever written); the novels *Jimbo* (1909; first draft written years earlier), *The Human Chord*, *The Centaur* (Blackwood's spiritual autobiography and the centrepiece of his entire work), and *A Prisoner in Fairyland* (1913): these volumes and others attest to the truth of Ashley's contention.

The rest of Blackwood's career was, however, a series of fits and starts. Ashley finds more value in *Julius LeVallon* (1916) than I do; he actually calls it "arguably the best of all his novels." Its loose sequel, *The Bright Messenger* (1921), is to my mind still less successful; Ashley charitably notes that it is "a courageous book—intelligent, unique, original. Alas, it is not a great book." It is, indeed, rather chilling to read at this point in Ashley's book that "Blackwood had said all he wanted to say." The last three decades of his life were devoted chiefly to plays (notably *The Starlight Express*, an adaptation of *A Pris-*

oner in Fairyland, with music by Edward Elgar), to works for children, and especially to appearances on radio and television. To my mind none of the later works for (or about) children can measure up to the utterly charming and patently autobiographical *The Education of Uncle Paul*, one of the lost classics of fantasy and a book desperately crying out for reprinting, perhaps in conjunction with *Jimbo*. Ashley, to my mind, considerably overpraises the late *The Fruit Stoners* (1934), saying of it: "Although deeply philosophical, the book is devoid of the oversentimentality of *The Education of Uncle Paul*, and the verbosity of *A Prisoner in Fairyland*, and has a stronger narrative drive than *The Extra Day*, which makes it the most accomplished of his childhood books." Well, perhaps a rereading is in order; however much one may disagree with Ashley's judgments, his opinions are always worthy of respect.

One could go on and on about Blackwood, and about Ashley's biography. The obscure facts that he has unearthed are endlessly fascinating. Who could have imagined that, as a reporter in 1893, Blackwood interviewed Lizzie Borden? that a 1925 revival of the play *Through the Crack* marked "the first professional theatrical work for Laurence Olivier" (he was "a second assistant stage manager and general understudy")? that Blackwood was saved from death by a German bomb by rushing out of his house to check on some burning sausages? If one must cavil, one might say that Ashley's discussion of Blackwood's works tends a bit too much toward plot summary (necessary in many cases because of their current unavailability) and not enough in the way of analysis. But that analysis can now be left to others—or to Ashley himself, if he wishes to write a companion critical study—since the fundamental facts of Blackwood's life have now finally been charted. One hesitates to use the word "definitive" for any work of scholarship, but it is difficult to imagine anyone writing a more detailed, more exhaustive, and at the same time a more empathetic and heartwarming biography. Through Mike Ashley, we come to know Algernon Blackwood, to admire him, and to wish that he had been our own "Uncle Paul."

Some years prior to completing his biography, Ashley had compiled *Algernon Blackwood: A Bio-Bibliography* (Greenwood Press, 1987). He toiled for a decade on this work, and it shows. With this volume the bibliography of Blackwood never need be done again (something, I fear, that cannot be said of the well-known bibliographies of Clark Ashton Smith and Robert E. Howard, which beg for recompilation by someone who actually knows bibliography).

Of the bibliography itself I am scarcely competent to speak—perhaps no one but Ashley is. Aside from bibliographical information, we are given brief plot summaries of every single work Blackwood ever wrote; the listing of shorter works supplies information on all appearances of the work—in magazines, anthologies, and collections (I mention this because in my Lovecraft bibliography I could only cross-reference this material in an index). The most tantalising thing is a listing of unpublished items: there are two incomplete novels and several short stories here, and it is stupefying to me that this material—along with the vast quantity of uncollected Blackwood (stories, radio plays, talks, essays, poetry)—has not been published or reissued. Presumably Ashley is working on the task. In some ways the bibliography is almost too complete: everything is indexed, re-indexed, and cross-indexed; we are even told which libraries in the United States, Canada, and England own Blackwood books and which specific titles they own—something I have never seen in a bibliography. A chronological index to Blackwood's publications, at the end of the book, will be enormously useful to someone tracing the course and development of his work. For the foreseeable future, this work, along with the biography, will be the Bible of Blackwood studies.

The indefatigable Ashley followed up his bibliography with a collection of rare and uncollected stories, *The Magic Mirror: Lost Supernatural and Mystery Stories by Algernon Blackwood* (Thorsons/Equation, 1989). Any collection of "lost" stories is unlikely to contain matter that is uniformly equal to what the author himself published (unless, as in the case of Lovecraft, the author never managed to assemble his work in his lifetime). Blackwood himself gathered his tales into a dozen collections, and it must be admitted that, on the whole, he selected his best work for these volumes. There is, certainly, no tale in *The Magic Mirror* that ranks with the very best of Blackwood—such stories as "A Descent into Egypt," "The Man Whom the Trees Loved," and "Sand"—and several stories fall flat or are curiously pulpish in style, such as "The Man-Eater," published in *Thrilling Mystery* after being rejected by higher-paying magazines. Nevertheless, there are a few gems. "The Kit-Bag" has an atmosphere of clutching horror, "The Singular Death of Morton" is an effective vampire story, and there are two exquisitely delicate war fantasies—"The Soldier's Visitor" and "The Memory of Beauty"—that are dimly reminiscent of Machen's similar efforts. Two later comic stories, "The Voice" and "The Magic Mirror," are surprisingly similar in tone and flavour to Dunsany's Jorkens tales, although any actual literary influence is highly unlikely. "Roman Remains," a very late tale originally published in *Weird Tales* for March 1948, would have been a superbly atmospheric story if Blackwood had not tacked on too much explanation at the end.

Ashley was wise to have included in this volume extracts from Blackwood's best novels—*Jimbo, The Education of Uncle Paul, The Centaur,* and *Julius LeVallon*—since it is these works that embody the core of Blackwood's thought and also contain some of his finest prose. All four novels are landmarks in weird fiction, and they are absolutely essential to a proper understanding of Blackwood. Few of them are explicitly horrific, but they all poignantly reflect in various ways the essence of Blackwood's mystic Nature-philosophy.

The revelation that Blackwood was a great success on radio opens up a whole realm of work that needs to be studied. Machen and Dunsany occasionally appeared on the BBC, but Blackwood found a virtual new career from the middle 1930s and through the 1940s as a teller of tales on radio and even television. Ashley has included several of Blackwood's tales written specifically for radio, and a critical analysis of them must take cognisance of this different medium in assessing them.

Mike Ashley, not merely the leading but virtually the only Blackwood scholar, has written a substantial introduction to this book, and his notes prefacing the stories are models of conciseness and lucidity. The critical study of Blackwood is still in its infancy, but we need volumes like this to comprehend the nature and scope of his achievement.

Arthur Machen: A Minor Classic

Arthur Machen is a writer who needs to be periodically rediscovered. Unlike Edgar Allan Poe, now firmly ensconced in the rolls of world literature, or H. P. Lovecraft, who after many fits and starts seems unlikely to fall back into obscurity, Machen has, ever since he began publishing his work widely, flirted intermittently with fame and oblivion. He horrified the timid and conventional in the 1890s; raised a furore over "The Bowmen" in the teens of the last century; was lauded by James Branch Cabell, Vincent Starrett, Carl Van Vechten, H. P. Lovecraft, and other American enthusiasts in the twenties; became a respected elder statesman of literature and recipient of a civil list pension in the thirties; and has been the subject of fleeting biographies, critical studies (notably by Wesley Sweetser), a landmark bibliography (by Sweetser and Adrian Goldstone), and articles for the last four decades. The Arthur Machen Society is occasionally active, but its publications are rarely seen beyond its limited circle. Two of those members, Mark Valentine and Roger Dobson, have produced a noteworthy compilation in *Arthur Machen: Apostle of Wonder* (Caermaen Books, 1985).

Machen's work has many flaws and many virtues. The latter speak for themselves: a magically evocative and musical prose style—easily one of the best in English whenever he is being honest and not derivative; a horrific imagination that invests the ordinary with a sort of transcendental wonder, as of marvels just out of vision's reach (in this sense his most typical work is the hauntingly pensive—and unjustly forgotten and inaccessible—*A Fragment of Life*); a power for summoning up the latent mysteries of Nature akin to and perhaps more powerful than that of Hawthorne. The flaws are equally obvious. First and foremost, Machen wrote too much—his countless articles and essays say the same things many times over; his work is full of inessential and unsuccessful attempts, such as *Dr Stiggins* and *The Canning Wonder*; he is very uneven, and many tales go nowhere (especially the disappointing late novel

The Green Round); his longer works have little structure or unity, and in all his work he is discursive and occasionally verbose.

Another feature of Machen's work is his inability to distance himself from his creations. It is obvious (and would be so even to one who knew nothing of Machen's biography) that he himself is the hero of *The Hill of Dreams* and *The Secret Glory*; in many other stories he uses characters as transparent mouthpieces for the views he upholds or (as in *Dr Stiggins*) rejects. In prior days this might have been considered a flaw, but newer critical theories have been breaking down the distinction between fiction and nonfiction, and Machen can be seen as a herald of that trend: his autobiographies read like novels, his novels read like confessions. And *The Hill of Dreams*—that poignant, agonising book about a man's attempt to express the inexpressible—can be seen as another curious foreshadowing of modernism, since (as many critics have wryly noted) the subject of most novels nowadays seems to be the difficulty of writing a novel. Machen was boldly facing what was to become the central issue of modern philosophy: is it possible for words to convey reality? Wittgenstein, after all his work in linguistic analysis, felt reduced to representing truth in a series of grunts and gestures; and Machen's Lucian Taylor at the last reaches a similar conclusion.

Arthur Machen: Apostle of Wonder reprints some older essays—Anthony Lejeune's and M. P. Shiel's memoirs of Machen—and contains fine new studies by Roger Dobson, Mark Valentine, Nic Howard, and—perhaps the best of all—Andy Sawyer on *The Hill of Dreams*. Dobson provides a "pilgrim's guide" to Machen's residences in England, and the editors have charmingly unearthed brief quotations by and about Machen (by Lovecraft, Starrett, Cyril Connolly, Jerome K. Jerome, and others) to serve as "fillers" to round out a page. There could be many such; one of my favourites (not cited in this book) comes from Robert Hillyer: "My first feeling was one of admiration for a writer who so robustly held to his own destiny, and compromised only the happiness of his existence, never the perfection of his style, to make a living." We can only think of Lovecraft.

When Machen's *The Secret Glory* was published in 1922, fifteen years after he had written it, it contained four long chapters narrating in loving detail the spiritual and physical journey of Ambrose Meyrick from school days at Lupton to his native Wales; there then followed a very brief appendix in which Meyrick's journey was hastily concluded. If this appendix reads like a sort of synopsis, that is because it is exactly that. The last two chapters of the novel, constituting some 143 pages of manuscript, were omitted by Machen, perhaps because the novel had already attained considerable size; these chapters were evidently given to Vincent Starrett, who deposited them at the Beinecke Rare Book Library at Yale University with Machen's stipulation that they never be published.

So the matter stood until a few years ago, when I finally secured the permission of Machen's agents and of his surviving daughter Janet (now deceased) to secure a photocopy of the manuscript from Yale. Having done so, I proceeded to make a transcript as best I could, although I did not find Machen's handwriting quite as easy to read as I do Lovecraft's. I sent both the photocopy of the manuscript and my transcript to various Machen enthusiasts in England, and eventually they found their way into the hands of Ray Russell, who prepared a new and better transcript and secured permission to publish the item. *The Secret Glory: Chapters Five and Six* (Tartarus Press, 1991) appeared in a handsome hardcover edition of 250 copies, and every Machen devotee ought to secure it.

I do not have the space here to conduct a full-scale analysis of *The Secret Glory*: it is a dense, rich novel with some of Machen's best writing in it. But I will say that I have always been troubled by the ill-fitting juxtaposition of a rather nasty (but probably justified) satire on the English school system with an ethereal account of Meyrick's quest for the Holy Grail. Machen—in an introduction to the novel published here for the first time—actually addresses this issue: "I myself have seen something of life—I mean of real life—and my experience teaches me that the veils of enigmas are drawn aside not so much by faery shores or in enchanted castles as in Pentonville and Lloyd square." This means—and it is something to which Lovecraft would have given full assent—that one must start with the real, the actual, in order to make the fantastic credible. This principle is, in the abstract, unexceptionable; I am simply not certain that Machen has executed it very well in *The Secret Glory*. I believe he accomplished the feat much better in *The Hill of Dreams* and especially in that unjustly forgotten masterwork, *A Fragment of Life*.

And yet, *The Secret Glory* as a whole, and these last two chapters in particular, embody some of Machen's most vital and intimate writing. He has a delightful section where Meyrick joins a roving band of actors, and it becomes clear that he is drawing upon his own experiences as a bit player in Frank Benson's company. Meyrick's romance with Nelly, narrated in the earlier sections of the novel, gives way to a romance with Sylvia Vaughan, the daughter of a relative in Wales with whom Meyrick stays; this relationship is portrayed with the utmost delicacy and grace—I do not know any weird writer who could have handled it better. As a whole, however, *The Secret Glory* (these two final chapters included) tends to meander: it is full of digressions, pseudo-philosophical set-pieces (several of which had previously appeared as magazine articles), and vicious attacks on those aspects of modern civilisation (and there were many) of which Machen did not approve. But even if it is not very unified, it is still worth reading for its exquisite prose and for what it tells us about the life and mind of Arthur Machen.

Critical work on Machen is still at a relatively primitive stage, and is still confined on the whole to Machen devotees. Ray Russell issued two volumes of *Machenalia* in 1990, and they contain some very meritorious material. Of the five articles in Volume 1, the palm must be accorded to Kenneth W. Faig's "Heaven and Hell: Abnormal Mental States in 'N' and 'The Exalted Omega,'" which occupies a full half of the entire booklet. Like Machen's own works, it tends to ramble, but one cannot help finding the ramble diverting and informative. Faig sheds fascinating light on these two late and relatively obscure tales, and the article complements Dale J. Nelson's piece on "N" which opens the volume. Mike Butterworth, beginning with a rumination on that imperishable opening line of *The Hill of Dreams* ("There was a glow in the sky as if great furnace doors were opened"), provides an earnest defence of Machen's visionary mysticism. V. Williams ably defends the late novel *The Green Round* while acknowledging its faults, and Roger Dobson suggests an intriguing link between the narrator of Machen's treatise on aesthetics, *Hieroglyphics*, with the narrator of "The White People."

Volume II of *Machenalia* is still more substantial, containing some of the best criticism on Machen in recent years. Roger Dobson contributes a superb essay on that superb collection of prose poems, *Ornaments in Jade*; Godfrey Brangham all too briefly touches upon the role of women in Machen's work; Jonathan Wood offers a highly stimulating piece on Machen's prefaces to the works of other authors and their importance to his life and thought (an article on his prefaces to his own works would be still more illuminating); John Howard studies boundary imagery in Machen's works—again briefly but suggestively; and Gregory Ventre provides a wide-ranging analysis of *The Three Impostors*, although he is perhaps a little too interested in summing up other critics' views of this work, and of Machen generally, rather than offering his own opinions. Every essay in this volume is solidly researched and conceived, and I only wish the authors had allowed themselves more room to develop their ideas.

The copyediting, proofreading, and general typography of all three volumes under review could perhaps have been improved; while considerably above the level of "fan" publications, they are not quite of professional calibre. I am referring, of course, purely to matters of production and design, not to the quality of material. It is, however, interesting that, of the nine different contributors to *Machenalia*, only one (Dale J. Nelson) is a university professor. This is still the situation even in the criticism of Lovecraft, and I am the last person on earth to be condescending toward amateur scholars. Machen is a writer eminently worth studying, and if academicians are not interested in him, it is their loss.

The ultimate fate of Arthur Machen is still not clear, and is perhaps not ours to determine. Such writers as Lovecraft, Robert E. Howard, and Tolkien command immense popular followings, and now require only increased critical attention to ensure their literary recognition; but Machen joins Lord Dunsany, William Hope Hodgson, M. P. Shiel, and Clark Ashton Smith in appealing only to a limited band of cognoscenti, and as a result they may never gain the academic attention they deserve. But perhaps it is better thus: there are few fates more horrible to conceive than of a writer who is nothing but fodder for dissertations.

What is Machen's place? Perhaps Andy Sawyer's concluding statement in *Arthur Machen: Apostle of Wonder*, in reference to *The Hill of Dreams*, can be applied more generally to Machen himself: "A minor classic? Yes, I think so." There is no condescension in this remark.

William Hope Hodgson: Writer on the Borderland

The degree to which William Hope Hodgson has been ignored even by critics of weird fiction is remarkable to the point of being offensive: author of four of the most powerful horror novels of his time, as well as of many superb short stories, Hodgson has yet to receive anything approaching comprehensive treatment. Ian Bell notes toward the end of his slim but substantial collection of essays, *William Hope Hodgson: Voyages and Visions* (Bell, 1987), that "a full-scale biography and critique are much to be desired." That is putting it mildly. In recent years R. Alain Everts and Sam Moskowitz have done much on the biographical side, but we may well have to confess that Lovecraft's treatment of Hodgson's work in "Supernatural Horror in Literature" and Brian Stableford's in *Scientific Romance in Britain 1890–1950* (1985) are still the best and most "comprehensive" discussions—best, that is, until Bell's heaven-sent booklet.

Bell devotes a certain amount of space to biographical matters: articles by him, Richard Dalby, and Mark Valentine fill in little-known aspects of Hodgson's life, and Dalby reprints some fascinating brief articles by Hodgson on physical exercise—one of them evidently his first published work. But the rest of the book is devoted to criticism—by Peter Tremayne, Michael Goss, Valentine, Brian Stableford, Bell, Andy Sawyer, and Roger Dobson. Cumulatively, these articles add up to the most exhaustive and penetrating treatment Hodgson's work has ever received.

There is an understandable inclination on the part of some Hodgson devotees to be wildly hyperbolic as to his merits: Tremayne soberly informs us that "no writer has ever described a storm at sea with such skill as Hodgson" (momentarily forgetting, no doubt, Poe's "Descent into the Maelström" or any number of passages in the works of Joseph Conrad), and Dobson quotes the dubious Lin Carter as saying that "not Conrad—not Melville—could have done what Hodgson did in *The Ghost Pirates*." All this is harmless enough, and is rather reminiscent of the early stages of serious Lovecraft criticism; scholars will eventually learn that floridity of this sort is actually self-defeating by inspiring outraged incredulity. It is fortunate that most contributors to this volume simply address Hodgson's work and only indirectly convey its brilliance by the subtlety of their interpretations—a subtlety impossible for work that does not deserve to survive.

While there is universal praise for *The House on the Borderland* (Stableford's philological conjectures as to Hodgson's possible stages of composition of the novel are as fascinating as Sawyer's analysis of it as literally a "borderland" between old-time Gothicism and forward-looking science fiction), the sea tales and novels do not seem to have won over as many readers. But Goss's essay, perhaps the best in the book, is wonderfully illuminating in showing how the ship isolates human beings from normality and leaves them terrifyingly alone in the face of the supernatural. Analogously, Valentine largely succeeds in defending the Carnacki stories as more than merely clever twists on the "infallible detective" theme; they are more integral to the rest of Hodgson's work than we suspected.

But the greatest controversy rages over *The Night Land*; and the controversy, interestingly enough, is by no means settled in this volume, where Bell and Sawyer present quite different evaluations of this sprawling work. I am entirely willing to believe Bell in regarding the love element as central to the novel, Lovecraft's derisive comments notwithstanding (Dobson makes the same point and rightly chastises Lovecraft for his similar—and still more myopic—dismissal of Shiel's *The Purple Cloud*); but I am less certain whether any critic in this volume really comes to terms with its peculiar style. Whereas Sawyer flatly declares that the style is "excruciatingly awful," Bell maintains that the "archaism" is necessary "in establishing the distinctive (and all-important) sombre atmosphere of the work." These two views are not necessarily contradictory, but what both of them overlook is that the style is not "archaic" in any meaningful sense of the term. The style of *The Night Land* is a schoolboy archaism written by someone who had absolutely no conception of what seventeenth- or eighteenth-century style actually was. Lovecraft gets to the heart of the matter by remarking in a letter: "Tsathoggua! but what sort of insanity gets hold of some of these birds (W. H. Hodgson is the classic and memorable offender . . .) when they try to represent the diction of an age which after all is, historically speaking, essentially modern? Haven't they ever read Goldsmith and Fielding and Johnson and Gibbon and Sterne and Smollett and dozens of other prose writers of that fairly recent yesterday?" (*Selected Letters* 5.430–31). One could accept the style of *The Night Land* if only it were not premised to be the style of a very well-known historical period.

But arguments of this sort are healthy, especially when we are at an early stage in the critical analysis of an author. There is much to be done in Hodgson—his uncollected work needs to be gathered (and is now being gathered in Night Shade's five-volume edition of his complete fiction), more biographical research (particularly as regards the actual writing of his work and its possible sources) must be done, and his place in literary history more precisely fixed. Ian Bell and his associates have made a notable first step in that direction.

E. F. Benson: Spooks and More Spooks

I have often wondered how one goes about reviewing a reprint of an established classic. The accustomed practice, from my experience, is to discuss everything except the text itself: the elegance of the typeface; the quality of the illustrations (if any); the skill of the editor in preparing the text (or, as in the case of some recent editions of *Ulysses*, the lack of it). In a sense, this sort of reticence is understandable, for there is a certain impertinence in a reviewer giving his offhand critical judgments of a work that has already stood the test of time and become suitably canonised.

If I take the opposite approach here, it is because the ghost stories of E. F. Benson are not established, but neglected classics. I can attest to this personally in that I have not even been able to find, much less read, the bulk of the stories in the mammoth and landmark volume *The Collected Ghost Stories of E. F. Benson* (Carroll & Graf, 1992); for Benson's four collections of weird tales are among the rarest jewels for the collector of fantasy and horror, and it is precisely their fabulous scarcity that has made them undeservedly neglected when a case could, and should, be made that they ought to take their place next to the stories of M. R. James, Oliver Onions, and Walter de la Mare as a watershed in the British ghost story tradition.

The Collected Ghost Stories of E. F. Benson contains an ambiguity found in all titles that utilise the word "collected": it can either be a synonym for "complete," or (somewhat disingenuously) simply refer to those works that happen to have been collected for this edition. Here it is the latter meaning that applies. All that Richard Dalby has done is to print, unchanged, the contents of Benson's four collections of weird tales—*The Room in the Tower* (1912; RT), *Visible and Invisible* (1923; VI), *Spook Stories* (1928; SS), and *More Spook Stories* (1934; MSS)—along with an introduction by himself, a foreword by Joan Aiken, and an early article by Benson on a witchcraft trial. He has not printed the few weird tales found in Benson's otherwise mainstream collection, *The Countess of Lowndes Square* (1920), and (a little uncharitably) does not so much as mention Jack Adrian's admirable volume of Benson's uncollected weird tales, *The Flint Knife* (Equation, 1988). Adrian's edition of Benson's *Desirable*

Residences and Other Stories (Oxford University Press, 1991) also contains a few more weird specimens not in Dalby's volume. Dalby has not even been very helpful in indicating the breakdowns of the four collections he has printed; let me therefore state here that, as printed in this volume, *The Room in the Tower* comprises the first seventeen stories, *Visible and Invisible* the next twelve, *Spook Stories* the next twelve, and *More Spook Stories* the final thirteen.

This range of writing—covering more than two decades in a literary career than spanned almost five—must testify to the persistence of a sense of the weird in Benson. Benson was, of course, in his time better known for his mainstream novels, stories, and nonfiction works; and in some bizarre fashion his "Mapp and Lucia" society novels experienced a resurgence in popularity some time ago. But it would not be unkind to Benson to say that his weird tales will survive—and deserve to survive—long after all this other matter has fallen into merited oblivion.

And yet, Benson does not appear to have had a very exalted or carefully worked-out view of the writing of ghost stories. In his autobiography, *Final Edition* (1940), he writes offhandedly, "Now ghost stories . . . are a branch of literature at which I have often tried my hand," going on merely to speak of certain fairly obvious points of technique ("The narrator, I think, must succeed in frightening himself before he can hope to frighten his readers"). Benson was, at least in his own mind, pretty much of a traditionalist in the ghost story tradition—a fact emphasised by his presence at a celebrated meeting of the Chitchat Society in 1893 at which M. R. James read his earliest ghost stories. It would be nearly twenty years before Benson's own first weird volume would appear, by which time James had already published the first two of his collections; and yet, I do not believe that Benson can be passed off merely as an imitator of James, or even one who followed very closely in his footsteps.

The curious thing about Benson is that, almost in spite of himself, he modernised or updated the Jamesian ghost story in several ways. James's tales always hark backward, sometimes to the very distant past, as is perhaps fitting for an authority on mediaeval manuscripts; Benson's tales rarely do so, and are sometimes aggressively set in the present. One of his earliest stories, "The Dust-Cloud" (*RT*), involves the ghost of an automobile ("Seems almost too up-to-date, doesn't it?" one character remarks). In "The Confession of Charles Linkworth" (*RT*) the ghost of a man who has been executed for murder communicates by telephone to a chaplain, pleading for absolution; "In the Tube" (*VI*) takes place in the London underground. Other stories, in order to introduce the weird subtly and covertly, are written in that archly sophisticated manner found in his society novels, but in so doing they create a "modern" atmosphere precisely analogous to contemporary writers' setting weird tales at rock concerts or nightclubs. The opening pages of "The Shootings of Achnaleish" (*RT*) involve a comic banter and emphasis on the mundane

("Rent only £350!") that suggest anything but the weird, so that the supernatural phenomenon is the more striking and powerful when it finally does emerge.

But there is more to this than merely using the observable tokens of the present in a tale. It must be declared that Benson was a confirmed spiritualist—his brief discussion of ghost stories in *Final Edition* is prefaced by a perfectly serious account of an apparition he and a friend claim to have seen—and many of his tales present elaborate pseudo-scientific justifications of ghosts and other weird phenomena on spiritualistic grounds. This also serves to "modernise" his tales, and in two ways: first, Benson was riding a wave of spiritualism that gathered strength after the first world war; and second, Benson's very need to account for his apparitions by means of philosophy or science (or what for him passes for such) betrays his unconscious absorption of the positivism of his day, whereby spiritualistic phenomena could not be accepted on their own but required a (usually specious) "proof" to overcome the scepticism that had already become ingrained in the majority of intelligent people.

It should be pointed out that Benson was not exactly an occultist, in spite of his passing mention in "The Dust-Cloud" of "occult senses" by which the supernatural can be perceived. But his tales (as well as some of his otherwise mainstream novels) are full of Ouija boards, séances, and other paraphernalia of the spiritualism popular in his day, and there is no question—in spite of the flippancy of some of his treatments of these matters—that he took the whole subject quite seriously. The canonical spiritualistic/philosophical "defence" for the weird occurs in "The Other Bed" (*RT*):

> "Everything that happens," he said, "whether it is a step we take, or a thought that crosses our mind, makes some change in its immediate material world. Now the most violent and concentrated emotion we can imagine is the emotion that leads a man to take so extreme a step as killing himself or somebody else. I can easily imagine such a deed so eating into the material scene, the room or the haunted heath, where it happens, that its mark lasts an enormous time. The air rings with the cry of the slain and still drips with his blood. It is not everybody who will perceive it, but sensitives will."

This is all very elegant, even though upon analysis it devolves into mere poetic metaphor instead of science or philosophy. But it neatly accounts for the "haunting" of a given spot (which in nearly all Benson's stories is the product of a crime—usually murder or suicide—committed there) and for why only "sensitives" can perceive it rather than most of us hard-headed materialists. In effect, what Benson is arguing for is (as he says in an another story, "Outside the Door" [*RT*]) "how inextricable is the interweaving between mind, soul, life . . . and the purely material part of the created world"—an utterance, incidentally, that betrays the flaw in Benson's thinking at this point in its invalid distinction between "mind, soul, life" and what he fallaciously takes to be "dead" matter. But let that pass; the mere fact that Benson felt the need for such justifications—rather laborious on occasion—is telling. No longer could the weird be presented merely as such, without at least a gesture of rationalisation.

It is perhaps not a wise thing to read Benson's weird tales all at once, for they (like nearly all their kind, including James's) become repetitive and monotonous after a time. I do not see much development, either conceptually or aesthetically, in the corpus of Benson's stories; if anything, his first two collections represent (again like James) a pinnacle from which he only declined in later years. And all those séances really do become a little tiresome after a while. Benson has great fun with them in some tales, especially "Mr Tilly's Séance" (VI), in which a real spirit exposes a fraud medium; but at the very time that this fraud is being exposed, the "reality" of the spiritual world is confirmed.

The truth of the matter is that some of Benson's most successful tales are not ghost stories at all (note that he never used that phrase in the titles of any of his collections, as James did for his first two) but pure "weird tales" where the phenomena are of a much more unclassifiable sort. Already in "Between the Lights" (RT), an early tale, Benson is declaring, "The paraphernalia of ghosts has become somehow rather hackneyed." His best tale may be "The Man Who Went Too Far" (RT), in which a young man, Darcy, seems to have developed some unnatural sense of communion with the natural world. And yet, phrased this way, it becomes clear that what Darcy has actually done (whether from psychic possession by Pan or not) is to have sloughed off the "unnatural" encumbrances of civilisation and returned to the purity of Nature. But because Darcy has adopted a perhaps one-sided view of Nature as pure benevolence and joy, he is overwhelmed by the revelation of the violent side of creation. "The Man Who Went Too Far" is a tale that deftly combines ecstasy, awe, and horror into an inextricable union.

Other non-ghost stories are nearly as effective. "Mrs Amworth" (VI) is a classic vampire tale; "Caterpillars" (RT) introduces us to an image—huge writhing slugs—that Benson uses frequently in his tales; "'And the Dead Spake'" (VI) chillingly tells of a scientist who has found some way to "tap" into the brains of the dead; in "The Horror-Horn" (VI) we find a hideous race of dwarfish quasi-human beings said to live in caves in the Alps; elementals are put on stage in "'And No Bird Sings'" (SS); and so on. Later tales utilise seemingly conventional ghost-story scenarios to convey moral or social messages, usually the anguish of marital discord, a theme to which the lifelong bachelor Benson recurs with anomalous frequency. Then there is the delicate "Pirates" (MSS), a poignant story of a lonely elderly man recovering his childhood. An autobiographical reading can scarcely be avoided here.

There is much more one can say about the weird tales of E. F. Benson, and a substantial account of his work has yet to be written. Neither Joan Aiken's foreword (which harps on Benson's possible misogyny, as if literature were designed to promote proper social behaviour) nor Dalby's chatty biographical introduction do much to lay the groundwork for such a piece, but all the evidence one needs is in the actual tales in this volume—along, of course, with the other volumes of Benson's work mentioned earlier. Once such an analysis is made, it may well become evident that Benson was a key transitional figure between the "classic" ghost story of M. R. James and the psychological ghost stories of Walter de la Mare, Oliver Onions, and L. P. Hartley. In the meantime, *The Collected Ghost Stories of E. F. Benson* is a volume no weird library can afford to be without; if nothing else, it will save us all a great deal of time and money hunting for those rare collections that have vanished like all the will-o'-the-wisps Benson saw in every haunted wood or lonely cottage.

A. M. Burrage: The Ghost Man

For my sins, I had not read a word of A. M. Burrage before I came upon *Someone in the Room: Strange Tales Old and New* (Ash-Tree Press, 1997)—not even the famously obscure *Some Ghost Stories* (1927), a reprint of which I have owned for some time. *Someone in the Room* is the third of four volumes assembling all Burrage's weird tales, and whatever one may think of the overall level of quality of his work, praise must be extended to Ash-Tree Press for this effort in preserving the literary remains of a writer who at least commands our respect for his tenacity and devotion to the cause of weird literature.

The two previous volumes of Burrage's work—*Intruders: New Weird Tales* (1995) and *The Occult Files of Francis Chard: Some Ghost Stories* (1996)—have, indeed, evoked mixed responses. The genial Chet Williamson, always responsive to the classic British ghost story, reported that, although *Intruders* "is very much a potluck dinner," the "good [stories] outweigh the bad, and the best are very good indeed" (*Necrofile* No. 19 [Winter 1996]: 6–7). Conversely, Darrell Schweitzer, who is perhaps a little harder on old-time weird work than he should be, dismissed most of the tales in *Some Ghost Stories*: "These are not horror stories. There is no fear in them. As stories of any kind they are just too simple" (*Necrofile* No. 28 [Spring 1998]: 10). My own opinion of *Someone in the Room* is perhaps a little between these poles, but much more toward Williamson's than Schweitzer's.

There is, indeed, some justification for Schweitzer's irritation that Burrage feels the need to insert an actual ghost into nearly all his tales; but this is a limitation of the entire subgenre of the "ghost story," and it applies as much to the more sophisticated work of M. R. James as it does to James's resolutely second-rate imitators. And it is perhaps no surprise that many of the most effective tales in *Someone in the Room* are those that unexpectedly depart from this standard scenario.

The first half of the volume consists of uncollected tales taken from the many magazines in which Burrage appeared; some had been collected in a volume assembled by Anthony Skene, *Between the Minute and the Hour* (1967), but this volume is itself now quite scarce. There are some surprisingly fine moments in them. Schweitzer may not think there is any fear in Burrage, but I for one got an authentic chill out of the very first story, "The House of Unrest." A family has moved into a new house, and everything seems placid and even rather tedious—except for the fact that the family's first visitor suffered an epileptic fit on the doorstep. What could have caused it? Later another member of the family sees what he takes to be a tramp lurking in the garden. Finally the family friend, Noel, who had had the fit tells that he suffered his attack when he saw some strange woman looking out the window of one of the rooms. Now the narrator, another family friend, sees the woman himself:

> Now a great fear was on me, that fear which we feel in nightmares, but which is happily strange to our waking hours. I knew that only a thin pane of glass divided me from something which was not of this world and not of God. Yet I could not take my eyes from her, and some force beyond my control compelled me nearer and nearer to the window until our faces were only a few inches apart. And through the galloping panic in my head I heard, as it were, an echo of young Noel's voice: "Go right up to the window as I did, and have a good look at her throat!"

It is to Burrage's credit that he restrains himself from describing in detail what the narrator saw.

In other tales Burrage manages to mingle horror and pathos effectively. One of his best tales is "Little Bride-of-a-Day," in which a man returns after twenty years to the inn where he had spent a tragic honeymoon, his young bride dying the very evening of their marriage. The poignancy comes not merely in the reappearance of the bride's ghost; rather, it comes from the fact that she actually fails to recognise her husband, who has become haggard and dissipated through the two decades of his loss. We learn from the dust jacket of *Someone in the Room* that Burrage's "specialty was the light-hearted love story"; here he renders that trope supernatural and extraordinarily moving.

"Oberon Road" is a departure for Burrage in that the ghosts are not the focus of the story. Here we learn of a place that exists only in the imagination: the protagonist, Michael Cubitt, is told that Oberon Road is "the first on your left before you get to Norman Avenue," but he knows there cannot be any such road—he has been traversing the same route for twenty years of a dreary job and knows every inch of the place. And yet, he comes upon Oberon Road after all, finding it peopled with delightful boys, girls, and even some adults. We quickly learn that residence in Oberon Road comes at a high price—not in money, but in deeds. When he complains to an estate agent that he has lots of money to buy a house there but that another man he saw did not, the agent contradicts him: "Oh, yes, he did. He had a great deal. He had sixpence once, his week's pocket-money. And he gave it to a woman on the road who carried a baby which was starving because she was starving." Elementary and perhaps sentimental as this allegory is, I found it quietly touching. At any rate, Cubitt now learns what kind of coin is required for a residence in Oberon Road.

The stories in this volume reprinting the tales in the original *Someone in the Room* (1931) are actually rather disappointing. Here the presence of a relatively conventional ghost in nearly every story becomes mechanical; the tales are also virtually uniform in size, as if Burrage knew that the magazines in which he published had a fixed amount of space allotted to him, and he was anxious not to exceed it. The result is that, even when Burrage comes upon a potentially interesting conception, he fails to develop it properly. "The Case of Mr Ryalstone" features what I believe to be one of the most ingenious premises in weird fiction: in conscious contrast to *Dr Jekyll and Mr Hyde* (cited by name in the story), where one man has two separate personalities, we are here dealing with two clearly distinct individuals with a single personality; each of them dreams of the other every night, and these dreams are so vivid and realistic that they realise that they are both fragments of the same consciousness. But this conception—which might well be the subject of a fine novel by someone like Ramsey Campbell—instead merely peters out: one of the individuals dies, prompting the other to die as well.

"The Waxworks" appears to be singular in Burrage's work in being a non-supernatural horror tale; and yet, its execution is so ingenious that it still carries a delectable *frisson*. We are introduced to the seemingly hackneyed premise of a man, Hewson, who wishes to spend the night in a waxworks museum, specifically in the exhibit containing the models of notorious murderers. One of them, a Dr Bourdette, is a very recent addition. Hewson undergoes the usual sense of disquiet, then alarm, then actual terror as he passes the night with his cheerful company; then he becomes convinced that the image of Dr Bourdette has moved. At this point two alternatives occur to us, one supernatural and the other non-supernatural: (1) the wax figure has magically come to life; or (2) Hewson is imagining things. But as the figure speaks, another alternative becomes apparent: this is the real Dr Bourdette, who "mysteriously disappeared" when the police became too hot on his trail; he explains to Hewson that he entered the waxworks, switched himself with his wax image, and simply waited for everyone to leave. He then calmly approaches Hewson with a razor (his preferred method of extermination) and apparently kills him. This seems to be nothing more than a tale of gruesome pseudo-supernaturalism, but Burrage adds a final twist: when the authorities come down to the exhibit the next morning, they indeed find Hewson dead—but there is no mark on him, and the wax figure of Dr Bourdette is standing placidly as before. In fact, Hewson had indeed imagined everything—to the point of imagining his own throat being cut.

Burrage is capable of this type of ingenuity all too infrequently. Other tales are all quite competent, smoothly and elegantly written, but rarely deliver a punch. They become hackneyed and predictable. No doubt Burrage wrote too much, even within the realm of weird fiction, to say nothing of his other voluminous work. And yet, it would be churlish not to appreciate those few masterworks that did emerge out of his prodigality of output, and we should be grateful to Ash-Tree Press for collecting all his weird work, good and bad, in easily accessible volumes. It may well be the case that Burrage produced only one single, perhaps rather slim, volume of truly outstanding weird work; but that is more than can be said of all too many others.

Herbert S. Gorman: Where Is the Place Called Dagon?

I am sure I am not the only person to have been intrigued when, many years ago, I first read Lovecraft's comment in "Supernatural Horror in Literature" about Herbert S. Gorman's *The Place Called Dagon* (George H. Doran, 1927), "which relates the dark history of a western Massachusetts backwater where the descendants of refugees from the Salem witchcraft still keep alive the morbid and degenerate horrors of the Black Sabbat." Now I knew that Lovecraft himself had written a story early in his career called "Dagon"; and in my youthful naiveté and ignorance I wildly conjectured that Gorman might have been a friend of Lovecraft who had written this novel as a tribute to his mentor. Perhaps Gorman was the first "Cthulhu Mythos" writer!

It did not take me long to ascertain that this was impossible, and that Gorman almost certainly knew nothing of Lovecraft's existence. Still, that plot description sounded uncannily Lovecraftian, and I sought out this rare book with fervency. Finally locating it (with the assistance of the late proprietor of Fantasy Archives), I read the book at last and came to the conclusion that the novel, rather than being influenced *by* Lovecraft, may well have influenced Lovecraft, specifically in "The Shadow over Innsmouth" and "The Dreams in the Witch House." But this is by no means the most important thing about *The Place Called Dagon*; the fact of the matter is that it is a thoroughly entertaining and substantial horror novel.

Herbert Sherman Gorman (1893–1954) does not, on the face of it, seem a very likely candidate to have written a minor weird classic. Having spent his early life as a journalist in Springfield, Massachusetts, he later achieved considerable renown as a literary critic and biographer. He was a friend of James Joyce and wrote one of the earliest biographies of him, *James Joyce: His First Forty Years* (1924), only two years after the publication of *Ulysses*. Fifteen years later he wrote a more formal biography of Joyce. He also produced biographies of Longfellow (1926), Hawthorne (1927), Dumas (1929), and Mary Queen of Scots (1932). Although his first two books were poetry collections, Gorman did write a fairly substantial body of fiction; but none of his other novels are weird. *Gold by Gold* (1925) is an experimental novel adapting the stream-of-consciousness style of *Ulysses*; one critic believes this is the first time that this style was used in an American novel. Most of Gorman's half-dozen other novels are historical novels set usually in Napoleonic France or in Mexico.

It is clear that Gorman drew upon his Massachusetts upbringing for *The Place Called Dagon*. In this novel he evokes—as powerfully as any writer aside from Hawthorne and Lovecraft—the hoary antiquity of New England and the long, dark shadow cast by the region's Puritan heritage. The tale is set in Leominster (pronounced LEM-inster) and Marlborough, small towns northeast of Gorman's native Springfield. Through the eyes, ears, and voice of his protagonist, Daniel Dreeme, a young doctor who takes up his practice there, Gorman reflects on the Puritan past:

> Into this sequestered place came the sons of Pilgrims and the Puritans . . . They had no time for the lighter pleasures of living, and, indeed, their ethical conception of existence forbade them. They eschewed the colored ribbands of life. . . . They had no time for love or laughter but they had plenty of time for labor and a taciturn doggedness not always unbroken by sighs. Surely the women must have sighed. Life was not a career but an onerous duty.

But Dreeme is not, in fact, the central figure in the novel. This role is shared between two individuals, Doctor Humphrey Lathrop, a huge and ancient man who chose Dreeme as his successor upon his retirement, and Jeffrey Westcott, a learned and sinister individual who has entered the area for purposes of his own. Lathrop appears to be the fount of all knowledge in the region; and when Dreeme, who has had strange encounters with Westcott, with George Burroughs (the local minister), and others, confronts him with the blunt query, "Where is the place called Dagon?," Lathrop advises him to proceed with caution. Something is going to happen at the place called Dagon, but Lathrop either does not know what it is or is unwilling to say. He and Dreeme ponder the situation. Is there, Dreeme asks, anything actually supernatural going on? Lathrop dismisses it out of hand: "Against the supernatural I turn my face. It isn't reasonable. It isn't even spiritually reasonable." But, he continues: "'I believe in mysteries. . . . I believe these mysteries to be intellectually suspected at rare moments but never actually solved. I do not believe that we will ever solve them. So far as I know they move on another circle of time or in another dimension or anything you choose. But I demand that they be called supernormal and not supernatural.'"

But Westcott emerges as the Faustian villain of the novel, a figure of unknown, perhaps unimaginable, power and knowledge who ponders crumbling old books of cabbalistic lore and who plans some secret rite at the place called Dagon for some nameless purpose. Why has he even come to this remote locale when he himself is not a farmer and seems to have no relationship with its stolid and unimaginative denizens? Dreeme challenges him on this matter, and Westcott is ready with a rejoinder:

> "Years ago the peculiar circumstances of my birth pushed me into a specific line of investigation. The seeds of that particular knowledge for which I sought were buried in this valley and I settled here with the determination to foster them and cause them to grow. You say that I have nothing in common with the farmers of Marlborough but that only reveals your ignorance. I have this in common with them,—they, too, know of the seed. They, too, keep the ground fertile that it may grow in its appointed time. Their lives and the lives of their forefathers are but a preparation for the time when that seed will sprout. I am the self-constituted gardener. I am the man who directs."

It is clear at this point even to Dreeme that the "seeds" Westcott is speaking of do not refer to agriculture.

Dreeme finally learns what the place called Dagon is: it is a lonely valley with a set of standing stones, under the altar-stone of which the bones of the Salem witches are buried. Gorman postulates that there actually was a coven of witches in Salem, who may have exercised some sort of psychic influence over the community (Lathrop reminds Dreeme: "There is nothing supernatural in that, after all"). But after the trials the witches were either killed or scattered. Some of them fled west, and they settled here in Marlborough. (Gorman is only slightly bending the truth. The small town of New Salem, in central Massachusetts, really was settled by people from Salem, although a good forty years after the witch trials. Marlborough was in fact settled in 1657.) These settlers had carried with them the revered bones of the hanged witches, and they buried them under the Devil Stone. Lathrop imagines what their ceremonies there might have been:

> "I can picture that place lighted by torches at midnight. I can picture the rapt faces of the witches and the compelling eyes of the Black Man as he stood above them and called on Satan, on Beelzebub, on Asmodeus, the fiends that he imagined served his purpose. I can hear the laughter of the women and see their glistening eyes as the madness took them. By day they were taciturn people, carrying on the quiet masquerade of pioneers, building up homes in the clearing, pushing the forest farther and farther back, but when the moon rose the madness that was in their blood swept them out of themselves and they became other creatures employing pagan symbols and ancient phallic ceremo-

nials. They existed in a domain out of place and time, then, a land of hallucinations and dreams and primitive urges."

Lathrop recounts the story of Thomas Morton of Merry Mount, a man of the early seventeenth century who, disliking Puritan religious and social repression, established a small colony south of Boston whose members tweaked the noses of the Puritans with their licentious and pagan behaviour. The Puritans took quick action, scattering the colony and calling the region Dagon, from the Philistine god who, in the Old Testament, serves as an epitome of heathenism. Lathrop then concludes the tale by maintaining that the former residents of Merry Mount founded Leominster. (Gorman again takes liberties with the historical record here: not only was Leominster not settled by Morton's clan, but it was the Pilgrims, not the Puritans, who were horrified by Morton's antics and drove him from the place.) It should be clear by now that nothing supernatural actually occurs in *The Place Called Dagon*. And yet, just as Thomas Tryon did in *Harvest Home* (1973), Gorman achieves an uncanny atmosphere of the pseudo-supernatural throughout this work, especially in its concluding tableau, where Westcott attempts to reenact a pagan ritual at the place called Dagon. This scene, which takes up a full quarter of Gorman's novel, is remarkably akin to the concluding scene in *Harvest Home*, where a similarly hoary rite is in question. Gorman cannot resist adding one final rumination on the lurking menace of this ancient land:

> This is New England, he thought. This is the tired land of forgotten pioneer enterprises. . . . But it is more than this, as well. How if all this glittering commercial civilization is no more than a huge shell, an incrustation of years, beneath which lurk the old pagan madnesses that were corollaries of the Puritan repression? How if the ancient Dionysiac urge did not perish but remained like an ominous monster in a deep cavern biding its time and waiting its day? Suppose that the May Pole of Merry Mount and the Witches' Sabaoths of Salem were to be reborn with disastrous consequences because of their long suppression?

It is because *The Place Called Dagon* is as much a social commentary as it is a tale of horror—or, rather, because it finds horror festering in the dark social heritage of a centuries-old community—that it is so uniquely convincing. Each of Gorman's principal characters is etched sensitively and realistically; and although the pace of the novel may be a trifle slow by present-day standards, its culminating scenario is as dramatically riveting as anything written today.

It would, I suppose, be invidious to compare *The Place Called Dagon* with current works in the horror field. It is not merely that it stands head and shoulders above other novels that have been written in the last two or three decades; it is that, in spite of its non-supernaturalism, it is actually a weird *novel* in the sense that its themes and conceptions require the novel form for execution. Thomas Ligotti among others has rightly deemed most horror novels today as being merely mystery or suspense stories with horrific interludes; but the cumulative power of *The Place Called Dagon* attests to the unity of its design.

This novel—along with such other distinctive works as Francis Brett Young's *Cold Harbour* (1924), Leonard Cline's *The Dark Chamber* (1927), and R. E. Spencer's *The Lady Who Came to Stay* (1931)—could only have been written, and published, at a time when there was no such thing as a "horror genre." All these novels were issued by mainstream publishers, and all these works were produced by writers who by no means specialised in horror or published in pulp magazines, but who simply happened in this one instance to be attracted to a supernatural or weird scenario. I suppose something of the sort has always gone on, and perhaps in some senses still goes on today, as mainstream writers write the occasional horror novel in order (as Lovecraft piquantly put it) to "discharge from their minds certain phantasmal shapes which would otherwise haunt them." It is too early to say whether the novels of Peter Ackroyd or Michael Cadnum will ever have quite the charm of the works I have just mentioned. Perhaps they may in fifty years. In the meantime, Gorman's *The Place Called Dagon* is a book that the ardent weird bibliophile will no longer have to scour used bookstores or rare-book catalogues to secure, thanks to its recent (2003) reprinting by Hippocampus Press. It is very much a minor classic of our little realm.

Andrew Caldecott: The Well-Crafted Ghost

In all honesty, Andrew Caldecott's *Not Exactly Ghosts: Collected Weird Stories* (Ash-Tree Press, 2002) is more interesting for its mere existence than for its actual contents. We are here presented with the collected horror tales (the complete contents of two short story collections) of a highly unusual man—Andrew Caldecott (1884-1951), a high-ranking member of the British colonial service. The great majority of Caldecott's career was spent in the Malay peninsula, where he remained from 1907 to 1935; thereafter he served in Hong Kong (1935-37) and Ceylon (1937-44). Along the way he received several knighthoods, and, as Stefan Dziemianowicz remarks in his richly detailed introduction, he is perhaps the only author of weird tales to receive a full page in the prestigious *Dictionary of National Biography* and a lengthy obituary in the *New York Times*. Those weird tales were a product of Caldecott's retirement; in quick succession he published *Not Exactly Ghosts* (1947) and *Fires Burn Blue* (1948), although it is an open question whether the twenty-five tales in these two volumes were actually written just prior to publication or years earlier. Purely internal evidence—such as the setting of some stories in the 1920s and 1930s—might point to earlier composition, but this is mere conjecture.

So what does one make of Andrew Caldecott as a weird writer? Competence, ingenuity, and wholesome geniality are the descriptives that spring to mind. I find no single story in this volume that stands out over the others; all are ably written, cleverly conceived, and satisfyingly executed. If Caldecott lacks the hypertrophied prose of Poe or Lovecraft, the esoteric mysticism of Blackwood, or the shivering sense of the unholy that typifies Machen, he at least reveals a vigorous pleasure in writing that makes him representative of the best kind of amateur storyteller.

It would be misleading to consider Caldecott merely another in the long line of M. R. James disciples, even though James is mentioned by name (along with John Metcalfe) in some of the stories. The majority of his tales are indeed "ghost stories" in the narrow sense of the term, and many of these embody a relatively conventional supernatural-revenge motif that is one of the sad limitations of the ghost story as an art form. But on occasion Caldecott abandons the ghost for more bizarre horrors. In particular, he is able to use his colonial experience in the remoter provinces of Asia to good effect both for convincing background and for some actual legendry. Only a civil servant could have depicted the daily peregrinations of a "Government House calling-book":

> Punctually every morning at nine o'clock it was deposited there, and as punctually every evening at half-past six removed, by two scarlet-hatted, scarlet-sashed peons. This function they performed with such evident satisfaction to their personal vanity as to make of it almost a ceremony. Indeed the aide-de-camp referred to it in his Routine Orders as "the Procession of the Book".

Let it not be assumed, however, that Caldecott exhibits even the remotest tinge of the racism and classism so typical of the British colonial service of the great days of the Empire: he was, in fact, a notably progressive figure, and no doubt earned his honours precisely because of the respect he accorded to the natives in his charge.

Many of Caldecott's stories are filled with verse—not merely a couplet or a quatrain, but several lengthy poems. The curious thing is that most of these poems are presented precisely in order to be made fun of; it appears that Caldecott enjoyed the task of writing bad poetry. As Dziemianowicz notes, "At least one story, 'Autoepitaphy,' seems to have been conceived for no other purpose than to showcase his skill in composing amusing doggerel." We are certainly at the farthest remove from Ann Radcliffe, who was apparently under the impression that the poetry she liberally scattered through her Gothic novels was actually good.

There does not seem to be any advantage in analysing any single story of Caldecott's, or even the whole of them as a lot. They are set either in England or in the colonies with which Caldecott was familiar. Ghosts abound, but sometimes other kinds of supernatural entities, such as the huge spiders in "Grey Brothers," which is a kind of poor man's "Heart of Darkness" in its study of an Englishman who has retreated to the depths of the jungle to cultivate the large arachnids that dwell there; music is featured in a number of tales, in such a way as to reveal Caldecott as sensitive and knowledgeable in the art; and a few stories (especially in *Fires Burn Blue*) seem to peter out into confusion and inconsequence, as if Caldecott had no idea where he was going with the narrative and merely brought it to a close out of weariness. But these are rare instances, and on the whole *Not Exactly Ghosts* can afford any devotee of the weird a certain mild satisfaction in well-crafted and well-conceived tales written in pure if unadventurous English. At the very least, they will allow all but diehard collectors to forego spending hard-earned cash searching out the original editions of what must be two fabulously rare volumes.

Rescuing Shirley Jackson

I was under a peculiar handicap in reviewing Shirley Jackson's *Just an Ordinary Day*, edited by Laurence Jackson Hyman and Sarah Hyman Stewart (Bantam, 1997). In early 1991, while conducting research for a lengthy essay on Shirley Jackson for my forthcoming study, *The Modern Weird Tale* (McFarland, 2001), I came upon dozens of stories, sketches, and essays by Jackson in magazines and anthologies that had not been reprinted in the lone collection of stories she assembled in her lifetime, *The Lottery* (1949), nor in the posthumous collection, *Come Along with Me* (1965), edited by her husband, Stanley Edgar Hyman. (The omnibus volume, *The Magic of Shirley Jackson* [1968], contains stories taken from either *The Lottery* or *Come Along with Me*.) I wrote to Brandt & Brandt, the agents representing Jackson's estate, and sent them all the texts I had at that time acquired; but I was informed in a letter from Brandt & Brandt dated 16 July 1991 that Jackson's children did not approve my proposed collection. Five and a half years passed, and now this volume of unpublished and uncollected stories appears.

In their introduction, Jackson's two eldest children report discovering a cache of unpublished Jackson stories in a Vermont barn several years ago. They followed it up by what they announce as a stunning revelation—the discovery that twenty-six cartons of Jackson's manuscripts were at the Library of Congress. It seems a trifle hard to believe that her own children did not know of this repository, but there it is. They could have learned of it just as easily from Joan Wylie Hall's monograph, *Shirley Jackson: A Study of the Short Fiction* (Twayne, 1993), which cites some of the unpublished material and has a complete bibliography of the uncollected work. The Jackson children maintain that they secured these uncollected stories either through Jackson's brother and sister-in-law, Barry and Marylou Jackson, or in the San Francisco Public Library. Well, maybe so; but it is certainly odd that all but two of the twenty-two uncollected stories in this book were stories I had supplied them in 1991.

Of course, I did not know of the unpublished material, and it is quite conceivable that the Jackson children came upon the other items independently of me. At this point it hardly matters; what does matter is that we are now presented with a substantial cache of "new" Jackson stories, many of which we would be much the poorer without.

I fear, however, that we would not be much the poorer without the thirty previously unpublished items. They span the entire range of Jackson's work—tales of horror and the supernatural, tales of crime and suspense, "mainstream" stories of interpersonal conflict, delightful accounts of her children (always among the most refreshing of her writings), and entirely unclassifiable stories that only she could have written. Perhaps the only true gem among these unpublished stories is a very simple tale called "Summer Afternoon," which tells of two little girls who decide to go and visit a friend, but merely see her peeping over the ledge of her bedroom window. When they tell this to the mother of one of the girls, the latter is alarmed; for she knows that that child recently died. Have the little girls seen a ghost? are they teasing the mother? or are they themselves so traumatised by the death of their little friend that they desperately "make believe" she is still alive? We never know, and never can know.

Otherwise, I fear it is a pretty sorry lot. "The Smoking Room" and "Devil of a Tale" are flippant stories about the devil; "Nightmare" appears to be a transcript of a nightmare, but it is not a story in any sense; "Dinner for a Gentleman" is a moderately clever supernatural tale masquerading as a comic story about a woman who is hopeless in the kitchen and a mysterious "friend" of her mother's who magically helps her; "Lovers Meeting" uses bits of the Shakespearean song from *Twelfth Night* ("Journeys end in lovers meeting") that runs like a harrowing leitmotif through *The Haunting of Hill House*, but does not otherwise seem to have any relation to that novel and is in itself perfectly incoherent; "Lord of the Castle" is a curious supernatural historical tale, but is not well developed; "The Story We Used to Tell" is a fantasy that bears some dim connexion with Jackson's magnificent haunted house story, "A Visit" (in *Come Along with Me*), but is far inferior to it.

In her rather uncharitable review of this book in the *New York Times Book Review*, Joyce Carol Oates complained that the book was poorly arranged in that mainstream stories, fantasies, crime stories, and accounts of Jackson's children were haphazardly mixed together. There is some merit to this complaint, but an opposite view could be taken. Jackson is one of those rare writers who are genuinely "unclassifiable," and this may have much to do with her relative lack of critical acclaim: mainstream critics and readers seem taken aback by the unexpected intrusion of the supernatural into her work, while readers of fantasy are perhaps unprepared for the careful and precise character portrayal and other "mainstream" elements that are featured in all her stories. To Jackson, more than to almost any other writer, it would be grotesquely unfair to attempt some neat categorisation of her works; if the weird tales were grouped under the blunt and deflating banner of "Tales of Horror and the Supernatural," much of their power—a power resting precisely in the unpredictable entrance of the weird in an otherwise placidly and deceptively "ordinary" narrative—would be lost. If I had a complaint about the arrangement of the book, it would be that the distinction between unpublished and uncollected stories is somewhat arbitrary; although, barring any account of why these stories remained unpublished (were they rejected? did Jackson not wish to submit them anywhere?), perhaps the distinction has some use. Indeed, I gain a sense that some of the unpublished tales were mere exercises in narrative tone or style, and were never intended as "finished" stories.

Turning to the uncollected stories, I first wish to express regret—purely from the standpoint of a supporter of weird fiction—that some of the more interesting weird or science fiction pieces did not make it into the book. A three-page story called "Bulletin" that appeared in *Fantasy and Science Fiction* for March 1954 is a spectacularly potent piece suggesting the near-complete collapse of learning in the future. "Root of Evil" is a respectable tale from *Fantastic* (March–April 1954; rpt. June 1969). It involves a man who advertises in the paper that he is giving money away and the variously suspicious, incredulous, and angry responses to the ad. I am not sure there is any point to this story aside from delineating people's innate suspicion of unadulterated benevolence; but it is still a haunting and disturbing tale.

But, putting aside one's regrets as to what did *not* make it into this volume, let us relish what *did*. "One Ordinary Day, with Peanuts" is finally between the covers of a book bearing Jackson's name. This magnificently misanthropic tale (first published in *Fantasy and Science Fiction* for January 1955) was reprinted in several "best short stories of the year" anthologies at the time, which makes me wonder why Stanley Edgar Hyman failed to include it, or several other fine tales, in *Come Along with Me*. Reading Judy Oppenheimer's 1988 biography of Jackson, one develops the strong sense that Hyman resented Jackson's superior fame as a writer (Hyman was only moderately renowned as a literary and cultural critic); could he perhaps have been paradoxically attempting to demote Jackson at the same time he was purporting to preserve her work? I have no warrant for saying that in the absence of documentary evidence; but the very peculiar contents of that posthumous collection would make anyone wonder.

Then there is "The Possibility of Evil" (*Saturday Evening Post*, 18 December 1965), a story appearing four months after Jackson's death and the winner of an Edgar award from the Mystery Writers of America. This account of an aristocratic old woman who writes anonymous poison pen letters to other citizens so as to keep her town "clean and sweet" is a trifle obvious, but is redeemed by its unrelenting viciousness. In the end the woman is detected and someone repays her in kind by destroying her cherished rose garden. Oppenheimer believes, incredibly, that Jackson identified with the old woman: "Shirley wanted to see herself . . . as a proper lady, sure of her place, who sent forth her terrible messages to the world yet remained anonymously secure." But surely we are meant to loathe the old woman for her spitefulness and her injustice: "Miss Strangeworth never concerned herself with facts; her letters all dealt with the more negotiable stuff of suspicion."

"'All She Said Was "Yes"'" (*Vogue*, 1 November 1962; its title is not printed accurately in this book) speaks poignantly of a curious young girl whose parents have been killed in an auto accident. It is somewhat analogous to "The Intoxicated," the chilling tale that opens *The Lottery*, in that it suggests that the girl is clairvoyant; and like that story, it is told from the point of view of an individual who fails to perceive the girl's powers. This tale is also a little obvious (there is no ambiguity, as in "The Intoxicated," whether the girl really can see into the future or not), and a predictable ending does not help matters: the girl tells her neighbour repeatedly not to go on a boat, but the neighbour pays no attention and the story concludes: "we're all going to go on a cruise." But the delicate portrayal of the central figure—an unattractive, tight-lipped, morose girl who knows that her parents will die and is accordingly not shocked but merely saddened and stupefied, and now totally alone in the world—makes this one of Jackson's later triumphs.

These are among the better weird tales in the volume; there are also a number of "mainstream" stories that ought to be read by anyone interested in Jackson or in good writing. But the fact remains that there is at least another entire collection's worth of material—some of it better than the items included here—that lies ready to hand. Some trained scholar like Joan Wylie Hall ought to go through both the remaining uncollected stories and the other unpublished material at the Library of Congress and put together such a volume, one assembled with perhaps a little better understanding of Jackson's place in American literature than that exhibited by her children. In any event, *Just an Ordinary Day* will provide a few delightful and startling revelations to readers who only know Jackson through her commonly available volumes; and lovers of the weird should be grateful for even a few crumbs to gratify their taste.

III. CONTEMPORARIES

Les Daniels: The Sardonic Vampire

Les Daniels is the forgotten man in modern horror fiction. If one had taken a survey in 1982 as to who were the leading figures in the field, Daniels would no doubt have been close to the top of the list. After writing two nonfiction studies of the horror tale, Daniels in 1978 published *The Black Castle*, one of the best first novels in the genre; it introduced his sardonic hero-villain, the vampire Don Sebastian de Villaneuva. The very title of the work signalled Daniels's allegiance to the traditional roots of weird fiction, but his work was no mechanical pastiche: Sebastian was clearly the creation of one who knew the field well and consequently knew what liberties to take with this old theme. With *The Silver Skull* (1979), one of the best horror novels of the last thirty years, Daniels seemed already worthy of the company of Campbell, Klein, King, and Straub; and *Citizen Vampire* (1981), the third Sebastian novel, did nothing to diminish his standing. But in the last several years Daniels has suffered some setbacks and has virtually disappeared from the scene; but *Yellow Fog* (Tor, 1988) has brought him back with a vengeance.

What makes Daniels's work unique is his fluid intermingling of genres. In his novels there is a little of the classic horror tale, a little of the detective story, a little of the historical novel, and a little of the mainstream novel. The result is a distinctive texture found in the work of no other living writer; perhaps only some works by John Dickson Carr offer a dim parallel. (I am personally indebted to Daniels for introducing me to Carr's remarkable supernatural mystery, *The Burning Court*.)

Yellow Fog is a considerable expansion of a novelette published in 1986 by Donald M. Grant for the World Fantasy Convention in Providence. I have not had access to the Grant edition, so cannot judge the difference between the two versions; but the revised edition is certainly seamless and unified. I had somehow fancied, when reading *Citizen Vampire*, that old Sebastian himself was appearing a little tired of his repeated resurrections; but in *Yellow Fog* he is as vibrantly evil as ever.

And yet, much of the secret to Daniels's effectiveness is that no one is purely good or purely evil in his work. Sebastian certainly lusts after the delicate Felicia Lamb, but only reluctantly makes her a vampire after warning her of the direful consequences ("The dead will fear you as much as the living, for we are alien to both"). Reginald Callender, Felicia's fiancé, seems no more than a wastrel, dandy, and fortune-hunter, but toward the end even he gains a certain forlorn dignity as he vainly tries to win back Felicia from Sebastian's clutches. Nigel Stone appears to be Reginald's stalwart cousin, but conveniently marries Felicia's now-wealthy maiden aunt at the end. All the characters are vividly realised in this work.

Daniels has always done well in capturing the historical setting of his novels. Here we are in 1847, and see glimpses of the aged Madame Tussaud and her Chamber of Horrors; Samuel Sayer, who remembers his far-off days as a Bow Street runner before the advent of Scotland Yard and the Metropolitan Police; and the genial whore Sally Wood, who finds herself engrossed in the best-selling penny dreadful of the day, *Varney the Vampire*.

Daniels has a remarkable skill at etching certain scenes with a pitiless clarity and precision, but conversely can also write delicate prose-poetry or even dream-fantasy when the occasion calls for it. This novel gains a tragic dimension when Felicia, having become a vampire, refuses to partake of human blood and wastes away to a pale shadow, as Sebastian looks on ineffectually. The great vampire of course survives at the end, but it took Daniels another three years to feature him in a new work.

In that work, *No Blood Spilled* (Tor, 1991), Daniels treads water. In saying this I mean no especial disrespect, but am rather trying to define, as precisely as I can, this novel's place in the totality of Daniels's work. *No Blood Spilled* is an avowed sequel to *Yellow Fog*, which saw Don Sebastian de Villenueva resurrected in the half-elegant, half-seamy world of early Victorian England. The relation of *No Blood Spilled* to *Yellow Fog* is far closer than the relation of Daniels's three prior novels to one another; indeed, I understand that another novel will complete a sort of trilogy with *Yellow Fog* and *No Blood Spilled*. This, in fact, is part of the problem: *No Blood Spilled* seems to have virtually no *raison d'être* save to serve as a link between *Yellow Fog* and the forthcoming novel, and has trouble standing by itself as an independent aesthetic entity. The plot meanders, the characters seem rather one-dimensional, and the book fails to build to a suitable climax at the end. It is as if Daniels has decided arbitrarily to cut off his novel at a certain point and start the next one from there.

No Blood Spilled takes us to India, where Sebastian has gone to pursue his quest for knowledge—specifically, knowledge of the nature of death. In the first three novels in which he appeared, Sebastian had become increasingly weary of suffering the indignity of periodic resurrection, and began to devote himself to the pursuit of utter extinction. Here, as a result, he comes to Calcutta to penetrate the mysteries of Kali, the Hindu goddess of death. He is pursued by the maniacal Reginald Callender, who escapes from the madhouse in which he has been interred and vows to hunt down Sebastian and despatch him for causing the death of his fiancée Felicia Lamb. Callender actually becomes a little more interesting than Sebastian here: the latter, in fact, does not even make much of an appearance in the novel, while the former wavers between cringing sycophancy and a surprisingly dogged tenacity.

The keynote of Daniels's entire work is an opposition between natural and supernatural horror, with a subtle suggestion that the former—the horror of war, of fanaticism, and of what must tritely but no less accurately be termed man's inhumanity to man—is perhaps the more loathsome of the two. *No Blood Spilled* is no different. While Sebastian's thirst for blood is certainly described with verve, the many natural horrors usurp our attention: the madhouse in which Callender is confined (Daniels has read *Melmoth the Wanderer* with care); the savagery of the Indian rite of suttee—the burning alive of a man's wife after his death; the vileness of teeming and impoverished Calcutta, where beggar children are intentionally mutilated by their family so as to appear more pitiable; and the savagery of the Thugs, those assassins and worshippers of Kali who have been almost eradicated by the British, but who can still be found on the underside of Anglo-Indian society. And yet, some of the supernatural episodes are of considerable interest also, although curiously enough many of these involve Sebastian not as perpetrator but as victim. Even he has difficulty dispensing with a rubbery, pale-white ghoul who gnaws off most of the flesh from his leg; and in probably the most striking visual image in the book (and perhaps in the whole of Daniels's work), we find the following resurrection of Sebastian after he has been left for dead (assuming that word has any meaning as applied to him) in a monsoon puddle after being repeatedly bitten by a cobra:

> And from one of these little lakes a human hand emerged, its pale fingers groping toward the sky like the tendrils of a plant in search of nourishment. A face floated up beside it, plastered with wet black hair that obscured all of its features but an open, hungry mouth. Sloping shoulders hunched out of the water, and in the ghastly glare of the next lightning bolt the figure of a man emerged, his lean body encrusted with mud, small stones, and crawling creatures of the earth.

It is passages like this that make *No Blood Spilled* the entertainment that it is, but I miss the searching philosophical reflections of Sebastian on his anomalous state (the most interesting we get is this: "I am nothing. I am only part of the endless void where Kali rules, and where all men will someday be her subjects whether they are cowards or not"), reflections that make the Sebastian novels far more than mere exercises in bloodletting.

It is always a pleasure to read Les Daniels: his style is clean, spare, and stately; his moments of grue are never adventitious, but always emerge naturally from the logic of the scenario; his characters are on the whole vivid, piquant, and compelling. But I can't help feeling that Daniels has let us down a little in *No Blood Spilled*. It is simply filler: a bridge that will link *Yellow Fog* with the final chain of the trilogy. Perhaps it was not meant to be read on its own, just as no one would read only Tolkien's *The Two Towers* or Eddison's *A Fish Dinner in Memison* (but then, no one reads Eddison anyway, more's the pity). One of Daniels's many virtues is that he writes *short* novels; and yet, perhaps the best thing that could be done for *No Blood Spilled* is to publish it in an omnibus with *Yellow Fog* and whatever the third novel will be. This may result in an anomalously sizeable tome, but it may also give *No Blood Spilled* its true place in the Daniels canon.

To date, sixteen years have passed since the publication of Daniels's last novel, and the final component of the presumed trilogy is nowhere to be seen. Daniels has apparently expressed a certain vexation that word of his planned trilogy was leaked, referring a bit uncharitably to a "fan" (i.e., myself) who imprudently spilled the beans and claiming that he had no such trilogy in mind. This may be making a virtue of necessity: if, for whatever reason, Daniels has given up the writing of novels to pursue other career options, then surely he has only himself to blame for not following through on a work that I had on pretty good authority (i.e., himself) that he was going to write. As it is, Daniels will probably become only a footnote in the history of modern horror—but a most interesting footnote nonetheless.

Dennis Etchison and His Masters

Dennis Etchison's *The Death Artist* (DreamHaven, 2000) collects tales published chiefly in the 1990s, although one, "On Call," dates to as early as 1980. Etchison is a writer who must be emphatically urged to stick with the short story if he can possibly do so without starving in the streets; for his novels are uneven at best. His first, *Darkside* (1986), was a modest success, but the same cannot be said for his next two, *Shadowman* (1993) and *California Gothic* (1995), both of which are marred by diffuseness, prolixity, and a failure to come to grips with the full range of social and political issues raised by their scenarios. And yet, no praise can be too high for Etchison's previous story collections, *The Dark Country* (1982), *Red Dreams* (1984), and *The Blood Kiss* (1988), and *The Death Artist* can takes its place in this worthy company.

Not all the stories in the collection are weird tales, or even tales of mystery and suspense; but they are fine works for all that. "The Last Reel" is a poignant account of a young woman lured inexorably into the pornography industry by ruthless, uncouth entrepreneurs preying upon her loneliness and yearning for stardom. "Call Home" grippingly depicts what appears to be a little girl lost on a California street, but who turns out to be something quite different. "No One You Know" is the tale of a love triangle, made complex by a spare narration relying almost entirely on transcripts of telephone conversations.

As Campbell is the poet of the British urban terrain, so is Etchison a master in portraying, with strokes simultaneously loving and cynical, the freeway-choked sprawl of southern California. "Deadtime Story" features this crisp glimpse of the landscape:

> The gas station on the corner fired a volley of soft bells at him as cars wheeled past the pumps, their lights wavering coronas through a descending mist. At the Apple Pan customers were lined up three deep behind the stools for pie and hot coffee. He smelled the warmth blowing out the open door as he passed, thought of eating but knew he wouldn't be able to hold it down, not now. He cut left at the first side street and pressed north through a residential neighborhood, moving away from the open boulevard and the traffic.
>
> He crossed Olympic, then the tracks at Santa Monica Boulevard, moving up Glendon so fast that his ankles began to hurt. As he drew closer he felt less protected than ever despite the darkness, with the Mormon Temple to his right as brightly lighted as a movie set, its golden angel with trumpet raised as if to announce his passage. By the time he hit the alley behind the Club he could no longer be sure that he was not being followed.

This richly textured, metaphor-laden passage reveals Etchison to be one of the finest prose writers in the entire realm of weird fiction. And the fact that, in this collection as elsewhere, he chooses to convey his message largely by means of dialogue shows that he trusts the reader to read between the lines of the often childishly simple words of his protagonists, weighing every phrase and sentence for the emotional undercurrents they bear.

Not everything in *The Death Artist* is of the highest merit; indeed, two of the longer tales, "Deadtime Story" and "Inside the Cackle Factory," are among the most disappointing. On the other hand, we have several stories that we would be very much the poorer without: "When They Gave Us Memory," in which we are uncertain whether a successful actor's parents have gone mad or senile in failing to recognise him or whether the actor himself is living in some kind of fantasy world he has invented for himself; "The Detailer," about what a young employee in a car wash discovers in an expensive car he is asked to clean; and "The Dog Park," about what happens to dogs (and people) if they venture too close to a gorge near the edge of a park. From the simplest, most ordinary situations, Etchison can fashion a scenario that slides with exquisite subtlety from the prosaic to the disturbing to the appallingly horrific.

Etchison has also distinguished himself as an editor and anthologist, if such volumes as *Cutting Edge* (1986) and *MetaHorror* (1992) are any gauge. His *The Complete Masters of Darkness* (Underwood-Miller, 1991) is a reprint of a series of anthologies that came out in paperback from Tor in 1986, 1988, and 1991 respectively (anomalously, the last paperback volume, apparently delayed, postdates the hardcover edition). Etchison asked forty-five authors to select what they themselves feel to be their best or (as Etchison remarks in the peculiar introduction to the first volume) "choicest" short stories, allowing them to add an author's note at the end explaining why or how they wrote the stories. This procedure, Etchison believes, allows him to escape the pitfalls of standard reprint anthologies, which reflect "the idiosyncratic tastes of their various editors." He wants to spare "an already confused readership" yet another anthology that merely reflects his (Etchison's) tastes, fancying somehow that if the authors themselves select the stories all such problems of idiosyncrasy will be solved.

This is all very curious. In the first place, it is exactly such "idiosyncratic" editors—from Dorothy L. Sayers to Dashiell Hammett to Alfred Hitchcock (whoever in fact compiled his anthologies) to Hugh Lamb and Richard Dalby—who have given us the most memorable collections of weird tales. In the second place, it rapidly becomes evident that the authors have *not* (or not simply) chosen their best work for inclusion, and that there are just as many different agendas operating here as there are authors; the result is not one idiosyncratic viewpoint but forty-five. The very first story, Ray Bradbury's mediocre "The Dead Man," was selected because "it has rarely been reprinted and most of my readers hardly know of its existence." Can one really think that this story represents Bradbury to best advantage, as opposed to such masterworks as "Skeleton" or "The Fog Horn"? By the second volume Etchison is forced to confess that the authors are now selecting "a personal best or a favorite that somehow did not reach a wide audience on original publication." This is already a significant equivocation. By the third volume Etchison is in full retreat, noting that in some cases "the representative piece . . . is a relatively obscure entry worthy of greater attention, one that for subjective reasons is close to the author's heart and at odds with what is popularly perceived as the author's strong suit." Now it appears that we should clearly *not* expect to find what is commonly believed to be the author's best or "choicest" story! Who, in any case, decides what is the "best"? The author? readers? critics? editors? publishers? All this has not been thought through very well, and the result is a serious confusion of purpose and a series of anthologies that is actually more idiosyncratic and less unified than those compiled by a single human being. (I use this term in contradistinction to the computer-generated anthologies of Martin H. Greenberg.)

Then there are the author's notes. I fear there is much room for mischief here. In other anthologies that have commentary of this type, such as *The Arbor House Celebrity Book of Horror Stories*, where someone else is commenting on an author's work, the worst that can happen is that the commentator can be accused of effusiveness or vapidity. (The ideal case, of course, is an anthology like *Lost Souls*, were editor Jack Sullivan, a profound scholar in the field, has offered much useful information on the authors and works he has reprinted.) When, however, authors write on their own work, all sorts of bad things can result—anything from pure self-congratulatory arrogance (William F.

Nolan, Thomas F. Monteleone, Hugh B. Cave) to sanctimoniousness (Chelsea Quinn Yarbro, Richard Matheson, and—though I hate to say so—Ramsey Campbell) to flatulent attempts at humour (too many to mention—only L. Sprague de Camp's note was to my mind genuinely amusing). The sanctimonious ones are the worst: Yarbro, Matheson, and Campbell evidently feel that it is their duty to tackle, respectively, environmental pollution, the spread of violence, and religious fundamentalism in their stories. They remind me of what Lovecraft called "People With A Purpose": "These good folk write because they want to make others do or believe in something which they believe in, and of course their main purpose is propaganda and persuasion—and not that reflection of real life or exaltation of sheer beauty which is authentic literature." How Campbell could have selected his trick story "The Words That Count" (an idea that T. E. D. Klein has executed vastly better in "Ladder") over any of the magnificent tales in *Demons by Daylight* or *Dark Companions* utterly befuddles me. In the end only a few of the author's notes are really enlightening: George Clayton Johnson speaks fascinatingly of the origin of his fine tale, "Sea Change," as a treatment for "The Twilight Zone"; Karl Edward Wagner reproduces the commonplace book entry that records the nucleus of his amusing story, "Neither Brute Nor Human"; and Kate Wilhelm's note turns out to be rather more interesting than her actual story.

Etchison is also at great pains to emphasise how he is boldly spanning the barriers of genre that evil publishers and booksellers have imposed on this field. This becomes rather tedious (it is repeated in all three introductions), and in any case Etchison is protesting too much. The barriers have been systematically attacked for the last decade or more, and two of the contributors—Fritz Leiber and Robert Bloch—are pioneers in genre-leaping from, respectively, the science fiction/fantasy and mystery/suspense realms. And yet, it is an indication of Etchison's own predilections that he is more interested in probing the boundaries between science fiction and horror than between mystery and horror. Among the predominantly science fiction authors included are Kate Wilhelm, Damon Knight, Barry N. Malzberg, Avram Davidson, Algis Budrys, and L. Sprague de Camp, while on the mystery side there is really only Bloch. There is relatively little non-supernatural horror here: Bloch's "The Animal Fair" and George Alec Effinger's "Glimmer, Glimmer" can classify, but both are undistinguished; Budrys's vicious *conte cruel* "The Master of the Hounds" is perhaps the best of the lot.

This brings us to the touchy subject of who is included in this series and who is not; I shall not be so tactless as to suggest that not all the forty-five writers deserve inclusion (although to my mind some do not), but some of the omissions are startling. Where are T. E. D. Klein and Thomas Ligotti? Almost any of the stories in *Dark Gods* or *Songs of a Dead Dreamer* would be better than almost any of the stories actually included in this series. Some other omissions are perhaps quibbles, but here goes anyway: Peter Straub, Les Daniels (neither of them have written much short fiction, but I for one would have welcomed reading again Straub's "The General's Wife"), Dan Simmons, Thomas Tessier, Robert R. McCammon, Iain Banks—and how about Etchison himself? Some would lament the general absence of the splatterpunks (aside from their reluctant mentor, Clive Barker), but I am not one of them. Then there is the inclusion of Richard McKenna, who died as long ago as 1964. If this series claims to represent *contemporary* writers, how can his inclusion be justified? His is the only tale that does not have an author's note, and one imagines that it was included simply because Etchison happened to like it. This now makes forty-six editorial viewpoints! And if one is going to include the recently deceased, where are Shirley Jackson (d. 1965) or Rod Serling (d. 1975) or John Collier (d. 1980) or Robert Aickman (d. 1981) or . . .? You get the point. It is unfortunate that Etchison devotes so little space to explaining the basis for his selections; he offers only a single sentence—"A few renowned authors declined the invitation for personal reasons, and others proved frustratingly elusive in my efforts to locate them"—and it is not very helpful.

It should be clear by now that the conceptual difficulties and paradoxes in this series would not be an insuperable obstacle were the actual stories better than they are; but they are not. As a whole, the tales are flat, routine, mundane, and essentially pointless; the prose is lifeless, the characterisation superficial and stereotypical, the supernatural phenomena not carefully thought through, and the stories themselves as a rule simply seem to have no compelling *raison d'être*. It would be tedious to discuss individual tales, but I cannot help singling out two for particular dispraise: Charles L. Grant's "A Garden of Blackred Roses," his usual mishmash of tepid supernaturalism and soap-opera romance, and George R. R. Martin's disastrous attempt at mingling humour and horror, "The Monkey Treatment," every one of whose plot twists I predicted well in advance of its occurrence.

But let us turn to the good stuff: Steve Rasnic Tem's "Preparations for the Game," a pure nightmare; Frank Belknap Long's recent story "Cottage Tenant," a fascinating combination of Jungian psychology and Greek mythology; and two stories that genuinely combine humour and horror, Nigel Kneale's "The Patter of Tiny Feet" and L. Sprague de Camp's "Judgment Day," with its imperishable opening sentence ("It took me a long time to decide whether to let the earth live"). Easily the best story in the entire series is Joyce Carol Oates's "Family," which shows what a *real writer* can do with a horrific subject—a writer who knows the nuances of language, who can draw character in a few deft strokes, and who can convey her message by subtle implication rather than obvious statement. The cavernous gap between real writing and clumsy hackwork is no better demonstrated than by the juxtaposition of this story with Dean R. Koontz's fatuous and maundering "Twilight of the Dawn." The spectacle of Koontz attempting to be a philosopher of religion would be somewhat amusing—rather like watching a dancing bear—were it not so pitiable. And yet, the series ends ably with Stephen King's "The Woman in the Room" (from *Night Shift*), which has a terseness and stinging wit that King can only dream of now that he has babbled himself out into empty verbosity. But it is not in any sense a weird tale: it is, instead, a powerful mainstream story of a man experiencing the trauma of his mother's slow death by cancer.

So there you have *The Complete Masters of Darkness*. Probably it could, if properly pruned, make one rather slim but excellent anthology. Even if the bulk of the stories will no doubt find the oblivion they richly deserve, there is enough good—indeed, outstanding—material here to make at least the three paperback volumes well worth picking up. As for the hardcover: although it is moderately priced for so large a volume, in these lean times it may still be a luxury.

Thomas Tryon: The Return of the Posthumous Collaboration

Thomas (or, as the title page has it, "Tom") Tryon's *Night Magic* (Simon & Schuster, 1995) is a very strange book. It is strange not in its substance—which is disappointingly mundane for a work supposedly in the realm of fantasy or horror—but in its genesis and its appearance at this late date. For its author died four years before the appearance of the volume.

In an article published in 1992 and later included in *The Modern Weird Tale* (McFarland, 2001), I wrote:

> In 1971 Thomas Tryon (1926-1991), a minor Hollywood actor, published *The Other*; to everyone's surprise, it became a best-seller. Two years later Tryon published *Harvest Home*, followed by *Lady* (1974) and *Crowned Heads* (1976). After a long hiatus Tryon then issued *All That Glitters* (1986); most recently he published *The Night of the Moonbow* (1989) and *The Wings of the Morning* (1990), the latter being the first of a projected four-volume saga of a Connecticut family in the nineteenth century on which Tryon was working prior to his death. The second novel in this series, *By the Waters of Babylon*, as well as a children's book, *The Adventures of Opal and Cupid*, are apparently forthcoming.

What is missing from the above list is, of course, the novel under discussion.

Tryon's work divides, rather schizophrenically, into four relatively discrete units, just as his own life divides between acting and writing. There are his horror novels, *The Other* and *Harvest Home*; there are his novels and tales about Hollywood life, *Crowned Heads* and *All That Glitters*; there are two tantalisingly elusive works, *Lady* and *The Night of the Moonbow*, which are tangentially aligned to his horror novels; and there are historical novels set in Connecticut, *The Wings of the Morning* and *In the Fire of Spring* (1992), which latter may or may not be the novel cited in various reference works or obituaries as a work-in-progress under the title *By the Waters of Babylon*. The children's story *The Adventures of Opal and Cupid* also appeared in 1992.

All this has been gone into at such tedious length because there are serious questions concerning the authorship and authenticity of *Night Magic*. As I was reading this novel, I gradually sensed that this was unlike—and inferior to—everything else of Tryon's I had ever read (and I have read all his work with the exception of his Hollywood tales and the children's story). I had noticed the coy statement tucked away at the very end of the dust jacket, "Tom Tryon . . . died while revising *Night Magic*"; but the novel did not, to my mind, read like an *unrevised* or *unfinished* work, merely an *inferior* one. Then I read the following on the press release: "Tom Tryon . . . died while revising *Night Magic*. Valerie Martin, author of *Mary Reilly* and many other novels, and John Cullen were brought in to finalize and polish the manuscript."

Well.

I confess that I have not read *Mary Reilly*, but I have heard good things of it from those who have. I know nothing about John Cullen. It would be uncharitable of me to decry their work in preparing this novel for publication, but there is something gravely wrong here. It has also not escaped my notice that *Night Magic* is the only book of Tryon's not to have been published by Knopf. Was it rejected by them? When, indeed, was this novel actually written? Is it an early work that Tryon perhaps wrote even before *The Other*? What little biographical material exists on Tryon leads me to doubt it. And I frankly doubt whether Tryon was working on *Night Magic* at the end of his life, since he had apparently turned his attention definitively to the historical novel. His obituary in the *New York Times* states: "Despite his illness [Tryon died of cancer], Mr. Tryon recently met with his editor and typed and dictated revisions to the second and third novels of a proposed four-volume historical series dealing with 19th-century New England and China and collectively titled 'Kingdom Come'" (5 September 1991). (This itself is an anomaly, since this third volume has apparently not been published.)

I suppose I have put off actual discussion of *Night Magic* long enough; but, after reading it, I am forced to echo Clara Schumann's response to hearing Brahms's first symphony: "I cannot disguise the fact that I am painfully disappointed." Whereas *The Other* was a masterpiece of psychological terror, *Harvest Home* a deeply textured novel of the horror to be found in the primitive countryside, *Lady* a delicately sensitive character study, *The Night of the Moonbow* a poignant novel of childhood (shamelessly misadvertised by Knopf as a horror story), and the historical novels rich panoramas in the manner of R. F. Delderfield, *Night Magic* is a lacklustre novel that—like Peter Straub's *Shadowland*—tries and fails to invest weirdness and wonder into prestidigitation and sleight-of-hand. Whose fault this is, it is difficult to say: I suppose some blame must fall on Tryon himself, if indeed he wrote any significant part of the work; but his posthumous collaborators do not appear to have helped any.

Night Magic proposes a continuity of magic going back to Egyptian times and passing through Simon Magus, Merlin, and Cagliostro (who are all reincarnations of the same figure), until the present day, with one Max Wurlitzer, an aged and apparently over-the-hill magician. The link between all these reincarnations is the Eye of Horus, an Egyptian gem "possessed of strange and wondrous properties," which Wurlitzer cleverly steals from the Metropolitan Museum in New York in order to perform his final and most spectacular magic show. He needs, however, an assistant to pass on his knowledge and supernatural powers, and conveniently finds one in the figure of Michael Hawke, a skilled young magician who works humble little magic shows in Central Park and whose girlfriend, Emily Chang, becomes increasingly concerned about his involvement with the cadaverous Wurlitzer. There are also other bit players, such as Wurlitzer's elderly longtime lover, the much put-upon medium Beulah Wales, and Samur Abdel-Noor, a fabulously wealthy Egyptian who hires Wurlitzer and Hawke to perform a lavish magic show for his birthday.

Night Magic never comes to life. Its prose attempts to invest magic shows with a sense of wonder, but ends up sounding merely pompous, pretentious, and overblown. There is never any attempt to specify the nature of Wurlitzer's powers: are they merely sleight-of-hand, or some sort of hypnosis (Wurlitzer can affect people's behaviour merely by speaking to them in a certain way, and Hawke learns this trick as well, although—in a scene all too reminiscent of *The Sorcerer's Apprentice*—he is unable to control it and ends up creating a scandal in Washington Square Park), or something more sinister altogether? All we get is this:

> "What is real magic?" Michael asked at once.
> Something almost like a smile of indulgence for Michael's impetuous youth crossed the old man's face. "First of all," he said, "it's a matter of learning to see things differently . . . Once you learn that, at certain times it's possible to enter a world—a fantasy world, if you like—where you can do things ordinary people consider mysterious. To the magician, however, they are only clear and natural, because he brings his imagination to bear on the ordinary and makes his fantasy real."

This is not helpful, and the matter is never clarified any further.

What has distinguished Tryon's previous work is a remarkable gift for language whereby every single word contributes to the final end. His novels, lengthy as some of them are, have all the "unity of effect" that Poe sought in the short story. *The Other* and *Harvest Home* in particular build to an inexorably cumulative climax that make them among the pinnacles of modern horror fiction. This sort of thing cannot be said for *Night Magic*. If it required two different writers to bring this manuscript into publishable shape, then clearly much reconstruction and revision had to be accomplished. It would perhaps be of some moderate interest to know the actual circumstances of this posthumous patch-up; but, in all honesty, the whole matter is not important enough for anyone to care about.

In my earlier article I wrote, "If Thomas Tryon had continued in the vein of *The Other* and *Harvest Home*, he could easily have rivalled Shirley Jackson and Ramsey Campbell for preeminence in modern weird fiction." I see no reason to take back that sentence, nor any reason to think that *Night Magic* will affect that judgment, since I do not regard it as part of the Tryon corpus at all. Those who study literary anomalies can make of it what they will.

Stephen King and God

The plot of Stephen King's *The Girl Who Loved Tom Gordon* (Scribners, 1999) can be summed up in one short sentence: A girl gets lost in the woods but eventually finds her way out. This doesn't sound like a prepossessing theme for a novel, and it isn't: this little book begs comparison with *Cujo* as perhaps the very nadir of King's work. It is not surprising that *Cujo* is also nonsupernatural: King seems to have much difficulty with this form. (He has troubles with the supernatural as well, but that's another matter.) While there is some merit in *Misery* (1987) and considerable merit in *Gerald's Game* (1992) and *Dolores Claiborne* (1993), *The Girl Who Loved Tom Gordon* is a work we would be much better off without.

Nine-year-old Patricia (Trisha) McFarland gets lost with remarkable ease in the Maine woods when she deliberately falls behind her quarreling mother and brother (the novel provides much opportunity for King to wring his hands about divorce, the breakup of the family, and such), and suffers a variety of other indignities—continual mosquito and wasp bites, shortage of food (she lives for more than a week on nuts and berries), exhaustion that leads to hallucinations, and on and on. What carries her through her ordeal, apparently, is her devotion to Tom Gordon, a (real) pitcher for the Boston Red Sox, whose performances she hears on her handy Walkman.

The first problem with this novel is that King takes too many literary short-cuts. Early on, Trisha falls head over heels down a precipitous incline, and much of the contents of her backpack—food, a video game, etc.—are seriously damaged; but of course her Walkman survives intact. King knows that the advancement of the plot—at least the plot he has in mind—depends on the operation of the Walkman as a radio, so he defies plausibility and simply decrees that the Walkman will work. King immediately compounds this error by another one: the moment Trisha turns the Walkman on to check its condition, she hears a news report of her disappearance! This is simply laziness on King's part: the coincidence here strains credulity to such an extent that the entire novel from this point onward seems unreal. We know we are only reading a book, not an account of something that might actually have happened.

Trisha gains the feeling that if Tom Gordon (a "closer") gains a save at the end of the game she is listening to, then she will herself be saved. Sure enough, he does, and so is she—although not for another week or so. King is straining hard to make a variety of baseball elements stand as metaphors for real life; and the most egregious one occurs toward the end. The religiously devout Gordon has evidently stated (and King presents his utterance in pompous italics): *"It's God's nature to come on in the bottom of the ninth."* This kind of TV-commercial philosophy may be entirely appropriate for a writer who has himself become a brand name, but to any serious reader it will seem shallow and implausible to the point of grotesquerie. And yet, King intends us to see this as the guiding metaphor of the entire book. In a fatuous letter that accompanies the novel as a press release, King states: "*The Girl Who Loved Tom Gordon* isn't about Tom Gordon or baseball, and not really about love, either. It's about survival, and God . . ." How so? How, exactly, has God "come on in the bottom of the ninth"? A bear threatens Trisha just as she is about to be rescued; are we to think that the hunter who clips an ear off the animal, and so drives him away, is a manifestation of God? The very notion that God has somehow intervened to assist Trisha is an unintentional insult, for it is abundantly clear that Trisha has survived entirely through her own determination and willpower. It would be a good idea if King were to refrain in the future from ludicrous theologising and stick to telling a good story. And it would be even better if he actually came up with a good story to tell.

Peter Straub and the Blue Pencil

Peter Straub does not write a great many short stories; his taste inclines more toward hefty novels like *Koko* (1988) or *The Throat* (1993). Indeed, even the short stories he writes are not especially short. In Straub's first collection, *Houses Without Doors* (1990), the best and most substantial items were two stories, each of a hundred pages or more in length—"The Buffalo Hunter" (a powerful tale of psychological horror, perhaps meant as a homage to Ramsey Campbell) and "Mrs. God" (a subtle, allusive work meant as a homage to Robert Aickman). When *Houses Without Doors* appeared, I hailed it as showing two positive tendencies in Straub's work: an ability to convey his message in a somewhat shorter compass than in his frequently bloated novels, and a return to overt supernaturalism, something that had seemed on the wane in light of such novels of suspense as *Koko* and *Mystery* (1989). I regret to report that Straub's new collection, *Magic Terror* (Random House, 2000), forces me to eat my words in both regards.

Straub's career certainly is a puzzle—a dance on either side of the line separating suspense from the supernatural. I mean no criticism of Straub's ventures into the former domain: indeed, I am so bold as to pronounce *The Throat* the finest mystery novel I have ever read—superior to anything by Agatha Christie, John Dickson Carr, Dorothy L. Sayers, or Margery Allingham, and perhaps surpassed only by the aggregate work of P. D. James. But, for purely selfish reasons, I would find it comforting if Straub could venture a bit more into the supernatural, a realm for which he has in the past displayed such marked ability. *The Hellfire Club* (1996) is an able work of psychological suspense and a fit companion to *The Throat*; but it is not a work of horror. *Mr. X* (1999) *is* supernatural, but I do not think it a success: his attempt to work in a Lovecraftian mode (the novel is a riff on "The Dunwich Horror") forces him into stylistic and thematic tropes that do not seem to fit him, and the result is unsatisfactory both as pastiche and as a self-standing work.

One would think that the very title of *Magic Terror* points to a return to the supernatural, but every one of the seven stories is a mystery or suspense tale; and, to my mind, not one of them is a success even in this domain. Each is crippled by verbosity, lack of focus, and anticlimax. Straub, I fear, has grown too fond of his own literary voice. He seems to think that every word he writes is golden, and so he grows unwilling to use the blue pencil (or, to be a bit more up-to-date, the delete key) on anything he has written. I am reminded of R. Boerem's comment on certain other talented writers: "There are writers who are very good by the sentence and the paragraph . . . I think of Styron and Updike. If you read a paragraph by them, you think to yourself after you read the paragraph, 'This is a well-written paragraph; this is nicely balanced; this is well-stated; this shines.' But when you've read the book, you come away with nothing." This is exactly my sentiment after reading *Magic Terror*.

It would be unprofitable to examine the stories in the volume in detail; but I cannot forbear commenting on the final two, "Hunger, an Introduction" and "Mr. Clubb and Mr. Cuff." In both of these stories Straub has, for reasons I cannot fathom, deliberately adopted a pompous, stilted, pretentious style that makes all the events seem artificial, contrived, and (even though they describe acts of gruesome physical horror) flippant. Consider this passage from the latter tale:

> What an abyss of shame I must now describe, at every turn what humiliation. It was at most five minutes past six P.M. when I learned of the desertion

of my most valuable client, a turn of events certain to lead to the loss of his cryptic fellows and some forty percent of our annual business. Gloomily, I consumed my glass of Dutch gin without noticing that I had already far exceeded my tolerance. I ventured behind the screen and succeeded in unearthing another stone flagon, poured another measure, and gulped it down while attempting to demonstrate numerically that (a) the anticipated drop in annual profit could not be as severe as feared and (b) if it were, the business could continue as before, without reductions in salary, staff, or benefits.

I am entirely at a loss to understand the purpose of this absurd diction—the arch use of "consumed" instead of "drank," the use of the rare and preposterous word "flagon," the clumsy enumeration of (a) and (b). Even if it is meant as a means of character portrayal, the effort fails; for the only result is that we cease to care what happens to this bombastic individual. One can only urge Straub to return to the vibrancy of style and substance that he showed in *Ghost Story*, *Mystery*, *The Throat*, and other works—works that have given him his deserved place in the higher echelons of horror and suspense fiction.

Ramsey Campbell: Alone with a Master

I am on record as saying that Ramsey Campbell is the most significant weird writer of our time, and perhaps the most significant since Lovecraft. *Alone with the Horrors: The Great Short Fiction of Ramsey Campbell 1961–1991* (Arkham House, 1993), gathering together thirty-nine of what Campbell himself feels to be his best tales, offers about as definitive a proof of the truth of that statement as could be desired.

This volume will inevitably beg comparison with *Dark Feasts: The World of Ramsey Campbell* (Robinson, 1987), of which this book is a sort of augmented edition. Twenty-seven of the thirty stories in *Dark Feasts* are in *Alone with the Horrors*, and it is interesting to note which tales were dropped. They are "The Whining," "The Words That Count," and "Horror House of Blood"; evidently Campbell decided (or was persuaded by Arkham House's editor James Turner) that these were no longer among his best or most representative. I think the omissions were wise; indeed, Campbell's fondness for "The Words That Count"—a trick story whose supposedly blasphemous use of the Lord's Prayer in reverse could only be shocking to lapsed Catholics like himself—is wholly inexplicable. I am also happy to note that the appalling typographical errors in *Dark Feasts* have here been entirely eliminated.

Alone with the Horrors dates the commencement of Campbell's literary career to 1961. There is no compelling reason why this date should have been chosen over several others one could name, and one develops the impression that it is simply a marketing device. On the one hand, we could go back to

1957/58, when the delightful juvenile stories in *Ghostly Tales* were composed; on the other hand, it might be thought that all the Lovecraftian pastiches of the *Inhabitant of the Lake* (1964) period are really juvenilia. *Alone with the Horrors* contains, as its opening story, "The Room in the Castle"—which is, to be sure, one of the better tales of its kind, lapsing into absurdity only with the actual appearance of the tentacled monster—but then skips ahead to 1966 with what is in effect Campbell's declaration of independence from Lovecraft, "Cold Print." Although this story also purports to be an addition to Lovecraft's "Cthulhu Mythos," it—along with its predecessor, "The Cellars" (1965)—is really the first of Campbell's tales to feature many of the themes and tropes of his mature work: the gritty urban milieu, the mingling of violence and aberrant sex, the dreamlike, prose-poetic style that simultaneously probes the psyche of a neurotic mind and impressionistically paints the twisted and distorted world as seen by that mind.

These techniques served Campbell well in his second collection, the landmark volume *Demons by Daylight* (1973), whose contents had mostly been written by 1968. We have three stories from this collection in *Alone with the Horrors*, but easily twice as many could have been included. I still maintain that *Demons by Daylight* is Campbell's best and most unified collection, and regret that he did not include in *Alone with the Horrors* what I believe to be the two best tales in the volume—"The Franklyn Paragraphs" and "Concussion." But this sort of complaint could be made over and over again: how can a single volume even begin to house the "best" of Ramsey Campbell?

By 1968 Campbell had already mined the *Demons by Daylight* vein nearly to its limit; and he seemed for the next several years to be searching for a new or different style to express his vision. *The Height of the Scream* (1976) strikes me as in some ways more experimental than its predecessor, or at any rate more tentative and heterogeneous: the very diversity of tone of the tales in this collection makes it less coherent than *Demons by Daylight*, and many of the stories seem uninspired, overly obscure, and even a little self-indulgent. It is significant that *Alone with the Horrors* now contains (with the elimination of "Horror House of Blood") only a single story from this collection, and that is the early tale "The Scar" (1967).

Campbell's next collection, *Dark Companions* (1982), shows that he had found a new voice as a short story writer. The dream-imagery of the *Demons by Daylight* period is not abandoned but harnessed: the stories are now set more firmly in the mundane world, but Campbell's focus on individual psychology allows dreamlike effects to enter precisely at the moment when the horror is beginning to manifest itself. Campbell's fascination with the complexities of human relationships, typical of *Demons by Daylight*, has given way to an intense concern with loneliness, both physical and psychological. It was, let us remember, in this period that Campbell wrote his masterwork of solitary paranoia, *The Face That Must Die*. A full twelve stories from *Dark Companions* find their way into *Alone with the Horrors*, and several others—"Napier Court," "The Little Voice," "The Pattern"—could or should have been included.

Between *Dark Companions* and his next major collection, *Waking Nightmares* (1991), Campbell issued several smaller volumes of tales: *Cold Print* (1985), *Night Visions 3* (1986), *Black Wine* (1986), *Scared Stiff* (1986), and, of course, the juvenilia in *The Tomb-Herd and Others* (1986) and *Ghostly Tales* (1987). Only three tales from all these subsidiary collections are included in *Alone with the Horrors,* and one again wonders at the parsimony: where is the nightmarish "In the Trees" and "Beyond Words" from *Night Visions 3?* or "Broadcast" and "The Previous Tenant" from *Black Wine?*

With the stories of the *Waking Nightmares* period we see Campbell at the very height of his short story technique. He is now no longer content to work in a single style or mood, but varies them as the theme or subject warrants. Perhaps this is a result of Campbell's relative sparseness of output in the short story: in the ten-year period of 1981-90 Campbell wrote only twenty-eight short stories; in the years 1981, 1982, and 1989 he wrote none. In any event, *Alone with the Horrors* reaps four stories from this latest collection, and again one begs for more.

It is difficult to specify the exact nature of Campbell's appeal as a short story writer. On the one hand there is style—one of the most fluid, supple, and allusive in modern fiction (not just modern weird fiction)—and on the other there is subject-matter: the city, the perplexities in what Lovecraft scornfully dismissed as "man's relations to man," the warped mentalities that the grinding phantasmagoria of the modern age produces in such abundance. Campbell is the poet of urban squalor and decay. More so than T. E. D. Klein's New York or Clive Barker's London, the Brichester or Liverpool of Campbell's mature stories evokes not merely the noise, grime, and dangers of the city but those inhabitants—both lower- and middle-class—who find themselves crushed within its omnipresent coils. Only Campbell could instil horror in the commonest objects of our daily existence: plastic bags ("In the Bag"), a perambulator ("Baby"), a raincoat ("Old Clothes").

"The Depths" (1978) provides the philosophical justification or rationale for Campbell's emphasis on the horrors of the city. It contains one of the most ingenious premises in modern weird fiction: an author finds that if he does not frantically write down his horrible nightmares of violence and sadistic crime, they come true in actuality:

> Before he'd begun to suffer from his writer's block, there had been occasions when a story had surged up from his unconscious and demanded to be written. Those stories had been products of his own mind, yet he couldn't shake them off except by writing—but now he was suffering nightmares on behalf of the world.

No wonder they were so terrible, or that they were growing worse. If material repressed into the unconscious was bound to erupt in some less manageable form, how much more powerful that must be when the unconscious was collective! Precisely because people were unable to come to terms with the crimes, repudiated them as utterly inhuman or simply unimaginable, the horrors would reappear in a worse form and possess whoever they pleased.

This is, of course, a scarcely veiled metaphor for the indifference to society's ills that typifies urban—and especially middle-class—life. Just as the repression of dreams causes them, in *Incarnate* (1983), to emerge in a still more bizarre and dangerous form, the repression of our sense of responsibility for urban violence causes it to erupt in a still more explosive manner.

Many of Campbell's stories seem to be what I would call *supernaturalisations* of the horrors of the city; in other words, they are metaphors for the very real and chilling dangers of urban life. "The Scar" tells of what might happen in a dark alley in a bad part of town; "Down There" hints of what might lurk in the basement of an office building; "The Man in the Underpass" is a magnificent tale of the dangers of a pedestrian underpass, that distinctively British topographical landmark which has exercised a great fascination for Campbell; and perhaps the early "The Cellars" is an exemplification of a mother's warning to her daughter not to go to strange places alone with a man.

"Mackintosh Willy" (1977) is perhaps Campbell's masterpiece of this type; it may well be the single most horrifying story he has ever written. This triumph of suggestiveness tells, through a boy's eyes, the relatively simple story of a derelict who dies, haunts the bicycle shelter he used to occupy in life, and then pursues a boy who mutilated his corpse by putting bottle caps over his eyes. No reason is given for the resurrection of the derelict's body; but the subtlety of the prose and the richness of the atmosphere cause such a detail to fall to the background. Consider the hideous description of Mackintosh Willy drowning the boy in a pond: "When I tried to raise him, I discovered that he was pinned down. I had to grope blindly over him in the chill water, feeling how still he was. Something like a swollen cloth bag, very large, lay over his face. I couldn't bear to touch it again, for its contents felt soft and fat." That "swollen cloth bag" is reminiscent of a famous climax in M. R. James's "The Treasure of Abbot Thomas," in which a supernatural entity is described as resembling "some rounded light-coloured objects . . . which might be bags." Indeed, the elusiveness of the supernatural manifestation in "Mackintosh Willy" is very Jamesian, but with a power and poignancy drawn from the decaying urban milieu that James could not have imagined.

Paranoia is, for Campbell, the inevitable outcome of the ceaseless and grinding squalor and decadence of the urban milieu. The palpably real horrors of the inner city—crime, violence, poverty—compel its inhabitants to adopt an eternal vigilance that can easily metamorphose into irrational suspicion and vigilante justice. The paranoid character stalks through the length and breadth of Campbell's work—from the pervert in "Cold Print" to the harried telephone operator in the most recent tale included in *Alone with the Horrors*, "End of the Line" (1991)—and may be, in addition to and working in conjunction with his portrayal of decayed cityscapes, his most distinctive and easily recognisable contribution to weird fiction. Hawthorne, Machen, and Lovecraft found the sinister in the untenanted wilderness; but Campbell is the archetypal weird fictionist of the metropolis. Jobs that lead nowhere and accomplish nothing; sex, drugs, and crime as the only escapes from crushing poverty or aimless ignorance; caution and vigilance devolving into irrational suspicion and freakish violence: this is Campbell's city, and it is something that those who dwell in the urban landscape can recognise very plainly.

There is, however, more to Campbell's success in short fiction than a deft style and a powerful subject-matter. What makes his tales stand so far above those of his contemporaries is what must nebulously be called *point of view*. Campbell's stream-of-consciousness technique compels us to see his psychotic characters' minds *from the inside*, so that we come to gain a faint awareness of the twisted logic by which they justify their beliefs and the vicious actions based upon them, with Campbell refraining from passing any easy moral judgment. It is not, to be sure, that we are somehow meant to sympathise with such characters; rather, it is what Lovecraft said of Poe in "Supernatural Horror in Literature":

> Poe . . . perceived the essential impersonality of the real artist; and knew that the function of creative fiction is merely to express and interpret events and sensations as they are, regardless of how they tend or what they prove—good or evil, attractive or repulsive, stimulating or depressing—with the author always acting as a vivid and detached chronicler rather than as a teacher, sympathiser, or vendor of opinion.

Indeed, it is this perspective that makes Campbell's short stories generally superior to his novels, where I sense that he tends to side more openly with his normal middle-class characters. (Campbell has solved this problem in the masterful *Count of Eleven*, where the seemingly normal middle-class character Jack Orchard turns out to be a weirdly sympathetic psychopath.)

Those who criticise Campbell as a sort of "Johnny-one-note" for his relentless harping on the horrors of the city and on violent psychotics ignore, I think, the many variations of tone he can play upon his basic themes. In particular, some of his later tales appear to be subtle parodies of himself, such as "Seeing the World" (where a bland bourgeois couple come back from a vacation as zombies) and perhaps "End of the Line." "The Voice of the Beach" (1977) attempts—not entirely convincingly, to my mind—to duplicate Lovecraft's cosmicism; "The End of a Summer's Day" (1968), among many in *Demons by Daylight*, exquisitely unites horror and pathos; and "Loveman's Comeback"—as with all the tales in *Scared Stiff*—mingles sex and horror to produce a distinctive amalgam. Every great short story writer tends to develop a certain mood that is uniquely his own, and the brooding and cheerless atmosphere that inheres in Campbell's best work is in effect his signature upon the horror field.

Alone with the Horrors is a landmark on the scale of Machen's *The House of Souls* (1906), Blackwood's *Incredible Adventures* (1914), Lovecraft's *The Outsider and Others* (1939), Shirley Jackson's *The Lottery* (1949), and Robert Aickman's *Cold Hand in Mine* (1975). It contains the best—or at least some of the best—work of the best living weird writer; it has been meticulously edited by Campbell and James Turner; and its fourteen full-page photomontages by J. K. Potter visually interpret Campbell's work in a singularly felicitous manner. And yet, this monument may only represent Campbell at the midpoint of his career: I cannot even begin to imagine what a sixty-year retrospective of his work would contain.

Ghosts and Grisly Things (Tor, 2000), first published in 1998 by Pumpkin Books, is Campbell's first story collection of new tales since *Strange Things and Stranger Places* (1993). It does far more, however, than merely gather the relatively small number of stories Campbell has written over the past several years: it reaches back to reprint such things as "Through the Walls" (written as early as 1974 and published as a booklet from the British Fantasy Society in 1985) and four of the tales in *Night Visions 3* (1986), an anthology containing stories by Campbell, Lisa Tuttle, and Clive Barker. Several other tales were written in the mid- to late 1970s, although some were first published considerably later. Accordingly, the volume provides a capsule of Campbell's short story work over the past quarter-century—a compressed glimpse that shows why Campbell remains the leading short story writer in the horror field today.

The overriding motif of Campbell's work might be called urban paranoia. For Campbell, who spent his formative years in the gritty, crime-infested city of Liverpool, the pressures of urban life—rapid modernisation that wipes out both the physical and the metaphorical traces of the past and its traditions; the blight of crime that spreads well beyond lower-class environs to engulf the middle and upper classes; the overwhelming juxtaposition of heterogeneous humanity (what Evelyn Waugh called "those vile bodies")—make for a psychological pressure-cooker that can lead to unthinkable violence and tragedy. The family unit itself can crumble under the strain: "Through the Walls" is a nightmarish the story of a man, Hugh Pears, who comes to harbour evil designs on his own family, developing in particular an incestuous desire for his ten-year-old daughter. Seen entirely through Pears's point of view as he goes about his mundane activities with his wife, son, and daughter, the tale gains exceptional power as Pears's reason inexorably gives way. The tale, however, is not simply one of obsession. It ventures into the supernatural in its suggestion that Pears's psychosis is the result of powerful drugs that are somehow seeping through the walls of his house from the flat of his next-door neighbors. And what of the blood that Pears sees repeatedly appearing on those walls? Is it symbolic of the blood his daughter might shed were he in fact to have intercourse with her—or kill her? The one previously unpublished story in the collection, "Ra*e," is thematically related to "Through the Walls" in hinting at who is really responsible for the rape and murder of a fourteen-year-old girl. "The Sneering" is another masterful tale, in which the sneers that an elderly couple receive from youths seem symbolic of the cynical, modern attitude they cannot understand.

Several recent stories show that Campbell can absorb new developments in technology to augment the horror of his scenarios. "Going Under" focuses on a man's desperate effort to secure a working cellphone to contact his estranged lover while running in a charity race through a dark tunnel. "The Alternative," in which a prosperous man is haunted by a recurring dream that he and his family are living in a slum, not only hints at the shuddering guilt felt by many of the middle class at the existence of grinding poverty, especially in cities where the propinquity of rich and poor makes it all too evident, but reveals how sterile life can be to many modern-day denizens without such seeming necessities as a television or a computer.

In several tales I find a misanthropy—the idea that human beings are intrinsically loathsome and disgusting—that is as refreshing as it is uncommon. A throw-away sentence in "Going Under," in reference to some body-builders—". . . both appeared to have devoted a good deal of time and presumably machinery to the production of muscles, not only beneath shoulder level"—gets at the point exactly. The brief but pungent "A Street Was Chosen"—vaguely reminiscent of the "Twilight Zone" episode, "The Monsters Are Due on Maple Street"—suggests that very small disruptions in the daily habits of modern city-dwellers can produce the most appalling results.

The stories in *Told by the Dead* (PS Publishing, 2002) were written from as early as 1968 to as late as 2001, running the gamut from the ghost story to the tale of mental breakdown, from science fiction to grim psychological realism. The volume offers a fascinating recapitulation of Campbell's progression as a short fictionist. His first story collection—after the engaging but insubstantial *Inhabitant of the Lake and Less Welcome Tenants* (1964)—was *Demons by Daylight* (1973), a volume that in many ways remains the pinnacle of his work as a short story writer. What makes those tales so haunting is their intense, almost obsessive focus on the shifting moods and sensations of an individual consciousness, to the degree that we can scarcely separate dream, hallucination, or madness from the perception of objective reality. "Return Journey" (1998), in *Told by the Dead*, is a splendid replication of that early manner, especially in its rapid shifting between past and present. "The Previous Tenant" (1968), the earliest tale in this volume, similarly utilises the supernatural for purposes of psychological analysis, but here the scope is broadened to encompass the complexity of human relationships: a painter becomes obsessed with the physical tokens (and possibly the ghost) of a young woman who had committed suicide in the apartment he occupies, but his wife's half-unconscious destruction of these tokens points not only to her jealousy of her dead rival but to the difficulty of fusing aesthetic accomplishment with domestic harmony.

In such later collections as *Dark Companions* (1982) and *Waking Nightmares* (1991), Campbell focused on urban blight and squalor, and in "Becoming Visible" (1998) he continues the topos:

> I let my bicycle off its chain on the cold sweaty pipe in the Gents and carry it down the worn concrete stairs and out of the side door. A puppy or a rat scuttles down the alley, away from the bins outside the Chinese restaurant, where the kitchen is full of jabbering not much more alien than the talk that surrounds me every day. Above the senseless assortment of roofs the clouds are a slab of grease, holding down the heat of all the drudges who tramp the streets at lunchtime. They've gone home now to pretend they've lives worth living, only some have changed into this season's uniform and are swarming to the lights of clubs and pubs. I pedal past couples stuck together by their hands and imitating dummies in shop windows, past people who've given up pretending that a home is worth the effort and are nesting in the doorways of dead shops. Then there are buildings that are being smashed and burned, and a park with a lake that litter is soaking up and trees that move about so much I have to keep my curtains shut. I cycle through, past two children undressing each other in a shelter, and then I'm where I try to live.

This entire scene evokes the urban paranoia of *The Face That Must Die* (1979/1983), the first and greatest of his non-supernatural novels. In *Told by the Dead*, "Agatha's Ghost" (1997) comes close to equalling it in its cheerless portrayal of an elderly woman who believes herself to be haunted by her dead nephew.

Campbell's skill at depicting, insidiously and with a cumulative accretion of bizarre details, the madness of seemingly ordinary people is highlighted in "Little Ones" (1996) and "No Strings" (1998). But perhaps his greatest accomplishment in this regard is "The Word" (1993), a novelette that concludes *Told by the Dead*. Aside from being a devastating send-up of the dreariness of science fiction and fantasy conventions ("There'll be a woman whose middle is twice as wide as the rest of her, and someone wearing no sleeves or deodorant, and at least one writer gasping to be noticed, and now there's a vacuumhead using a walkie-talkie to send messages to another weekend deputy who's within shouting distance"; and later the magnificent one-liner, "The hotel is booked solid as a fan's cranium"), this tale grimly depicts the gradual psychological decline of an embittered critic, Jeremy Bates, who can scarcely conceal either his scorn or his envy of the sudden popularity of a hack science fiction writer, Jess Kray, who achieves immense notoriety with a possibly blasphemous book called *The Word*. It is no accident that Kray's name brings Jesus Christ to mind, nor that Bates writes a letter signed Jude Carrot (Judas Iscariot). Bates's murder of Kray on a television talk show seems all but inevitable.

Told by the Dead also includes Campbell's harrowing science fiction story "Slow" (1975), as well as several tales, on the borderline between supernatural and psychological horror, depicting the terrors to be encountered in travel ("The Entertainment" [1998], "All for Sale" [2001]). "The Worst Fog of the Year" (1970) features two variant endings, one supernatural, the other non-supernatural. In an afterword Campbell explains that Karl Edward Wagner, who wished to use the tale in a volume of *The Year's Best Horror Stories*, objected to the latter ending (which causes the story to conclude with a deflatingly comic anticlimax) and requested that the author write a new one; Campbell did so, much to the benefit of the tale.

Campbell's array of short stories must now number over 300, five times as many as H. P. Lovecraft's and a hundred more than Algernon Blackwood's. While his output of short fiction has understandably decreased during the past quarter-century, when he has written a full score of novels, it is gratifying to see that the short narrative—so uniquely amenable to the kind of intense, clutching, nebulous horror Campbell has made his own—is still in the forefront of his aesthetic vision. To be sure, we would be much poorer without such novels as *Incarnate*, *Midnight Sun*, and *The House on Nazareth Hill*, but the absence of such masterworks of concentrated terror as "Mackintosh Willy" and "The Word" would impoverish us even more. Fortunately, we are able to sample the Campbellian narrative in both the long and the short mode, and seem destined to do so for many years to come.

Campbell's novels of the 1990s and early 2000s similarly reveal a provocative progression of style and manner. Every new novel is a revelation. *Midnight Sun* (1990), *The Count of Eleven* (1991), and *The Long Lost* (1993) are all virtuoso performances—but how different they are from one another! Lovecraft remarked that M. R. James stood "at the opposite pole of genius" from Lord Dunsany; and this expression seems to me very apt in regard to Campbell's two novels, *The One Safe Place* (Tor/Forge, 1996) and *The House on Nazarath Hill* (Headline, 1996), which might represent the opposite poles of his literary output.

It would be cumbrous to give a detailed plot summary of *The One Safe Place*, one of the longest of Campbell's novels. Suffice it to say that it deals with the accidental but violent intertwining of two families—the Travises, who have come from America to England as husband Don pursues his bookseller's trade, his wife Susanne becomes a university professor, and their adolescent son Marshall strives to fit into the British school system; and the Fancys, a lower-class clan almost every one of whose members seems involved in some sort of low-level criminal activity. Phil Fancy pursues Don Travis in his car because of some perceived slight; later he pulls a gun on Don, and still later he hunts down the Travises at their home, threatening Marshall but being caught by the police when he breaks his ankle. His eighteen-month prison term seems mild enough, but even this punishment enrages the other members of his family, who continue the persecution of the Travises until Don is actually killed in front of his bookshop by two of the Fancys. Don had unwisely procured a gun to defend himself (guns are, of course, exceedingly difficult to obtain in England, as they should be in the violence-racked U.S.), but had not loaded it; when the Fancys, confronted by the gun-wielding Don as they come to his bookshop to threaten him, learn this, they kick him to death while a busload of commuters watch.

But the true foci of the novel are not the adult members of the respective families but the children, Darren Fancy and Marshall Travis. Traumatised by the events overwhelming his family (which also include an outrageous confiscation of videos owned by Susanne and used in her classes, on the grounds that they lack a British censor's certificate), Marshall flees school one day and falls unwittingly into the hands of Darren, who finds in this development an opportunity both to avenge the wrongs he feels the Travises have caused his family and—possibly by an act of actual murder—to raise his standing in his criminous clan. *The One Safe Place* is as relentlessly cheerless a work as any Campbell has written, *The Face That Must Die* not excluded. After the death of Don Travis, who in life cracked his share of jokes (as many of Campbell's later characters do), the novel becomes almost unbearably depressing. To say this, however, is only to praise the powerful atmosphere of gloom in the work and its ruthless display of the tragedy of wasted lives. The character portrayal is particularly fine. Campbell knows that the clearest way to etch the differing sociocultural status of the Travises and the Fancys is by their speech; the latter can hardly utter a sentence without monotonously lacing it with profanity, and their scornful references to the police ("the filth") and women (who are all "tarts") betray their attitudes far more than their actions.

But the depiction of the Fancys, while harsh, is far from being uniformly contemptuous. Campbell is careful to show that Darren in particular is largely the product of his environment and upbringing. Brutalised since youth by both his father and his mother, raised in a filthy, impoverished home where the only money comes from crime and where his mother blandly takes to prostitution to raise money after her husband goes to jail, Darren can scarcely be expected to be other than he is—ignorant, ill-tempered, smouldering with hatred and resentment, and thirsting avidly for the violence of which he himself has been the victim. "He wasn't going to let her [his mother] see how much she was hurting him, he was saving it up until he could pass it on to someone else": this single sentence laconically exposes the unending cycle of violence engendered by domestic abuse.

As for the Travis family, almost to the end they desperately maintain that their coming to England was not a mistake, even though Don has died, Susanne is outraged at the lack of freedom of expression, and Marshall is a little confused by British ways and British English. The fact that they are Americans is significant: having come from a country where violence has become endemic and gun ownership a supposed right, they are scarcely prepared for the level of violence they face in a land where the murder rate is a fraction of what it is in the United States.

The censorship issue is perhaps the one facet of the novel that disappoints, for its sudden resolution when the police decide not to prosecute Susanne seems somewhat of a copout. An American readership might be very interested to pursue the legal ramifications of the matter in a country where there is no First Amendment. In particular, Campbell has no discussion of the university's position in the whole situation, even though Susanne hopes and believes that it will support her contention that the confiscated videos are educational in nature. Campbell had treated the issue previously if glancingly in *Ancient Images*, and perhaps he wishes here to do no more than to draw attention to the general problem: on the one hand, the possible effect of actual pornography (as in some bestiality videos owned by the Fancys) on impressionable people; and, on the other hand, the arbitrary nature of government censorship—supported, perhaps, by a majority of unthinking individuals in the society at large who find in "nasty" videos a simple answer to the difficult issue of crime and its causes. Campbell is, of course, manifestly on the side of freedom of expression, even though he has now and again delivered a warning to the purveyors of explicit horror fiction that cannot be ignored: "I think it is high time some of them considered that they may be producing something more deplorable and more pernicious. The best I can hope is that their work, with the tedium of its excesses, destroys nothing but itself." But in *The One Safe Place* he somehow fails to come to grips with the issue.

The overriding question in regard to the novel, of course, is whether the work is within the realm of horror fiction at all. The question is only of interest for purposes of classification and can scarcely affect one's evaluation of the work itself. Not only is *The One Safe Place* non-supernatural, but it is not really even a suspense novel with horrific interludes (as, say, the novels of Thomas Harris are): only the passage involving Marshall's wandering out of school and falling into the hands of Darren can be said to be remotely weird. Consider this description of a derelict as seen by Marshall:

> . . . he almost tripped over a figure seated against the wall under the window of a clothes shop—a man dressed in a sack or an old coat, which he'd pulled up over his head and draped around a grey dog on his chest. The animal must

be dead, because it was grey with dust, and so was the stubble covering much of the man's caved-in face. Were his eyeballs coated with dust, or were his eyes shut? The head fell back, the face began to move, which ought to mean he was alive, except that it appeared to be coming to pieces.

Only much later do we learn that this and other hallucinations were engendered by some LSD secretly slipped into his drink by an individual who ran into him at the mall—none other than Darren Fancy. Otherwise, *The One Safe Place* is a mainstream novel, pure and simple.

And yet, it is difficult to deny *The One Safe Place* a high standing in Campbell's work overall, however anomalous it may be and however puzzled many of his devotees may find themselves upon reading it. It is an unpleasant novel that leaves a bad taste in one's mouth, but that is its purpose. It lays bare the culture of criminality and violence that is ripping apart the fabric of both English and American society and is leaving no one, however exalted in social or economic rank, unscathed. It offers no hope and sees no solution to the problems it exposes; and if this be deemed a flaw, it is a flaw with which society as a whole is afflicted.

The House on Nazareth Hill, conversely, might seem on the surface merely an artfully executed haunted house novel, but it proves to be much more. This work is indeed a triumphant return to the supernaturalism that had seemed to be becoming increasingly rare and attenuated in Campbell's recent novels, but it is also as searing a portrayal of domestic tension as any in his entire body of work.

Here again a plot summary of this long novel would be tedious and cumbrous. We are here dealing with another small family—Oswald and Heather Priestley and their daughter Amy—who move into a place called Nazarill (short for Nazareth Hill), a structure that was built centuries ago but which, after serving as offices in the nineteenth century and then standing deserted for decades, is refurbished as apartments. In an early scene, the eight-year-old Amy is sitting on her father's shoulders looking into the deserted pile, but then falls into the place after seeing something scuttling away out of sight. That night she has a horrible dream in which her father says to her grimly, "Your mother's dead, and you're mad; and you're staying here in Nazarill."

The novel proper opens when Amy is nearly sixteen. She seems in many ways a typical teenager—playing loud heavy-metal music, wearing an array of metal ornaments in various pierced parts of her body, and having a boyfriend, Rob Hayward—but we quickly learn that her mother had died years before in an automobile accident. Amy and Oswald also have what appear to be no more than the disagreements to be expected of a somewhat rebellious teenage daughter and her ageing father.

Weird phenomena begin to manifest themselves both to Oswald (who thinks he sees spiders lurking in the corners of his own flat) and to the other tenants of Nazarill. Amy, meanwhile, is increasingly obsessed with the history of Nazarill (especially in what it may have been before it was a set of offices) and also increasingly troubled by what she takes to be her father's overprotective and dictatorial behaviour, almost as if he were her jailor. Her discovery of a Bible that had been somehow trapped in the huge oak tree outside the house leads her to the truth: Nazarill had been an insane asylum. Moreover, there is a rumour that the Partington witches—assuming they existed at all—used to dance upon the hill before Nazarill was built. Could the strange skeletonic creatures whom the tenants see out of the corners of their eyes be the ghosts of witches who had been locked up in the place? Later an estate agent grudgingly mentions that Nazarill had been gutted by a fire that had killed all the inmates and the staff.

Meanwhile, relations between Amy and Oswald deteriorate rapidly. As they seem to reenact some of the brutalities that the staff had practised upon their hapless inmates, the reader comes to wonder whether Oswald is in fact possessed by the spirits of the erstwhile asylum staff. Why does he begin speaking in archaic language and forgetting the use of common objects like the building's intercom? The viciousness of Oswald's treatment of his own daughter rivals any of the supernatural manifestations in the novel, and it can only lead to tragedy for them both.

The House on Nazareth Hill will not be long in taking rank as one of the finest haunted house novels in literature, perhaps surpassing even Shirley Jackson's masterful *The Haunting of Hill House* (1959). Readers will welcome it as a return to supernaturalism, which was wholly absent in some of Campbell's recent novels, such as *The Count of Eleven* (1991) and *The One Safe Place*; but more than that, it is a magnificent fusing of the intense, clutching supernaturalism that we find in his short stories with the wrenching domestic conflict we have seen in his later novels, along with the gripping depiction of paranoia (in the figure of Oswald, who becomes a crazed religious maniac in the latter stages of the work) found in such an early novel as *The Face That Must Die*. In essence, *The House on Nazareth Hill* is a grand summation of the best of Campbell's many-faceted work.

Some of the supernatural effects in the novel are as chilling as any in his entire oeuvre. One tenant catches an actual glimpse of the entities haunting the place, and is appalled by its curiously *incomplete* appearance:

> a shape which, as she began to distinguish it, Hilda took at first to be a large plant or small tree which had withered after thrusting itself up through the floor and against the wall to the right of the window. Then she saw the remains of hands at the ends of both branches fastened to the wall on either side of a shrivelled, lolling head. There was no question they were hands, because as she located them in the dimness they began to writhe all the fingers they had left, beckoning her into the cell.

Later on, Amy, creeping downstairs, finds all six doors of the ground-floor flats slightly ajar. A bony hand emerges out of one door; worse, the entity actually speaks to Amy. As she mutters to herself, "I never wanted to live here in the first place," the other replies: "None of us did." Then the creature reveals itself: "The grey wispy coating of the skull was certainly not hair. The figure still had some of a face, or had somehow reconstructed parts of one, which looked in danger of coming away from the bones, as the scraps of the chest were peeling away from the ribs to expose the withered heart and lungs, which jerked as though in a final spasm as Amy's gaze lit on them."

The inevitable question that the student of Campbell's work must raise is the degree to which the novel is autobiographical. At the time of the novel's writing, Campbell's own daughter, Tamsin, was exactly Amy's age, while Oswald appears to be in that period of middle age in which Campbell finds himself. Speculation on the point is of course useless in the absence of evidence, and the likeliest theory is that Campbell used his imagination to exaggerate what might be the customary disputes between teenagers and their parents—loud music, body piercing, personal untidiness—into a Grand Guignol of supernatural and domestic horror. It is, certainly, of interest that the narrative urges the reader to sympathise very largely with Amy rather than with Oswald, who is clearly depicted—even before his supernatural transformation—as a somewhat overprotective parent. Oswald, however, is not lacking in sympathy himself at the beginning, since his plight in raising a headstrong teenage girl in the gaping absence of his beloved wife is an affecting one. And yet, one wonders how we are to interpret Amy's perception of her father at one point:

> She gazed at him . . . and saw a furtively anxious old man in an out-of-date grey overcoat and black scarf. His face seemed to have devoted its recent years to producing more of itself, its lower cheeks bellying on either side of the jaw and pulling down the corners of the mouth, while the underside of the chin had settled for adding itself to the throat. His eyebrows had always been prominent, but their greyness made them appear heavier, and to be weighing down his eyes.

However much this may or may not tally with Campbell's own impression of himself, it emphasises a point that many of Campbell's novels have made: the difficulty of dealing with change, specifically change of character. Oswald's change in outward appearance from the vibrancy of young manhood to the stodginess of middle age is later echoed by a psychological transformation that makes Amy feel that the father she once knew is no longer even present, but has been replaced by some hideous gorgon whom she refuses to recognise or acknowledge.

For such a lengthy novel, *The House on Nazareth Hill* is remarkable for having, basically, only two central characters, Amy and Oswald. The narrative focus alternates at critical junctures: the death of one tenant is seen through

Oswald's eyes, as are the encounters of two others with the ghostly entities. These scenes allow the reader to be fully aware of the supernatural nature of the phenomena, and also bring further reader sympathy to Amy, whose own glimpses of the weird are seen to be unmistakably genuine. The alternations of narrative perspective between Amy and Oswald in the latter stages of the novel are also psychologically telling, in that they clearly delineate both her own fears (of the creatures hovering around her as well as of her demented father) and Oswald's crazed rationalisations of his detestable abuse of his daughter.

The House on Nazareth Hill testifies that Ramsey Campbell remains at the peak of his form in his fourth decade of writing. With this novel he has unified several of the themes of his earlier work—pure supernaturalism; exploration of social and domestic trauma; chilling portrayal of psychosis—into a seamless fusion. The work infuses new life into one of the most venerable motifs of weird fiction—the haunted house—but is by no means merely an exercise in antiquarianism, as its searing displays of social and family conflict attest. *The House on Nazareth Hill* shows that readers can look with confidence to Campbell's continuing innovations in the multifaceted modes of horror fiction.

Campbell's next novels, *The Last Voice They Hear* (Tor, 1998) and *Silent Children* (Tor, 2000), may perhaps not rank among the very best of his works, but even middling Campbell is better than the best that nearly anyone else has to offer. Campbell has told me that the two novels comprise "a pair . . . in terms of shared themes"—specifically, the theme of the peril that can so easily befall children.

The Last Voice They Hear weaves several seemingly unrelated narrative strands together into a unified and gripping climax. The bulk of the novel focuses upon Geoff Davenport, the host of a TV news show whose half-brother disappeared when he was eighteen. Throughout the novel we are provided with glimpses of the shoddy, abusive treatment Ben received from his parents, who clearly preferred Geoff. Ben begins to make enigmatic phone calls to Geoff and also to leave him a succession of envelopes at various locations, usually containing photographs of sites associated with their childhood. Things take a sudden turn for the worse when Ben causes a car driven by Geoff's wife Gail's parents to crash in Scotland. He then performs the sadistic ploy that he has used on the eight elderly couples he has previously killed: he uses glue to bind their arms around each other and to seal their lips in an everlasting kiss—a grotesque parody of the affection he himself failed to receive from his own parents and grandparents.

Ben then contrives a still more heinous act: pretending to be Gail's father, he kidnaps Geoff's three-year-old son, Paul, from the television station's day care centre in London and takes him back to his hometown, Liverpool. Geoff eventually tracks Ben and Paul to an amusement park in Blackpool; Geoff manages to save Paul, but Ben jumps off a tower to his death.

The Last Voice They Hear manages, without overstating the matter, to convey a variety of social messages at once, but its central point is clear: the abuse of children can have lasting and catastrophic effects, and can engender psychopathic behaviour years later. Some readers might perhaps wish a more exhaustive dwelling on Ben's ill-treatment during his youth, but in a few deft strokes Campbell portrays the humiliation a boy must feel when his own parents or grandparents—figures whose authority he has been brought up not to question—display contempt or loathing for him.

Silent Children is a still finer work than its predecessor and ranks close to the summit of Campbell's non-supernatural work. The novel deals largely with Hector Woollie, a handyman who has murdered several children; one of them Woollie had buried under the floor of a house in the suburb of Wembley, which he was renovating. The house is owned by Roger and Leslie Ames, a married couple who subsequently divorced. After months of trying to sell the house, Leslie and her thirteen-year-old son Ian decide to move back into it, despite the unsavoury reputation it has now gained throughout the placid middle-class neighbourhood.

Leslie takes in Jack Lamb, an American horror writer, as a roomer. At this point we are led to expect a hackneyed romance between Jack and Leslie, and sure enough they become attracted to each other and engage in sex not long after Jack moves in. Leslie envisions marrying Jack, who might also provide an adult male authority figure for her wayward son.

But Campbell has lulled us into a false sense of security. Jack, it turns out, is none other than the son of Hector Woollie. Although by no means afflicted with Hector's psychosis, he is haunted by the possibility that, as a teenager, he may on occasion have unwittingly helped Woollie dispose of children while assisting in his father's renovation work. Much of the tension in the novel arises from repeated attempts by Hector—who is believed dead, having staged his own apparent death so as to escape the police—to contact Jack. At one point Hector voices Jack's most deep-seated fear: "I wonder how much like your dad you really are deep down." Later Woollie kidnaps seven-year-old Charlotte, daughter of the woman Roger Ames has now married, as well as Leslie's son Ian; the rest of the novel is devoted to efforts to rescue the children.

The one overriding feature of *Silent Children*—above its smooth-flowing prose, its tense moments of suspense, and its revelations of a diseased mind—is the vividness of its character portrayal. Even minor characters are rendered so crisply and vitally that they immediately come to life. Major figures such as Leslie and Jack are fully formed, complex personalities who are etched with increasing subtlety with each passing chapter. Campbell has depicted the teenager Ian Ames with especial felicity, capturing in all its paradoxical confusion the burgeoning character of a boy on the verge of young manhood. A distinctly satirical edge enlivens many descriptions of character and incident: Campbell is relentless in exposing the pettiness, hypocrisy, and selfishness that can typify middle-class suburban life. Few characters in the novel emerge as wholly admirable. Although the reader's sympathy resides chiefly with Leslie, and secondarily with Jack and Ian, even they are flawed individuals struggling as best they can to live up to their own ideals.

Oddly, Hector Woollie seems somewhat cloudy, specifically in regard to the psychological aberrations that led him to his multiple murders of children. There is, by design, no such intense and relentless focus on his psychotic mentality as there is on Horridge in *The Face That Must Die* or even on Jack Orchard in *The Count of Eleven*: Woollie is merely one of a network of characters whose accidental intermingling has produced the chilling scenario.

In Campbell's next novel, *Pact of the Fathers* (Tor, 2001), even the crime/suspense element is reduced to a minimum. Like classical Greek tragedy, all the "horrors" take place offstage and come to us only at second hand. This need not imply a diminution of the power of these episodes; it is only that those who want a more obvious jolt as part of their literary nourishment had best go elsewhere.

Pact of the Fathers reveals, with exquisite pacing and tempo, a scenario whose implications are appalling and grotesque. A young woman, Daniella Logan, grieves over the sudden death of her father in a car accident; but adding to her trauma is a scene she witnesses a few days later, in which a group of men appear to act out some mysterious ritual with knives over her father's new grave. Compelled to investigate the matter, she learns that her father had been one of a number of fathers who, to insure their success in business, had formed a pact to kill their first-born children. Described in this way, it can be readily seen that the novel bears some parallels to *The Long Lost*, in which we similarly see the working out of an age-old ritual in a modern world that seemingly has no place for such things. But the differences are also striking. There is never any suggestion in *Pact of the Fathers* that those who fulfil this pact receive supernatural aid; rather, it would appear that the others involved in the covert group provide assistance to those who carry through their dreadful mission and, conversely, destroy (as Daniella's father had been destroyed) those who lose courage and spare their first-born.

What distinguishes *Pact of the Fathers* is the suppleness, fluidity, and richly textured elegance of its prose. Campbell's writing has never been better; his etching of character has never been more telling and shrewd; his modulation of the narrative has never been surer. Consider this passage, describing a scene in Greece (where Daniella has fled to escape vengeance on the part of the other fathers):

A line of squat white houses not much less rough than rocks straggled down the lumpy road to the harbour. Old women sat unmoving outside two adjacent houses, their faces wizened as dried fruit, their eyes black as their headscarves and the dresses that hid them from the neck down, their expressions no more welcoming than the priest's had been. A moped leaned in a doorway beyond which she heard the thumps and grunts of a martial arts game a solitary silhouette was playing on a television almost blank with sunlight.

Passages like this should make every other writer despair of ever hoping to equal the smooth rhythms, sharp observation, and painterly elegance that Campbell has developed over a lifetime of unremitting work as a prose stylist.

But is it horror? Is it even suspense? We are, at the outset, puzzled as to why Daniella has fled to Greece, away from all her friends and family, but the astute reader will have resolved this point some time before Campbell himself reveals it; and the only obviously horrific scene might be one that describes the hideous fate of another father who failed to offer up his first-born. As I say, those who want a book to make them jump out of their skins on every other page will surely be disappointed; but other readers—may they not be few!—who look to a novel for some insight into how people actually act and think will find *Pact of the Fathers* one of the quiet triumphs in Ramsey Campbell's novelistic output.

As for *The Overnight* (PS Publishing, 2004), it is a perfect embodiment of the adage of "Write what you know." Early in his career Campbell made the unnerving admission that the crazed murderer in *The Face That Must Die* was, in many fundamentals of his character and attitudes, based upon his mother as she descended into madness in her final years. More recently, *The House on Nazareth Hill* might—in its intense focus on the troubled relations between a man and his teenage daughter—be seen as a (presumably exaggerated) reflection of his own relations with his then-teenage daughter, Tamsin. And who can forget "The Chimney," an early tale that chillingly echoes the estrangement of Campbell's parents? No event in Campbell's life, however innocuous, seems out of bounds for fictional treatment; but that event frequently serves as little more than a springboard for imaginative voyagings in the best traditions of supernatural horror.

In the spring of 2000, as Campbell announces in a brief preface to *The Overnight*, he began working fulltime at a Borders bookstore in Cheshire Oaks. I am sure I was not the only one to be astounded and dismayed when I heard at the time that the leading horror writer of our generation felt the need to take on this work to help support himself and his family; one thinks of Lovecraft toiling away at poorly paying revision work (and even, on one occasion, securing temporary employment as a ticket-taker at a movie theatre) to make ends meet, or Machen grinding out reams of vapid journalism before he received his Civil List pension. Even though Campbell's bookstore stint lasted only a few months, it seemed to reflect badly on a number of facets of contemporary society—the state of horror publishing, especially in the UK (Campbell no longer has a major commercial publisher to issue his works in his native land); the inequities of a capitalist system that consistently fails to reward excellence but only rewards popular appeal—even though it reflected supremely well on Campbell himself in his willingness to make sacrifices for his art and his family. We should therefore not be surprised that, in a few years' time, Campbell transmuted his reasonably pleasant descent into wage-slavery in the crucible of his imagination, the result being *The Overnight*, a supernatural novel that ranks high among the achievements of his long and varied career.

We here encounter—in a present-tense narration that Campbell has used relatively infrequently for long works, most notably in the novella *Needing Ghosts* (1990)—a succession of workers at a bookstore, Texts, in a small shopping plaza (Campbell calls it a "retail park") in the Manchester/Liverpool area. A setting less promising for the incursion of the supernatural would seem difficult to imagine, but Campbell manages it through shifting narrative perspectives—each chapter is seen through the eyes of a different bookstore worker—and the extraordinarily subtle accumulation of bizarre details.

Texts is run by an American named Woody, whose attempts at introducing a kind of brash, cheerful efficiency are not well received by his largely British staff of young professionals. Interpersonal tensions also add their weight of unease to the narrative: one employee has just left his partner (a fellow employee) and taken up with another coworker; another employee named Agnes (she pronounces it Anyes) is harried by overprotective parents; another, a gay man named Jake, is predictably harassed by an intolerant bigot named Greg. But these emotional complications are only the unnerving backdrop to increasingly harrowing supernatural manifestations that eventually become too plain to be ignored. A constant and ever-thickening fog seems to hover around the retail park; computers develop minds of their own, failing to correct typographical errors even after repeated proofreading; elevators malfunction; books continually seem to get misshelved; and, most disturbing of all, small grey animate objects are half glimpsed skulking around shelves, in the stockroom, or in the workers' staffroom. What could be the cause of these manifestations?

It is here that *The Overnight* might perhaps be criticised for excessive reticence. Campbell does not wish to spell out the matter in an obvious way, but the hints that are sprinkled throughout the narrative—hints based upon the sinister history of the region as a focal point of violence and death for centuries or millennia—seem just a trifle too vague and imprecise to account for the horrors on display. It also takes a pretty large leap of faith to assume that such age-old horrors—many of which are exhibited during an all-night shelving session that Woody insists upon, lending the book its title—could have the wherewithal to affect the most sophisticated paraphernalia of modern life, from computers to electronic elevators to the very essence of contemporary published books, whose text and illustrations hideously melt into an amorphous mass before one horrified worker's eyes.

But this cavil seems insignificant in contrast to the many deft images of terror and bizarrerie, as well as the gripping sense of cumulative horror that envelops *The Overnight*. As the novel develops, such seemingly innocuous words as "gritty," "grimy," "fog," and even "smile" take on appalling overtones. The novel may also be open to the flaw of introducing too many characters (we encounter such bookstore employees as Woody, Madeleine, Jill, Connie, Wilf, Geoff, Greg, Jake, Gavin, Ray, Angus, Agnes, and Nigel, along with cameos by the authors Brodie Oates and Adrian Bottomley), few of whom seem sufficiently different from one another to take on distinct personalities of their own. But there is a certain perverse fascination in seeing each of these characters killed off one by one toward the end of the novel, in scenes that are narrated by the doomed workers themselves as they encounter a fate they strive haplessly to avoid.

The Overnight also reveals Campbell's finest melding of humour and horror since *The Count of Eleven* (1991). Aside from some moments of extraordinary wordplay, the novel features moments of pure hilarity that in some inexplicable way only augment the horror of the general situation. One scene in which the relentlessly cheerful Woody strives to encourage his reserved British underlings to greet their potential customers with grinning smiles and a robust "Welcome to Texts!" is a comic vignette that Wodehouse could not have surpassed. And Campbell has also developed an enviable skill at portraying the finest shades of emotional nuance in the interpersonal exchanges between his characters. All apart from its merits as a supernatural novel, *The Overnight* can be read with pleasure as a dissection of the societal and personal complexities of life in the twenty-first century. And the manner in which Campbell successively shifts the narrative voice to exactly those characters whose actions or sensations carry the story forward is a remarkable feat of literary architecture.

With *The Overnight* Campbell proves what is already beyond the need of proof—that he is the most consistently gifted and rewarding writer of supernatural horror now in practice. He has, in the past forty years, produced hundreds of short stories and a score of novels that have set an increasingly higher mark for other writers to aim at, and with few exceptions he alone has reached that mark with any degree of regularity.

Secret Stories (PS Publishing, 2005) features one of the most ingenious openings in contemporary horror fiction. We are plunged into the narrative of a nameless male protagonist who comes to the assistance of a young woman being victimised by a gang of surly men on a subway train in Liverpool. But the man is not content to act as the woman's rescuer; he himself pursues her, perhaps hoping for some reward beyond mere thanks—and in the end pushes her on to the train tracks, where she is killed by an oncoming vehicle. Only gradually do we learn that this is in fact a short story written by the central figure of the novel, Dudley Smith, a young man who, although working for a living (at a job assistance bureau), still lives with his mother. Although he calls her by her first name, Kathy, it quickly becomes evident that her seemingly benign overprotectiveness has smothered and infantilised him.

Actually, the above narrative is the second chapter of the book; the first chapter—consisting of a single sentence ("'. . . Dudley, there's something I haven't been telling you,' she said, and at once he was terrified that she knew")—is similarly puzzling until we learn that Kathy has surreptitiously submitted the story, entitled "Night Trains Don't Take You Home," to a newly formed magazine, the *Mersey Mouth*, which is sponsoring a contest for unpublished writers. But why would Dudley be "terrified that she knew"? What is it that he fears she knows? This, too, is something we learn only gradually. When Dudley's story wins the contest, a staff writer for the magazine, Patricia Martingale, is assigned to write a piece on Dudley to accompany the story. She interviews several of Dudley's friends and colleagues, including a schoolteacher who had disapproved of Dudley's early writings for reasons he does not make entirely clear: Is it that these stories—all involving the killing of women—are too graphic? Is it that they seem to be based on actual occurrences? The teacher, Mr. Fender, wonders, "I should want to ascertain how fictitious the stories are," and later: "Smith was wholly devoid of imagination." It is not entirely unusual for a writer to base his tales on actual events; but what are we to make of the remark about Dudley by Walt Davenport, the owner of the *Mersey Mouth*: "I've never met a writer who was closer to his creation"?

Slowly the truth dawns on us: Dudley has actually committed the murders about which he is writing.

This revelation, coming relatively early in the novel, colours our perceptions of all the subsequent events, and furthermore turns virtually every statement made by the central characters into a kind of *double entendre*. Patricia, when first meeting Dudley after having talked with Kathy, remarks: "I hope you don't mind, but your mother has been letting us into your secrets." At this point, Dudley does not know how much Kathy knows about his activities. When, a little later, Kathy protests against staging Dudley for a photograph holding a knife, commenting, "He's a writer, not a murderer," we are already sensing that she is merely engaging in a pitiable wish-fulfilment fantasy.

Dudley is initially offended that his mother went behind his back in submitting the story, but gradually he comes to look forward to appearing in print. But things begin insidiously going wrong. First, the insufferable boss at his office, Mrs Wimbourne, expresses doubts about whether Dudley can even allow the story to be published and accept the prize money, for this would constitute "competing employment" that might be prohibited by the conditions of his employment. Campbell is brilliant at portraying the petty office politics that make Dudley's life there a slow-burning hell. Then follows the incident with Shell Garridge. She is a comedian with a ferocious and aggressive feminist streak; as a columnist for the *Mersey Mouth*, she had cast a vote against Dudley's story and continues to protest its publication. At a club one evening she provides what proves to be a telling psychological portrait of Dudley:

> "Tortured animals when he was a kid. Scared of women. Hasn't got a girlfriend. Likely brought up by a single mum. I'm not dissing him, but she'd have kept telling him how he was better than everyone else, treating him like every time he farted somebody should bottle it and sell it. Only deep down he'll know he's nothing and hate her for not stopping him knowing. That'll be another reason he's got it in for women even more than most men have. So whenever he's feeling more than usually knobless, because I don't reckon he'll have much to play with and anyway he won't be able to get it to salute, he goes creeping after women on their own so he can pretend he's worth knowing about. Most of the time he can't catch them, because women aren't as stupid as him. Just now and then one of them's unlucky, thinks he's so pathetic he has to be harmless."

Shell has spoken better than she knew; for she proves to be Dudley's first victim—or, rather, the first victim whose gruesome murder Campbell allows us to see.

But if Shell, through her cruel verbal abuse of Dudley, seems a not entirely sympathetic victim, Patricia Martingale is very much otherwise. As things continue to go badly for Dudley—the family of the woman who had died in the train station, having heard of the imminent publication of Dudley's story, protests against it and forces the magazine to withdraw it, although they promise to publish another of his stories; a short film that was to be based upon his story is similarly protested by the friends and family of the dead woman; Dudley finally walks out of his job, having come increasingly close to losing his hold on reality—he comes to blame Patricia for his troubles, and in the end kidnaps her, ties her entire head, along with her hands and ankles, in package-sealing tape (he refers to her as the "package," a classic dehumanising gesture), and confines her in his bathtub. Her struggles to escape provide fodder for the story Dudley is now writing.

Secret Stories ranks high among Campbell's output for the deftness with which the central figure is drawn, and his gradual but unremitting descent into paranoia and madness. The slightest of touches—as when Kathy wipes Dudley's mouth at dinner, with Patricia present—conveys how Kathy has unwittingly kept her son tied to her apron-strings and prevented his maturation into a healthy adult. Nearly every one of Dudley's utterances comes across as juvenile and sophomoric. Campbell's final, poignant comment on his protagonist—"he looked like a child outraged and terrified by the unfairness of the world"—perfectly encapsulates the boy that Dudley has remained into manhood. And yet, Dudley is far from being the only vivid character in the book: Kathy, Patricia, Shell, and others come to vibrant life under Campbell's hands.

But it would be unfair to *Secret Stories* to suggest that it features the unrelieved gloom of *The Face That Must Die*. Indeed, one of the best-kept secrets of Campbell's writing is the degree to which he has, especially in later years, become a comic writer. To be sure, this novel does not seek to reach the levels of grotesquerie found in *The Count of Eleven*, but clever touches abound. My favourite, perhaps, is when Dudley sits down at breakfast to eat a bowl of Sticky Rotters. (I say this as one whose favourite cereal remains Count Chocula.) Kathy's unsuccessful attempt to make a pie is described as follows: "Kathy brought out of the oven a pie so collapsed that it seemed bent on negating its own shape." Whole scenes—as when Dudley is beaten up by the brother of a woman who claims Dudley insulted her at his office, or when Kathy, staying at a hotel to keep out of Dudley's way, makes the acquaintance of a seemingly normal man who in fact is a masochist and wants Kathy to whip him—are full of comic buffoonery. But they do not counteract the prevailing mood of grimness, even tragedy, that hangs as a pall over *Secret Stories*.

The Tor edition (*Secret Story* [2006]), aside from altering the title, is abridged. Although Campbell himself prepared the abridgment, readers owe it to themselves to read the complete version. No detail in this novel is too insignificant to lend its weight to the final cataclysmic outcome.

Clive Barker: Weird Fiction as Subversion

In assessing *Clive Barker's Shadows in Eden*, edited by Stephen Jones (Underwood-Miller, 1991), I am working under somewhat of a handicap, in that I am not entirely convinced that Clive Barker is an especially good writer. And yet, the problem with criticising Barker—as is even more the case with the splatterpunks whom he has reluctantly and perhaps unwittingly spawned—is that an attack upon him is frequently interpreted as an ideological and narrowminded condemnation by the squeamish, the prudish, and the conventional. Let me assert, then, that I have no intrinsic objection to Barker's extensive use of sex and violence in his work, and that I can relish his handling of both the former ("The Age of Desire") and the latter ("Jacqueline Ess: Her Last Will and Testament"). It is my belief that *The Damnation Game* is one of the finest weird novels of our time—rich, dense, complex, and beautifully written—and that *Weaveworld* is a very interesting experiment, even if it does not have very much in the way of philosophical or even aesthetic substance. My problems with Barker can be divided into three general rubrics: (1) he frequently does not think through his supernatural conceptions very well, so that they lack the internal logic that weird fiction must have if it is to be anything more than a cheap *frisson*; (2) his style can be very careless and slipshod, full of solecisms and even spelling mistakes; and (3) he seems to be unable to imagine any horror beyond the harm that can be inflicted upon the human body. I do not have the space here to justify these complaints (although they will be elaborated in some of my remarks below), and I trust that I can refer readers to my lengthy chapter on Barker in *The Modern Weird Tale*.

Having said all this, let me immediately add that *Clive Barker's Shadows in Eden* is a magnificent compilation. It has just about everything the Clive Barker fan could want: rare materials by Barker, many interviews of him, appreciations by his colleagues, a few serious critical analyses, and a rich abundance of photographs of and drawings by him. Most of the items are reprinted: of the fifty or so pieces here, thirty-seven are previously published; of the thirteen original pieces (two by Barker), at least three are reworkings of earlier articles. The arrangement of articles (as well as a large number of sidebars and marginal comments) has been accomplished with exceptional skill, and presents about as complete a picture of Barker the man and writer as we are likely to have for a long time. The overriding question of whether Barker genuinely deserves this sort of treatment is one that this volume cannot, I suppose, be expected to answer.

Among the many distinctive features of this book is the amount of nonfiction by Barker—interviews, essays, lectures, introductions to books by other writers—included here. Some of the interviews might have been trimmed or omitted, as they can on occasion be somewhat repetitious, insubstantial, and even bathetic ("What do you think about *Moby Dick?*" "Well, *Moby Dick* is a great novel as far as I'm concerned"); and one very interesting lecture—delivered at UCLA in February 1987—ought to have been printed as a unit rather than being cut up into a great many sidebars. All this material reveals Barker to be a highly articulate and stimulating spokesman for weird fiction in general and for his brand of weird fiction—explicit, physically extreme horror—in particular.

Even here, however, I have some problems. Barker speaks repeatedly of the need for weird fiction to be grounded in "metaphysics." We live, Barker feels (surely correctly), in a world where the "banal" reigns supreme—in television, in newspapers, in most of our daily lives. Accordingly, weird fiction must be "confrontational" and "subversive," waking us up from our listlessness and lethargy. I believe Barker is on firm ground here, but I am not convinced that his own fiction actually embodies these principles. (This is what used to be called the gap between intention and achievement, before intention was banished from critical theory.) Barker criticises Stephen King for his all too frequent good-vs.-evil scenarios where the monster is portrayed as a "pure other" that must be extirpated for the good of the world; but I regret to say that Barker has himself fallen into a naive good-vs.-evil pattern in some of his own work, notably *Weaveworld* and *The Great and Secret Show*. Perhaps the clearest and most succinct expression of Barker's own view occurs in a sidebar taken from a 1988 interview:

> I'm not just writing to horrify, I'm writing to disturb, excite and subvert. Those functions are best served by the clearest possible views of the imagined scenes. I never cut to shadows—never cut away the moment of maximum revelation. What is revealed can be a moment of transcendence or disgust or self-comprehension or all three. It can be erotic, it can be funny, it can be foul. Those ambiguities and paradoxes are best arrived at if you show all there is to see.

This sounds good in theory, but in practice I fear that repeated doses of mere physical horror do not excite horror or disgust so much as . . . boredom. Barker says in a cocksure fashion that "What you can't do to most of the images in my books is ignore them": well, yes you can, since after a while they all start sounding the same. The only solution for someone in Barker's position is either to increase the dosage (as in *The Damnation Game* and his films) or to opt for a different mode of writing altogether (as in *Weaveworld*). In a sense I can understand and even sympathise with Barker's impatience with the subtlety, indirection, and suggestiveness of much traditional weird fiction, which can on occasion lead to excessive obscurity (Robert Aickman) or mere tameness (some of M. R. James and most of his disciples). But Barker's own frenetic pyrotechnics have drawbacks of their own. I defy anyone to read Barker's "The Midnight Meat Train" and T. E. D. Klein's "The Children of the Kingdom" and not come away with a vastly greater impression of the horrors that may dwell on the underside of New York City in Klein's tale than in Barker's. Klein cannot possibly be accused of pulling any punches—his denouement is about as horrifying as anything I have read in modern literature; it is simply that his tale is written with an elegance, meticulousness, and atmospheric tensity that Barker's cannot hope to achieve.

Two other strains that emerge in Barker's nonfiction are a denigration of mainstream fiction and an extreme hostility to critics ("I don't give a fuck about the critics"). These are, in the end, two aspects of the same phenomenon: Barker's impatience with the stodginess of mainstream critics who refuse to acknowledge weird fiction as a recognised means of expression. Barker finds most mainstream fiction lame and tiresome, and he and J. G. Ballard produce a witty parody of the average novel: "Barker gives it a generic title,

Adultery on Campus, and Ballard satirizes the typical mainstream plot: 'George and Mildred live in Highgate; he's a securities dealer; she teaches at the local comprehensive; and they have problems!'" Clever and even telling as this is, it really does to mainstream fiction what (as Barker himself recognises) mainstream critics do to weird fiction: judge it by its poorest, not its best, examples. Bad horror novels could be parodied in an exactly analogous way, but this would say nothing about the merits of genuine artists like Machen, Dunsany, Lovecraft, and Campbell. And Barker's very naive view of criticism—"I've never been interested in that: I hate the vivisection of literature, which is a necessary part of analysis, and I hated the idea that they took this stuff apart and they talked about the bits they understood and avoided the bits they didn't"—does the same thing. Barker seems not to allow that good criticism can actually enhance the reader's appreciation and enjoyment of a text.

The end result is that Barker has developed a highly confrontational view of his place in the literary arena, and has come to feel that shocking and outraging people is in itself a virtue. This is best encapsulated by an exchange between him and Ramsey Campbell:

> CAMPBELL: But I look forward to being censored and being pilloried with great glee . . .
> BARKER: Why is that? Would it be the proof of the success of your art?
> CAMPBELL: No, I just think it would be a lot of fun.

For Barker, being banned is in itself a testament to aesthetic worth; he forgets that, while many worthy books (e.g., *Ulysses*) have been banned, not all things that are banned (e.g., child pornography) have aesthetic value.

After all this, Barker then turns around and says: "I'm writing popular fiction. . . . You get your material to the largest cross-section of people you possibly can." There are two problems here: first, if Barker is simply a popular writer, why all the talk about metaphysics and *le fantastique* (as Barker has taken to calling his writing—rather strangely for one who claims to be nonelitist); second, *why* should one get one's work to the largest number of people possible? Do mere numbers of readers really signify anything? Art is not a democracy, but only an aristocracy of excellence. Stephen King, James Michener, and Danielle Steel are not the most significant literary figures of our time, though they are read by vastly more people than are, say, John Fowles and Gore Vidal. It is the latter who will prevail in the end; and this is not because of any sort of conspiracy on the part of highbrow critics who are hostile to "popular" literature, but because there *really is* more substance in Fowles and Vidal than in King, Michener, or Steel.

But I do not wish to be unjust to Barker as essayist. His introduction to *Night Visions* 4 (1987) is a really fine articulation of the aesthetic purpose of weird fiction. "Ramsey Campbell: An Appreciation" (1986) is a moving tribute, combining personal reminiscence with keen critical insight. Even his essay on Stephen King (for *Kingdom of Fear,* 1986), although rather effusive, manages to direct some telling blows at King's verbosity and conventionality of outlook. There are also a number of charming little surprises. Who would expect Barker to say that "I want to do a 'bodice-ripper' very much"? or that "*Peter Pan* is, I suppose, the book I would want to be buried with"? More seriously, a stimulating discussion of censorship between Barker and Dennis Etchison is one of the highlights of this book (this was in a forum at UCLA in 1987, but has been unpublished until now). I wish, however, that Barker would not, in his interviews and essays, be quite as self-congratulatory as he is, lumping himself matter-of-factly with Goya and Blake and expatiating about the profound depths in his own work. It is almost as if he is trying to talk himself into literary greatness rather than letting his actual creative work do it for him.

There is, in the end, not much about Barker in this book. The table of contents appears to suggest a number of articles—by Stephen Jones, Douglas E. Winter, Lisa Tuttle, Kim Newman, Neil Gaiman, and many others—but a good many of these turn out to be interviews. There is one interminable article on *The Great and Secret Show* by Gary Hoppenstand that manages, incredibly, to be almost as vapid and fatiguing as the book itself. There is considerable discussion of Barker's films, and this is among the most useful and illuminating material in the entire volume; Barker's work in comics is also treated interestingly, if briefly. A large bibliography at the back of the volume will no doubt be welcomed by collectors, as it lists everything from prices of foreign editions to proof copies of Barker's books; but scholars will not find it of much use, as it is lacking in volume numbers, page numbers, and other bibliographically essential features. There is no listing of critical work on Barker at all; this is perhaps because, aside from countless interviews, reviews, and newspaper write-ups, there simply isn't any.

The only genuine critical articles in the book are two long pieces by Michael A. Morrison on *The Books of Blood.* These are unexceptionable, although to my mind they vastly overpraise Barker and fail to point out the serious plot holes in many of his stories. This is, I think, not an insignificant cavil. The whole trick of weird fiction is to convince the reader that "what could not possibly happen" (in Lovecraft's phrase) is actually happening; one either accomplishes this with the sheer hallucinatory power of prose (Ramsey Campbell and Thomas Ligotti in their very different ways) or through meticulous realism and atmosphere (Lovecraft, T. E. D. Klein). Barker attempts to do both, but fails on a great many occasions; and the result is that his scenarios simply become preposterous and collapse of their own absurdity. (This is notably the case with that utter fiasco *Cabal,* which is—significantly—very little discussed in this book.) Morrison ignores all this, and also ignores Barker's curiously limited imaginative range: virtually everything he writes about concerns the purely physical transformation of the human body. This is to say not merely that Barker is utterly incapable of adopting the "cosmic" point of view of Lovecraft, Hodgson, and Klein but also that he lacks even that ability to probe psychology (normal or abnormal) which distinguishes the work of Shirley Jackson, Aickman, and Campbell. Occasionally Barker attempts some sort of political symbolism, but some of these stories—"The Body Politic," "Babel's Children," "Hell's Event"—present such ludicrous premises that no serious political implications can be derived from them.

One rather strange feature of this book is the meagre amount of space devoted to Barker's plays, his first literary work. We are given a completely incoherent group interview with Barker's production company and a slightly more informative interview-article by Anne Billson; and excerpts of some of his plays are scattered throughout the volume in sidebars. I am utterly mystified why these plays have not been published, since they were evidently successful both critically and popularly; I can only imagine that Barker himself does not want them published as yet.

It is not to be expected, perhaps, in a book of this sort—in which Barker himself has lent much assistance—that anything especially negative would be printed. Certainly none of the actual articles are, and some of them—as well as the interviews—are so effusive that in the end they become a little sick-making. Some of the sidebars, however, print negative reviews of his plays, books, and films, and these are rather entertaining. Charles L. Grant's comment—"what Clive needs is a good editor"—hits the mark exactly, although I have a feeling that it and the other negative comments were printed almost in order to make fun of them and to show the limited and conventional mentalities of those who don't lap up everything of Barker's with gleeful relish. Still, these things provide a little balance in a work that would otherwise be wholly panegyrical.

It is interesting that this book, largely compiled around 1989 (there is very little material from 1990 or 1991 here), is in a sense already dated. Barker wowed everyone in 1984-85 with *The Books of Blood*, leading to Stephen King's celebrated remark (cited far too often here) that "I have seen the future of the horror genre, and his name is Clive Barker." And yet, Barker is now only one of many writers on the cutting edge of the field, and the wily veteran Ramsey Campbell may yet overtake him even in popular esteem (let alone critical respect, in which he will always be leagues ahead) with such stunning products as *Needing Ghosts* and *Midnight Sun*. Also, the splatterpunks have in some sense displaced Barker as the new kids on the block, even though they are on the whole vastly inferior to him literarily. Barker himself has not helped things any: since the superb *Damnation Game* he has come out only with *Weaveworld* (an interesting but highly atypical work), *Cabal*, and *The Great and Secret Show*, which almost everyone admits to have been a cataclysmic failure. (There is also, of course, his work in comics, but it has not received much serious attention; and his films after *Hellraiser* have been greeted rather unenthusiastically.) I wonder whether Barker has already had his fifteen minutes of fame. As a result, the long delay in the appearance of *Clive Barker's Shadows in Eden* may have doomed it, even though, as I say, it is a highly skilful and devoted compilation. My own belief about Barker is that, although he has a powerful imagination and an ability to write with verve and piquancy, he has yet to harness his talents such that he can consistently produce work of lasting merit. And he may well be spreading himself too thin, as many appear to believe. No one wants to muzzle or censor Barker, and his views on the subversive nature of weird fiction are very refreshing; but please, Clive, get a good editor.

David J. Schow: Zombies, Tapeworms, and Kamikaze Butterflies

It is regrettable that David J. Schow both coined the term "splatterpunk"—at the World Fantasy Convention in Providence in 1986—and, shortly thereafter, got saddled with the dubious sobriquet "The Father of Splatterpunk" (which appears on the cover of his paperback collection, *Lost Angels*). He deserves better. Let it pass that the true father—or, at least, grand-uncle—of splatterpunk is Clive Barker, for it is he who really popularised the sort of tough, in-your-face writing that later writers have used and abused. Let it also pass that, as recently as Spring 1990 (when an interview with him appeared in *Weird Tales*), Schow was still defending—and glorifying—the movement: "And here come those nasty old Splatterpunks, their hair is strange, their clothes are weird, their fiction is often noisy, and they do things like cross over to films, to music, to a whole audience uninterested in haunted New England towns besieged by the Old Ones and malignant, demonic children coming through the doorway to Hell and making deals with the Devil." It would be just as easy to parody the splatterpunks as Schow is parodying old-time "classic" horror of the Lovecraft-Machen-Blackwood type; indeed, the splatterpunks themselves in many cases unwittingly provide excellent parodies of their own slipshod, crude, and morally unchallenging work. At least Schow refused to participate in Paul Sammon's monument of mediocrity, *Splatterpunks* (1990), although Sammon coyly (and uncharacteristically for the coat-tail-rider of a movement that prides itself on leaving nothing to the imagination) declines to say why: "His decision arrived in the form of a note enumerating a number of reasons for turning me down; none, to my mind, seemed particularly deal breaking." Well, maybe Schow was just prophetic:

maybe he saw that the movement he named would fizzle out in a few years, its promulgators deflated by their towering lack of talent.

What, then, causes David J. Schow to remain worth considering while his pals John Skipp and Craig Spector—not to mention other buffoons now promoting "erotic horror" such as Lucy Taylor and Adam-Troy Castro—flounder in the abyss of hackdom? To put it simply (and here I paraphrase—with a certain chagrin, I must confess—John Farris's otherwise fatuous introduction to *Black Leather Required*): this guy can write.

The career of David J. Schow is certainly a curious one. Four of his books (not counting the anthology *Silver Scream* [1988]) appeared in 1990. This was, to be sure, an odd circumstance, and I am not sure how to account for it. Schow had been writing short stories throughout the 1980s, not to mention many adventure novels written under a pseudonym or a house name and even some novelisations of films and television shows, including some episodes of "Miami Vice." But it is only the works written under his own name— the collections *Seeing Red* and *Lost Angels*, the novels *The Kill Riff* and *The Shaft*, and a new collection, *Black Leather Required* (Mark V. Ziesing, 1994)— that are worth considering. And they are indeed worth considering.

Schow is, to my mind, the only writer in the splatterpunk or "erotic horror" movement who can actually write worth a damn in the idiom they have created—the slangy, profanity-laden style that is presumably representative of our age. Only Schow has distinguished himself by going beyond the mere adolescent hurling about of obscenities to write with a vigorous, arresting, richly metaphorical style that lays bare our hypertrophic, technology-choked, morality-vacant century. His compatriots seem, on the contrary, like schoolboys scribbling "fuck" on a wall. How does he do it? Let us take a random example (from "The Shaft," a short story in *Black Leather Required* that was the nucleus of his novel)—a simple description of a Floridan's first trip to Chicago:

> My first taste of bonafide snow was pretty comical. After four straight weeks of what the imbeciles on the news here called "medium to light flurries," my neighborhood had become a Dantean vision of the Arctic Circle. Lumbering automobiles skidded ass-sideways into each other, providing a lot of employment for Chicago's fender, body and paint people. Dead black slush, like concentrated air pollution mix, obliterated the curbing while the sidewalks simply vanished beneath a four-foot snowpack that settled into solid ice. Pedestrians pretended it was nothing abnormal. Cursing, they teakettled about and broke their bones. No big deal. Everybody slouching along, muffled into anonymity, necks bowed by the forces of nature, defeated and pissed off, avoiding eye contact and snarling at all comers—the Chicagoan in full wintertime flower. It was positively medieval.

This passage is really a prose-poem of urban life—impressionistic, blandly cynical, mixing highbrow ("Dantean vision") and lowbrow ("ass-sideways") with studied insouciance, and even coming up with a piquant neologism (the verb form "to teakettle") more typical of poetry than prose. But don't be fooled. Although Schow manages this style without a single false step and pulls it off with a dazzling verve and panache, he is no Johnny one-note. Consider now this passage from "Sand Sculpture," a story original to *Black Leather Required*, describing a man whose young wife has just died:

> Hadn't he become just a bit overwrought? Obsessive? Hinged to the past, bereft of new emotions and stagnantly content to convert their home into a ghoulish shrine to her memory? Balance had been misplaced. In here, it was Lorelle who was favored, and as a consequence of an ailment he called love, he was now in mortal danger of being dragged under by the riptide of what she had meant to him.

Here again are startling metaphors—"ghoulish shrine to her memory," "the riptide of what she had meant to him"—but it is all expressed in a clean, refined prose that the likes of Skipp and Spector couldn't even dream about.

I shall have to resist the temptation to talk about Schow's previous work—a temptation made the more irresistible because, in all honesty, *Black Leather Required* is a somewhat uneven collection that does not always represent Schow at his best. His best collection is still *Seeing Red*; although *Lost Angels* purports to be a thematically linked volume of tales, several of the individual stories therein tend toward diffuseness and lack of focus. And in some of the longer tales in *Black Leather Required*, Schow seems so caught up in his own vibrant virtuosity of style that the narratives fail to advance crisply. But perhaps I can have my cake and eat it too by discussing the short story "The Shaft"—which Schow here states is "the first piece of short fiction I completed after the fanfare garnered by 'Red Light'" (the lead story in *Seeing Red*)—in conjunction with the novel. It is, quite frankly, a major crime that *The Shaft* has not yet appeared in an American edition; I myself don't even own a copy of it but have a mere Xerox of the Macdonald edition. This novel—one of the best in our field in the last twenty years—is the one genuine contribution of splatterpunk to literature; Barker's *The Damnation Game* (1985)—his one and only good book—is a close second, although perhaps it must be considered presplatterpunk.

"The Shaft" is a relatively simple tale of a low-level drug runner, Cruz, who is forced to hole up in a seedy Chicago boarding-house whose central ventilation-shaft is the haven of some loathsome and ill-defined monster. While the tale packs a considerable wallop, it doesn't hold a candle to the novel, in which several additional characters flesh out the picture and make it a searing portrayal both of the drug culture and of the safe, moronic flaccidity of middle-class life. If the novel has any flaw, it is in the nature of its supernatural entity. We are asked to believe that, initially, a huge and loathsome tapeworm emerged from the stomach of the tenement's seedy landlord and stationed itself in the shaft. Fed by a kilo of cocaine that Cruz dropped down the shaft to escape the police, and which burst from its wrapping and mixed with the standing water at the bottom of the shaft, the tapeworm grew to huge size and strength. All this is tolerably believable, but then a further metamorphosis occurs: somehow the building itself becomes animate, bleeding when its walls are damaged and able to enlarge and contract its rooms to trap some hapless tenant; on top of this, the human beings it dispatches come back to life as hideous zombies. This is a mighty tall order for a tapeworm to accomplish.

Schow, in fact, is not always comfortable with the supernatural. In many tales in *Black Leather Required* we are presented with conventional vampires, zombies, werewolves, and the like; and Schow's flip tone causes these tales, perhaps unwittingly, to lapse into self-parody. Actually, Schow is rather good at treading the borderline between humour and horror. "Last Call for the Sons of Shock" puts Frankenstein's monster, Count Dracula, and the Wolfman on stage, and the scintillating mix of supernaturalism, B-movie references, and low farce produces an effect I have never encountered anywhere else. But when Schow attempts to give a "serious" treatment of the vampire myth ("A Week in the Unlife"), even he can't pull it off. Conversely, "Pitt Night at the Lewistone Boneyard" starts out as mere buffoonery—all the occupants of a family gravesite have somehow become zombies, and the one surviving member of the family encounters each of them in turn—but gradually turns serious and even poignant; for what this tale really is about is the effort of this one survivor to say and do the things he could not or did not say or do to his relatives when they were alive. By doing so, he relieves himself of the guilt he has felt at their passing and can now go on with his life.

Other stories are simply outrageous. "Scoop Makes a Swirly" is also original to this volume, and is nothing more than a cheerfully gruesome crime story narrated with arch sarcasm. This is the second tale involving the petty criminal Scoop, the first of which appeared in some anthology I've never heard of called *Look Out He's Got a Knife*; Schow tells us that "Scoop isn't done, yet; oh, no. I think the next one is called 'Scoop Sucks the Troposphere.'" All this is good fun, but the final tale in the volume, "Bad Guy Hats," doesn't quite come off. It too is a rather nasty and violent crime story, but written without the good humour of its predecessor. Schow reports, with a certain cheerless glee, that it "was recently solicited (enthusiastically), then rejected (vehemently), by the publishers of a German splatterpunk anthology because it was 'too violent and sexual.'" That certainly is absurd, and it allows Schow in an afterword to get on his high horse about censorship and middle-class timidity and suchlike; but the fact is that the story's violence and sex seem to me aesthetically unmotivated. Here we have two sets of criminals, one pursuing the other; Schow is, to be sure, careful to deny any moral superiority to either group by portraying both as bloodthirsty and amoral, but his concluding reflection—that it is nowadays hard to tell the good guys from the bad guys—somehow doesn't strike me as very deep. You need something better than this, Dave, to justify your bloodletting.

Some of the stories border on science fiction. "Sedalia" is an entertainment about dinosaurs having come back to life in our day and the social and logistical problems this causes; the tale goes on a little too long, but is amusing enough. Rather more substantial is "Kamikaze Butterflies," a conscious tribute to Ray Bradbury's story "A Sound of Thunder," in which a man, going back in time, treads on a butterfly and thereby changes all future history. In his story, Schow displays a group of soldiers of fortune who go back in time and intentionally do as much damage as possible in an effort to wipe out entire future civilisations or perhaps all human life:

> The story went that the tiniest death, the soundless pulverization of a butterfly's fragile body in the past, could grow, in the future, to a thunderstroke, a palpable floodtide of sound that touched all, and changed all it touched. The payoff for death on a massive scale was therefore seductive to Masterson. Although the mission he proposed was a guaranteed one-way op, each member of Omega Team had volunteered. Each volunteer realized that each of their actions, even the tiniest, like Mendoza's smoldering cigarette butt, would yield results too large to be contained by any history book, ever. That power, savored briefly but equally guaranteed, was enough to recruit them. A story of people who never were, a fiction printed on dead trees in cheap black, could change the face of a world they scorned.

This story brings up a crucial issue in modern horror writing, especially of the splatterpunk type. It is difficult to know whether Schow is endorsing his characters' misanthropy or tacitly condemning it; I fervently hope it is the former, for we need a little more honest misanthropy in the world. More seriously, for all the splatterpunks' talk of being "subversive" (and this is a term Clive Barker is now throwing about with monotonous frequency), the fact is that the majority of their work fails utterly to challenge bourgeois morality. I cannot help quoting a resounding utterance by Lovecraft, made so long ago as 1923:

> Popular authors do not and apparently cannot appreciate the fact that true art is obtainable only by rejecting normality and conventionality in toto, and approaching a theme purged utterly of any usual or preconceived point of view. Wild and "different" as they may consider their quasi-weird products, it remains a fact that the bizarrerie is on the surface alone; and that basically they reiterate the same old conventional values and motives and perspectives. Good and evil, teleological illusion, sugary sentiment, anthropocentric psychology—the usual superficial stock in trade, and all shot through with the eternal and inescapable commonplace. (Letter to the Editor, *Weird Tales*, March 1924)

This statement is truer now than when it was written. Sammon's *Splatterpunks* anthology is full of tales that are "subversive" and "unconventional" only in their explicitness, not in their ethical orientation. Consider Edward Bryant's "While She Was Out," which extends obvious sympathy to a middle-class suburban woman who is set upon by a gang of street youths; and improbably, she manages to kill them off one by one! Schow is, in "Kamikaze Butterflies" at least, a little different in refusing to come down on one side or other of the moral issue he has raised. And Schow's many stories of the drug culture are similar, especially *The Shaft*. Without either romanticising or moralising, he conveys the staggering human toll exacted by this lifestyle, in which money, drugs, and sex are free for the taking but security is harder to come by.

Black Leather Required is, as I say, a somewhat uneven collection, and is not helped by Schow's fatuous refusal to identify the first publication of most of the stories ("If you expect to discover 'original publication' data by reading this teeny paragraph, too bad, because I don't play that"). It is things like this—along with his ridiculous introduction to *Silver Scream* and the meandering afterword he has tacked on to this volume—that make me hope fervently that Schow will stick to fiction from now on. (Schow's work in film doesn't do much for me, either. He and John Shirley were responsible for the screenplay for the popular Brandon Lee film, *The Crow*, but one would never guess it from the simple-minded dialogue and predictable outcome, although in charity one can assume that the comic-book origin of the plot had something to do with that; and, of course, Schow cannot be blamed for the late lamented Mr Lee's singular lack of charisma and stage presence.) In the meantime, there must be a publisher somewhere who will want to introduce *The Shaft* to American readers. This and *Seeing Red* alone make Schow a formidable figure in modern weird fiction, and he is one of the few reasons to retain an interest in this field.

Donald R. Burleson: Enmeshed in the Bizarre

So you think Don Burleson is nothing but a highbrow academic who writes abstruse literary criticism and is an authority on H. P. Lovecraft? Think again. His dozens of short stories have already won a following of their own, and they have appeared in venues of the widest sort, from *F&SF* to the many theme anthologies compiled by Stefan Dziemianowicz and his cohorts.

One of the first glimpses of Burleson's fiction writing was in the slim pamphlet *Four Shadowings* (Necronomicon Press, 1994). It may seem odd that none of the four stories in this booklet is Lovecraft-inspired, but as a matter of fact very little of his bountiful fiction (a generous sampling was previously made available in *Lemon Drops and Other Horrors* [Hobgoblin Press, 1993]) is

Lovecraftian. It is, however, on the whole relatively traditional—and this too is a little peculiar from a critic who has caused considerable controversy by venturing into some of the more arcane reaches of poststructuralism.

Burleson's tales are competent, elegantly written (a teacher's voice is described as "a ship of sound cutting through a fog of daydream"), occasionally quite revolting, and in general entirely satisfying. Of the four stories in *Four Shadowings*, the first and the fourth are the best. "A Student of Geometry" adopts a Campbellian approach (the volume is dedicated to Ramsey Campbell) in probing the cloudy mind of a young girl who can't seem to pay attention to her geometry lessons. (Burleson is, incidentally, a professor of mathematics.) The atmosphere, however, is less that of Campbell than that of, say, Conrad Aiken's "Silent Snow, Secret Snow." "One-Night Strand" treads exquisitely on the borderline between grisly horror and farce in its account of what a solitary traveller finds in the adjoining room of a motel.

Beyond the Lamplight: Stories from the Dark (Lack O'Lantern Press, 1996) offers a much larger selection of Burleson's short fiction, containing thirty-four stories (eleven of them previously unpublished). I scarcely know how to express my approbation for what might become a landmark volume in modern weird fiction.

It may perhaps strike the reader as odd that Burleson writes stories that are on the whole orthodox, straightforward, and accessible. To say this, however, is far from saying that they are conventional or banal; instead, it is to say that Burleson has chosen—wisely—to work within the traditional framework of the modern weird tale, knowing that such a framework is still capable of providing abundant room for imaginative expression and horrific effect. Whether consciously or not, Burleson's fiction harks back to the work of Ray Bradbury, Richard Matheson, and (more recently) Ramsey Campbell; almost all his stories tell of ordinary people in ordinary, even mundane, circumstances becoming gradually, inexorably enmeshed in the bizarre.

What lends the tales a distinctive edge is Burleson's pungent and wickedly morbid imagination. Nothing is sacred to him. You will think very differently of a squalling baby in a restaurant after reading "A Little Place Off Elm Street"; a dog's shedding takes on loathsome qualities in "Hair of the Dog"; the abortion/right-to-life debate will take on some disturbing overtones after one reads "Mikey Joe." Some of Burleson's tales—"Frosty," "Leftovers," "Gums," "Milk," to name only a few—reach the utter limit of physical repulsion, but do so without any violence in diction or crudities of style. Indeed, this volume perhaps sets a record for the number of horror stories revolving around dentistry—the imaginative offspring, apparently, of some serious dental work Burleson himself was forced to undergo some years ago.

But it would be unfair and inaccurate to say that Burleson is interested merely in the physical shudder, however artfully he may accomplish it. "Down in the Mouth" (not, in spite of its title, a story about dentistry) is one of the most spectacularly cosmic tales I have ever read; and it achieves its effects not through the painstaking (and at times laboured) accumulation of details that we find in Lovecraft or Hodgson, but through a series of compact vignettes that take up all of sixteen pages. "Snow Cancellations" is extraordinarily subtle in its delineation of an unthinkable state of affairs in a small New England town deluged with snow. The delicate "Walkie-Talkie" fuses horror and pathos inextricably and poignantly. And "Ziggles" (a conscious Ramsey Campbell pastiche that was one of the high points of Dennis Etchison's *MetaHorror*) is one of many stories that neatly manage what Fritz Leiber called the "terminal climax"—the expression of the story's climax in its final line.

"Ziggles" is perhaps alone in being an avowed pastiche; in nearly all the other tales no dominant literary influence is observable. Even H. P. Lovecraft, the subject of the bulk of Burleson's critical work, appears only fleetingly. "Christmas Carrion" is an amusing takeoff of "The Terrible Old Man," while "Kokopelli" (whose basic theme is also found in Burleson's first novel, *Flute Song*) contains fleeting mentions of "Old Ones" and a blind idiot god named "Az-ah-tsot," but these prove to be only minor tips of the hat in a story whose basic imaginative focus is purely Burlesonian.

The only thing one might wish of Burleson is that he at times allow himself the space of a novelette—that intermediate length which has produced so many weird masterpieces from Joseph Sheridan Le Fanu to Ramsey Campbell—to develop some of his conceptions. It is certainly uncanny that this volume contains thirty-four stories and 340 pages—exactly ten pages a story, on average. Compactness is a far from unworthy skill in a field that has lately been plagued by a wearisome succession of overblown novels, but one might like to see some of these stories gain added weight and potency by expansion.

In *Flute Song* (Black Mesa Press, 1995) we are treated to the first of Burleson's published novels, and it ought both to delight the loyal followers of his tales and to win new converts tired of the same old formulas that have done much to end the late horror boom.

Flute Song—the delicate restraint of its title is only one of its virtues—concerns the celebrated incident in New Mexico in 1947, in which a UFO may have crashed and an extraterrestrial may have been captured alive but kept under wraps from that time till now by the U.S. government. In a prefatory note to the novel, Burleson gives a brief summary of these events and expresses his belief that the scenario is substantially true, which, if so, would represent "the most elaborate coverup in the history of humankind."

An incident of this kind is certainly a valid one upon which to base a horror novel, but I wonder whether Burleson would not have been wiser to place his prefatory note at the end, rather than at the beginning, of his work. It is not merely that the account tends to instil a certain incredulity in the reader (even though it is obvious that Burleson has done thorough research into the matter—he has even interviewed surviving witnesses to the event—and also that he is nobody's fool and scarcely to be lumped in with the UFO lunatic fringe), but it tends to drain the opening segments of the novel of their suspense, since we know exactly what is coming.

But no matter. As the novel gets underway, we become enthralled with the whole situation and find it of consuming interest whether we believe it to be "real" or not. Readers of Burleson's short stories—and, for that matter, his essays—have long been accustomed to the lean elegance of his style; they will not be disappointed here. *Flute Song*, though a full-fledged novel, has all the "unity of effect" that Poe sought in the short story; there is not a wasted word. Although the action is fast-paced, there is plenty of room for exquisite descriptions of character and landscape that reflect both a sure novelistic sense and a love of the region that Burleson—by birth a Texan who has spent the majority of his life in New England—has come to regard as his true home. Consider this tableau of the terror that the night desert can inspire:

> They sat for a long while in silence, the flashlight making eerie phantoms of their faces. For some reason Anne's view of this scene now swept up and away like a movie camera; in her mind she retreated to some distance away and seemed to see the three of them, goblin faces in the near-dark, clustered around the wan illumination of the flashlight in a strange little island of light floating in a sea of illimitable darkness. When she brought her mind back to the immediate scene, with Eric sitting by her side and Sage not four feet in front of her, the impression lingered, the feeling that they were wrapped in a tight little ball of pale light with endless, whispering, menacing seas of blackness stretching away around them in all directions. The effect, to her, was unspeakably, disturbingly eerie. She had never before been frightened of the desert at night, but it frightened her now.

Each of the characters in *Flute Song* is rendered vivid and distinctive—not through laborious repetition of surface details but through crisp emphasis on telling elements of their actions, their mannerisms, and their pasts. Even the extensive interior monologues whereby each figure reflects upon his or her situation are tailored, in language and tone, to that character's temperament. We have an array of seemingly ordinary individuals whose lives have all been touched by the bizarre: "Hap" Trujillo, an ex-army man who, when assigned to clean up the debris of the alien spacecraft (which he has been told by his superiors was a weather balloon), hides away a small piece of it and inserts it slyly into a copy of Cervantes, but who becomes a shattered alcoholic from the weight of the secret he must keep; Lucy Trujillo, Hap's daughter, who has been told of her father's secret by her mother and who winds up with the copy of Cervantes, to her great danger; Anne Hawk, a part-Indian linguist who has worked for twelve years learning the alien survivor's language and has developed considerable empathy for him; Eric Hayes, a old college flame of Anne's who, as an anthropologist, stumbles into the situation; Sage, an ancient Indian shaman who actually saw the crash of the spaceship and nursed the alien back to health before the government came to take him away; the alien himself, referred to merely as the Crewman and inscrutable in both his intellect and his emotions; and, of course, the villains of the piece—a variety of operatives in the most secret branches of the government.

It is in regard to these latter that some criticisms might perhaps be made. The three chief heavies—Roger Wynn and his underlings, Varelli and Blake— are one-dimensional caricatures. Wynn is an odious and ruthless individual who implausibly quotes Shakespeare at every opportunity and whose fanatical desire to keep the New Mexico incident secret leads him to murder, kidnapping, and other crimes; while Varelli and Blake are mere goons. A few shades of grey might have made these characters a little more interesting; as it is, they are all too predictably black.

But this blemish is a small one. *Flute Song* is compellingly, compulsively readable; once lured into the plot, no reader will be able to refrain from learning the outcome. It would make a superb film. In saying this I mean no covert insult, as I might in the case of some other recent works that, in their sketchiness of character portrayal and reliance on cheap tricks to keep the plot moving, read more like botched screenplays than novels. *Flute Song*, in its deft plotting, rich characterisation, and grace of style, is a thoroughly satisfying read; but its visual and aural magic almost demands translation to the screen. The "flute song" itself—a product either of the alien spacecraft or of the desert itself, or perhaps of both together—is, literally, the haunting leitmotif of the novel: "The sandy plains would seem to breathe forth a sage-scented breath redolent of unplaceable music, then, a dry sound vaguely like the husky sighing of some scattered multitude of nameless flutes whose elusive tones capered on the mesa tops and played among the chamisa and the mesquite bushes and fled laughing down shadowy reaches of arroyos in the desert night."

One final virtue of *Flute Song* is its compactness. At a time when some of our most popular writers (I think immediately of Stephen King, Anne Rice, and Clive Barker) have made fools of themselves with lumbering behemoths that produce in the reader a very different kind of horror from what was intended, Burleson's lithe gazelle of a novel glides along like an eerie melody itself, quickly absorbed but long remembered. All those who support the small press, and good literature, owe it to themselves to get *Flute Song*.

Burleson's second novel, *Arroyo* (Black Mesa Press, 1999), is in part a kind of revision—or shall we say revisitation?—of *Flute Song*, but in reality it is a very different kettle of fish. *Arroyo* deals more explicitly with the "Roswell incident" than did its predecessor, and on a superficial level adopts the same scenario—valiant townspeople battling against the evil machinations of a supersecret branch of the government. But, as its title suggests, it draws even more vividly upon the very landscape of the region, to the extent that it becomes perhaps the most significant "character" in the novel. Arroyos are "great long dry rivercourses that ran for leagues through the desert, sandy riverbeds flanked by canyonlike walls of sand shallow in places, but so high in places that one could not see over them, could not see out into the surrounding desert plain." One particular arroyo, near the town of Chasco, New Mexico, has gained the sobriquet Arroyo Encantado (Enchanted Arroyo), for reasons that become quickly evident as the novel progresses.

That Burleson is gifted with a keen—almost uncanny—ability to grasp the essence of a place (the *genius loci*) was long ago evident in his painstaking researches into Lovecraft's New England; and now he has brought the same insight into his new adopted region:

> In the east, where a sable depthlessness of night had cast a bewilderment of stars over the New Mexico desert like a magic dust, the faint glimmer of golden sunlight crept into the fabric of the night, infusing the darkness with a pastel blur that slowly, slowly broadened, brightened, ripened into the crimson riot of oncoming day. Long, somber shadows edged out from the hunkered forms of mesquite and cholla and spiky-headed yucca, shadows that played over the sand like the impalpable touch of ghostly fingers, played quietly over the sand and edged slowly back to the source, contracting in the shifting light, ebbing away like a dusky tide as the sunrise, regal and undeniable, filled the whole turquoise sky with blinding brilliance.

I am reminded of Clark Ashton Smith's remark after reading Lovecraft's "The Shadow over Innsmouth": "[The story] has an atmosphere that one can't shake off in a hurry. I can still smell and taste it!" Similarly, one can see, smell, taste, and touch the dust, sand, and cactus of Burleson's New Mexico, and it would be no surprise to me if he were one day recognised as a local colourist of note. With passages like the above, we can perhaps excuse the fact that the actual human characters seem a trifle stereotypical: Lisa Jamarillo, a divorcée trying to pick up the pieces of her life after the messy breakup of her marriage, who drifts into Chasco and becomes involved in the anomalous scenario; her young son Jerry, who does the same; Bill Weston, another visitor who strikes up an acquaintance with Lisa and finds himself facing the unutterable; and so on. The old—possibly preternaturally old—Indian witch Araña is a little more distinctly realised. Indeed, perhaps the most interesting human character, surprisingly, proves to be the government agent Truman Lloyd, whose metamorphosis from cardboard villain to sensitive, guilt-ridden ally adds a piquant touch to a novel that might otherwise have lapsed into conventionality.

It is, perhaps, a bit of a parlour game to read a Burleson novel and hunt for Lovecraftian allusions or influences, knowing as we do that he is a leading

Lovecraft scholar. But in this case the hunt is fruitful, showing how thoroughly he has absorbed the essence of Lovecraft and made it his own. The general setting of the novel, while of course authentic because of Burleson's first-hand knowledge, brings Lovecraft's "The Mound" to mind—especially when, in the opening chapters, we are cast back to the time of Coronado, one of whose party experiences a UFO encounter in the very arroyo that will serve as the focus of the novel. Later we learn the truth about the "Roswell incident": it was not merely that the UFO crash was hushed up by the government, but that the technology derived from the wrecked spaceship had led to spectacular advances (including the microchip and a cure for cancer), some of which had to be kept secret because it would have been all too evident that the advances had been inspired by extraterrestrial science. Who cannot think of Lovecraft's "The Shadow out of Time," with its dark suggestions that many advances of our time are in reality the product of the transferred minds of the Great Race?

But the most obvious Lovecraftian touch becomes evident when Lisa and Bill, after several days in Chasco, begin to sense that some of the townspeople took a little—shall we say peculiar? Large, almond-shaped eyes, heads a little too big for them, and the like? It comes as no surprise that, as in "The Shadow over Innsmouth," these individuals are the product of sexual union between aliens and the human inhabitants of Chasco. To Burleson's credit, this phenomenon is not portrayed with the furious racial horror of Lovecraft; instead, the offspring of such "miscegenation" seem merely a bit more sensitive, gentle, and perceptive than their neighbours.

The manner in which Burleson portrays his aliens might seem a tactical mistake:

> The figure . . . was barely half the height of a man. Its arms and legs were long and thin, but somehow, paradoxically, these limbs appeared both frail and oddly strong. Each hand had four fingers, and no thumb. The head was disproportionately large, pear-like, with dark almond-shaped eyes a little larger than a man's eyes . . . The face of the thing featured only a thin slit for a mouth, and indentations that might have been orifices suggestive of nostrils and rudimentary ears.

We seem to have come upon this sort of thing all too often in the wake of Whitley Strieber and his ilk. But of course Burleson is suggesting that the oddly similar descriptions of aliens supplied by these "abductees" are based on reality.

Arroyo is a thunderously good read—fast-paced, with engaging characters, some stupendously cosmic suggestions, and enough episodes of suspense, terror, and awe to keep any reader engrossed to the end. Over and above all its events and characters, though, is the omnipresent terrain of New Mexico, whose otherworldly character—tailor-made, it would appear, for alien incursion—is brought to life with vividness, poignancy, and affection by Burleson's pen.

Permit me, however, a brief harangue. I regard the possibility of UFO visitation as unlikely in the extreme; but even more egregiously unlikely is the possibility that our esteemed government could have covered up such a thing for any significant amount of time. It appears to be a common view in some regions of the American West that the government is both supercompetent and oppressive—a view that inspires in us world-weary Easterners nothing but cynical amusement. Those of us who know the inner workings of Washington political life are too plangently aware of the incalculable number of buffoons and blabbermouths who occupy all levels of our government—from the highest to the lowest, the military and intelligence communities included—to have any belief that they could possibly refrain from talking about any concealed alien bodies to their spouses, friends, or cronies on the *Washington Post* or the *New York Times*. Surely any number of events of the not too distant past ought to have convinced anyone that keeping a secret in Washington is not easy to do. No one need worry that anything like the final scene of *Arroyo*—the military marching in and attempting the "containment" (i.e., incarceration and eventual elimination) of the inhabitants of Chasco—would be possible: even if some may not have much trust in the Bill of Rights, they can always place abundant and unfailing trust in the inefficiency and incompetence of the municipal, state, and Federal government.

All this may not have much to do with Burleson's novel; but I am forced to record it as one of the reasons why some features of *Arroyo* created obstacles in my willing suspension of disbelief. But perhaps others will react differently.

Norman Partridge: Here to Stay

So far as I am aware, Norman Partridge (b. 1958) was introduced to the weird fiction public with a slim short story collection, *Mr. Fox and Other Feral Tales* (Roadkill Press, 1992). This volume evidently attracted some attention in its day, but only the title story—a convoluted and strangely beautiful tale of love and murder—is worth notice. If *Mr. Fox*, in spite of the windy praise of its supporters, only showed an inkling of promise, then Partridge's first novel, *Slippin' into Darkness* (Cemetery Dance Publications, 1993) displays that promise fulfilled. This is one of the finest horror novels of the last decade. Although entirely non-supernatural, *Slippin' into Darkness* evokes an atmosphere of dreamlike weirdness by its fragmented narration and tough but strangely poetic prose.

Partridge also creates an illusion of the supernatural by the ghostly hovering of April Destino—a young woman who, gang-raped in high school, descends into prostitution and ultimately kills herself—over the entire scenario. She is already dead when the novel opens, but she is nevertheless the central character in the book, the character against whom each of the vividly realised figures—the four high-school jocks who raped her, the black man who filmed the rape and who becomes a shabby producer of child pornography films, the woman who was April's best friend in school but who betrayed her through jealousy—must define themselves.

This *tour de force* of a novel, whose entire surface action occupies exactly one day but whose flashbacks skilfully paint an affecting picture of high school life, is a relentless psychological portrait of people who showed youthful promise but have lapsed into mediocrity, amoral criminality, and humiliating failure. As horrible as the rape of April Destino and her subsequent suicide are, the true horror of *Slippin' into Darkness* is the horror of wasted lives and futile violence. Although a profoundly depressing work, this novel is as compelling a read as any I have had in a long time. It is one of those very few books which one wishes would never end.

The Man with the Barbed-Wire Fists (Night Shade Books, 2001) presents a much more substantial collection of Partridge's short stories, and supplies as good an introduction to the many virtues and few deficiencies of his work as anyone is likely to require. In his engaging and illuminating introduction, Partridge—a Northern Californian by lifelong residence—makes an unashamed confession of the significant influence of horror films (many of which he initially saw at a drive-in theatre near his home in a town he fails to specify) upon his work. It would be an interesting study to ascertain whether Ramsey Campbell, T. E. D. Klein, and Thomas Ligotti are the last writers in our field to have been chiefly influenced by print rather than by film. This is not necessarily meant in disparagement, and Partridge himself admits that he and his young pals "read Bradbury and Bloch and that weird guy Lovecraft," but his almost exclusive focus, in his introduction, on horror films carries its own implication.

Whatever the case, it is evident that all those horror, vampire, werewolf, and other monster films have left a decided impress upon Partridge's work. The tales in this volume are replete with these standard creatures: vampires in "Do Not Hasten to Bid Me Adieu," werewolves in "The Pack," and zombies in "In Beauty, Like the Night," a tale that (aside from the fact that these zombies are otherwise lovely supermodels) manifestly betrays the influence of *The Night of the Living Dead*, the film that had the greatest impact on the young Partridge's imagination. Nor is Partridge particularly concerned with providing a plausible rationale—or, indeed, any rationale at all—for the existence of these redoubtable entities. This is because the true merit of his work lies not in its conception but in its execution and style. His prose does not quite reach the gonzo pyrotechnics of a David J. Schow, although it is heading in that direction; but its hard, chiselled tensity, its rugged, slashing beauty is what carries the reader along in spite of the occasional mundanity of the root idea. Consider a passage describing those zombie lovelies in "In Beauty, Like the Night":

> His Grimesgirls were still beautiful. Miss July, her stomach so firm, so empty above a perfect heart-shaped trim. Miss May, her skinless forehead camouflaged with a wreath of bougainvillea and orchids. The rounded breasts of Miss April, sunset bruised and shadowed, the nipples so swollen. The sunken yellow hollows beneath Miss August's eyes, hot dry circles, twin suns peering from her face with all the power of that wonderful month.
> Twin suns in the middle of the night.
> She walks in beauty, like the night . . . in beauty, like the night . . . of cloudless climes and . . . starry skies and all that's best of dark and bright . . .

But Partridge does occasionally expend his imagination into his monsters as well as his prose. "The Bars on Satan's Jailhouse" features (aside from a coyote-lycanthrope that seems thrown in rather haphazardly into an otherwise predominantly crime/suspense narrative) a character who wears boots made of live bats. "The Hollow Man," if I understand it correctly, is an atmospheric tale narrated in the first person by a Wendigo.

The tales alternate between supernaturalism and non-supernaturalism, the latter perhaps slightly in the majority. In my opinion Partridge works best in the non-supernatural vein (as he did in *Slippin' into Darkness*), although one clever story, "Coyotes," begins as an apparently routine tale of sadism and verges suddenly off into the supernatural at the end. "Minutes," "Last Kiss," and "Red Right Hand" are only a few of Partridge's triumphs of suspense and psychological terror. It is here that his *noir* prose finds its perfect match in the scenario he has orchestrated. His story construction frequently features a fragmented narration that can be highly effective, but on occasion produces obscurity and confusion. I am not ashamed to confess that in several stories I am quite unable to ascertain what has actually happened. Every sentence is jewelled, but the overall effect is opaque even on the level of the surface plot.

A word on the production of *The Man with the Barbed-Wire Fists*. Almost everything about this book, from the evocative dust-jacket art by John Picacio to the typeface and design of the volume as a whole, is impeccable (although one wishes that small-press publishers would learn not to place running heads on blank pages). The signed limited edition of the book features, as a separate chapbook, a charming juvenile tale, "Castle of the Honda Monsters," that may go far in elucidating the origin and character of many of Partridge's later tales. All in all, a book that any connoisseur of horror or suspense would find it difficult to be without. Mr Partridge is here to stay.

Thomas Harris: Lecter as Albatross

Thomas Harris has never written supernatural fiction: after abandoning journalism, he began his literary career with a dreadful potboiler, *Black Sunday* (1975), followed by the admirable *Red Dragon* (1981) and *The Silence of the Lambs* (1988), to which *Hannibal* (Delacorte Press, 1999) is a much-awaited sequel. In refreshing contrast to the dreary prolificness of some of our other best-selling authors, Harris has habitually taken years to write his novels, and on the whole they are rather good. They will by no means enshrine him in the higher echelons of the literary pantheon, but they are among the more engaging works of popular fiction in recent years.

To my mind, however, none of his works falls into the realm of the horror tale, chiefly because Harris deliberately chooses to emphasise detection rather than the psychological aberration of his villains. The serial killers in both *Red Dragon* and *The Silence of the Lambs* are, to be sure, quite perverse; but because Harris is determined to keep their identities (and, largely, their motivations) a mystery until the end, he only infrequently allows himself the opportunity to depict their twisted psyches—as, say, Robert Bloch does in *Psycho*, making that work an authentic tale of horror. It need hardly be pointed out that this decision by Harris has no bearing on the qualitative evaluation of his novels; it merely affects the works' genre classification.

Hannibal is an avowed sequel to *The Silence of the Lambs*, and it features many characters familiar from its predecessor. Dr. Hannibal Lecter, the psychiatrist-turned-serial-killer (and occasional cannibal), was a shadowy figure in Harris's two previous novels, but is very much at centre stage in this one; so is Clarice Starling, the FBI operative who hunted down the serial killer in *Silence*. *Hannibal* opens superbly, with a gripping confrontation between Starling and some drug dealers in Washington, D.C.; the resulting loss of life, fueled by biased press reports, causes Starling to be vilified, even though she acted in self-defence. After years of silence, Lecter writes to her, urging her to resist her superiors, who are seeking to make her a scapegoat. We ultimately learn that Lecter is living well in Florence, Italy, disguised as a museum curator.

About a quarter of the way through the novel, however, things start to go downhill. We learn that the wealthy Mason Verger—one of Lecter's first victims (he survived, although much of his face was eaten away by the hungry villain)—has offered a $3 million reward for the capture of Lecter alive; Verger naturally wishes to exact some particularly loathsome revenge on his nemesis. Accordingly, an unscrupulous Italian police officer strives to catch Lecter, whose disguise he has seen through; but he ends up being Hannibal's next victim. This entire Florence segment reads rather like an overenthusiastic travelogue: Harris cannot resist including every possible bit of information he has soaked up about Italy, going well beyond the bounds of verisimilitude and sounding on occasion like an encyclopedia.

But if the first half of *Hannibal* is somewhat of a disappointment to those who admired Harris's two previous works, the second half plummets into realms of dreadfulness not seen since the heyday of Harold Robbins. Several flashbacks portray Lecter's childhood in Lithuania; and we are asked to believe that he became a serial-killer-cum-cannibal because he saw his sister caught, killed, and eaten by starving soldiers in World War II. This may be bathetic enough, but the ending of the novel is worse still. It was only to be expected that Verger's cohorts would suffer the very fate—being eaten by a herd of man-eating wild pigs—they had outlined for Lecter; but Harris goes on and destroys the uneasy relationship between Lecter and Starling that lent such vivid tension to *The Silence of the Lambs*. Lecter, it appears, sees in Starling a kind of replacement for his devoured sister, and so he rescues both himself and her from Verger, drugs her, and hypnotises her so that she becomes his companion (and presumable lover). At the conclusion of the novel we see them enjoying an opera in Buenos Aires.

All this is really too preposterous. Would Starling be so amenable to hypnotic control? And could Harris really have thought that this conclusion would prove satisfying to the readers of his previous novels? It has become obvious that Harris himself has, after a fashion, fallen in love with Lecter: he takes care to portray Hannibal's enemies as even more repulsive, hypocritical, and avaricious than Hannibal himself; and of course they lack his elegance, refinement (the first thing Lecter does after he settles in Virginia is to purchase a clavichord), courage, and psychological fortitude. And then there is an absurd and irrelevant subplot involving Mason Verger's sister, a lesbian bodybuilder who is so determined to bear a child that she secures some of her brother's sperm and promptly kills him.

There has been much speculation as to why Harris wrote *Hannibal*—or, rather, wrote it as he did. Some think it is a self-parody; others think that Harris has simply lost the ability to write well. I am sceptical of both these theories, especially the latter: the first 100 pages of Hannibal are scintillating, not only in their brisk action but in occasional flashes of tart wit ("There is a common emotion we all recognize and have not yet named—the happy anticipation of being able to feel contempt"). Another theory—that Harris wrote this book merely to fulfil a contractual obligation to write a sequel to *The Silence of the Lambs*—is more plausible. I have no evidence of its truth, but it seems likely to me.

Many readers and reviewers appear to believe that Harris's next novel, *Hannibal Rising* (Delacorte Press, 2006) is even worse than *Hannibal*, but, oddly enough, I am not one of them. In some ways it is superior to *Hannibal*—more, perhaps, for what it lacks than for what it actually contains.

The central theme of the novel is the issue of moral responsibility. Harris provides a much more detailed account of Hannibal's youth: the novel starts when Hannibal is eight years old and ends when he is about eighteen or twenty. We learn that he and his family are forced to leave their castle in Lithuania in the face of the Nazi blitzkrieg early in World War II. During the Germans' retreat in 1944-45, the family manages to reoccupy the castle, but all its members, with the exception of Hannibal and his beloved younger sister Mischa, are killed before Hannibal's eyes: throughout the novel he is plagued by visions of his mother dying by fire. But the worst is to come: a gang of looters, led by one Vladis Grutas, takes over the castle, imprisoning and brutalising Hannibal and his sister; desperate for food, they decide to eat Mischa, and he can never forget her pleas as she is taken away.

We move to a period just after the war. The Lecter castle has been turned into an orphanage, and Hannibal, now thirteen, is a resident there. Presently his uncle, Robert Lecter (who has married a Japanese woman, Murasaki), comes to take him away to his chateau in France. It is at this point that Harris begins to engage in the issue of moral responsibility. Hannibal had already exhibited some violent tendencies at the orphanage, chiefly in response to bullying by other boys. But now, in France, he performs his first murder: he pummels a butcher who had directed some lewd remarks to Murasaki. Later, Robert accosts the butcher, but in so doing he dies of a heart attack. Hannibal now confronts the butcher and brutally kills him. The body is later found, with the head missing; still later, when the head turns up, it is lacking its cheeks—and we are immediately meant to recall what the Lecter family cook told Hannibal a short while before: "The best morsels of fish are the cheeks. That is true of many creatures."

In spite of this instance of cannibalism, we are led to sympathise with Hannibal and to believe that the butcher has received his just desserts—and this scenario is repeated throughout the novel, which is largely engaged in recounting how Hannibal systematically hunts down and kills the other looters who had eaten his sister. Given that most of the erstwhile looters have since entered a life of crime, we can scarcely waste any sympathy upon them. In any event, Hannibal reveals himself to be both intellectually brilliant (he is the youngest man ever to be admitted to medical school in France) and culturally sophisticated (perhaps, indeed, a bit more so than his creator: Harris commits such gaffes as leaving the accent off of "Place de l'Opéra" and "Ile de la Cité" and noting Hannibal's listening to a "Bach string quartet," although the string quartet as a musical form did not exist in Bach's time), so that it becomes easy to root for him in his vigilantism.

Hannibal is, indeed, careful not to harm anyone except the specific individuals he is pursuing. One of these, a man named Kolnas, has a wife and two children. At one point Hannibal confronts him, tossing at him a bloodstained bag that he suggests are portions of his family. Although Kolnas had given to one of his children a bracelet that had been worn by Mischa, this fact in itself does not confer moral guilt upon the child, and we are momentarily outraged that Hannibal could have committed such an act of wanton murder; but in fact the bag contains only a "beef roast," and was therefore designed merely to taunt Kolnas with his own former cannibalism.

Harris, however, does suggest that there is nonetheless something anomalous, perhaps even inhuman, about Hannibal. After the death of his sister, he apparently lost his power of speech for years, not regaining it until his uncle's death. Hannibal subsequently exhibits incredible powers of coolness under pressure: he passes a polygraph test given by the police after the death of the butcher (the polygrapher remarks that Hannibal has "a monstrous amount of self-control"); when waiting to kill the ringleader of the looters, Vladis Grutas, Harris notes: "Hannibal was calm. His pulse was 72." A police detective, fully aware that Hannibal is engaging in a murderous rampage, delivers a telling comment: "'The little boy Hannibal died in 1945 out there in the snow trying to save his sister. His heart died with Mischa. What is he now? There's not a word for it yet. For lack of a better word, we'll call him a monster.'" But this is one of the few moments of reflection and analysis that we find in the novel. The greatest failing of *Hannibal Rising* is its author's unwillingness—one can hardly call it an inability, given his past work—to engage in a psychological portrait of Hannibal. Harris evidently wishes the reader to infer Hannibal's overall mental and psychological condition merely from the events of the novel; and while there is some plausibility in this exercise (adhering as it does to the standard writer's advice to show rather than to tell), the novel ends up being nothing but a flat succession of incidents. A little more of the author's ruminations on the significance of Hannibal's actions would have been welcome: Is Hannibal truly justified in his murderous onslaught, or has he now already become a "monster"?

As it is, Harris is in danger of becoming so enraptured with the figure of Hannibal that he loses his manifest skill as a writer of suspense novels. Hannibal Lecter has indeed become an icon of popular culture, but there is only so much aesthetic nourishment that Harris can squeeze out of him. Harris is clearly relying on the heavy overtones of horror and evil that the figure of Hannibal brings to any work in which he appears; taken by themselves, *Hannibal* and *Hannibal Rising* are quite undistinguished as novels, and even Hannibal's "star quality" cannot carry them. Long ago, H. P. Lovecraft warned of the dangers of the serial character: "Now this is manifestly inartistic. To write to order, and to drag one figure through a series of artificial episodes, involves the violation of all that spontaneity and singleness of impression that should characterise short story work. It reduces the unhappy author from art to the commonplace level of mechanical and unimaginative hack-work" (*Selected Let-*

ters *1911–1924*, p. 158). Harris has, to be sure, not quite reached the level of "unimaginative hack-work," but one suspects that the figure of Hannibal Lecter may now be something of an albatross whom he would be well advised to throw overboard.

Thomas Ligotti: The Long and the Short of It

Thomas Ligotti (b. 1953) long ago ceased to be a secret. Although the first edition of his first book, *Songs of a Dead Dreamer* (1986), was released almost surreptitiously by a small-press publisher, it was picked up three years later by major firms in both America and England and very properly received enthusiastic reviews ("Put this volume on the shelf between Lovecraft and Poe, where it belongs"). His second volume, *Grimscribe: His Lives and Works* (1991), seems to have been reviewed even more favourably, as was only right for a collection that continued its author's unique and quite twisted vision of the world in tales that were still more deft in style, theme, and substance than those of its predecessor. Ligotti's third collection, *Noctuary* (Carroll & Graf, 1994), gathers much of his hitherto uncollected work and adds one lengthy new story.

What I have found refreshing about Ligotti up to this point is not merely his distinctive contributions to the literature of the weird but his remarkable aloofness from the cliquishness that currently dominates commercial horror writing. He has flatly claimed his inability (perhaps a humble euphemism for unwillingness) to write a "horror novel"; he avoids the mutual backpatting (I'll blurb your book if you blurb mine) that has made such a mockery of critical standards in the field; he appears content to appear in the small press, largely because he is one of those "professional" writers who actually has a real job (he was, until recently, an editor at Gale Research Co. in Detroit) and therefore does not need to churn out fiction by the yard to put food on the table. What all this boils down to is that Ligotti has so far demonstrated a high level of artistic sincerity that keeps him resolutely fixed on his own aesthetic goals as a writer and allows him to scorn the siren's song of quick profits that leads so often and so deservedly to quick oblivion.

And yet, what are we to make of a writer who has issued two collections in less than five years? This may not perhaps seem excessive, especially as his last two collections are quite slim and as there is only one original work in this newest volume. Certainly, the example of Ramsey Campbell is always there to remind us that quality and quantity need not be mutually exclusive. And yet, if I am less than enthusiastic about *Noctuary*, it is only because I do not wish to see Ligotti being pressured by his publishers or his readers into producing more than he comfortably can or assembling what frankly comes dangerously close to barrel-scrapings. That Ligotti's barrel-scrapings are generally superior to most other writers' best offerings is beside the point.

Noctuary is, for no especially compelling reason, divided into three sections, preceded by an introduction that reprints his "Dark Chamber" essay from *Necrofile* #1. That introduction is a discussion on the notion of "weird," both as a word and as a conception; but its title, "In the Night, in the Dark," points to the essence of Ligotti's work—the incursion of dream-elements into "ordinary" life. But, as I have said elsewhere, this is a misconstrual of Ligotti's method: it is not that he simply inserts the dreamlike into the "real," but that he shows that what we take to be "real" is itself a sort of mad dream. Although in his introduction Ligotti declares that "the supernatural itself cannot exist without the predominant norms of nature," those "norms"—if meant as a realistic portrayal of mundane life—are so lacking in his work that no genuine contrast with the unreal is established. This is by no means a flaw—it is meant merely as a characterisation of Ligotti's work. On the whole he seems so devoid of interest in the "real" world that he cannot take the trouble to describe it. The occasionally vivid tableau or sharp insight into human character that we stumble upon in his tales may make us aware that he does not lack the ability at either topographical or psychological realism; but Ligotti finds the real world itself so prosy and wearying that he prefers merely to plunge the reader directly into the unreal. This method has both its virtues and its drawbacks. Its virtues are an extraordinarily distinctive texture that sets his work apart from all others in the field; its drawbacks are occasional lapses into obscurity, insubstantiality, and seeming pointlessness. I fear that *Noctuary* seems to me to present more of the drawbacks than the virtues.

Ligotti makes a great error in opening the volume with "The Medusa," which displays him at his worst in a long-winded tale full of self-indulgent, smart-alecky, high-sounding sentences that in the end mean nothing. The problem with Ligotti is that much of the horror in his work is engendered purely by language, and is also of a sort that cannot be absorbed directly by the emotions but must be filtered first through the intellect. He is as disdainful of the conventional "rules" of fiction-writing as Lovecraft or Dunsany was; one of the cardinal "errors" he commits is talking about an event or scenario instead of actually displaying it. In his best work this is not an error at all, for what Ligotti is attempting to do is to worry out all the weird overtones and atmospheric bizarreries of a given scenario, something that can only be accomplished by a sort of intellectualised rumination, not by a straightforward account of events. It is true that Ligotti's prose, even in fiction, has an uncannily nonfictional feel (so does Lovecraft's and Poe's); but in his poorer work, as in "The Medusa," it lapses into a sophomoric pretentiousness that ill conceals the fact that he is writing very elegantly about absolutely nothing.

The other items in this first section—"Conversations in a Dead Language," a subtle tale of supernatural revenge; "The Prodigy of Dreams," which comes very close to realising Ligotti's goal of presenting the real world as the quintessence of nightmare; and "Mrs. Rinaldi's Angel," a less successful disquisition on dreams—range from the successful to the undistinguished; but I see no thematic links between them and no rationale in grouping them together.

The one original work in this volume, "The Tsalal," is almost worth all the other stories combined. This tale concerns an individual, Andrew Maness, who is the incarnation of the Tsalal (a term taken deliberately from Poe's *Narrative of Arthur Gordon Pym*), or *"a perfect blackness."* Maness's father, a clergyman, has written a book called *Tsalal,* and Andrew ponders its significance:

> "'There is no nature to things,' you wrote in the book. 'There are no faces except masks held tight against the pitching chaos behind them.' You wrote that there is not true growth or evolution in the life of this world but only transformations of appearance, an incessant melting and molding of surfaces without underlying essence. Above all you pronounced that there is no salvation of any being because no beings exist as such, nothing exists to be saved—everything, everyone exists only to be drawn into the slow and endless swirling of mutations that we may see every second of our lives if we simply gaze through the eyes of the Tsalal."

I do not know if this accurately represents Ligotti's philosophy, but it is an ideal instance of that intellectualised horror of which he is such a master. Somehow Andrew Maness is the embodiment of this nihilistic existentialism, and only Ligotti could have written so compellingly hypnotic a tale around such a dryly philosophical conception.

"The Tsalal" opens the second section of the book, which presents other such memorable tales as "Mad Night of Atonement" (which utilises Ligotti's frequent humans-as-mannekins metaphor) and "The Voice in the Bones," a pure nightmare with no realism of setting or coherence of plot to speak of but with as potent an atmosphere of the strange as I have ever encountered. These stories, in their various ways, are an encapsulation of what makes Ligotti so distinctive a voice in modern weird fiction.

The third section is a series of nineteen prose-poems, many under 500 words in length. It might be thought—given Ligotti's general scorn for the mechanics of plot and his emphasis on mood—that this would be an ideal form for him, but it is exactly here that his single-minded emphasis on pure verbal witchery presents its greatest drawbacks. Ligotti has failed to note that even the most delicate prose-poems—whether by Baudelaire or Clark Ashton Smith or Dunsany (*Fifty-one Tales*)—must present some unified or coherent narrative if they are to have any effect. Most of these items are simply too insubstantial, fragmentary, and directionless to amount to much. A passage from "The Spectral Estate" typifies their essence: "Long exasperated by questions without answers, by answers without consequences, by truths which change nothing, we learn to become intoxicated by the mood of mystery itself, by the odor of the unknown. We are entranced by the subtle scents and wavering reflections of the unimaginable." This is an ideal that Ligotti does not always fulfil; and most of these items, written with undeniable panache as they are, simply leave no impression upon the reader and are forgotten the moment they are finished.

I cannot sufficiently emphasise that my reservations about *Noctuary* stem only from the very high regard with which I regard Ligotti's work as a whole: he has set so exalted a standard for himself that anything that doesn't measure up to it seems a disappointment. Ligotti still remains the most refreshing voice in weird fiction, the one writer who can never be mistaken for someone else. I do confess, though, that I am a little concerned at the seeming lack of development in his work. He has been writing for about fifteen years—the same length of time that separates Lovecraft's "From Beyond" from "The Shadow out of Time." Where exactly is Ligotti going? Has he said all he has to say in his present mode? What further goals has he set for himself? It is, thankfully, inconceivable that Ligotti could ever write a novel unless he reverted to the idiom of his early "Last Feast of Harlequin" or some other nominally realistic style; but he has surely written enough "noxiously hideous fragments" (as Lovecraft characterised Shiel's "Xélucha") that one would like to see him do something different. And one does not want to see him resurrect, merely to fill a volume, old failures that are better left buried in the small-press journals where they first appeared.

There were rumours some years ago that Ligotti was written out, or that he was unsure what direction to take in his work, but I am unable to vouch for the truth of these reports. At any rate, any notion that Ligotti has already finished saying what he has to say has been put triumphantly to rest in his latest volume, *My Work Is Not Yet Done: Three Tales of Corporate Horror* (Mythos Books, 2002).

The subtitle is of some significance, and I make no apology for drawing upon the facts of biography to provide some background. Ligotti worked for many years at Gale Research Co. in Detroit (the volume is dedicated to a coworker, Marie Lazzari), and he has drawn upon his corporate experiences with great panache in these three tales. One would not wish to read any excessive autobiographical significance in the crazed murderer who is the protagonist of the long title story, but Ligotti's familiarity with the petty office politics that renders work at many companies a living hell is evident on every page.

And yet, the first thing that strikes us when we contemplate the story "My Work Is Not Yet Done" is its very existence. Here is a nearly 150-page novella— perhaps 50,000 words in length—that fills three-quarters of the book. This length would not be intrinsically anomalous in the work of someone like Blackwood, Lovecraft, Le Fanu, or Campbell (remember *Needing Ghosts?*), who have discovered that the novelette or novella is particularly suitable for the creation of cumulative horror; but for Ligotti it calls for some explanation. This is because, in an interview published in the magazine *Dagon* in 1988, he stated bluntly: "Critics of supernatural horror fiction have repeatedly observed that the novel is a difficult form for telling a tale of terror. After brooding for years over this matter from the viewpoint of a potential novelist, not to mention the many aborted attempts at actually writing the things, I find this form too difficult for me." To be sure, "My Work Is Not Yet Done" cannot be considered a full-scale novel, but it is certainly about as long as Lovecraft's *At the Mountains of Madness* or *The Case of Charles Dexter Ward*, or (to switch genres) any of the short novels of Dashiell Hammett.

I certainly welcome Ligotti's expansion of his fictional palette in the direction of the novel, although I share with him a grave doubt as to the aesthetic feasibility of the "horror novel" as conventionally written. Ligotti rightly maintains that such a work, except in the hands of a master, tends to lapse into merely a mystery or suspense narrative with horrific interludes—an indictment that could, regrettably, apply to nearly all the "horror novels" written over the past thirty years. In "My Work Is Not Yet Done" Ligotti has ingeniously found several ways to avoid this dilemma—specifically by the use of first-person narration (which thereby allows the tale to achieve the "unity of effect" that Poe recognised as the *sine qua non* of the short story), and by writing what appears at the start to be merely a mundane (if elegantly narrated) tale of a serial killer, but which slowly metamorphoses into something very different and much more alarming.

"My Work Is Not Yet Done" introduces us to Frank Dominio, a longtime worker at a company that is never named, and whose actual business is also never specified. Like many employees, Frank deliberately seeks to maintain his level of mediocrity in order to remain in a stable job that does not require from him any notable degree of mental acuity. Through a series of accidents, Frank finds himself forced to resign; blaming a brace of coworkers for what appears to be deliberate malice on their part in causing his departure, he undertakes to murder them one after the other in systematic fashion. At this point we seem involved in nothing more than a tedious and predictable suspense tale in which each victim will suffer worse torments than his or her predecessor; but in some (wisely unexplained) fashion Frank lapses into a bizarre half-dead, half-alive state, with the power of leaving his body and also, apparently, with the power to transform the very atoms of his victims into something very much worse than their already grotesque human forms. It is at this point that the particularly twisted imagination that we know from the rest of Ligotti's work comes into play.

This novella in particular, and the volume as a whole, displays an augmentation of the pungent, misanthropic wit that Ligotti has gradually made his own, and which signals him as an authentic heir of Ambrose Bierce. "My Work Is Not Yet Done" is, for all its grisly horror, really quite funny, albeit in a bitter, sardonic manner. Consider a pen-portrait of one coworker, Sherry:

> If she closed her eyes and didn't speak Sherry could indeed pass for an attractive human female. But the moment she spoke or the moment her thing-like eyes came into view, she became a Gorgon (no mythic significance intended or necessary). This duality that Sherry embodied could often be a source of tremendous conflict to those around her, who one moment would experience the tide-pull of her figure and the next moment, when she happened to speak or the image of her eyes loomed up, would be inwardly retching with disgust at the very existence of this Sherry-thing, as well as heaving away inside with self-revulsion for having felt an attraction to this creature.

Lest one fancy that Ligotti has lapsed into misogyny, he makes clear that his disgust at what Evelyn Waugh called "those vile bodies" is gender-neutral:

> . . . Richard's stature was more than that of someone who purchased his suits at clothes stores catering to large-bodied men. His physical conformation, straight and solid from head to toe, was imposingly athletic, the anatomy of an erstwhile ball-player of some kind who had kept his shape into middle age. In all probability Richard had garnered his share of shining trophies for the glory of Self and School. He wouldn't be the first member of middle- to upper-level management with a background in the world of sport, with all the playing-field metaphors they borrowed from that milieu, chief among them being all that puke-inducing nonsense about teams (the characterization of someone as a "team player" was at the top of my line-up of emetic expressions of this sort).

As will be evident from these extracts, Ligotti has tempered what in the past might have been regarded as his excessively tortured prose, and has instead evolved a smoothly flowing narrative style that, if perhaps a bit more spartan in its exotic metaphors than before, is nonetheless capable of powerful emotive effects.

After the Golconda of horror we find in this richly textured novella, the two tales that round out the volume—"I Have a Special Plan for This World" and "The Nightmare Network"—seem almost like afterthoughts, but they offer aesthetic rewards of their own, plunging us into a far more surreal world than that presented in "My Work Is Not Yet Done," and thereby reassuring those devotees of Ligotti who might have been alarmed that he was abandoning his uniquely bizarre vision for the mundanities of the mystery-suspense tale, however artfully managed.

My Work Is Not Yet Done displays a Thomas Ligotti at the height of his form—in imaginative range, in verve of style and precision of language, and in cumulative power and intensity. And it reveals several new sides to Ligotti's work—an ability to draw upon workaday experience, a tart, biting wit that spares no person or object within the range of its jaundiced vision, and, most of all, an expansiveness of plotting and character development that may one day allow us to witness that most anomalous and unexpected of eventualities, a Thomas Ligotti novel.

A special word of commendation must be given to David Wynn's Mythos Books. This is far and away the most attractive volume he has published to date, and his choice of Harry O. Morris to execute his typically fantastic collage illustrations was an inspired one. It has long been a truism that much of the best work in our field comes from the small press, and with more volumes like this one Mythos Books may well come to stand at the forefront of independent publishers of horror and fantasy literature.

Michael Cisco: Ligotti Redivivus?

Michael Cisco burst on to the horror/fantasy scene with *The Divinity Student* (1999), a short novel of bizarre, obsessive fantasy that won him the International Horror Guild award for best first novel. He has followed that success with the novels *The Tyrant* (2004) and *The San Veneficio Canon* (2005), the latter set in the same realm as *The Divinity Student*. He now displays both his short and his longer work in two recent volumes.

Cisco has frequently been compared with Thomas Ligotti, and the comparison is apt for more than one reason. Both engage the reader with a complex, at times tortuous, prose that deliberately seeks to create hallucinatory effects in an effort to shatter the bland façade of mundane reality; both thrust us into realms that are not quite those of pure imagination, but that, while continuing to have random connections or parallels with the "real" world, feature unexplained bizarreries that can be deeply disturbing—disturbing on a profound, metaphysical level that is chiefly intellectual in nature.

I am, however, not quite ready to crown Cisco as the next Ligotti. A close examination of his two most recent books might give some reasons why.

Secret Hours (Mythos Books, 2007), Cisco's first short story collection, was published by Mythos Books because, I take it, a substantial number of the tales were inspired by Lovecraft, even though only one or two of them (most notably "Translations") can qualify as tales of the "Cthulhu Mythos." Robert M. Price's rather unhelpful brief introduction doesn't give us much to go on, but perhaps no introduction—or review—could. What does strike me after a reading of these fourteen stories, is the frequency with which they are inspired, not by "life" or "reality," but by literature. I make this comment not in criticism, but merely to state a fact. Lovecraft himself remarked of Coleridge: "The fact that his experience came through books rather than life does not militate against him, because he had the rare faculty of accepting the contents of books in an abstract way, as if the material came directly from life without literary filtration. Bookishness becomes tepid and artificial only when one looks *at* the books instead of *through* them" (letter to Frank Belknap Long, April 1928). This could serve as an exact description of Michael Cisco's art, at least in the present story collection.

Hence we have stories inspired by Lovecraft's "Pickman's Model" ("I Will Teach You") and, of all things, "Herbert West—Reanimator" ("The Chaos into Time"); by Frank Belknap Long's "The Hounds of Tindalos" ("The Firebrands of Torment"); by Robert W. Chambers's *The King in Yellow* ("He Will Be There"); and more generally by various Lovecraft conceptions or images ("Translations," "The Water Nymphs," "What He Chanced to Mould in Play"). There is also a story called "The Death of Edgar Allan Poe," although its connexion with the known facts of Poe's final days seems to me rather opaque. In one of the several brief notes that are scattered throughout the volume, Cisco notes that "Ice Age of Dreams" is a kind of combined homage to T. E. D. Klein and Arthur Machen.

But Cisco is anything but a mere pastichist. He has managed somehow to lend substance and even a kind of cosmic dignity to the trashiest of Lovecraft's tales, "Herbert West—Reanimator," by making that buffoonish figure strive not for the reanimation of mere human remains but of the universe itself. "Translations" goes well beyond being merely another hackneyed tale of Nyarlathotep (it was designed for a second Chaosium anthology of Nyarlathotep stories edited by Price).

And yet, probably the most striking tale in the volume is one that does not betray any obvious literary parentage. "Dr. Bondi's Methods" takes us to an imaginary European country, Godavia, in which evil has triumphed over good. But this has had the awkward result of a shortage of "victims" for the evil citizens to prey upon; whereupon the Moral Institute was born, designed to instil good moral qualities into selected individuals so they can in turn be the fodder for the evil ones. The writing and execution of this tale—which remains just on this side of self-parody—must be read to be appreciated.

I am, however, troubled by some, indeed most, of Cisco's other tales. He seems to be content with throwing out provocative ideas and images, but fails all too often to round them out into finished stories. The result is a series of sketches, vignettes, fragments, prose-poems, or what have you. (The volume begins with a work called "Two Fragments.") Cisco is a writer of immense talent, with a prose style of vivid exoticism, conceptions of daring bizarrerie, and the power to create atmosphere with a single deftly crafted sentence. But, if *Secret Hours* is any gauge, he is like an extraordinarily skilled pianist who is content to execute difficult improvisations but unwilling to sit down and play a finished composition from beginning to end. A certain lack of discipline seems evident.

Consider "Translations." The story is really two stories in one, but neither segment is developed adequately. In the first, we are concerned with two people, Theodore and Eleanor, who are set to the task of translating a recently discovered text of the *Book of Nephren-Ka*. Along the way we receive tantalising and apocalyptic visions of a future New York where civilisation has come close to collapse. But then this scenario is dropped and we are given the actual text of the *Book* (a rather short one)—but it too peters out to inconsequence. "Ice Age of Dreams" proposes the striking possibility that dreams from the past can leave behind physical traces, but the story ends before this idea can be developed properly.

The Traitor (Prime Books, 2007) exhibits both the virtues and the failings of Cisco's shorter work. It too is written with impeccable prose; it too throws out provocative ideas, images, and conceptions; but it too fails to shape itself into a coherent and well-rounded narrative. We are in an unspecified fantasy realm, where the inhabitants have been subdued by a neighbouring people called the Alaks. The narrator-protagonist, Nophtha, first under the influence of his uncle, Heckler, and then of a friend or colleague, Wite, and his sister, Tdzde, becomes an "apostate" (Cisco deliberately avoids specifying the orthodoxy—religious or political—from which Nophtha is an apostate). Nophtha tells his story from prison, and as a result the novel has a chillingly oppressive pall of melancholy hanging over it. Nophtha, Heckler, and Wite are all "spirit-eaters," and early on he explains what this entails: "The world being full of spirits, many of them dangerous or at least irritating and troublesome, . . . the spirit-eater is the supernatural rat-catcher."

It would, however, be profitless to attempt any kind of outline or synopsis of the plot, which meanders in a fashion that would render any kind of summary next to impossible. *The Traitor* is full of striking images and tableaux—perhaps the most striking of which is the killing of Wite by Nophtha, narrated in a mesmerising stream-of-consciousness manner that renders every event almost intolerably clear and vivid—but as a whole it seems to go nowhere and ends inconclusively. Cisco might also be advised to devise somewhat more euphonious names for his imaginary realms and personages: such names as Yestyy, Tdzde, Xchte, and the like do not make for pleasant reading.

In spite of the above criticisms, I, for one, will welcome every new work that emerges from Michael Cisco's pen. I am not entirely sure that he has found his voice yet, and I am hopeful that someday he will learn—as his masters, Ligotti, Klein, Ramsey Campbell, and Lovecraft himself learned—that a little more coherence in narrative will bring ample rewards; not merely rewards in popularity (although that is not something to be entirely despised), but in the more effective conveyance of the powerful message he has to convey.

Sherry Austin: The Southern Ghost Story

In Sherry Austin's *Mariah of the Spirits and Other Southern Ghost Stories* (Overmountain Press, 2002) we are presented with thirteen ghostly tales chiefly set in the South—whether it be the author's native North Carolina, or New Orleans, or Atlanta, or other sites. Wisely, Austin places most of her tales in rural or remote coastal locales where the incursion of the weird seems an almost natural consequence of the forlorn decay brought on by abandonment and the wistful pathos of glory days long past. As the author states in her introduction, ". . . the Old South of some of these stories it itself a ghost . . ."

One should, however, not expect the blood-and-thunder spectres of a Stephen King or Clive Barker, or even the subtler but nonetheless aggressively violent wraiths of M. R. James and his ilk. Instead, Austin's tales evoke the faded delicacy of a Mary Wilkins Freeman, the topographical rootedness of Sarah Orne Jewett, the emphasis on searing personal and domestic tragedy of a Fred Chappell (who has also supplied a justifiably cordial blurb to a fellow North Carolinian). In prose of admirable suppleness and pungency, Austin can introduce the weird with a subtlety that makes her noisier contemporaries in the horror field seem clumsy and clownish.

Austin never loses sight of the fact that a ghost is chiefly a metaphor—a symbol for some human drama whose plangency is enhanced by the evocation of the supernatural. Hence, in the story "The Other Woman," we find the *doppelgänger* motif used to good effect to emphasise marital discord. "Come, Go Home with Me" tells with extraordinary delicacy of the end of an old man's life and his recognition that the time for him to join the ghosts of his past has come. The supernatural is reduced almost to the vanishing point in "Lost Soul," but this tale captures with heart-rending eloquence the pangs of youthful love and rejection. A very different type of story is "The Dressmaker's Mannequin," a whimsy that is almost reminiscent of Lord Dunsany (I think particularly of his tale "Blagdaross," in *A Dreamer's Tales*) in its depiction of the shifting thoughts and moods of a mannequin in a New Orleans curio shop.

Not every tale, perhaps, is equally successful. Several attempt a revivication of the days of Southern slavery, but only the title story is effective in its grim account of an African-American mother who seeks to prevent the execution of her rebellious son. As a grammatical purist I also find the bland and repeated use of "alright" highly offensive. No matter how widespread this solecism becomes, it will always remain a solecism. Austin hurts her cause by maintaining in her introduction that, although she is "both a skeptic and a believer" as far as ghostly phenomena are concerned, the frequency with which such phenomena are found in folklore (and particularly in sacred texts) represents "a great cloud of witnesses to an ancient and enduring belief." I am not sure what she is asserting here, surely the universality of a belief is no guarantor of its truth. Prior to 1450 there was a pretty universal belief that the sun revolved around the earth.

But these are small blemishes in a book that is on the whole a highly creditable first offering to the literature of the weird. Skilled as Austin is in the short story, and perhaps knowing that ghostliness is most effective in the short compass, I for one was interested to see if she can maintain her distinctive atmosphere of quiet pathos in a novel. As if by magic, I received my wish in Austin's next book, *Where the Woodbine Twines* (Overmountain Press, 2006), a short novel that fulfils every reader's prediction of her creative development. Once again set in the South, this time in South Carolina, *Where the Woodbine Twines* introduces us to thirteen-year-old Nan Ayler, who develops a complex, paradoxical friendship with eleven-year-old Catherine Wiley. Can Catherine's dour hostility to Nan be attributed entirely to her perceived membership in a fading Southern aristocracy? Has she, even at her tender age, suffered a trauma of which she is unwilling to speak? A trip to the beach, with an almost phantasmagoric episode at a carnival that Ray Bradbury could not have surpassed, culminates in . . . what? All we, and Nan, know is that something strange occurred. *Where the Woodbine Twines* may perhaps be only on the fringe of supernatural fiction, but that is not to deny its extraordinarily fluent prose ("Moonlight lay like giant pearls between the tree trunks"), its subtle but telling character portrayal, and its etching of an anomalous incident that has haunted a young woman for the duration of her life. If one is looking for the perfect antidote to the excesses of contemporary supernatural fiction, this is surely it.

Shades of Edgar and Ambrose

It is not surprising that writers of all stripes have been fascinated with the lives of the great horror writers. Their distinctive work has led to a compelling interest in the quirks of personality and background that inspired it; and in some cases their lives are of intrinsic interest. Of the three great American weird writers—Poe, Bierce, and Lovecraft—Bierce probably led a life of the greatest surface interest, having seen action in some of the bloodiest battles of the Civil war and then becoming a notoriously fearless journalist in San Francisco. It would seem that the relatively tame lives of Poe and Lovecraft would not offer much fodder for the novelist, but several have made the attempt nonetheless. We are now presented with two novels that centre, respectively, around Bierce and Poe. Both of them are mystery novels, in which our celebrated authors lay down their pens and, as it were, pick up their magnifying glass and meerschaum pipe.

Oakley Hall risks comparisons with Carlos Fuentes's *The Old Gringo* (1985) in writing an historical novel about Ambrose Bierce; but whereas Fuentes has written what amounts to a novel-length prose-poem, a kind of historical fantasy about the last days of Bierce's life (about which we know nothing), when he wandered down to Mexico and was probably shot by one faction or the other of the Mexican Civil War, Hall's *Ambrose Bierce and the Queen of Spades* (University of California Press, 1998) puts Bierce on stage in the very midst of his literary and journalistic career—a period in which much is known of his life and writings, but nevertheless enough gaps remain to allow Hall not implausibly to involve Bierce in a murder mystery. Accordingly, Hall's objectives are rather less grandiose than Fuentes's, and it may well be said that he fulfils those objectives more satisfactorily.

In Hall's novel, we are introduced to Tom Redmond, a young journalist who has become Bierce's assistant on the San Francisco satirical weekly, the *Hornet*, for which Bierce writes his regular "Tattle" column. Hall, oddly enough, is never explicit about the date of his novel's events, but they clearly take place in 1885 (when Bierce was, in fact, writing his "Prattle" column for the San Francisco satirical weekly, the *Wasp*). Two whores are murdered in the seedy Morton Street red-light district, each of them appallingly mutilated; a playing card—the ace and the two of spades, respectively—is left on their bodies. All this leads Bierce to suspect that the murders are an outgrowth of the seedy dealings, twenty years earlier, involving the Jack of Spades Mine, in which a madam, Caroline LaPlante, and her husband, Nat McNair, fleeced several other partners to gain spectacular wealth. For a time Caroline's son, Beaumont McNair, comes under suspicion. His fiancée, Amelia Brittain, persuades Tom Redmond—who is much taken with her—to pursue the investigations himself. Redmond ends up being a bit more active than Bierce, who rather resembles Rex Stout's Nero Wolfe in remaining sealed up in his editor's office much of the time, merely digesting the information brought to him by Redmond.

Bierce's interest is doubly piqued when an elderly lady, a Mrs. Hamon, is also murdered, apparently by the same serial killer. Mrs. Hamon was to have seen Bierce to supply evidence of serious chicanery by a leading San Francisco judge, Aaron Jennings, who is hand in glove with the railroad interests. Bierce—who, in Hall's portrayal, wages a fanatical and single-minded vendetta against the Southern Pacific railroad, which has a stranglehold on the political and economic structure of the entire state—is convinced that Jennings is somehow involved, and devotes much of his energies to proving the point. In the end, the truth is a bit different from what Bierce initially suspected, but nevertheless he and Redmond solve the case.

This is all great fun, and the portrayal of Bierce is pretty much on target. I find myself, however, a bit annoyed at some of Hall's careless and easily correctible errors of detail. I lost count of how many times the celebrated railroad baron Collis P. Huntington was referred to as Collis B. Huntington. (Evidently the University of California Press has no fact checkers for novels, even those that draw heavily upon the historical record.) Bierce is also made to utter a solecism that, given his penchant for correct English, he would never have said ("different than" for "different from"). The most puzzling aspect of Hall's depiction is his decision to make Bierce the editor of a fictitious magazine and the author of a fictitious column. Why not—in a novel in which so many other real facts of late nineteenth-century San Francisco's literary and political history are paraded—go ahead and refer to Bierce as the author of "Prattle" and the editor of the *Wasp*? And—to compound the error—why not actually quote portions of Bierce's "Prattle" column (which, to a San Franciscan like Hall, should be easily available to him in several local libraries) rather than come up with bogus quotations that, although based in part on some of Bierce's other writings, in the end do not sound like Bierce at all?

But one need not be too hard on Hall. His novel is not intended for those very few individuals who are authorities on Bierce, but for those many who find him a compelling figure. Let it pass that many features of the conventional picture of Bierce—in particular, that he was an unrelenting cynic and misanthrope—are unwitting caricatures. Hall manages to avoid the extremes of this caricature, presenting Bierce as furiously independent, tartly satirical, and unrelenting in his pursuit and exposure of deceit, folly, and hypocrisy, but also troubled by an uneasy relationship with his wife and not entirely consistent in his philosophical outlook: here was a man who repeatedly claimed that "Nothing matters" but to whom many things seemed to matter passionately.

Where Hall perhaps fails is in the very construction of his novel. He is trying to do too much: *Ambrose Bierce and the Queen of Spades* is at once a murder mystery, an historical novel, and a love story, and these elements do not mix very well—or, rather, Hall does not integrate them into a unified whole. At times his book reads like undigested research notes, as when we are given samples of Redmond's journalistic pieces on the railroad: they are, for the most part, factually impeccable, but completely halt the flow of action, and to no discernible purpose. The mystery itself is none too complex or even interesting, and its exposition is a bit on the languid side. Still, the novel is a thoroughly entertaining read, and most will come away with a broader, more nuanced image of Ambrose Bierce than they had before.

Oakley Hall is a respected novelist of fifty years' standing. By contrast, Harold Schechter has enriched the literature of our nation with several lurid volumes about serial killers, each of them blessed with one-word titles (*Depraved, Deranged, Deviant*). Whereas Hall's novel shows us Bierce through the eyes of an imaginary narrator, Schechter adopts a different strategy. In *Never-*

more (Pocket Books, 1999) he has written a novel about Edgar Allan Poe, *written in the first person as if by Poe!* What imp of the perverse could have led him to such a risky enterprise is beyond my powers of conjecture. To say that he has descended into the very maelström of hideousness would be more charitable than his wretched novel deserves.

 The mere effrontery of thinking that one can write an entire novel as if one were Edgar Poe would be bad enough; but Schechter compounds the damage by a multitude of gaffes. Would Poe have repeatedly split infinitives as Schechter does? Would Poe have repeatedly used the bogus word "thusly," so favoured by illiterate writers wishing to sound impressive? (The word "thus" appears 513 times in Poe's fiction and 69 times in his poetry; the word "thusly" never appears.) Would Poe have written erroneous French (*dishabille* for *déshabillé*)? (The word is spelled correctly in "The Duc de L'Omelette" [1832].) Would he have misspelled Sprenger and Kramer's celebrated witchcraft treatise, *Malleus Maleficarum?* Would he have made reference to Robert [sic] Scot's *Demonogly* [sic]? (There is of course no such work. Possibly Schechter is trying to refer to Reginald Scot's *Discoverie of Witchcraft* [1584].) I don't think so.

 It gets worse. At one point Poe takes a book off his shelves—Ovid's *Metamorphosis* [sic] as translated by John Dryden. This is a neat trick, since Dryden never translated the *Metamorphoses*—not all of it, at any rate. Schechter is no doubt attempting to allude to "Garth's Ovid" (1717), a translation of the *Metamorphoses* stitched together by Samuel Garth from sections of Ovid's poem translated by Dryden, Pope, Congreve, Gay, and a host of other poets of the day. A bit later on, Poe's aunt Maria Clemm pulls off an even greater stunt, recollecting how in 1810 she read "one of Mr. Dickens's novels"—two years before Charles Dickens was born. And the very apex of the preposterous is achieved by Schechter's writing a poem and passing it off as Poe's—a poem several of whose lines don't scan and none of whose lines have the least bit of sense or poetry in them.

 These errors may seem picayune, but Schechter invites this kind of scrutiny by writing not merely in the manner of Poe, but as if he *were* Poe. Schechter apparently believes that by expressing himself in the most orotund and verbose manner possible—throwing in all sorts of words that Poe habitually used ("dreary," "halcyon," "chamber door"), and peppering his text with the kind of overused italics that represents Poe at his worst—he will persuade the ignorant masses to whom his book is clearly intended that this is something Poe might actually have written. To any educated reader, however, Schechter's Poe merely sounds like a windy buffoon—an unwitting caricature of himself. He is nothing more than a dummy, a mannikin, a puppet—a kind of M. Valdemar made to mimic what the ignorant might believe are Poe's mannerisms but capturing nothing of Poe's inner personality.

Schechter, of course, tries to make things a bit more interesting by including a variety of schoolboy allusions to stories that Poe would write later, suggesting that the adventure recounted in this novel served as the nucleus of some of his greatest tales. Hence we are introduced to Roger and Marilynne Asher (get it?—Roderick and Madeline Usher); elsewhere Poe imbibes some Amontillado sherry; still later we come upon the Baltimore coroner's physician, Augustus Bedloe, later to become the protagonist of "The Tale of the Ragged Mountains." There are other things of this type, still more inane and puerile than these.

Even all this might have been forgiven—or at least overlooked—if Schechter had an interesting story to tell. But he doesn't. We are asked to believe that, in the year 1834, Poe teams up with, of all people, Davy Crockett (who was known to have been in Baltimore at this time, promoting his recent book of memoirs, which Poe savaged in a review), to hunt down a serial killer who murders with apparent randomness. But with Schechter tied up in knots by his own windy verbiage, the tale moves at such a glacial pace that few readers will have the patience or the interest to wade through to the end; on top of which, the basic plot is so simple-minded that any reader who has managed to stay awake will have easily guessed the outcome before the novel is two-thirds finished.

Schechter makes much of the mystery of why the word "Nevermore" is scribbled in blood by the murderer next to most of the victims. Poe solves the mystery in the end, but I have my own views on the matter. Perhaps it is what some critics would term self-referential—i.e., referring to the author himself. One can make some plausible conjectures: "I, Harold Schechter, will nevermore write a novel involving Poe or any other well-known writer in literary history whose style I cannot imitate and whose work and personality I do not understand." Or, better still: "I, Harold Schechter, will nevermore write another book as long as I drag out my wretched existence on this earth." Yes, I like that. I like that very much.*

---

*Alas, my prediction did not come true. In addition to writing several more books about serial killers, Schechter has gone on to write at least two more "Edgar Allan Poe Mysteries" and shows no signs of abating. Ah, conqueror worm, where are you when we need you?

IV. SCHOLARSHIP

The Charting of Horror Literature

In some ways the criticism of horror literature is still at an incredibly primitive stage. To my mind, there is still no sound general history of the field (the study by David Punter, seemingly comprehensive, is in reality so full of grievous omissions and so replete with idiosyncratic judgments as to be nearly worthless). Some good theoretical work has been done by Rosemary Jackson (*Fantasy: The Literature of Subversion*, 1981), Noël Carroll (*The Philosophy of Horror*, 1990), and a few others, but much more scholarship of this kind is necessary before we can begin to say that we understand the philosophical and aesthetic bases of horror fiction. Certain authors (notably Poe and Lovecraft) have been treated exhaustively, but even such luminaries as Ambrose Bierce, Arthur Machen, Algernon Blackwood, and the best of our contemporaries (chief among them Ramsey Campbell and Thomas Ligotti) have suffered inexplicable critical neglect.

The one aspect of the field that perhaps has been treated thoroughly is the realm of reference works, especially bibliographies. Several encyclopedias of horror literature afford sound guides to the bountiful work that has been done in the past two or three centuries, although even these have their elements of idiosyncrasy. Scholarship seems to have picked up a bit in the 1980s, and two books, both titled *Horror Literature*, published about ten years apart, give some idea of the state of criticism of the field during this period.

Horror Literature: A Core Collection and Reference Guide, edited by Marshall B. Tymn (R. R. Bowker, 1981), is a large volume that seeks to provide a history and bibliographic guide to weird fiction from the inception of the Gothic romance to the present day. Tymn assembled a band of seven scholars to cover the field, each writing a brief history and analysis of a given period or genre and supplying an annotated bibliography of important works as is found in Barron's *Anatomy of Wonder*. Such a collaborative effort can have both great virtues and great flaws: each scholar is generally a specialist in his own period, but there is oftentimes an annoying repetition of material (or a corresponding dearth of it on the borders of each period), and the quality of the individual contributions varies greatly.

I shall pass over in merciful silence the contentless foreword by Peter Haining—in the course of which he pats himself on the back for his countless (and almost uniformly mediocre) horror anthologies and declares inanely that literature's prime concern is to entertain (in which case one supposes that pornography and "women's Gothics" would be the most deserving of critical approval)—as well as the preface by Tymn, on a single page of which he splits an infinitive and produces the impossible verb form "underly" (p. xii). Indeed, the volume could have done well with better copyediting, for we encounter dozens of annoying grammatical blunders, misspellings, and the like: *conte cruel* is thrice rendered as *cante cruel* (224, 230, 254) and once as *contes cruel* (299); "garishly" becomes "garrishly" (180); once we find the impossible superlative "most perfect" (234) and the ugly neologism "him- or herself" (4); and there are dozens of misspellings of names, such as "Corcosa" for "Carcosa" (238), "E. Hoffman Price" for "E. Hoffmann Price" (291), "Marguiles" for "Margulies" (361), "*The Three Imposters*" for "*The Three Impostors*" (255), etc., etc.

Trivial as these errors may appear, they cumulatively confirm the impression that little care has been taken in the compilation of this volume—a fault to be ascribed more to editor Tymn than to his various contributors. In the bibliographical portions of the respective chapters in particular we find bizarre repetitions of information: Wise and Fraser's *Great Tales of Terror and the Supernatural* is listed in three different chapters (2, 3, and 4); the fantasy work of Le Fanu and Thomas Hardy appears in both chapters 2 and 3. Conversely, because chapter one ends at the year 1820 and chapter two begins at 1824, we find no significant discussion of Maturin's *Melmoth the Wanderer* (1820) or Mary Shelley's *Frankenstein* (1818) in either chapter: apparently each contributor felt that it was the task of the other to study the content and influence of these and other such works.

Omission, in fact, is the greatest failing of the book for all its deceptively bulky appearance. Only the first chapter ("The Gothic Romance: 1762-1820" by Frederick S. Frank) is entirely satisfactory: here we are not only given one of the most illuminating short discussions of the origin and significance of the Gothic novel, but are treated to an immense 150-page annotated bibliography of 422 English and German novels—a listing that forms a monumental landmark in the mapping of Gothic fiction. Regrettably, this fine beginning is confounded by chapter two ("The Residual Gothic Impulse: 1824-1873" by Benjamin Franklin Fisher IV), almost unquestionably the worst chapter in the volume. I am astonished—indeed, appalled—that Fisher fails even to mention Hawthorne's *House of the Seven Gables*, which Lovecraft labelled "New England's greatest contribution to weird literature"; other of Hawthorne's works—"The Ancestral Footstep," *Dr Grimshawe's Secret*, *The Marble Faun*—are passed over in equal silence. The brief and superficial discussions of Poe, Hawthorne, Le Fanu, and other important figures of this period (both in the introductory section and in the bibliography) neither reveal the historical development of the genre nor give any significant analysis of their work. It is amusing that Fisher discusses Hawthorne and the insignificant William Gilmore Simms in roughly the same amount of space—about half a page.

Chapter three ("Psychological, Antiquarian, and Cosmic Horror: 1872-1919" by Jack Sullivan) is an admirable and lucid discussion, providing both a coherent history of this very bountiful period (called by Philip Van Doren Stern the "golden age" of the genre) and penetrating discussions of such authors as M. R. James, Blackwood, Wilde, Bierce, and others. Sullivan also valiantly defends the artistry of the weird tale: there is no dichotomy between whether a tale is artistically brilliant and whether it frightens; rather, a tale frightens *because* it is artistically brilliant. The highest standards of literary criticism can and ought to be applied to weird fiction; and if the overwhelming majority of works (especially in modern times) cannot stand up to such scrutiny, there is yet no denying that the work of Poe, Bierce, Lovecraft, Machen, and others can hold its own as literature in every way comparable to mainstream work.

Gary William Crawford's discussion of "The Modern Masters: 1920-1980" is again inadequate, and omits citation of countless modern practitioners, from Roald Dahl to L. P. Davies to Charles G. Finney to Rod Serling and many others. I shall not say much about his analysis of Lovecraft (which generally parrots Barton L. St Armand), but may well question whether Lovecraft is as much an ironist and "Absurdist" as Crawford claims. These are strange terms to apply to a mechanist materialist who disliked the irony of a Cabell. Similarly, Crawford applies the terms "teleological progression" and "teleological regression" in a manner that frankly baffles me: what do these terms really mean? Crawford refers, apparently, to the descent upon the evolutionary scale of the narrator of "The Rats in the Walls" (which Crawford, like St Armand, appears to regard—quite wrongly, to my mind—as the prototypical Lovecraft tale, to the point of giving very little attention to Lovecraft's myth-cycle, which surely gives him his unique place in literature), but the word "teleological" is bizarre (especially regarding such a thinker as Lovecraft, who rejected Aristotelian metaphysical teleology as strongly as Epicurus), and typifies the misuse of philosophical terminology common among literary scholars. Crawford in any case does not seem to understand (nor, significantly, does St Armand) the importance of Lovecraft's cosmicism and rationalism, which (as Matthew H. Onderdonk pointed out decades ago) produce that fusion of science fiction and fantasy which we know as a Lovecraft tale. Still, Crawford's brief comparison of Lovecraft and Faulkner might well be worth pursuing. (Amusingly, Lovecraft is subordinated to Faulkner because the former presumably could not draw character—and this in spite of such distinctive figures in Lovecraft as Charles Dexter Ward, Edward Derby, Henry Wentworth Akeley, and others; but one wonders whether Crawford realises that characterisation in the conventional sense is inessential—nay, detrimental—to Lovecraft's "cosmic" approach, which minimises the significance of mankind.)

(Parenthetically, I must express my amazement in learning that, according to Crawford, "The Loved Dead"—cheap hackwork if ever there was any—is hailed as the "most noteworthy" tale in *The Horror in the Museum and Other*

Revisions, while "Beyond the Wall of Sleep"—a verbose early tale whose themes were developed to much better advantage in later works—is "undoubtedly" the best tale in *Dagon and Other Macabre Tales*. This sort of idiosyncratic opinionation runs through the whole of Crawford's chapter.)

Robert Weinberg's erudite section on "The Horror Pulps: 1933-1940" certainly displays his comprehensive grasp of this field, although I am not quite certain why 1933 was chosen as the starting date, hence causing the omission of any discussion of *Weird Tales* (touched upon briefly by Crawford) and other early pulps. Similarly, Steve Eng's section on "Supernatural Verse in English" is crammed to the bursting point with names and titles, but space considerations seem to have forced him merely to mention examples of supernatural verse with little discussion of the historical progression of this branch of literature or of the significance of individual works. Eng ought to write a large volume on this largely unexplored subject.

The bibliographies of biography and criticism by Mike Ashley are sadly unreliable and inadequate. We are told to consult Richard O'Connor's mediocre and superficial "popular" biography of Bierce, but no mention is made of Carey McWilliams's landmark biography or M. E. Grenander's important critical study. The bibliography of Poe criticism is cluttered with trivial and inessential volumes by Haining, Mankowicz, and Symons, without mention of the work of G. R. Thompson (especially *Poe's Fiction: Romantic Irony in the Gothic Tales*), Burton R. Pollin, and other leading modern Poe scholars.

In general, I find three large omissions that detract significantly from this volume's worth: (1) no mention is made of weird literature before the middle of the eighteenth century (although Eng cites early ballads and Spenser), which might run the gamut from Greek epic and tragedy to Shakespeare and the "Graveyard Poets"; (2) almost no mention is made of foreign weird writing (Balzac, Flaubert, La Motte Fouqué, Maupassant, Baudelaire, Huysmans, etc.)—a parochialism typical of American scholarship; (3) no account is given of the fantasy fandom movement of the 1930s and following, which initiated much criticism of fantastic fiction and continues to do so today. One could also quarrel at length with the intentional exclusion of certain authors (e.g., Dunsany) and the inclusion of others of very doubtful literary value (e.g., Seabury Quinn).

Still, all criticisms aside, this volume represents a significant first step in the charting of the immense field of horror literature; and if Lovecraft's "Supernatural Horror in Literature" remains a better historical guide to the genre, the work of Tymn's staff will provide the nucleus for a more comprehensive treatment of a field that will remain, as Lovecraft wrote, "a narrow though essential branch of human expression."

Horror Literature: A Reader's Guide, edited by Neil Barron (Garland, 1990) begins with the startling announcement that this and its previously published companion, *Fantasy Literature,* are "the most comprehensive critical introductions" to this body of work, and that Barron's *Anatomy of Wonder* (now in its fifth revised edition) is "the standard in the field." The jury is still out on these assertions, and even if they were true, it is rather bad form for Barron himself to say so. His work is good, at times superb, but it has its share of flaws and shortcomings.

Horror Literature begs comparison Marshall Tymn's previous volume of the same time, as both books use a virtually identical format. A closer examination, however, shows more and more divergences both in particulars and in overall design. And I regret to say that Barron's volume does not always emerge as the superior. (It is, accordingly, rather churlish of Barron to snipe at Tymn's book, criticising it for errors when his own volume has its share, including the systematic misspelling of Walter de la Mare's name.)

The first section of both books presents an historical survey of the weird tale with accompanying annotated bibliography of important titles. The first chapter of this section in both volumes is written by Frederick S. Frank; and his discussion of Gothic literature up to 1824 is impeccable in both accounts. The palm, however, must be handed to Tymn's volume, as Frank has there supplied his massive and brilliant bibliography of 422 Gothic novels, whereas in Barron's we find only 112.

Brian Stableford has two chapters in Barron's book dealing with weird fiction from 1825 to 1949; this covers more ground than the chapters by Benjamin Franklin Fisher IV and Jack Sullivan in Tymn's book, covering the period 1824 to 1919. Stableford's first chapter has little difficulty being superior to Fisher's, but he cannot match either the scholarship or the eloquence of Sullivan. Indeed, Stableford appears to have been allowed so little space that at times he resorts merely to rattling off names simply in order to get them into his chapters. The bibliographies for these chapters are also not, on the whole, as good as those in Tymn. Although Stableford writes with both academic precision and flair ("Crowley was no great shakes as a writer of fiction"), he simply does not have the space for detailed analyses of any given writer (although he devotes several illuminating paragraphs to the unjustly obscure work of Robert Hichens), having to content himself with a very broad thematic approach.

It finally dawned on me why neither Frank nor Stableford had the elbow room they needed for a proper evaluation of their respective periods: Barron has evidently decided that the contemporary horror scene (1950-1988) is deserving of extended treatment, and so he has had Keith Neilson write a chapter on this period that is as long as the three previous chapters combined. This is a serious mistake, and for more than one reason.

First of all, the emphasis is all wrong. Surely it ought to be obvious that the most literarily valuable work in the field was done in the period from Poe to Lovecraft; but Stableford, because of space constraints, was not able to provide any significant discussion either of these two titans or of other important writers like Le Fanu, Machen, Blackwood, Bierce, Benson, Onions, Hartley, and so many others from this period. (Some actual omissions are apparently the result of a dubious decision to relegate such authors as Lafcadio Hearn and John Collier to the companion fantasy volume.)

Secondly, Neilson may not have been the ideal person to write the chapter on contemporary weird fiction. He accords uniform praise to everyone—whether it be the high (Shirley Jackson, Ramsey Campbell, T. E. D. Klein) or the low (Charles L. Grant, James Herbert, and—imagine this—John Farris). He, and he alone, laments the fact that the occult potboilers of Dennis Wheatley are already achieving merited oblivion. (In the course of this discussion he reveals a serious misunderstanding of Lovecraft, but let that pass.) Indeed, it does not appear as if Neilson has anything bad to say about anyone. He falls into the trap that has caught so many academic critics: the desperate desire to find profundity in even the most banal and superficial work. This does everyone a disservice. The volume's prime goal (in spite of its subtitle) is to help librarians build up a choice collection of weird fiction. This requires critical judgment and discrimination, neither of which Neilson provides. The mere fact that a greater quantity of weird fiction (or what passes for it) is being produced today than in prior ages says nothing about the quality or endurance of this material; indeed, almost every commentator agrees that the vast majority of contemporary work is rubbish. There is no sense in advising underbudgeted libraries to go out and buy dozens or hundreds of works that will be forgotten in twenty years' time. Did it not occur to anyone that, on the scale of literary merit, Algernon Blackwood ranks a little higher than Charles L. Grant, or that Ramsey Campbell ranks a little higher than John Farris? One would never know it from reading this book. Barron's motivations in printing this bloated chapter can only be conjectured; all I can think of is that he wished to be more up-to-date than Tymn by giving emphasis to work that was published subsequent to Tymn's volume. If so, this is a misguided undertaking; and it results, ironically, in a book that may actually "date" much faster than Tymn's.

And yet, the volume is saved by the second section ("Research Aids"), in particular by Michael A. Morrison's brilliant and comprehensive survey of critical work in the field. These chapters far surpass Mike Ashley's superficial and inadequate chapter in Tymn's book. Morrison takes an actual critical stance toward his material, rightly censuring such works as Glen St John Barclay's wretched *Anatomy of Horror* or Lenemaja Friedman's lacklustre Twayne book on Shirley Jackson; Morrison also has no compunction listing small press or fan publications, which in many cases are the only works of scholarship on some authors and are often rather good.

The volume includes a fair amount of material on film, television, and art—a rather anomalous circumstance given the book's title, but a welcome addition in any event, as Tymn's book was largely lacking in such material. Michael Klossner and Walter Albert have contributed these sections, and have done an able job. Mike Ashley's listing of horror and fantasy magazines is superb.

In the end, how does Barron's book stack up to Tymn's? With the exception of Fisher's chapter (as well as that by Gary William Crawford on weird fiction from 1920 to 1980), the historical surveys and bibliographies in Tymn's are uniformly better than Barron's. But the entire second part of Barron's is vastly superior to Tymn's. I wish there were some way of melding these two volumes together; or, better yet, of compiling a volume that takes the best features of both without skewing the historical section all out of proportion as Barron does. I am not contesting, of course, that Barron is indeed more up-to-date than Tymn; but, as I have suggested, this virtue may prove to be rather short-lived.

The problems with Walter Kendrick's *The Thrill of Fear: 250 Years of Scary Entertainment* (Grove Weidenfeld, 1991) begin with its subtitle. Kendrick, a professor of English at Fordham University, has taken it upon himself to write a history of horror fiction from the Gothic novels of the late eighteenth century to the most recent books, films, and television shows; but he finds no virtues in this material other than that of providing "scary entertainment." This implies two things: first, that to "scare" is a prime or, indeed, the only purpose of horror fiction; and second, that the only value of such fiction is as (popular) "entertainment." "I've gone in search not of meanings but of feelings, those momentary prickles of the scalp and sudden intakes of breath that provide mysterious pleasure," Kendrick writes. That is, I suppose, refreshingly philistine if nothing else.

But wait a minute. Haven't there been a fair number of scholars who have actually found literary worth in the best horror fiction? With these people Kendrick will have nothing to do. "Instead of forcing run-of-the-mill work to yield up deeper, richer, more stable meanings, I've tried to read culture's throwaways on their own terms." This seems to imply that Kendrick will be dealing only with run-of-the-mill work in the field, but the whole tenor of his book suggests that *all* horror writing is run-of-the-mill, so that there is hardly any point in seeking deeper meanings in it at all. It's just scary entertainment.

Much of this hostility to scholarship lies in Kendrick's own deficiencies as an analyst. He spends most of his time either giving interminable plot summaries of books and films (*Bride of Frankenstein* takes up five pages) or quoting liberally from texts and then remarking, in effect, "Gee, isn't this scary!" When he actually tries his hand at interpretation, he can be astoundingly inept: It's news to me that Christopher Burrell's "Elegie" (1653) "reads like a guide for today's special-effects technicians." As a cultural critic Kendrick fares no better: "We no longer bury our dead as they were buried in the middle of the eighteenth century."

Kendrick's ignorance of the literature—both primary and secondary—is cavernous. It is bad enough that he has failed to read the best scholarship on horror fiction, from H. P. Lovecraft's "Supernatural Horror in Literature" (1927) to Peter Penzoldt's *The Supernatural in Fiction* (1952) to Rosemary Jackson's *Fantasy: The Literature of Subversion* (1981) to Noël Carroll's *The Philosophy of Horror* (1990). But surely even a popular history must cover the leading writers of the horror tale—Edgar Allan Poe, Joseph Sheridan Le Fanu, Arthur Machen, Ambrose Bierce, Algernon Blackwood, Walter de la Mare, H. P. Lovecraft, L. P. Hartley, Lord Dunsany, Oliver Onions, and on and on. These are the T. S. Eliots and James Joyces of the field; and their work reveals a richness, substance, and complexity that even Kendrick might be forced to acknowledge. Of these Kendrick covers only Poe and Le Fanu in any detail. It is typical that, of all the works by Lovecraft—the most significant American horror writer of the century and the subject of more scholarly commentary in the last two decades than any writer in the field, including Poe—Kendrick discusses only the minor collaborative tale "The Loved Dead," although even here he fails to realise that the story is a conscious parody of itself.

When Kendrick gets to the post–World War II period he falls completely on his face. He turns his attention wholly to movies, television shows, and comic books; it is as if no one is writing horror literature anymore. His fleeting comment that "the best the twentieth century can do [in horror fiction] is Stephen King" tells the whole story. Modern horror fiction was essentially born in 1971, when William Peter Blatty's *The Exorcist* and Thomas Tryon's *The Other* simultaneously appeared on the best-seller lists. Kendrick not only fails to discuss these books, both of which are rather good, but (somewhat curiously, given his penchant for movies) also ignores the two fine film adaptations of them. And apparently Kendrick has not even heard of such writers as Robert Aickman, Ramsey Campbell, T. E. D. Klein, Dennis Etchison, Thomas Ligotti, and so many others whose work has a depth and substance fully equal to any contemporary mainstream work. Perhaps Kendrick has been intimidated by the masses of books found on the horror shelves in bookstores, most of which are indeed worthless (but then, how much contemporary mainstream work has any hope of survival?); but there are an increasing number of reference volumes to help the reader and critic to separate the wheat from the chaff. Kendrick, however, cannot be bothered to make such an effort.

This book has no reason for existence. Its massive omissions and self-confessed anti-intellectualism bar it completely from the realm of serious scholarship, while even as a popular study it is far inferior to many other works of its kind. Les Daniels's *Living in Fear: A History of Horror in the Mass Media* (1975) is written with a thoroughness, flair, and perspicacity Kendrick cannot hope to match, although of course it is now far out of date. Scholars of the weird tale have long been battling against hostile mainstream critics who refuse on principle to grant any literary significance to horror fiction; with friends like Walter Kendrick, who echoes this myopic position but paradoxically glories in it, we don't need any enemies.

After reading Kendrick's sorry excuse for a book, it is in every sense of the word a profound pleasure to pick up Faye Ringel's *New England's Gothic Literature: History and Folklore of the Supernatural from the Seventeenth through the Twentieth Centuries* (Edwin Mellen Press, 1995). Because weird fiction continues to be a pariah to standard literature, it is one of the few fields where otherwise competent mainstream critics such as Leslie Fiedler and Walter Kendrick can reveal staggering ignorance of horror literature but nevertheless be praised for their acumen. The only academically respectable branch of the field—the Gothic novel—has been so overworked, and the critics who treat of it seem so unaware of its thoroughgoing mediocrity and of the vast array of outstanding work that followed it that a new book on the Gothic is more likely to evoke dismay than enthusiasm in the aficionado.

Faye Ringel, however, has chosen to approach the subject from an entirely different and, so far as I can tell, absolutely novel direction: the intermingling of folklore and fiction. The result is a stimulating and refreshing study that displays the author's wide range, exhaustive erudition, and aesthetic sensitivity, and constitutes one of the most signal contributions to the field in recent years.

Ringel's provocative thesis is stated at the outset:

> For New England, Gothic fiction can be at least as faithful a mirror of reality as so-called realistic or mimetic fiction. Despite the best advances of reason and science, belief in the reality of the unknowable or supernatural persists. While no one can prove beyond a shadow of a doubt that the machinery of the Gothic—the vampires, witches, sea serpents, devils—exists, throughout the history of New England, in one way or another, that machinery has been and still is believed to be true. More important, these beliefs have continued to inspire interest even among those who . . . have not yet settled the question of the reality of wonders and horrors.

In other words, the surprising frequency of belief in witchcraft, vampires, and the like throughout the history of New England both inspired writers to treat these subjects in literature and readers to read about them. Before one concludes that Ringel is a kind of Whitley Strieber or John Mack of literary criticism, let it be made clear that she is of course highly sceptical whether there ever were any real witches, vampires, etc. in New England—or, rather, whether they were of the supernatural variety. Certainly, there were isolated individuals who *thought* that they were witches and vampires, and many others who believed that they or others were; that is not in question. What actually is in question, in terms of Ringel's formulation, is how genuinely widespread such beliefs were and whether they had any direct or even indirect role in the way horror fiction was written or read. It is on this last point that I find some causes for doubt; at least, I do not see that Ringel has proved her point, or that it is even possible to do so. Did the believers in witchcraft actually read horror fiction? Did their attitudes toward it differ from those who read it as mere escape or those who, like Lovecraft, read it precisely because their scepticism as to the reality of supernatural phenomena led them to seek it out as a kind of imaginative liberation from the mundane? There is simply no evidence on these points, so that Ringel's hypothesis will have to remain merely a suggestive conjecture.

But none of this actually matters very much. *New England's Gothic Literature* is so full of remarkable research—that old-time philological and historical research which involves poring over old newspapers, obscure treatises, and little-read works of fiction—that each page contains some illuminating insight. Some parts of the work read like a novel, as Ringel acts as a kind of scholarly detective hunting down some faint thread of superstition through the ages. The scope of the book is even larger than its subtitle, for Ringel begins with voyagers' accounts of New England from as early as the sixteenth century—accounts that hint of strange sea-monsters lurking in New England waters. Encounters between European settlers and Indians evoked masses of weird folklore on both sides; it is scarcely to be wondered that the heritage of Puritanism inspired those settlers to find the Devil both in landscape and in their coppery foes. Ringel spends two full chapters giving an exhaustive account of New England witch belief culminating in the Salem outbreak of 1692; but I was a little disappointed that she did not state more clearly her own views as to the causes of that outbreak. She reviews the various theories of other scholars but does not give much of an account of the direction of her own opinions.

A chapter on New England vampire belief leads to a substantial disquisition on H. P. Lovecraft, since he treated that belief with novel twists in "The Shunned House" (1924). It would be a little uncharitable of me to point out some very small blemishes in this chapter, but their insignificance only underscores the general soundness of Ringel's scholarship. Her assertion that Lovecraft "never saw his works between commercially printed hard covers" ignores the fact that William L. Crawford's *Shadow over Innsmouth* (1936) was a purportedly commercial, not amateur, venture (the book sold for a dollar). Ringel repeats L. Sprague de Camp's assertion (entirely unsupported by any documentary evidence) that Lovecraft's racial views were derived from the work of Houston Stewart Chamberlain, when several other sources are far more likely. Ringel cites E. F. Bleiler, of all people, for the derivation of the Greek word

Necronomicon, not aware that Bleiler is as pitifully ignorant of Greek etymology as almost all the other poor devils who have had a go at this matter. And Ringel's strange assertion that there is some mystery about the actual address of the Shunned House (135 Benefit Street) only testifies to the fact that Henry L. P. Beckwith (who asserted that it was 133 Benefit Street) is simply wrong. Ringel of course discusses many other Lovecraft stories beyond "The Shunned House," and in fact her chapter can stand as an excellent introduction to Lovecraft (at least from a New England Gothic perspective) for readers and academicians alike.

From a purely critical point of view, Ringel's most valuable chapter is her last, in which she discusses the work of New England writers (or, at any rate, writers who wrote about New England) subsequent to Lovecraft. Here Ringel focuses on Shirley Jackson, Joe Citro, Rick Hautala, Stephen King, and a host of other writers who have largely been strangers to academic criticism. (Some of them, I regret to say, will probably remain so.) Ringel tries to cover so much ground that some of her work ends up being mere plot summary rather than analysis, but I believe she is chiefly attempting to show that there indeed *is* a lot of ground to cover and that further analysis should be done on some of these writers. She herself is one of the few who may be capable of doing this work.

Classics and Contemporaries

As I have repeatedly mentioned, the criticism of horror literature still seems, in many regards, at a rather primitive stage. If, as indicated above, general studies of the field have their difficulties, so do critical works on specific authors, which are either superficial "popular" studies or simply non-existent. Four recent studies—two of "classic" authors, two of contemporaries—provide some clues as to what has been done in this field and what remains to be done.

The one thing that struck me when I read Darrell Schweitzer's *Pathways to Elfland: The Writings of Lord Dunsany* (Owlswick Press, 1989) is *Probitas laudatur et alget*. When Juvenal wrote that tag ("Excellence is praised and left to shiver in the cold"), he could hardly have realised how prophetically it would have suited the work of Lord Dunsany (1878–1957), whom everyone acknowledges as a master of fantasy, a significant influence on H. P. Lovecraft, Ursula K. LeGuin, and others, and one of the great prose stylists of the twentieth century, but whom few nowadays actually read. Still less is he studied. Darrell Schweitzer has written the first full-length critical study of the entirety of Dunsany's work. To date we have had a charming memoir (Hazel Littlefield's *Lord Dunsany: King of Dreams*, 1959), a standard (and rather lifeless) biography in Mark Amory's *Biography of Lord Dunsany* (1972), and an old and mediocre critical study, E. H. Bierstadt's *Dunsany the Dramatist* (1917); but we have had to wait 111 years from Dunsany's birth for a true critical study; although even this book was apparently composed about a decade earlier.

Schweitzer is in the awkward position of having to say something about a writer of astonishing productivity and diversity about whom almost nothing has been said. There are, to be sure, many more articles on Dunsany than the few listed in Schweitzer's bibliography, but they are all entirely insubstantial and Schweitzer is to be excused for not listing them. As it is, he must devote considerable space to mere plot description (something he does very deftly), since the majority of Dunsany's work beyond the early short stories is unknown even to fantasy enthusiasts. Nevertheless, Schweitzer constantly manages to make pointed and perceptive critical comments as he goes.

Another difficulty with writing an introduction to Dunsany is organisation. Schweitzer has opted for the logical (if somewhat obvious) method of categorisation by genre (short stories, plays, novels, poetry, nonfiction)—a sensible enough arrangement even if it obscures the continuity or development of themes throughout the whole of Dunsany's work. But perhaps Schweitzer feels that such a thematic treatment is something better left to later studies, which can use his own as a foundation.

Although the book is largely a discussion, one after the other, of every major work by Dunsany in rough chronological order by genre, Schweitzer manages to convey his views of the totality and direction of Dunsany's writing. In a sense Schweitzer's division of works by genre is sound, since Dunsany really did proceed from one genre to another—although with much overlap—in the course of his career. Schweitzer in fact remarks: "Dunsany would begin well in any vein, writing his best stories of the type near the beginning, maintain a high level of quality for while, and then fall off to the point of utter exhaustion." I suppose this is true enough, although I see many late works by Dunsany as fully equal in style, conception, and execution to his earlier work. Indeed, my great plea to the fantasy community in general is the resurrection of such obscure but brilliant works as *The Story of Mona Sheehy* (1939), *The Man Who Ate the Phoenix* (1949), and *The Strange Journeys of Colonel Polders* (1950). Schweitzer would perhaps not agree with this exact list, but would certainly agree with the principle.

To a seasoned reader of Dunsany like myself, the book does not offer much that is new; but of course Schweitzer is not writing for the (literally) handful of individuals who have read the length and breadth of Dunsany's work but for the thousands of enthusiasts who have not. Even so, I found some points of enlightenment. A digression early in the book on why the countless imitators of Dunsany's *Gods of Pegāna*-type stories have largely failed is excellent; of Clark Ashton Smith in particular (who "may have followed in Dunsany's footsteps more than he cared to admit") Schweitzer notes: "He lacked the stylistic mastery to write as well as Dunsany, and if one doesn't write as well as Dunsany, one can't write like him at all." Schweitzer knows Dunsany's plays about as well as anyone, and a fascinating appendix supplies dates of writing, production, and publication of all the plays, even several lost or unpublished ones; this appendix shows that the dates of composition of the plays do not correspond at all to dates of publication, and this information must be digested by anyone interested in tracing the progression of Dunsany's dramatic work.

Any disagreements I have with Schweitzer are the personal and perhaps subjective disagreements of one who has read Dunsany thoroughly but read him differently. I would not rank the plays in general nearly so low as Schweitzer does—in particular, he seems insensitive to the mordant satire and cynicism in several plays in *Seven Modern Comedies* (1928) and *Plays for Earth and Air* (1937), although he keenly points out their deficiencies in characterisation and overall construction. As for the novels, I rank *The King of Elfland's Daughter* (1924) and *The Blessing of Pan* (1927) nearly as high as Dunsany's admitted masterpiece, *The Curse of the Wise Woman* (1933), although I have Schweitzer and others against me in vaunting *The Strange Journeys of Colonel Polders*. Neither of us is right or wrong in our preferences; indeed, such critical disagreements help to keep an author's work alive. As it is, Schweitzer's sensitive discussion of *The Charwoman's Shadow* (1926) may make me take another look at that novel. Schweitzer's merciless dissection of Dunsany's failings as a poet (someone should do the same for Lovecraft) is masterful, and in a stroke of genius he arranges a passage from the short story "Where the Tides Ebb and Flow" in free verse to show how much more genuinely poetical Dunsany's prose is than his verse. (In his foreword L. Sprague de Camp demurs a bit at Schweitzer's evaluation, although the principal value of the foreword is in offering some charming vignettes of de Camp's visits to Dunsany Castle.) Schweitzer has added an illuminating chapter (written after the bulk of the book) on the many uncollected works by Dunsany discovered by Schweitzer and myself in the course of our recent bibliographical work.

Darrell Schweitzer is a populariser in the best and most literal sense of the term. He is not interested in laborious critical analysis but instead seeks to make known the work of little-known authors or the little-known work of famous authors. As such, his writing will have far more wide-ranging effects than any amount of academic pedantry. Occasionally his style may lapse a little too far in the direction of colloquialism; refreshing as this is to one who has read more academic criticism than he cares to think about, it can sometimes create the impression of trivialising the subject in question. Nevertheless, Schweitzer has written a fine introduction to Dunsany; and if it is only the start of true critical work on this author, it is at any rate a sound start.

Some readers may, I imagine, look askance at my reviewing *The Barbaric Triumph: A Critical Anthology on the Writings of Robert E. Howard*, edited by Don Herron (Wildside Press, 2004)—an informal follow-up to Herron's admirable anthology, *The Dark Barbarian* (Greenwood Press, 1984)—as my views on Robert E. Howard have apparently been productive of a certain amount of controversy, and perhaps even of anger and hostility. I am entirely prepared to admit that my own knowledge of the scope and particulars of Howard's writing is inferior to that of any of the contributors to this book, so that the only perspective from which I can legitimately comment upon it is from the perspective of one who has done scholarly work in a related discipline (i.e., the study of H. P. Lovecraft) and who has been more generally involved in the study of weird fiction for the past twenty-five years and, accordingly, can possibly gauge the advances in scholarship that have occurred in this field during that time.

It strikes me, upon reading this anthology, that the field of Howard studies today is roughly where Lovecraft studies was at around the year 1980. I hope that this remark—and anything else I have to say in this review—will not be interpreted as patronising or condescending; such is not my intention. But I think it has to be acknowledged that the study of Robert E. Howard has not yet advanced to the current level of Lovecraft studies, and for reasons that have (or may have) nothing in particular to do with the respective merits of the two authors. Around 1980, there were a fair number of pretty bright people, most of them young (Donald R. Burleson, Robert M. Price, David E. Schultz, Will Murray, Scott Connors, Peter Cannon), who were on the brink of taking Lovecraft studies to a new level; but several of them (and I will include myself in this number) had not yet achieved a proper sense of intellectual or emotional distance from their subject, with the result that they exhibited a certain *resentment* at Lovecraft's relatively low standing in the canon of American literature. We took disparagements of Lovecraft personally; we reacted with bitterness and hostility at any perceived slight on our object of devotion. We tended to overpraise Lovecraft, to claim for him a loftier literary and intellectual status than he deserved, and we rained torrents of abuse down upon any who did not agree with us. We were not only young, but a tad immature.

Several Howard scholars in this book match this profile. They similarly have chips on their shoulders, and are deeply resentful whenever anyone fails to rank Howard among the luminaries of American or world literature. They have not yet learned the lesson—a lesson, admittedly, that it took Lovecraftians their own sweet time to learn—that merely producing sober, penetrating analyses of their subject would, in the course of time, be sufficient to convince the literary and scholarly communities that their author deserved a place in the American canon, even if that place might not be quite as exalted as they in our fervour had hoped for.

One of the chief ways in which Lovecraftians accomplished the raising of their subject in critical estimation was by the publication of their work in properly accredited academic venues. As someone who has not been affiliated with a university for the past twenty years, I am just about the last person to insist that the academy has any monopoly on critical judgment; but it is a cold fact of our culture that publication of scholarly work by academic publishers will indeed have an impact on how a given author is perceived by the literary community at large. It is, accordingly, somewhat unfortunate that Don Herron, who performed a notable coup by getting Greenwood Press, a legitimate academic publisher, to issue *The Dark Barbarian*, deliberately eschewed a similar venue for this book. In explanation, he states unhelpfully that "For any number of reasons, I decided to go with a popular press for this anthology." But Wildside is not a "popular" press; it is a small press—and that is a significant difference. What it means is that this book is likely to be read only by hard-core fans of Howard, rather than the general public (an audience that a true "popular" press could reach) or the academic community (which an academic press could reach).

Herron has made an additional error when he determined that the essays in this book be written without footnotes. The magnitude of this error can scarcely be exaggerated. It is not, as those unaccustomed to writing scholarly work appear to assume, that footnotes, endnotes, or references are merely meant to display a critic's erudition or, in the case of non-academic critics (and no one in this book is an academician with the exception of the French scholar Lauric Guillaud, whose essay has been translated by Donald Sidney-Fryer), to prove that they can write academic criticism as well as any old pompous-ass Ivy League professor; they are meant as a service to the reader. Exact citation of primary and secondary sources is vital in allowing readers to gauge the validity of the critic's argument. Do the citations actually support his argument? Has he perhaps quoted them out of context? In this volume, exact citations would have been helpful in a number of cases. The essays by Steven R. Trout, Scott Connors, and Steven Tompkins are particularly in need of them. Tompkins cites John Clute's *Encyclopedia of Fantasy* on a number of occasions; that book, as I recall, is more than 1000 pages, and in the absence of even the name of the entry quoted, it would be a trifle difficult to follow up these citations. Even more important, the critical reader—perhaps some youngster who is eager to do more scholarly work on Howard—would be stymied by the absence of citations. Where does one find, for example, the essay by Fritz Leiber cited by Tompkins without source? Perhaps it is the essay in *The Dark Barbarian*, but without a laborious comparison it would be difficult to tell. Or is it the introduction to *Marchers of Valhalla* that Connors cites? Who knows? Scholarship cannot grow and build upon itself without precision of this sort. It is all very well for Herron to say that he wants essays that are "enjoyable to read"; but having proper citations does not militate against readability. No one has to read footnotes if he doesn't want to.

The book could have used the services of a professional copy editor. Punctuational errors and irregularities are frequent (especially irritating is the placing of a quotation mark following, rather than preceding, a colon). Charles Hoffman uses "prophesy" as a noun, when it is only a verb in this form; Leo Grin unearths the impossible verb form "prophesize" and the impossible noun "prolificacy." (The English language provides only the clumsy "prolificness" as a noun form of *prolific*.) Mark Finn writes "one of who" rather than "one of whom." On a single page of Trout's essay we are introduced to the author of *The Hero with a Thousand Faces* as John Campbell and (correctly) Joseph Campbell.

Of the actual essays in the book, I am sorry to report that the two poorest are those by Edward A. Waterman and Leo Grin—sorry because Herron notes that these two individuals were instrumental in bringing this otherwise meritorious book to fruition. Waterman attempts an analysis of Howard's philosophy, but I regret to say that his grasp of the history and conceptions of philosophy are not sufficiently sound to write a proper article on the subject. He wants to maintain that Howard is an "irrationalist"; that is, that Howard stands in contrast to rationalism, which Waterman adequately describes as "the philosophical view that reason is capable of ascertaining all knowledge in the universe, that indeed all knowledge forms a single system with an inherently consistent structure following the laws and principles of logic." The problem is that there really is no coherent school or even philosophical method called irrationalism. As Patrick Gardiner states (entry on "Irrationalism" in *The Encyclopedia of Philosophy* [1967]): "Irrationalism . . . is an exceedingly imprecise term that is employed with a wide variety of meanings and implications. Consequently, any attempt to elucidate its sense within the confines of a clear-cut and tidy formula quickly runs into difficulties." This is exactly what happens to Waterman's analysis. He seems unaware that the true counterpoise to rationalism (as embodied in such seventeenth-century thinkers as Descartes and Spinoza) is not "irrationalism" but empiricism—a school of philosophy that rejected the deductive logic propounded by the rationalists and substituted inductive logic, or the gathering of hard facts pertaining to phenomena (chiefly from the sciences) as a provisional means of understanding those parts of the universe that come within the purview of our senses. This school dominated British thought for the better part of three centuries, extending from Sir Francis Bacon to John Locke to David Hume to John Stuart Mill to Bertrand Russell and many others; and contrary to Waterman's implication, the chief thinkers of the French Enlightenment (Diderot, d'Alembert, Voltaire, Condorcet, La Mettrie, Holbach) were all empiricists: the *Encyclopédie* is in fact a monument to empiricist thought. What is more,

Waterman presents evidence that Howard was a metaphysical dualist ("Howard's fundamental view of reality is therefore dualistic in nature, composed of two halves: matter and mind/spirit"), but this puts him in direct linkage with the rationalists, especially Descartes, rather than the empiricists, who largely rejected this dichotomy.

So far as I can tell, Howard did not have a coherent or well-rounded philosophy. This is not meant as a criticism—few creative writers (Lovecraft is one exception) devote any significant amount of time to studying philosophical questions or working out their own personal philosophies by detailed consultation of the philosophers of the past. If anything, Howard seems to me an extreme sceptic or agnostic ("My mind is open; I refuse either to deny or affirm"). It is difficult to link this relatively common attitude with any specific philosopher of the past or of Howard's own day. (Waterman commits the gaffe of being impressed that Howard followed Herbert Spencer is spelling *skepticism* as "scepticism." But the latter is simply the British spelling of the term, whereas the former is chiefly American; the latter had not quite gone out of fashion in the America of Howard's day, so his use of it is nothing remarkable.) Perhaps more work can be done on the particulars of Howard's philosophical thought, but it will have to be done by someone better versed in philosophy.

As for Leo Grin's essay, it is chiefly devoted to studying the notion of hatred as the guiding principle of much of Howard's work. It is a task he performs with considerable verve and learning, but he then tacks on a section, having no vital connexion with the rest of the essay, in which he attempts to champion Howard's greatness against those who have denigrated him. I will admit that I am one of the targets of his criticism, and I trust I might be allowed to defend myself. Grin quotes some uncharitable comments I made on Howard in my biography of Lovecraft and goes on to remark:

> S. T. Joshi . . . has made his name penning a number of books in praise of H. P. Lovecraft's batty life philosophies. To such critics weird fiction as defined by Lovecraft is sacrosanct, and anyone not parroting the cosmic emotionless horrors of their hero is rejected as a failure. . . . And so it was predictable to see Joshi, in his book *H. P. Lovecraft: A Life* (1996), offer sweeping generalizations in lieu of trying to explain Howard's formidable, *non-Lovecraftian* presence in the genre of weird fiction, a presence which otherwise would wreak havoc with his insular theories concerning the weird tale.

I scarcely know how to respond to this farrago of nonsense. In the first place, I have written exactly one book on Lovecraft's philosophy, *H. P. Lovecraft: The Decline of the West* (1990). (Both the title and subtitle of my book *A Subtler Magick: The Writings and Philosophy of H. P. Lovecraft* [1996] were supplied by the publisher and do not, to my mind, accurately describe the content of the book.) Second, I wrote that book not to "praise" Lovecraft's philosophy, but to analyse it and to show how it manifests itself in his fiction. Third, I have no idea what "batty life philosophies" can be—nor, it appears, does Grin, since he never specifies how Lovecraft's "philosophies" [did he have more than one?] are or are not "batty." Given that there are any number of similarities between Lovecraft's and Howard's world-views, and given that Grin himself declares Howard to have been afflicted with "suicidal depression," it is an open question whose "philosophies," Lovecraft's or Howard's, are the more "batty." Fourth, nowhere in my biography of Lovecraft (or anywhere else) do I declare that Howard was an inferior writer merely because he failed to embody in his work the philosophy of weird fiction enunciated by Lovecraft, nor can Grin find any such claim in my work. Indeed, if he had bothered to check my book *The Weird Tale* (1990), he would have quickly found that I specifically cite heroic fantasy as a legitimate (albeit hybrid) form of the weird tale, and mention Howard and Fritz Leiber by name as among its chief exponents. I go on to say that "Howard's evolution of this form is strictly dependent upon his philosophical concerns—his championing of barbarism over civilisation and his belief in the moral virtues of struggle and conflict"—points that several critics in this volume appear to have elaborated (without having deriving the idea from me, of course). I will state bluntly that I still think that Howard is not a particularly good writer—certainly not a great one—but my reasons for doing so rest upon relatively straightforward aesthetic criteria (his at times slipshod prose style, his wooden and stereotyped characters, the implausibility of some of his scenarios, etc.) and not upon any fancied philosophical deficiency or upon his failure to carry out Lovecraft's principles of weird writing.

One final point about Lovecraft and Howard, as seen by Grin, and I am done. Grin states that Lovecraft's preservation of Howard's letters proves that Lovecraft recognised Howard's "genius." I'm sorry to say that it proves nothing of the kind; it simply proves that Lovecraft found Howard a particularly interesting correspondent, all apart from the value of his creative work. Lovecraft also kept the letters of Ernest A. Edkins, an amateur journalist for whose writings Lovecraft certainly had some admiration, but which he certainly did not think the products of a genius. Don Herron, in his concluding essay, quotes a Lovecraft letter that gets to the heart of this matter. Lovecraft is discussing the wide array of correspondents to whom he writes:

> Take Bob Howard. There's a bird whose basic mentality seems to be to be just about the good respectable citizen's (bank casher, medium shopkeeper, ordinary lawyer, stockbroker, high school teacher, prosperous farmer, pulp fictionist, skilled mechanic, successful salesman, responsible government clerk, routine army or navy officer up to a colonel, &c.) average—bright & keen, accurate & retentive, but not profound or analytical—yet who is at the same time one of the most eminently interesting beings I know. (Letter to Kenneth Sterling, 14 December 1935)

And as for the praise lavished by Lovecraft in "In Memoriam: Robert Ervin Howard"—well, the occasion has to be taken into consideration (only H. L. Mencken, in his obituary of William Jennings Bryan, dared to violate the old rule of *de mortuis nil nisi bonum*), and Lovecraft was also habitually given to overrating the merits of his friends and colleagues. He thought Alfred Galpin would become one of the leading philosophers of the age, and August Derleth would become a kind of American Proust.

Grin brings further derision upon himself by fancying that the "millions of copies" of Howard's books that have been sold over the years, not to mention the high prices that the Arkham House *Skull-Face* brings on the collectors' market, are indications of Howard's lasting merit. But by these arguments, Erle Stanley Gardner and Agatha Christie would be the leading authors in world literature—or have they now been eclipsed by Stephen King, Danielle Steel, and John Grisham? And the collectability of a book, as is well known, has almost no bearing on its literary quality: entirely other criteria are used.

I repeat that, as the field of Howard studies develops, the perceived need for ham-fisted polemics of this kind will pass away. At the moment, they indicate only the critic's own insecurity, immaturity, and lack of critical judgment.

Of the other essays in the book, I need not speak in detail. Charles Hoffman's "Conan the Existential" strikes me as a good freshman paper—which, apparently, in large part it is. There is simply not enough evidence to declare Howard even approximately an existentialist or even a proto-existentialist. Mark Finn's "Fists of Robert E. Howard" is a sound analysis of Howard's fight stories, ingeniously structured around an actual fight in which Howard engaged; but I fail to derive any sense that these stories are of high literary substance. Perhaps Finn does not wish to make any such assertion. Steven R. Trout's essay on Howard and the frontier myth, Scott Connors's piece on Howard's utilisation of the German idea of the *Völk*, and Steven Tompkins's essay on Howard's suggestion of vast gulfs of time in his work are all competent pieces of work. George Knight's essay on Howard's use of nature and landscape seems to me marred by uncritical overpraise of Howard—again, something that one hopes will be felt to be needless as Howard studies gets more firmly on its legs. Don Herron's concluding essay, on the relations between Howard, Clark Ashton Smith, and Lovecraft, did not have much that was new to me, but perhaps others will benefit from it. I am sorry to say, however, that his recounting of the mere facts of this relationship does not go very far in confirming that these three figures are "the *great* writers indelibly associated with" *Weird Tales*—and even if it did, I don't suppose there is any great merit in such a distinction.

If I have concentrated on the possible shortcomings of this book, it is strictly in an attitude of constructive criticism. All in all, *The Barbaric Triumph* is itself a notable triumph: every essay has some value, and several go far in illumating the distinctive merits of Howard's work. If another such volume is compiled, perhaps a different publisher—one who, for example, does not print the front and back cover in nearly illegible red-on-black ink—can be found. And overall, certain basic tasks in Howard studies need to be accomplished before it can be placed on a sound footing. First, the texts of all his major work must be prepared in standard, textually corrected editions (perhaps the Wandering Star editions are a beginning in this direction). Second, his ancillary writings (especially poetry and letters) must be issued in sound annotated editions (I am at work, with Rusty Burke and David E. Schultz, on the preparation of the joint Lovecraft-Howard correspondence). Third, an exhaustive primary and secondary bibliography must be compiled (Glenn Lord's *The Last Celt* is an admirable effort, but will have to be reassembled in proper bibliographical format). Fourth, Howard scholars must get those chips off their shoulders. If Howard really is a great writer, then the mere analysis of his work will prove it. If he isn't, then no amount of bluster will convince any sensible person that he is.

Shirley Jackson is a writer *manquée*. Ignored by the mainstream critical establishment and uneasily regarded by the weird fiction community, she is deserving of at least a small place in the canon of American literature and a very significant place in the history of weird fiction. She might well be the most significant weird writer between Lovecraft and Ramsey Campbell, and some of her work—"The Lottery," "The Summer People," "The Lovely House," *The Haunting of Hill House*—is among the most powerful horror writing of the 1940s and '50s, although only the first and the last are so recognised.

It is, accordingly, not a surprise that critical work on Jackson is at an unbelievably rudimentary stage. Aside from an uninspired critical study by Lenemaja Friedman (published in 1975 by Twayne) and a workmanlike but critically naive biography by Judy Oppenheimer (1988), there are no books about Shirley Jackson, and only a random scattering of academic articles, ranging—as academic articles are wont to do—from the useful to the preposterous. Joan Wylie Hall, in her brilliant study, *Shirley Jackson: A Study of the Short Fiction* (Twayne, 1993), quotes with apparent approval Lynette Carpenter's belief that Jackson has been ignored by "traditional male critics" because of her "housewife humor" (by which, one imagines, Carpenter means Jackson's quite delightful collections of pieces about her children, *Life among the Savages* and *Raising Demons*). Hall wisely does not elaborate upon this foolish notion, for which not an iota of evidence exists. In fact, the ignorance of Jackson by the critical and the weird community rests precisely because she does not fits comfortably in either, presenting formidable problems of classification and orientation.

Hall's focus is not, of course, upon Jackson as a weird writer, but her careful examination of the short fiction makes it evident that Jackson was a titan in our field. Her Biercian misanthropy allowed her to write such scintillating *contes cruels* as "The Renegade," "The Witch," and "Seven Types of Ambiguity." She pioneered the tale of psychological horror in "The Daemon Lover," "Pillar of Salt," and others. *The Haunting of Hill House* may be her only explicitly supernatural novel, but several short stories—notably "The Lovely House" (also titled "A Visit")—introduce the supernatural in the most exquisitely subtle and indirect ways.

The format of Twayne's Studies in Short Fiction consists of three parts: first, a critical analysis of the author's short stories; second, a selection of writings by the author about his or her work; and third, a selection of previously published criticism about the author. This results in a highly felicitous conjoining of biography and criticism, of primary and secondary literature, and whoever designed this format is to be praised. In the present instance, the first and second parts of the volume are unfailingly illuminating, the third somewhat less so.

Hall's own critical analysis divides into three parts, the first discussing the stories in *The Lottery* (1949), the second on the stories in the posthumous collection *Come Along with Me* (1968), and the third on the dozens of uncollected stories that Jackson published in books or magazines and which, inexplicably, have still not been gathered in book form aside from the uneven collection *Just an Ordinary Day* (1997). There are some problems with this division, and Hall's failure to discuss the stories in *Life among the Savages* and *Raising Demons* in any detail—perhaps because, in the course of their incorporation in these books, the tales underwent such extensive revision that they became melded together into a single episodic narrative—obscures what seems to me a fundamental fact about Jackson's short stories: that they are vicious parodies or reversals of the genial domesticity of the family tales, where love among family members and integration into the community are replaced by hatred, envy, disappointment, and alienation. (This point is made by James Egan in his 1989 essay on Jackson in *Studies in Weird Fiction*, portions of which are reprinted here.) Also, Hall wants to believe that the *Lottery* collection is thematically unified; her arguments, made collectively throughout her analysis, are compelling, but I am not entirely convinced. It strikes me that the volume was hastily assembled to capitalise on the notoriety of the title story, and Hall's claim for a "loose coherence" for the volume is a significant equivocation.

On the whole, Hall's study of Jackson's short fiction is sane, acute, balanced, and terse—occasionally echoing the terseness of Jackson's own writing. She does not adopt any one critical approach in a doctrinaire way, or to the exclusion of other approaches. Hall also displays an uncanny ability to meld plot synopsis with critical analysis. This is by no means a slight accomplishment: many critics seem to feel that plot synopsis itself is sufficient for critical analysis, while at least one reviewer of my *Weird Tale* (1990) criticised me for not supplying *enough* synopsis of the work of Blackwood, Dunsany, and other obscure writers. A balance is very difficult to achieve, but Hall does so time and time again. Her analysis is a little old-fashioned, but in all the right ways: it is basically a sort of New Critical "close reading," with extremely careful attention to the actual text; and Hall has clearly benefited from the many hours she spent poring over the Shirley Jackson Papers at the Library of Congress, providing a wealth of information on original versions of Jackson's stories, their various stages of revision, and so on. It is heartening to see this sort of old-time philology still being practised and still yielding remarkable insights. If there are any shortcomings at all in Hall's study, it is a shortcoming imposed by the series: we find only passing discussion of Jackson's novels. Every reader will welcome a more unified study by Hall of Jackson's entire work, since that work is itself among the most thematically and philosophically unified of any I have read.

The material by Jackson included in the second part of the volume is wonderfully revealing; some of it consists of unpublished essays or letters, and their appearance here notably augments the value of the book. These pieces show that Jackson was an acute technician of the short story, and such essays as "Experience and Fiction" and "Notes for a Young Writer" are invaluable tutorial guides for transmuting one's life experience into usable fiction. Weird fiction enthusiasts may be a little disappointed at the understandable omission from "Experience and Fiction" of the passage discussing the genesis of *The Haunting of Hill House* (one day Jackson came down to her study to find the words "DEAD DEAD" on a sheet of paper in her typewriter); and space considerations no doubt impelled the omission from "Biography of a Story" of the hilarious and unbelievably nasty letters of comment received by the *New Yorker* upon publication of "The Lottery" ("Tell Miss Jackson to stay out of Canada"). On the other hand, "Notes for a Young Writer" is a perfect paradigm for the mingling of "weird" and "mainstream" conceptions in a story, and should be pondered by all prospective writers in our field.

I do not wish to say much about the critical extracts reprinted in this book; they make all too clear how inchoate is the work done on Jackson to date. Some of the best work is devoted to her novels, and as such could not be used. Helen Nebeker's symbolic interpretation of "The Lottery" is brilliant and has been foolishly attacked by Fritz Oehlshlaeger, who propounds an implausible feminist analysis of the story, and by Peter Kosenko, whose Marxist analysis makes wild assumptions—wholly unsupported by textual evidence—about the sociopolitical status of the community depicted in the tale. Hall had criticised these interpretations in her own study of "The Lottery," but was apparently forced to include these pieces for lack of anything better. Her bibliography reveals, significantly, almost no criticism on Jackson from the weird fiction community.

One of criticism's noblest functions is to drive the reader back to the primary texts, and Hall's study should make everyone initiate or renew an acquaintance with the remarkable short fiction of Shirley Jackson. Horror enthusiasts in particular owe it to themselves to see how much Jackson towers over most others in the field, especially those who have come after. Perhaps our diligent anthologists can get some of her work back into print. To those who are unfamiliar with Jackson, I can only say: you don't know what you're missing.

There are some books whose mere existence one should welcome irrespective of their quality or contents. Bette B. Roberts's *Anne Rice* (Twayne, 1994) is perhaps one of them, although in saying this I mean no disrespect to its author nor any disparagement of the book's substance.

It is well that there should be a critical study of Anne Rice in the Twayne's United States Authors Series, for these books—much pillaged by undergraduates, graduate students, and perhaps even professors—afford a compact and (especially of late) competent biographical, critical, and bibliographical overview of the author under discussion. One imagines that Anne Rice's work, aside from being popular, is being increasingly taught in schools, both because she is perhaps the only best-selling horror writer who happens to be a woman and, incidentally, because she is on the whole a pretty good writer. The dearth of actual criticism on Rice is signalled by Roberts's secondary bibliography, which—aside from Katherine Ramsland's two volumes, the biography *Prism of the Night* (1992) and a fluffy *Vampire Companion* (1993)—lists only book reviews and not a single critical article. (I appear to have written the first such article: "Anne Rice: The Philosophy of Vampirism," *Interzone* No. 75 [September 1993]: 47-50, 61; later reprinted in my *Modern Weird Tale* [2001].)

After a preliminary biographical chapter that draws heavily on Ramsland's biography, Roberts undertakes a general study of "Rice and the Gothic Tradition." This chapter is very peculiar. Roberts gives a fairly detailed analysis of the thrust of Gothic fiction from Walpole to Maturin, distinguishing a "female" Gothic tradition descending from Radcliffe with a more aggressive and explicit "male" tradition stemming from "Monk" Lewis. But why does the survey end with *Melmoth the Wanderer* (1820)? Why not carry it on through the landmark work of Poe, the later Gothic tradition (even Stoker's *Dracula*—surely of some possible relevance to Rice's work—is only cited in passing, and nothing is said of Le Fanu, Stevenson, and the rest), the great work of the early twentieth century (Machen, Blackwood, Dunsany, M. R. James, Lovecraft), and the outpouring of weird writing in the last two or three decades?

Roberts's study of the early Gothic school is certainly of interest, although she seems to reveal more knowledge of works *about* the Gothics than of the Gothics themselves. Perhaps her omission of later work is meant to suggest that Rice has not been much influenced by it (a debatable assertion, since it is manifest that *The Tale of the Body Thief,* at the very least, owes something to Lovecraft and Robert Bloch, both of whom are explicitly cited in the text), but then Roberts does nothing to demonstrate that Rice has much familiarity with the early Gothic tradition either. The failure to discuss modern work—or even to suggest that there was something called a "horror boom" in the 1970s and 1980s—is especially unfortunate. Rice may not—at the outset of her career, at any rate—have been an insider in the horror field, but it is unlikely that she would have turned to the writing of horror novels without the example (and sales) of Levin's *Rosemary's Baby* (1967), Tryon's *The Other* (1971), Blatty's *The Exorcist* (1971), and the early work of Stephen King. Though it may be unkind to say so, it appears that Roberts's omission of all this material is due merely to her lack of knowledge of it.

But let it pass. When she gets down to the actual analysis of Rice's work, Roberts does her job very creditably. Her analyses are somewhat unadventurous and expressed in a rather lifeless academic prose, but the points she makes in the course of detailed and analytical plot summaries of Rice's major novels—the vampire as outsider in quest of self-knowledge; the vampire motif as a symbolic exploration of polymorphous sexuality—are sound and made with vigour. If Roberts tends to be somewhat of a partisan (she can find very little bad to say about Rice's work except her unspeakable "erotics"), this is perhaps only to be expected. Most writers of weird fiction need a little drum-beating and pompom-waving to attract the attention of staid academics.

Let me take the opportunity here—since, in all frankness, I have run out of things to say about Roberts's book—to give some idea of Twayne's record in the study of writers in our humble field. It is certainly heartening that one of the earliest Twayne books was Wesley Sweetser's admirable study of Arthur Machen (1964). Vincent Buranelli's undistinguished Poe volume (1961) has been revised, but to no great effect. Some genuine Poe scholar should write an entirely new study. Mary Elizabeth Grenander's work on Ambrose Bierce (1971) is scintillating. I neither know nor care whether Twayne has published volumes on the older Gothic writers (Walpole, Radcliffe, Lewis, Maturin, Shelley); I imagine they have.

As for other writers in the century after Poe, Twayne's record is not so good. It took fifteen years and three prospective authors to get a book on Lovecraft out, although Peter Cannon's volume (1989) was well worth the wait. There is a good recent book on Bram Stoker by Phyllis A. Roth (1982), but none on Algernon Blackwood, Lord Dunsany, M. R. James, or Robert E. Howard. Blackwood is a particularly glaring omission. My recent book on

Dunsany (*Lord Dunsany: Master of the Anglo-Irish Imagination* [Greenwood Press, 1995]) might have served, but it is a little long for a Twayne book and I hate abridging myself.

Moving into the modern age, Lenemaja Friedman's mechanical study of Shirley Jackson (1980) ought to be replaced, although it is partially compensated for by Joan Wylie Hall's superb volume on Jackson's short stories in Twayne's Studies in Short Fiction series. There are already two books (by Joseph Reino and Tony Magistrale, respectively) on Stephen King. On the basis of abstract literary merit, it could well be wondered whether this is one (or two) too many, but I suppose even Twayne—which is almost exclusively a library publisher, although it tried and failed to issue paperback volumes two or three decades ago—must consider the market. In the neighbouring field of fantasy, perhaps M. P. Shiel, A. Merritt, Clark Ashton Smith (although more for his poetry than for his prose), and Fritz Leiber deserve studies. It is difficult to think of many more.

Twayne, of course, is not in the business of promoting writers of fantasy, horror, and the supernatural; but it has issued volumes on some mighty obscure mainstream authors, and there are a few critics in our field who are capable of producing good introductory works on the authors I have mentioned. If so, perhaps academicians like Bette B. Roberts (or the egregious Walter Kendrick) will become convinced that some tolerably good horror fiction has been written after 1820.

This whole issue has, regrettably, become academic, since the Twayne imprint has been suspended for the last several years and is not likely to be revived.

V. H. P. LOVECRAFT

Some Lovecraft Editions

This is not the place for anything approaching a comprehensive account of H. P. Lovecraft's publication history in book form. The broad outlines of such a history are known to most devotees. Arkham House's control of the Lovecraft texts—beginning with its first volume, *The Outsider and Others* (1939), and continuing almost down to the present day—was a decidedly mixed blessing. To be sure, the Arkham House editions brought Lovecraft's work to the attention of enthusiasts of weird fiction, but the relegation of Lovecraft's work to the small press hindered his acceptance by the mainstream community. Meanwhile, paperback editions of Lovecraft's stories achieved only sporadic success, and it not until the late 1960s that the so-called Arkham Edition of the Works of H. P. Lovecraft—initially published by Beagle Books and later subsumed under the Ballantine Books imprint—made Lovecraft a household word. These books sold, in the aggregate, in excess of a million copies in the first few years of their appearance, leading to the celebrated review by Philip Herrera in *Time* magazine (June 11, 1973) under the title "The Dream Lurker." The Arkham Edition consisted of eleven volumes, but only four of them contained work entirely by Lovecraft, the rest being "Cthulhu Mythos" writings by August Derleth and others. Lin Carter added two more volumes in the Adult Fantasy series.

In 1982, Ballantine reprinted these six volumes—*The Tomb and Other Tales, At the Mountains of Madness and Other Tales of Terror, The Lurking Fear and Other Stories, The Case of Charles Dexter Ward, The Dream-Quest of Unknown Kadath,* and *The Doom That Came to Sarnath*—with new cover art by Michael Whelan. The appearance of these books was certainly a mixed blessing from many perspectives; indeed, the only real blessing was their mere existence: the return of H. P. Lovecraft's fiction to the paperback shelves of the country's bookstores after at least a six-year lapse (excluding two unfortunately evanescent paper editions from Jove) was indeed to be welcomed, although one cannot help regretting that the presentation was not handled more competently. These six volumes were exact reprints of the Ballantine editions, and no notice was taken of the radical advances in scholarship made in the last decade. It is all too obvious that profit-making was the highest priority in the minds of the editors at Ballantine, for the volumes have been reprinted in the cheapest and most convenient manner possible, and the resulting inadequacies and anomalies are not pleasant to behold.

Every experienced reader of Lovecraft's fiction must be aware of the idiosyncratic selection of these volumes. Many major tales—"The Shadow out of Time," "The Whisperer in Darkness," "The Rats in the Walls," "The Thing on the Doorstep," "The Colour out of Space," "The Dunwich Horror," and many others—were left out (this due to the fact that Jove apparently owned the paperback rights to these tales, forcing Ballantine to pick up Lovecraft's barrel-scrapings to fill their volumes; it is a shame that Jove has not kept its two paperback volumes—*The Colour out of Space* and *The Dunwich Horror*—in print, for these are clearly the best selections of Lovecraft's fiction ever published in paperback), while many lesser tales—the "early" tales ("The Beast in the Cave," "The Alchemist," etc.) and the fragments—were included. The latter, however much they aid in understanding the genesis of Lovecraft's work, have no business being in a mass-market paperback; and insult is compounded to injury by the inclusion (in *The Tomb*) of a spurious "Complete Chronology" of Lovecraft's fiction (it is not even complete) reputedly from his own pen but actually fabricated by August Derleth. Kenneth Sterling's name was left off the collaboration "In the Walls of Eryx," as was that of Anna Helen Crofts in "Poetry and the Gods."

Other anomalies of arrangement have resulted from the attempt to integrate four volumes from the old Beagle Lovecraft edition with the two (*Dream-Quest* and *Doom That Came to Sarnath*) from the Adult Fantasy Series. Hence "The White Ship" appears both in *Dream-Quest* and *Lurking Fear*; "The Strange High House in the Mist" appears in *Dream-Quest* and *Tomb*; "In the Walls of Eryx," "Imprisoned with the Pharaohs," "The Tomb," and "The Festival" appear in *Doom That Came to Sarnath* and *Tomb*; "Beyond the Wall of Sleep" and "From Beyond" appear in *Lurking Fear* and *Doom*. Indeed, Lin Carter's two editions are surely the most satisfying of the lot—or would be if *Doom* were not marred by his fatuous and inane attempts at critical commentary. Carter pompously announces, in his "Partial Chronology of Lovecraft's Early Work," that "Whatever errors have crept into the chronology . . . are probably only a matter of weeks or of a month or so away from the truth" (this itself is paradoxical, since the tales are dated by year); but unfortunately his dating of "What the Moon Brings" to 1923 is at least six months off (the correct dating is June 1922). The selection in both these volumes, however, is notable, although obviously slanted toward Lovecraft's "dreamland" tales: *Doom* contains the four prose-poems (out of print since *Beyond the Wall of Sleep* [1943] save in Roy Squires's collector's editions of 1969-70), a poem ("Nathicana"), and other rare works.

Typographically, too, the volumes leave much to be desired. Only the two Carter volumes are set in a readable type; in the other four the type size is incredibly small, the pages are crammed to repletion, and (in *Tomb*) titles of stories are set in the same type size as the body of the text. It is almost a blessing that, in *The Case of Charles Dexter Ward*, the letters by Curwen and his cohorts are not set in reduced type (as they ought to be), else we might require a magnifying glass to read them.

A final matter is now of common knowledge. Since the Ballantine editions derive directly from the Arkham House volumes, the texts of the tales are seriously, sometimes appallingly, corrupt. We need not here repeat the sad tales of the two omitted passages in *At the Mountains of Madness*, the dropped half-paragraph in "The Statement of Randolph Carter," the dropped passage in the second paragraph of "The Silver Key," and the various dropped lines in "The Dunwich Horror" and "The Whisperer in Darkness"—all the result of following the corrupt Arkham House texts.

In sum, the advantages of these editions—the fact that some (but not by any means all) of Lovecraft's best work are again available to the reading public, in attractive covers by Michael Whalen (which, however, have nothing to do either with the stories included in the respective volumes or with Lovecraft's work in general)—are not offset by their manifest deficiencies.

Later in 1982, Ballantine released a large trade paperback, *The Best of H. P. Lovecraft: Bloodcurdling Tales of Horror and the Macabre*. It would be uncharitable to deny that the appearance of this volume was a welcome thing; clearly the time was long overdue for the availability of Lovecraft's greatest short stories and novelettes in a paperback edition. What inspires inevitable reservations in the reviewer is that the job could so easily have been done better.

The selection of Lovecraft's "best" tales was made by Robert Bloch, and the editors at Ballantine apparently respected Bloch's wish to reprint even a few stories from Ballantine's six-volume mass-market paperback series. I do not find this overlap as distressing as others seem to have done; for, although "The Outsider" and "The Shadow over Innsmouth" are indeed available elsewhere, there is every intrinsic justification for including them here, since this volume is clearly intended to serve as a general introduction to Lovecraft for the novice, who can then seek out the lesser fiction elsewhere. Indeed, my only dispute in the actual selection is the inevitable inclusion of "In the Vault" and "Pickman's Model"; the former in particular seems to me in no way representative of Lovecraft's best work, and has no place in a volume of this sort. Conversely, I welcome the inclusion of "The Silver Key" (although it is robbed of its setting in the "Randolph Carter cycle"), since I feel this is a much undervalued tale whose philosophical import will at least prove an antidote to such powerful tales of pure horror as "The Rats in the Walls" (properly leading off the collection) and "The Colour out of Space." Generally the selection closely follows that of the Arkham *House Dunwich Horror and Others* (1963).

I was much impressed by Mr. Bloch's introduction, which displayed both an up-to-date knowledge of Lovecraft scholarship and a profound insight into the appeal of horror in our age. Hence we find an intelligent explanation and dismissal of Derleth's "posthumous collaborations" as far inferior to Lovecraft's own work ("he [Derleth] sounded the notes but lost the music"); a valiant rebuttal to the claim (most recently voiced by Ted White) that horror fiction is written by the "sick" and read by such; a penetrating analysis of

American social mores from the 1920s to the present and their influence upon the popularity of the weird tale; a perceptive discussion of Lovecraft's attitude toward race as typical of his era and social position; and countless other illuminating details. Bloch makes interesting and amusing attempts to relate Lovecraft's work to the present day, as typified by the wry comment: "Wizard Whateley in 'The Dunwich Horror' is not exactly the sort of farmer the Department of Agriculture would approve of, nor would nutritionists endorse the diet of the elderly owner of 'The Picture in the House.'" We can well allow Bloch these moments of fun, for in this article (rather more subdued than is his wont, although still enlivened with wit) he interprets as well as amuses. I find no serious misstatements of fact or misinterpretations of Lovecraft's character (save perhaps Bloch's belief that Lovecraft "craved" fame through his writing; rather, Lovecraft seems to have been heedless of anything but the intrinsic merit of his work); and in conclusion Bloch contrasts the superficiality of the modern horror novel and film (because their creators were nurtured merely upon comic books and other cheap literature) with the permanence and profundity of Lovecraft's own work, raised as he was upon the "classics of the genre." Bloch's introduction to an excellent and thought-provoking summary of Lovecraft's life, work, and reputation.

The major improvement demanded in this volume is the presentation of the texts. The texts used are the same old corrupt versions disseminated by Arkham House, filled with hundreds if not thousands of errors, omissions, and mistranscriptions. One wonders why no effort was made to secure the corrected texts, especially since the entire volume was reset. Another detail which I find personally offensive is the appearance of a rather inane blurb by Stephen King on the front cover. Such could only have been expected, of course, for a volume intended for wide distribution; but Lovecraft's work certainly requires no imprimatur from such a writer as King. The back cover blurbs of individual tales are more than usually inept, and the front cover is emblazoned with a horribly lurid subtitle ("Bloodcurdling Tales," etc.!) which is thankfully not reproduced on the title page. In sum, the benefits offered by a volume certainly outweigh its defects; and no one concerned with spreading of Lovecraft's fame need regret its appearance.

It was only two years later that the first of my corrected editions of Lovecraft's work, *The Dunwich Horror and Others*, appeared from Arkham House; two further volumes of his original fiction were published in 1985 and 1986, followed by an edition of the corrected "revisions" in 1989. The paradoxical thing, however, was that, even though Ballantine was licensing its editions from Arkham House, they have failed to reprint these corrected texts, in spite of the numerous mass-market and trade paperback editions that they issued in the later 1980s and 1990s. One of them—*The Dream Cycle of H. P. Lovecraft: Dreams of Terror and Death* (1995) is particularly egregious. There are so many things wrong with this book that it would take a long commentary to enumerate them. The trouble starts with a bonehead introduction by Neil Gaiman. Consider a single sentence: ". . . he sold one tale—*At the Mountains of Madness*—to John W. Campbell's *Astounding Science Fiction*." There are no fewer than *four* mistakes here: (1) Lovecraft did not himself sell *At the Mountains of Madness* to *Astounding* (it was sold by agent Julius Schwartz); (2) he had *two* stories in the magazine ("The Shadow out of Time" is the other); (3) he did not sell either story to *Campbell*, who didn't like Lovecraft and in any case only took over the magazine two or three years after Lovecraft's stories appeared; and (4) the magazine was at the time called *Astounding Stories*. Think some of these errors are picayune? Well, they are nothing compared to what we find in the text proper. How about the failure to use the corrected texts published by Arkham House, which have been around for a decade or more? How about the inclusion of a work ("The Thing in the Moonlight") that is not by Lovecraft? (This item is still being regularly included in Ballantine editions of Lovecraft, most recently in *Shadows of Death* [2005].) How about the inclusion, in a book purporting to reprint Lovecraft's "dream" stories, of tales that have nothing to do with a dream-world (e.g., *The Case of Charles Dexter Ward*)? How about the omission of the hyphen in *The Dream-Quest of Unknown Kadath* and the diaeresis from "Celephaïs"? How about the omission of "The Unnamable" from a volume that reprints the other four Randolph Carter tales? But a catalogue is too painful. This trade paperback was meant as a companion to the egregiously subtitled *Best of H. P. Lovecraft: Bloodcurdling Tales of Horror and the Macabre* (1982), and was followed next year by another volume (*The Transition of H. P. Lovecraft*) that reprinted (also in corrupt texts) the remaining fiction. I have no idea what purpose this volume was meant to serve aside from lining Ballantine's pockets and revealing the stupidity of their editorial staff.

Then there is *Crawling Chaos: Selected Works 1920–1935* (Creation Press, 1993), edited by James Havoc and with an introduction by Colin Wilson. The most charitable thing one can say about this book is that there there does not seem to be any compelling reason for its existence—aside, of course, from putting a few pence in the pockets of James Havoc, the publisher of Creation Press. But given that Lovecraft is now regarded as being in the public domain in England, one suspects that more such supernumerary volumes might appear in the coming years.

Several questions emerge from the contemplation of this book:
(a) How is it possible that any responsible publisher can be unaware of the existence of the corrected texts of Lovecraft's stories published by Arkham House?
(b) What possible reason can there be in recycling corrupt texts that are already available in paperback in England in marginally better editions from Grafton?

(c) By what conceivable rationale can two stories not entirely by Lovecraft ("The Crawling Chaos" and "The Horror in the Museum") be included in a purported selection of Lovecraft's "best" work, one of which actually lends its name to the title of the volume?

(d) Who on earth (aside from August Derleth) would consider "From Beyond," "The Terrible Old Man," "Herbert West—Reanimator," "The Hound," "What the Moon Brings," and "In the Vault" among Lovecraft's best work?

(e) Who would *not* consider *At the Mountains of Madness* and "The Shadow out of Time" among Lovecraft's best work?

(f) Why is Colin Wilson such a twit?

The last few of these questions are somewhat easier to answer than the others. Colin Wilson's introduction is a slipshod rehash of what he has said before on Lovecraft, and proves that in the thirty-odd years since he encountered him he hasn't learnt much. Boasting that *The Strength to Dream* (1961) represented "the first time anyone had published anything about Lovecraft in England" (ignoring countless reviews of the Gollancz editions since 1951 as well as many articles in science fiction magazines), he goes on to say that in that book "the opinion I express of him is not high." This is an understatement: has Wilson forgotten that he called Lovecraft "sick" and "rejected 'reality'" (whatever that is supposed to mean)? He gives us one more warmed-over version of his simple-minded sociology of horror ("It was obvious that the peculiar violence and morbidity of [Lovecraft's] work was a typical 'outsider''s reaction against a world he found crude and unbearable"), then concludes (on the basis of "The Loved Dead," of all things—Wilson is wholly unaware that this story is a self-parody) that "behind all Lovecraft's work is disguised sexual frustration"! Assuming for the nonce that any of these views are actually worth taking seriously, let us consider them more closely. I have several points to make. (1) I do not find anything particularly "morbid" in Lovecraft's work—certainly, in comparison to writers ranging from Poe to Robert E. Howard to Clive Barker, Lovecraft is normality itself in this regard; (2) Lovecraft, it seems to me, had pretty good reasons for regarding his age "crude and unbearable"—or, to put it a little more rationally, lacking in the aesthetic and social graces he believed should exist in a civilised society; (3) the relation between Lovecraft's alienation from his time and his fiction is vastly more complex than Wilson conceives, and from all the evidence I have studied I do not find any straightforward correlation between the two; (4) I find considerably greater evidence of "morbidity" and sex frustration in Wilson's own work, notably *Ritual in the Dark* and *The Schoolgirl Murder Case*; and Wilson's naive pipe-dream that the human race will someday develop new mental faculties seems pretty indicative of Wilson's own distaste for his age!

Wilson's biographical sketch is full of errors large and small. He repeats his wildly erroneous claim that Providence was "a small provincial town of the type guaranteed to suffocate any person of talent" (hasn't Wilson read any of Lovecraft's paeans to the wonders and beauties of his native city? why would Lovecraft come running back so eagerly to Providence after two years in New York?), says that Lovecraft's Dunsanian tales "sound not unlike Rider Haggard" (!!??), repeats the false story that "The Loved Dead" saved *Weird Tales*, and otherwise produces a mishmash of half-baked sociology and psychoanalysis that would disgrace a freshman in college. One would think that Wilson's recent occultist work has destroyed whatever standing he ever had as a writer or thinker, but Creation Press evidently could not bother to find anyone more capable to write an introduction to Lovecraft.

The answers to questions (d) and (e) above are illuminated in the "Editor's Note" written by James Havoc. He denounces "The Whisperer in Darkness" and "The Shadow out of Time" as "boring . . . over-long, creaky, *misguided* [italics Havoc's] attempts at rationalization—for who can rationalize madness?" and concludes: "Give me ['The Horror in the Museum'] over the sterile contemporaneous ponderings of 'The Shadow out of Time' any day." I scarcely know how to respond to this piece of inspissated ignorance. "The Horror in the Museum" is a parody, Mr Havoc. Like anyone else, Havoc is entitled to his opinions (and, consequently, to his selection of contents for this volume). But he would save himself from looking like a damned fool if he would merely express his preferences and not try to utter ludicrous critical judgments that no one who has finished nursery school is likely to accept. The introduction ends by rhapsodising over the misprinted final line of "The Haunter of the Dark" ("titan blue"!), copied from the old Panther editions. There is, somehow, a weird appropriateness to this. This entire book seems like one long typographical error.

The Cthulhu Mythos

The Cthulhu Mythos is alive and well. We seem to have surpassed the eightieth anniversary of the Mythos, dating from the time when H. P. Lovecraft wrote "The Call of Cthulhu" in the summer of 1926. There seems little need to rehearse the development of the Mythos, either in Lovecraft's own day or thereafter. Suffice it to say that his colleagues—Frank Belknap Long, Clark Ashton Smith, Robert E. Howard, Donald Wandrei, Robert Bloch—made random "additions" to Lovecraft's myth-cycle in his lifetime, creating a shared body of cryptic allusion that appears to have intrigued numerous readers of *Weird Tales*, where most of their stories appeared. But it was August Derleth who, as early as 1931, wanted to give the Mythos the soubriquet

"The Mythology of Hastur" (Lovecraft, in his own whimsical references, did no more than call it "Cthulhuism" and "Yog-Sothothery"), and who, particularly after Lovecraft's death, both encouraged some writers to contribute to the Mythos and discouraged others, sometimes asserting his (or Arkham House's) copyright on the Cthulhu Mythos. Derleth, of course, not only wrote many "tales of the Cthulhu Mythos" himself, but fostered the idea that it occupied a central place in Lovecraft's own work.

But Derleth's own death appears to have opened the floodgates, and during the past three decades a veritable tsunami of Mythos novels, tales, and poems has found its way into professional, semi-professional, amateur, and online venues. In a work of almost frightening erudition, Chris Jarocha-Ernst's *A Cthulhu Mythos Bibliography and Concordance* (Armitage House, 1999), we find a total of 2631 contributions to the Cthulhu Mythos, from authors ranging from Louis G. Abbadie to Lee Clark Zumpe, and even including a work of juvenilia, "The Recurring Doom" (written at the tender age of seventeen, although Jarocha-Ernst tactfully omits the fact), written by one S. T. Joshi. The figure of 2631 may be somewhat misleading: it includes a surprising 211 contributions by Lovecraft himself, but about 160 of these are letters in which Lovecraft (usually in passing and in jest) drops the names of various gods or places he has invented. Nevertheless, Jarocha-Ernst's compilation stands as a monument to the fascination that Lovecraft's mythopoeic imagination has exercised, so that his own writings now constitute only a tiny nucleus within the multifarious and interrelated network of Mythos writings.

I appear to have become known as a rather intemperate opponent of the Cthulhu Mythos, but I suspect that my own motives and perspective have not been properly understood. I am not intrinsically opposed to anyone "adding" to Lovecraft's conceptions, nor do I object to anyone deviating from the themes or framework Lovecraft himself evolved. What I object to is (a) the imputation of erroneous ideas to Lovecraft's own myth-cycle (such as Derleth's notions that Lovecraft's "gods" are elementals, that his tales reflect a battle between "good" Elder Gods and "evil" Great Old Ones, or that his Mythos is parallel to the Christian mythos) and (b) ignorant or unimaginative contributions to the Mythos. Bad writing never serves any useful purpose, and I regret to say that most of the "tales of the Cthulhu Mythos" by writers other than Lovecraft strike me as being intrinsically poor. Someone could write a good story departing widely from Lovecraft's own conceptions (as Colin Wilson did in *The Mind Parasites* or Ramsey Campbell in "Cold Print"), but it does not seem to have been accomplished very often.

It is difficult to speak in small compass about the Cthulhu Mythos. Fortunately, there is no need for me to do so here, since I have just written a substantial treatise entitled *The Rise and Fall of the Cthulhu Mythos*, due out in 2008 from Mythos Books. Some analysis of various Mythos volumes that have been published in the last decade and a half may give some idea of where this curious literary (or subliterary) phenomenon is headed.

Tales of the Cthulhu Mythos (Arkham House, 1990) is labelled a "Golden Anniversary Anthology" commemorating fifty years of Arkham House, and constitutes a revision and expansion of the celebrated volume edited by August Derleth in 1969. Fifty years of Arkham House are indeed worth celebrating, although, unlike Derleth, the current editor, James Turner, does so in an almost excessively self-effacing manner: he fails to list himself as editor of this book (or even as co-editor with Derleth), and, instead of such crudely self-promoting ventures as *Thirty Years of Arkham House,* has contented himself with issuing a catalogue slightly more elaborate than usual and writing a reserved statement about Arkham House on the inside back flap of this book. He has also supplied an introduction, but more on this later.

I am not sure how many readers are aware of the surprising number of complicated critical issues this single book raises. I am not alluding to the reshuffling of the contents of the older anthology (four stories dropped and seven added); I am referring to the whole phenomenon of pastiche and in particular the way in which the Cthulhu Mythos has been imitated. The fundamental question is: Why? Why would any writer want to do this sort of thing? Surely it is clear that only those writers who have nothing of their own to say would stoop to pastiche, since by definition pastiche means the suppression of whatever individuality one might have and the duplication—within fairly narrow and specific parameters—of the tone, style, and substance of one's chosen model. If a story contains too much originality, it stops being pastiche and becomes something else—it is no longer a "Lovecraft pastiche" but is somehow nebulously "Lovecraft-influenced." And this raises a further critical problem: What, exactly, are the criteria to be used in evaluating such stories? They are evidently not to be regarded on their intrinsic merits, but rather on the fidelity with which they recall the originals on which they are based; but what virtue can we find in a work that copies someone else's vision? Just as literary criticism used to be conceived as a sort of second-order product, dependent upon the literature it was discussing (a view to which, incredibly, I still incline, even though it is completely antiquated and is derided by those critics who assert, by gum, that they're writing *literature* and don't you forget it), so pastiche must be regarded as a second-order phenomenon, one that by definition can never rise to the status of the model it strives to emulate.

Let me cease speaking in generalities. My first response on reading this book is a sort of overriding pity for certain writers who have wasted a large portion of their careers imitating something they have not understood. Some of the early stories in this book (those by Frank Belknap Long, Clark Ashton Smith, and August Derleth) make one painfully aware that some of these writers did not even know the rudiments of competent story-writing. These are the stories by adolescents (actual or arrested) written for other adolescents. They are now simply embarrassing. Let us consider a passage from Smith's "The Return of the Sorcerer": "Horror-breeding hints and noisome intuitions invaded my brain. More and more the atmosphere of that house enveloped and stifled me with poisonous, miasmal mystery; and I felt everywhere the invisible brooding of malignant incubi." No doubt Smith was congratulating himself for having successfully imitated Lovecraft's richly textured prose, but it is all bombast and fustian; it literally *means nothing* because it does not arise naturally from the story in which it is embedded. A passage from Derleth's "Beyond the Threshold" gets to the heart of the issue: "there were words—but not words I had ever heard before: a kind of horrible, primeval mouthing, as if some bestial creature with but half a tongue ululated syllables of meaningless horror." I am inclined to deconstruct this, since it is very easy to derive from this passage a meaning entirely opposite to what Derleth intended.

James Turner in his introduction says it all, although he is tactful enough not to single out any individuals: "The Mythos is not a concatenation of facile formulas and glossary gleanings, but rather a certain cosmic state of mind." David E. Schultz puts it another way: Lovecraft does not write about monsters, he writes about people—people who come face to face with their own appalling insignificance in a universe that has no awareness of their existence. *This* is a theme worth writing about; giant bugs and frogs are not.

Robert Bloch finally starts us in a somewhat better direction in "The Shadow from the Steeple" (1950), which shows a genuine extension of Lovecraft's way of thinking: the notion that Nyarlathotep is a sort of symbol for chaos and scientific hubris in impelling scientists to discover greater and greater engines of destruction is powerful, although the execution is rather awkward (I would not be so foolhardy as to try to shoot Nyarlathotep with a revolver). Bloch's "Notebook Found in a Deserted House" (1951) is a still greater success, not in conception but in style: the transposition of Lovecraft's cosmicism into the crude patois of an ignorant country youth is a masterstroke.

Indeed, the halfway point in this book (beginning with Fritz Leiber's "The Terror from the Depths" and continuing with stories by Ramsey Campbell, Colin Wilson, Joanna Russ, Karl Edward Wagner, Philip José Farmer, and Richard A. Lupoff) marks the transition from fiction intended essentially for children and fiction written by and for adults. It can hardly be denied that these latter writers are vastly superior in technique and sophistication to their predecessors. We do have, however, a relapse into juvenility in Brian Lumley's "Rising with Surtsey." Lumley's two contributions in the original anthology, "The Sister City" and "Cement Surroundings," are some of the most spectacularly awful stories ever written, and would have trouble finding their way even into such things as *Chronicles of the Cthulhu Codex* or *Revelations from Yug-*

goth; indeed, "The Sister City" has the merit of being positively the worst story by a professional writer I have ever read. But old Augie couldn't resist the stuff. "Rising with Surtsey" comes from *Dark Things* (1971) and is marginally better, although it is nothing but a cheap rip-off of "The Call of Cthulhu" and "The Shadow out of Time." (I was sorry, incidentally, to note the omission of my friend J. Vernon Shea's "The Haunter of the Graveyard" from the original anthology; it is not much of a story, but hardly worse than some others that were retained. Shea's best Mythos story, of course, is "Dead Giveaway" [1976], even though it has appeared only in the fan press. And I think Turner made a mistake in omitting James Wade's substantial story "The Deep Ones," a skilfully written tale with a delicacy of character portrayal that Lovecraft could not have matched.)

All this raises another troubling issue: not only are most of these stories dependent upon Lovecraft's vision, but many of them do little more than rewrite some of Lovecraft's own tales. Derleth was the most notorious example of this tendency, especially in his contemptible "posthumous collaborations." But I find that Leiber's "The Terror from the Depths," elegant and polished as it is, is not much more than a retelling of (presented in the form of a pseudo-sequel to) "The Whisperer in Darkness." Other stories show no especial advancement upon Lovecraft's conceptions. Stephen King's "Jerusalem's Lot" talks much of *De Vermis Mysteriis*, but is in the end simply a clever story about a giant worm.

Another curious phenomenon we can trace from the beginning to the end of this book—and, hence, from the beginning of Lovecraft's Mythos to the present day—is the unusual degree to which Lovecraft himself enters into these works. This is a more unusual matter than it may appear: to my knowledge, Sir Arthur Conan Doyle does not himself figure in very many Sherlock Holmes imitations. It is, I suppose, a tribute to the vigour of Lovecraft's personality and the near-legendary status he acquired even before his death. On the one hand we have Long's "The Space-Eaters" and Bloch's "The Shambler from the Stars," where characters thinly disguised as Lovecraft appear; then we have stories by Derleth, Bloch, Wilson, and others, where Lovecraft himself is named. This procedure is a little problematical, because it makes Lovecraft a believer and even an authority in the "myths" he was perpetrating. Bloch's "The Shadow from the Steeple" unwittingly echoes the claims of recent occultists when it says of Lovecraft: "For he wrote in parable and allegory, but he wrote the truth." Derleth (again) carries this device to shameless lengths: in "The Dweller in Darkness" he actually refers to *The Outsider and Others*, by H. P. Lovecraft, published by Arkham House last year"!

There can hardly be a doubt that Wilson's "The Return of the Lloigor" and Karl Edward Wagner's "Sticks" are the two most successful stories in this book. Wilson's long story hits home not merely because it brilliantly transports Lovecraft's vision into the contemporary world, but because it represents a fusion of both *Lovecraft's* and *Wilson's* world-views. In making his creatures, the Lloigor, "deeply and wholly pessimistic," Wilson has created a premise that is keenly frightening *to him* (since, as he admits in the preface to *The Philosopher's Stone*, he is "rather cheerful by temperament") and so to us:

> . . . the Lloigor, although infinitely more powerful than men, were also aware that optimism would be absurd in this universe. Their minds were a unity, not compartmentalised, like ours. There was no distinction in them between conscious, subconscious, and superconscious mind. So they saw things clearly all the time, without the possibility of averting the mind from the truth, or forgetting. . . . The Lloigor *lived* their pessimism.

The idea is not fully developed, but it is provocative and compelling.

On the whole, it is difficult to know what to make of this volume and of the whole phenomenon of Cthulhu Mythos imitations. The fact that the latest stories in this book date only from the late 1970s may mean that Turner could not find any worthy Mythos tales written in the last decade (or did not bother to look, something that is entirely understandable). One can sense in his introduction—although clearly it would not have been politic for him to have said so openly—that he has little patience with the whole "Cthulhu & Co." industry that still manages to keep the fan press stocked with new Shudde-M'ells and *Cthaat Aquadingens*; and when he says that a "very real injustice" has been done to the Mythos by all these half-baked imitations by talentless hacks, he is alluding to the spattering of this filthy slime upon Lovecraft's own work and reputation. Again the question is raised: Why bother to write this stuff? Original and skilful writers do not write pastiche; unoriginal and unskilled writers should simply shut up. But this is not likely to happen so long as fans and fan publishers continue to think that Lovecraft is about bugs and frogs and not about people.

It is not entirely clear to me what purpose *Lovecraft's Legacy*, edited by Robert E. Weinberg and Martin H. Greenberg (Tor, 1990), is meant to serve. It is all well and good that a major trade publisher in the field issues a volume commemorating the centennial of Lovecraft's birth—such a volume is bound to be more visible to the general literary community than specialised publications in the academic or small press—but in this instance there seems to be a confusion over what sort of continuity or unity these thirteen stories are supposed to have. It seems as if the editors simply selected thirteen writers at random and asked them to write anything they chose, however irrelevant to Lovecraft or his work it may be. I am reminded of a panel discussion held at the World Fantasy Convention some years ago. The idea was to gather as many living individuals who had known Lovecraft as possible, so that we could gain some first-hand account of Lovecraft the man. Unfortunately, those who knew

Lovecraft in the flesh are a vanishing breed. The panel featured Frank Belknap Long, certainly a logical choice: he had known Lovecraft for many years. Then there was Fritz Leiber: this was OK, since he had at least corresponded (briefly) with Lovecraft, although of course he had never met him. Then there was Manly Wade Wellman: a little problematical, since he had never known Lovecraft but was at least alive during Lovecraft's heyday and knew of him. Finally, to fill out the panel, was Ramsey Campbell: no, he had not known Lovecraft, was not even born during Lovecraft's lifetime, but at least he *liked* Lovecraft's stories and of course was heavily influenced by them. Don Burleson as moderator did the best he could to unite this diverse group of individuals, but the panel was inevitably a little disorganised. Alas, *Lovecraft's Legacy* is far more so.

This would not be an irreparable failing were the stories themselves of literary worth; sadly enough, for the most part they are not. I suppose there is an inherent danger in compiling "original" anthologies: What does one do if writers one has specifically asked to contribute produce deficient work? Can one tactfully reject it? Can one ask for revisions? If so, will those revisions in any way rectify a work that may be flawed in its very conception? If the original anthology is really replacing the magazine as the repository for new short work in the field, then I think all these matters must be thought through if we are not to be inundated with substandard material, even from professional authors.

Lovecraft's Legacy contains, as I see it, two "Cthulhu Mythos" stories (by Graham Masterton and Brian Lumley), two stories that use Lovecraft as a character (by Chet Williamson and Gahan Wilson), one rather interesting imitation of Lovecraft's non-Mythos fiction (by Brian McNaughton), one very bad Poe pastiche (by Mort Castle), five stories that have absolutely nothing to do with Lovecraft (by Ray Garton, Gary Brandner, Hugh B. Cave, Joseph A. Citro, and Ed Gorman), and—the best of the lot—two stories that actually utilise Lovecraft's philosophical conceptions in innovative ways (by Gene Wolfe and F. Paul Wilson). Of these thirteen stories, perhaps three are actually worth reading.

Masterton's and Lumley's stories are textbooks of how not to write Mythos fiction. Masterton's "Will" is so ludicrously implausible that one would be inclined to suspect parody if the author's tone were not so earnest and sincere. We are here presented with a corpse preserved in clay discovered during the excavation of the Globe Theatre in London. Lo and behold! this corpse turns out to be Shakespeare! It transpires that Shakespeare sacrificed his son Hamnet to Yog-Sothoth (or "Y'g Southothe," as Will refers to him) in order to gain literary genius (this is revealed in a letter found in the Shakespeare Library at Stratford-upon Avon—it is amazing that none of the thousands of Shakespeare scholars over the last 400 years ever came upon this document). Masterton imagines that all this illustrates Lovecraft's use of the "documentary" style, but if anything it reveals how far Masterton has to go to achieve the degree of believability that makes Lovecraft's stories so shuddersomely convincing. It is also rather offensive to conceive of Shakespeare's literary genius as anything but the product of his own intellect and imagination. Will needed no help from Outside.

Lumley's "Big 'C'" exemplifies another constant failing of Mythos pastichists: the peculiar, perhaps even unconscious, tendency to plagiarise Lovecraft's own stories instead of writing originally conceived stories. This tale is nothing but a ripoff of "The Colour out of Space" and "The Call of Cthulhu," and has no other *raison d'être* than to stir our memories of those stories. The writing of course is awful, and Lumley's afterword implies that he merely tossed it off and handed it to the editors because he had nothing better on hand.

The tales that use Lovecraft as a character are a little more interesting—but not much. Chet Williamson's "From the Papers of Helmut Hecker" is full of yuk-yuk in-jokes about Lovecraft and the horror field in general, including one hilarious nose-thumbing of Marty Greenberg himself ("these egregious and incestuous theme anthologies . . . about lesbian vampire dolphins"). The plot involves a Pulitzer Prize-winning writer who moves to Providence and produces unwitting Lovecraft pastiches, although he has never read Lovecraft; it turns out the the pet cat he obtained in Providence contains Lovecraft's spirit and is influencing his work. All this is moderately amusing, and an interesting testimonial to Lovecraft's possibly unconscious influence on writers who have not read much of him; but I fear that the story simply lacks subtlety: the portrayal of the arrogant Helmut Hecker is simply too crude and obvious to be effective.

Gahan Wilson's long story "H.P.L." is based on a very old premise: the Cthulhu Mythos is true! This is something that August Derleth was already utilising in his earliest Mythos imitations, and the only novelty that Wilson provides is in resurrecting Lovecraft himself (along with Clark Ashton Smith, who serves as Lovecraft's colleague and manservant [!]). Lovecraft has been saved from death by cancer by appealing to his own gods, who turn out to be the real McCoy. The problem is that Lovecraft, having converted to his own religion of Yog-Sothothery, ends up sounding like a rather harmless lunatic— one of the several lunatics I have met in the past few decades who have similarly been convinced of the reality of Cthulhu and Nyarlathotep. The story goes on too long and ends with Lovecraft's ascension into heaven, carried away in the arms or tentacles of one of the deities he has invoked. With all due respect to Mr Wilson, I think he had better stick to art.

The first truly meritorious story in this book does not occur until page 173. Brian McNaughton's "Meryphillia" is the first tale I have read to employ Lovecraft's ghouls as characters. This is a highly ingenious idea, and McNaughton's use of it in this elegant and atmospheric prose poem, involving a female ghoul who yearns to experience human emotions, is very effective. This story, along with those by Gene Wolfe and F. Paul Wilson, shows that a homage to or pastiche of Lovecraft actually requires some imagination and originality—it is not enough to mimic Lovecraft's prose style or appropriate his ideas without change. Wolfe's "Lord of the Land" is a powerful and subtle story about a scholar trying to track down the origin of the folktale of Anuat, "Opener of the North." There are no explicit Lovecraftian references, but the atmosphere and texture are distinctly Lovecraftian. F. Paul Wilson's story "The Barrens" is oddly similar, involving a researcher investigating the origin of the "pine lights" often seen in the Pine Barrens area of southern New Jersey. In this long and richly detailed story Wilson has succeeded in what C. Hall Thompson (and even Ramsey Campbell in his very early work) failed to do: to transplant Lovecraft's fictional Massachusetts topography to another locale. Wilson regrettably tacks on a rather blunt and obvious message at the end ("Who could find comfort in the knowledge that huge, immeasurable forces beyond our comprehension were out there, moving about us, beyond the reach of our senses?"), something Lovecraft would have left unsaid, but he has at least produced a genuine "Lovecraftian" story that yet retains its own individuality.

I have nothing to say about the other stories in this book. I hate to criticise Mort Castle's "A Secret of the Heart," since Castle was very eloquent in his praise of Lovecraft at a panel discussion at the World Fantasy Convention in Chicago in November 1990; but this Poe pastiche again tends to read like the parody I wish it were. Ray Garton's "The Other Man" is about a love triangle on the astral plane; Gary Brandner's "Ugly" is about a vengeful lizard; "The Blade and the Claw" is one more tiresome reprise of Hugh B. Cave's Haitian voodoo stories; "Soul Keeper" by Joseph A. Citro is about a religious fanatic who locks away a man in order to convert him (the plot seems borrowed jointly from a "Night Gallery" episode and Stephen King's *Misery*); and Ed Gorman's "The Order of Things Unknown" starts effectively as the story of a serial killer, but the psychological portrait of the protagonist is not etched carefully enough to be interesting. It should not be imagined that I am being inconsistent in condemning these stories for not having anything to do with Lovecraft while criticising Masterton and Lumley for an opposite failing. In the first place, the greatest flaw in these stories is simply that they are bad; secondly, Masterton and Lumley deserve censure for imitating Lovecraft too obviously, something Wolfe and F. Paul Wilson have deftly avoided.

I regret to say that the majority of these stories, although they are by supposedly professional authors, are not much above the level of "fan" fiction. What is more, the proofreading and copyediting of this book leave very much to be desired. Aside from an unusual number of typographical errors, we have mistakes that ought never to be made in a publication devoted to Lovecraft.

"Cthulhu" is once misspelled as "Cthulthu." *The Dream-Quest of Unknown Kadath* is twice printed without the hyphen; on page 107 we find "The Color [*sic!*] out of Space," on page 268 "The Colour Out [*sic*] of Space." *De Vermis Mysteriis* is rendered as *De Vermiis Mysteriis*. Joseph Curwen becomes Joseph Curwin. Gahan Wilson (who has made a number of the mistakes just noted) refers to Lovecraft's "novel" *Beyond the Walls* [*sic*] *of Sleep* in which Ooth-Nargai is featured (he is confusing the story "Beyond the Wall of Sleep," which does not mention Ooth-Nargai, with the 1943 Arkham House omnibus *Beyond the Wall of Sleep,* containing stories referring to Ooth-Nargai), and also talks of the resurrected Lovecraft buying back 66 College Street, moving it back to its original location (what happened to the Cyclopean List Art Building, now erected on this site?) and moving his aunts back into the house, when one of the aunts died in 1932, before Lovecraft (in real life) ever moved into the house, and the other in 1941. Did anyone who actually knows something of Lovecraft ever look over this book? These may be cosmetic points, but they are disturbing: there is now no excuse for these errors, when accurate information about Lovecraft is so widely disseminated. I also could have done without a certain amount of self-congratulatory back-patting that goes on in the authors' afterwords to each story, which are supposed to be a tribute to Lovecraft. If this is truly Lovecraft's legacy, then that legacy is a sorry and worthless one indeed; fortunately, his legacy lies elsewhere.

In the early 1990s Chaosium, Inc., creator of a very successful role-playing game based on the "Cthulhu Mythos," began trying to cash in on the interest in this phenomenon by issuing a series of books of Mythos fiction; they enlisted the services of the erudite Robert M. Price, who in recent years has become an even greater drum-beater for the Mythos than his mentor August Derleth ever was. In the process Price has, in the name of revisionism, attempted to rehabilitate Derleth's views on the Mythos. In 1992, in the introduction to *Tales of the Lovecraft Mythos* (Fedogan & Bremer) he defended Derleth's idea that Lovecraft's gods are elementals; with the emergence of *The Hastur Cycle* (Chaosium, 1993) and Robert Bloch's *The Mysteries of the Worm* (Chaosium, 1993), Price has become the definitive cult leader of the Branch Derlethians.

I shall perforce devote most of my attention to the introductions to these two books, since their actual contents are either well-known or negligible. In *Mysteries of the Worm* (an expanded edition of a volume of Bloch's Mythos tales published by Zebra Books in 1981) Price expatiates on what he fancies to be a critical issue of the Mythos: whether the Mythos is the stories themselves (by Lovecraft and others) or a body of lore or legendry upon which the stories draw. Price maintains that the latter view was "fundamental" to the dismantling of the Derleth Mythos by recent critics, but he appears to be in error: it is actually a very minor point, and has nothing to do with Derleth's major blunders (that the Mythos "gods" are elementals; that there are Elder Gods in Lovecraft; that the Mythos is somehow similar to Christianity); I fail to see why Price is so exercised about the matter. He adopts the former view, saying that a legend is nothing more than a story and that we have no other sources for the Mythos than the actual written stories.

This seems a truism, but Price has either failed to understand or has deliberately misinterpreted his opponents (especially Dirk W. Mosig, who has become his favourite whipping-boy). Let us consider an analogy. We know of Greek mythology largely from the various written accounts of it (by Homer, the tragedians, etc.); but no one would say that Greek mythology *is* those stories. There is still a reasonably strong likelihood that people once actually believed in the Greek pantheon, and that the various written accounts are drawing upon some body of legendry. Now no one (not anyone sane, at any rate) actually believes in the "Cthulhu Mythos"; but what Lovecraft was trying to do in his work was to create the *illusion* that he was drawing upon a body of actual lore or legendry. This is all that Mosig meant when making this distinction. In any case, Price has himself unwittingly adopted it in some of his articles, especially in a piece on the genealogy of the Old Ones, which not only extracts information ("lore") from stories out of context but also draws upon Lovecraft's letters.

Price's introduction to *The Hastur Cycle* is a more formidable proposition. He begins by attempting to defend Derleth's preposterous view that Poe, Bierce, and Chambers somehow "contributed" to Lovecraft's Mythos. Price fails to perceive two critical issues: (1) How can a writer "contribute" to something that doesn't exist at the time he is writing? and (2) Do the stories in this volume have any *genuine thematic links* that somehow make it illuminating to group them together? It is manifestly clear that the answer to the first question is no; the second needs further analysis.

This volume is very largely an excuse to reprint "The Whisperer in Darkness" (although Price disingenuously denies "centrality" to it) and other works that randomly mention Hastur, Carcosa, and other such things created by Bierce. But Price has failed to make the distinction (and perhaps fails to understand that there can even be such a distinction) between glancing allusions (as in Chambers and Lovecraft) and actual sequels or follow-ups. When Chambers lifted such terms as Hastur, Carcosa, Hali, and the like from Bierce, he not only did so clearly for the sake of mere allusiveness (none of these terms figure centrally in any stories in *The King in Yellow*) but did so with deliberate inconsistency—not only inconsistency with Bierce but with himself. Price is wrong to state that Hastur is a city in Chambers: in fact, it seems to me from references in the first five stories in *The King in Yellow* that Hastur is sometimes a constellation, sometimes a human being (see "The

Demoiselle D'Ys"), and sometimes merely a name mentioned for its evocative qualities.

So what are we to make of the fact that Lovecraft casually refers to terms from Bierce and Chambers in "The Whisperer in Darkness," and in such a way as to be entirely unclear (deliberately so, of course) what these entities signify? Is it really the case, as Price claims, that "We are seeing Lovecraft's 'The Whisperer in Darkness' as one link in a chain beginning with Bierce and Arthur Machen and continuing on through Derleth, James Blish, Lin Carter, Karl Edward Wagner, and other contemporary writers"? Is there any way in which the fundamental themes and conceptions of "The Whisperer in Darkness" owe anything to Bierce, Chambers, Machen, or anyone else? I am not talking about literary influence. Price attempts to prove some significant influence of Chambers on Lovecraft, but his account merely shows that Lovecraft picked up random bits of detail from Chambers and used them for his own purposes. The influence of Machen on Lovecraft is, of course, more significant, and it is what allows Price to reprint Machen's "Novel of the Black Seal" in the volume, in spite of the fact that there are no mentions of Hastur, Carcosa, etc., in it, which thereby belies his claim that "The Whisperer in Darkness" is not central to the theme of the volume! But I repeat that we do not require even Machen to make sense of "The Whisperer in Darkness," which stands up as an independent entity regardless of passing allusions or literary influence; but this cannot be said for the tales by Blish, Derleth, James Wade, and others in this volume, which are consciously predicated upon the existence of works by Chambers, Lovecraft, and others and cannot be made sense of without them.

I shall have to be mercifully brief in discussing the actual contents of these two books. Price does not seem to understand that the most significant complaints about the post-Lovecraft "Cthulhu Mythos" that modern scholars have is not its purported departure from Lovecraft's own conceptions (any writer who actually has something to say—like Colin Wilson in *The Mind Parasites*—will naturally depart from Lovecraft), but the undoubted fact that the stories themselves are so *bad*. The result is that this inferior work besmirches Lovecraft's own reputation, especially among those careless critics who cannot distinguish between Lovecraft's work and the cheap spinoffs. I suppose it is very elitist and anti-democratic to bring in such a notion as actual literary merit, but there it is. Is anything really to be gained by reading such rubbish as Derleth's "The Return of Hastur"? Richard A. Lupoff's "Documents in the Case of Elizabeth Akeley" purports to be a "sequel" to "The Whisperer in Darkness" but ends up being nothing but a half-baked rewrite of it. Price soberly calls the story "important." James Blish's cryingly stupid attempt to write the play *The King in Yellow* would make a good parody if it were so intended. Blish criticises Lovecraft (his "poetic gifts were feeble at best"), but at least Lovecraft knew the difference between blank verse and free verse, which Blish does not. Lin Carter, adapting Blish's play, at least makes it metrical, but that is all. And in all respect to Robert Bloch, the stories in *Mysteries of the Worm* are an embarrassment: they are not adult reading.

As for *Cthulhu's Heirs*, edited by Thomas M. K. Stratman (Chaosium, 1994), it had me in stitches. I do not know when I have laughed so hard—not, at least, since I read Peter Cannon's *Scream for Jeeves* a few months ago. I have proclaimed that Mr Cannon has distinguished himself as the leading humourist in the Lovecraftian tradition, but he had better look to his laurels, for several items in the present compilation afford him strong competition.

There's only one problem: none of this humour is intended.

Thomas M. K. Stratman starts things off quite well with an introduction entitled "The Nameless Manuscript" (I'm not going to touch that with a ten-foot pole). Nearly every paragraph contains some error or fatuity. Did you know that among the writers whom Lovecraft "openly encouraged . . . to use and add to his creations" were T. E. D. Klein, Ramsey Campbell, and David Drake, all of whom were born after Lovecraft died? And doesn't Stratman know enough to understand that the stories that bear the names Hazel Heald and Zealia Bishop are almost entirely the work of Lovecraft? Stratman concludes his screed with the following: "You will notice that I have chosen not to include a tale of my own in this anthology." (No, I hadn't noticed—only Lin Carter would fail to think it gauche for an anthologist to include one of his own tales.) "Three stories had to be cut, for space, and I chose to cut mine first. It just did not seem right to do it any other way." Big of him.

The one thing Stratman does not do is to explain the "rules" that were evidently sent out to prospective contributors to this anthology. I know them only by hearsay: there was to be no actual imitation of Lovecraft's prose style (thank God for small mercies), and no parodies were to be considered (I won't touch that with a twenty-foot pole). There may have been other stipulations, but they escape me now. The single most horrifying passage in this entire book is Stratman's remark that he received 120 submissions, of which the nineteen original stories and two reprints that comprise the volume are all that remain. I cannot even begin to conceive what was rejected.

Let us deal with the reprints first. Ramsey Campbell's "The Franklyn Paragraphs" is just about the only respectable story in the book—and it is, indeed, a superb piece of work. It is on my (very) short list of genuinely meritorious "additions" to the Mythos (the others: Colin Wilson's *The Mind Parasites*, Fred Chappell's *Dagon*, Fritz Leiber's "The Terror from the Depths," T. E. D. Klein's "Black Man with a Horn," and Basil Copper's "Shaft No. 247"). Why Stratman says that it has "seen only limited publication in his own collection *Cold Print* (Complete Edition)" is beyond me: it is one of the many great tales in *Demons by Daylight* (1973), which, if my eyes deceive me not, is currently in print in a mass-market paperback and pretty widely available. Stratman refers to this and the other reprint—Hugh B. Cave's "The Death Watch" (*Weird Tales*, June–July 1939)—as "rare and welcome additions to this diverse work." Cave's piece may be rare but it is anything but welcome; it only shows what an utter fool a cheap pulp hack can make of himself when trying to "add" to Lovecraft's Mythos.

Stratman does not mention what appears to me the real reason for the inclusion of "The Franklyn Paragraphs": one of the other stories in the volume is Robert M. Price's "Behold, I Stand at the Door and Knock," an avowed sequel to that tale. Here is what Price's story is about: A man buys *The Revelations of Glaaki* and as a result develops a gigantic penis that rips through the body of a Pakistani whore. (But remember, there are no parodies in this book!)

It has always puzzled me that supposed "sequels" or pastiches of Lovecraft seem content merely to be half-baked retellings of the original story, with only the feeblest attempt at any new ideas. In this book, "The Return of the White Ship" by Arthur William Lloyd Breach is little more than a retelling of "The White Ship," and t. Winter-Damon's windy "poem" "Kadath" is nothing more than a retelling of *The Dream-Quest of Unknown Kadath*. The only merit in these pieces is their evocation of the original works; they have no other reason for existence. The one good original story in *Cthulhu's Heirs* is "Those of the Air" by Darrell Schweitzer and Jason Van Hollander, which takes elements of "The Dunwich Horror" and "The Shadow over Innsmouth" and actually elaborates upon them. It is a delicate fusion of Lovecraft's cosmic horror with the "intimate" horror of much recent weird fiction.

Nothing else in this volume is worth even a moment's notice by any adult or intelligent reader. D. F. Lewis and Craig Anthony have written such pitiably confused and directionless narratives (Anthony's is a drama, no less) that one wonders how the authors themselves got through them. Lewis is evidently under the impression that obscurity is equivalent to genius, unaware that in most cases obscurity is equivalent to—obscurity. He is the most profoundly sophomoric writer I know. Scott David Aniolowski has invented a new Mythos god—Q'yth-az—while Crispin Burnham (a nice guy who has no business doing anything but editing *Eldritch Tales*) has transferred Dunwich country to Kansas. The only merit in Joe Murphy's "1968 RPI" is in its relatively recherché Lovecraftian references (one character is named Nathicana), while Marella Sands creates amusement (not entirely at her own expense) by making Nyarlathotep a woman in a virtual-reality scenario. Her tale almost approaches respectability.

"Pickman's Legacy" by Gordon Linzner comes pretty damn close to parody (and not of the self- or unintentional kind) in my view, and I'm surprised it made it into this book. It is a light amusement and works as a piece of Lovecraftian humour. Victor Milán's "Mr. Skin" begins quite promisingly by transferring the Lovecraftian atmosphere to the gritty slums and whorehouses of Los Angeles, but lapses into hysteria and bombast at the end. And I'm not giving away anything by saying that Dan Perez's "The Likeness" is about a tattoo that comes to life: this is telegraphed almost from the first page.

But enough is enough. Making fun of the contents of *Cthulhu's Heirs* is like shooting fish in a barrel; there's really no sport in it. One could even amuse oneself with the title (*Cthulhu's Errors?*). It is certainly of interest that almost no "name" writers are in this book (doesn't Chaosium pay enough?)—not that they do much better with this subject-matter, as everything from Stephen King's "Crouch End" to the complete works of Brian Lumley are sufficient to attest. The feeling that I came away with after reading this book is a sort of objective pity over the follies of the human species. I still do not know what would possess anyone to write a "Cthulhu Mythos" story; surely there must be something better to do with one's time—like staring off into space.

The sheer quantity of recent Mythos fiction makes the task of covering it difficult if not impossible. The books that have come my way are the following: Stanley C. Sargent's *Ancient Exhumations* (Mythos Books, 1999); W. H. Pugmire's *Dreams of Lovecraftian Horror* (Mythos Books, 1999); Joseph S. Pulver, Sr.'s *Nightmare's Disciple* (Chaosium, 1999); and E. P. Berglund's *Shards of Darkness* (Mythos Books, 2000). I have no idea whether these books are representative or not, but they do feature the work of several writers currently prominent in fostering the Mythos.

I am sorry to say that none of these books strike me as satisfactory. I was particularly disappointed by the lacklustre and clumsily written tales in Sargent's collection, for I know he can do better. His story "The Black Brat of Dunwich" (*Cthulhu Codex* #10, May 1997) is a genuinely clever deconstruction of Lovecraft's "The Dunwich Horror," and I am surprised it was not included in his volume, as it is far and away superior to any of the tales that actually were included.

As for Berglund, all he can claim is an E for effort. The first story in his volume, "The Feaster from the Stars," would be an excellent Mythos parody if it were not so tedious and long-winded. We are introduced to a baleful deity, nicknamed That Which Relentlessly Waits Outside—which immediately made me think of this redoubtable entity's cousin (or is it half-brother?), That Which Patiently Twiddles Its Thumbs on the Back Door of the Cosmos. Berglund is, prototypically, He Who Cannot Write His Way Out of a Paper Bag. Consider this passage: "He felt for the protrusion that would open the entrance for him. Feeling all over the plaster surface, he could not find any evidence of the protrusion that opened the fireplace entrance." In one story he begins six consecutive sentences, over two paragraphs, with "He . . ."

In many ways Pugmire's little book is the best of the lot, even though it is by far the slimmest. In many of his brief tales Pugmire reveals a genuine flair for poetic prose and the creation of a dreamlike atmosphere of shimmering fantasy. It is not only my prejudice that leads me to think that the best of his stories are the ones that mention no Mythos names, places, or deities.

The most superficially imposing book under consideration is Pulver's *Nightmare's Disciple*, a gargantuan 400-page novel. We are here concerned with one Gregory Bradshaw Marsh, a resident of Schenectady, N.Y., who becomes a serial killer as a means of reintroducing into the world the dreaded entity Kassogtha, evidently some relative or former spouse of Cthulhu. The mingling of the serial killer novel with the Cthulhu Mythos is a potentially interesting idea, especially as we are held in suspense throughout the novel as to whether Marsh is merely a lunatic who has become so fascinated with Lovecraftian fiction that he now believes it to be fact, or whether there actually is such an entity named Kassogtha whose return he will effect. I am giving away nothing by saying that the latter hypothesis proves to be correct.

What cripples *Nightmare's Disciple*, however, is its unrelenting, appalling prolixity. The one thing a novel of this sort needs is narrative drive and pacing; and it is the one thing it lacks. It begins finely, but rapidly gets so bogged down in tedious and windy expositions of the Mythos by various characters (in particular a self-styled expert named Cosmo who runs a horror bookshop) that the core of the plot—Marsh's successive murders and the efforts of a police detective, Chris Stewart, to solve them—is frequently all but forgotten. This is not a work of the Cthulhu Mythos, or even the Derleth Mythos, but the Kitchen Sink Mythos. Every Mythos name that could possibly be thrown in is thrown in, as in the following catechism that Marsh undergoes in his youth: "Can you name the three mates of Cthulhu? Which one is dead? Which was abandoned on Xoth? Do you know of the ancient priests Tchotghtguerele, Hnas-ry-Gij, Kreuhn, Ankh-f-n-Khonsu, or Varnsenda-Rasu? Have you read Clithanus' *Confessions*, the *Celaeno Fragments*, or the *Occultus of Hierarchus?*"

It is of interest that Pulver resolutely adheres to the Elder Gods/Great Old Ones dichotomy in this novel. His character Cosmo initially attributes this view to Lovecraft; later he grudgingly acknowledges that there actually is no battle between Elder Gods and Great Old Ones in Lovecraft, although he can't bring himself to admit that there are in fact *no* Elder Gods in Lovecraft at all, but that they were entirely an invention of Derleth. The rationale for preserving this dichotomy is of some interest. Chris says at one point: "I sure hope the school of the Mythos you told me about, the one that throws out Derleth's war between the Elder Gods and the GOO [sic!], is wrong. I'd hate to be some puny little human facing these monsters without hope of divine intervention, or without the Elder Sign." In this, Pulver exactly echoes Derleth's own motivations for inventing the Elder Gods: he could not endure Lovecraft's unflinchingly bleak vision of the universe, so he had to introduce a radical alteration into it to make it more palatable.

Once again, I emphasise that I do not criticise Pulver merely for writing about the Elder Gods, or introducing any other revision of Lovecraft's Mythos. All I say is that the result is a little less than scintillating. Is it more compelling to envision us "puny" humans as the helpless pawns of immensely greater forces who care nothing for us, or as the centre of a cowboys-and-Indians struggle between one set of morally "good" entities and another set of morally "evil" entities? Which one accords more with the actual state of the universe rather than the vain hopes and wish-fulfilment fantasies of the great mass of humanity?

And yet, Pulver is a good writer. When not riding his Mythos hobby-horse, he can produce such passages of quiet eloquence as this, describing his ageing police detective: "Thirty-two somehow became forty-three as he watched the years pass—some in the bottle, all in pain—leaving few dreams and no illusions. Now the files and photos spread across the desk in his den were fast removing what little remained of his battered belief in human decency." With more prose like this, and with a little less piling on of the Mythos, Pulver could do highly creditable work.

It is possible that the Cthulhu Mythos might best be expressed in verse. The compressed, allusive, figurative language of poetry can mask the potentially absurd or ridiculous elements of the Mythos in a haze of symbolism and metaphor. Of course, it takes a poet of high calibre to pull off the feat, and Lovecraft himself was not always up to the task. One poet who might be is Ann K. Schwader, whose *The Worms Remember* (Hive Press, 2001) presents some of the most powerful weird verse I have read in a long time. Her focus is not exclusively on the Mythos; instead, she takes the whole of Lovecraft's work as her springboard. Schwader works largely in standard metres and rhyme-schemes; in fact, the few examples of free verse that are included in the book are almost uniformly her poorest. She has specialised in the sonnet, and it is not going too far to say that a number of these could easily take their place with Lovecraft's own *Fungi from Yuggoth*. There is too much good work in this book to cite any individual poem or poem-cycle. Suffice it to say that Schwader's verse is superbly crafted and richly evocative; it will repay many rereadings.

Some of the Mythos tales I have discussed have featured liberal doses of unintentional humour. A work of Mythos humour that is decidedly intentional is Mark McLaughlin's piquant little booklet, *Shoggoth Cacciatore and Other Eldritch Entrees* (Delirium Books, 2000). We are told on the back cover that McLaughlin "is a regular participant in the World Horror Con Gross-Out Story-Reading Contest, and is currently the reigning champion"—a point not in his favour, if you ask me. But I am much relieved to report that McLaughlin does not rely merely on "gross-out" to achieve his effects: the fellow can actually write, and he writes with verve, pungency, and wit. Several of the items in this book are mere sketches or vignettes, but the most substantial entry (or entrée), "She's Got the Look," involves a gang of supermodels conspiring to usher in the Great Old Ones' return to world domination. But this item is exceeded by the book's final contribution, "The Brouhaha of Cat-hula," probably the single most outrageous example of Lovecraftian humour I have ever come upon. You will have to read it for yourselves to figure out what that title means.

At this point it would seem to be beating a dead horse for me to make any extensive comments on *The Children of Cthulhu: Chilling New Tales Inspired by H. P. Lovecraft*, edited by John Pelan and Benjamin Adams (Ballantine, 2002). And yet, I cannot forbear commenting on at least a few specimens in this book of all-original stories, mostly by young writers.

Let me state at the outset that, if my overall response to this anthology is not very enthusiastic, the fault cannot be placed entirely on the shoulders of the editors. I know nothing about Benjamin Adams, but John Pelan's astuteness as a writer, editor, and publisher can hardly be questioned. Why, after all, he has published two of my own books with Midnight House. I am therefore compelled to assume that the stories in this volume represent the best of a bad lot, and that what was rejected was, on the whole, even worse. One begins to wonder whether it is even possible to write a good "Cthulhu Mythos" story today.

I am obliged to single out Richard Laymon's "The Cabin in the Woods" for especial dispraise. Here we have what purports to be some kind of imaginative extension or elaboration upon Lovecraft's "The Whisperer in Darkness," but proves instead to be merely a crude and incompetent rewrite of that story. No new ideas, no new perspectives (except, perhaps, a clumsy attempt at depicting interpersonal conflict) can be found here. Laymon has a particular penchant for what might be called onomatopoeic horror: "I listened and heard a quiet, heavy *whup . . . whup . . . whup . . .*" and later: "A huge shape of blackness descended upon Arthur: *KRAWBOOM!*" (Wasn't there once a breakfast cereal with that name? Er, no, that was Kaboom.)

Why is this story in this book? It is not merely sub-professional; it is wellnigh subliterary. Laymon is certainly not to be classed with the mostly young, hip writers who largely fill this volume. I can only assume that his celebrity and reputation—the basis of which continues to befuddle me, since what little of his work I have read has been uniformly mediocre—impelled his inclusion in a book that is otherwise somewhat short on name recognition. (I am aware that Laymon has now shuffled off this mortal coil and is therefore not able to defend himself—as, in life, he was rather vociferously inclined to do, since he apparently did not take criticism very well. But no doubt his legions of devoted fans will come to his defence by raining imprecations upon my head.)

No other story in the book is quite as bad as Laymon's—or is bad in quite the same way. I could have done without the precious and pretentious stories by China Miéville and Caitlín R. Kiernan. "A Victorian Pot Dresser" by L. H. Maynard and M. P. N. Sims is a hackneyed tale of a tentacled monster and a virgin sacrifice. Tim Lebbon's "The Stuff of the Stars, Leaking" is the pointless story of an unexplained tentacled sea-monster that has apparently killed off the protagonist's wife. Poppy Z. Brite's "Are You Loathsome Tonight" has no relevance to Lovecraft at all, being instead a boring story about Elvis's last days; it concludes with a quotation from "Supernatural Horror in Literature" that has not the slightest connexion with the narrative. In Yvonne Navarro's "Meet Me on the Other Side" we learn that Lord Dunsany's Bethmoora is apparently somewhere in Arizona. Matt Cardin's "Teeth" is a lame attempt at mimicking the philosophical horror of Lovecraft's best narratives. Then there is Paul Finch's "Long Meg and Her Daughters," in which a monster attacks the protagonist in a library—by hurling books at him. In Weston Ochse's "A Spectacle of a Man" we are presented with "visions of Christ on a cross with tentacles"!

But the volume is by no means a total loss. Indeed, the editors' own story ("That's the Story of My Life") is one of the better ones in the book—a grim tale of a weird family in Arkham. James Van Pelt's "The Invisible Empire" is the poignant account of a Colorado mining town; its exact relationship with Lovecraft (aside from its citation of the *Necronomicon*, under the erroneous translation *Book of the Names of the Dead*) remains unclear, but it is a fine piece of writing. Meredith L. Patterson's "Principles and Parameters," perhaps the best tale in the book, is an effective tale that combines the scholarly erudition of Lovecraft (a professor of linguistics attempts to translate the Pnakotic manuscripts) with the Lovecraftian theme of ghouls.

And yet, even some of the better stories are marred with irritating flaws. W. H. Pugmire's "The Serenade of Starlight" displays its author's customary flair for prose-poetry, but proves upon analysis to be little more than a partial rewrite of "The Call of Cthulhu" and "The Shadow over Innsmouth." Brian Hodge's "The Firebrand Symphony" is a long and complex tale that brings "The Shadow over Innsmouth" vaguely—but only vaguely—to mind; but it is spoiled by an appalling use of contractions: *would've, could've, might've,* etc. This may be acceptable in dialogue, but in expository prose it is unacceptably slangy and slipshod. Was there no copy editor at Ballantine who had the critical judgment to fix this? Apparently not, since Paul Finch's repeated use of the solecism "Alright" also passed everyone's notice without, apparently, a second thought.

Lovecraft as a Character in Fiction

Lovecraft as a character in fiction has a very long history; in fact, we could date it so early as 1921, when Edith Miniter wrote a story, "Falco Ossifracus: By Mr. Goodguile," which features a thinly disguised version of Lovecraft. Didn't Vincent Starrett say that Lovecraft was his own most fantastic creation? The image of the gaunt, lantern-jawed horror writer, sleeping during the day and writing at night, often mislabelled as an "eccentric recluse," has definitively become a pop culture icon. However inaccurate the popular conception of Lovecraft may be, it fits our conception of what a writer of cosmic horror tales should be, and the genuine force of his personality—as exhibited both among those who knew and met him for decades as well as among those who were lucky enough to receive his interminable epistles—has made Lovecraft a larger-than-life figure.

One of the most distinctive treatments of Lovecraft as a fictional character can be found in Peter Cannon's thoroughly enjoyable short novel *Pulptime* (Weirdbook Press, 1984). The careers of the fictional Sherlock Holmes and the very real H. P. Lovecraft overlap sufficiently such that one wonders why an adventure conjoining them—as Holmes has been conjoined to Freud, Jack the Ripper, and other notables of the turn of the twentieth century—has not been written before now. The very idea of mingling fact and fiction in this way is essentially a light-hearted one, and this is what we get from this engaging work.

Peter Cannon's articles on Lovecraft have graced the pages of *Lovecraft Studies*, *Nyctalops*, *Crypt of Cthulhu*, and other journals; and the keen follower of the Cannon canon will have observed that he has frequently considered the possible influence of the Sherlock Holmes tales on Lovecraft. Some time ago Cannon ventured into fiction with the fine novelette, "The Madness out of Space" (serialised in *Eldritch Tales*), one of the best Lovecraftian pastiches of recent years; now he introduces the aged and goateed Sherlock Holmes into the seedy tenements of Brooklyn where, by coincidence, H. P. Lovecraft was dragging out his cheerless "New York Exile" early in 1925. Eventually all the members of the Kalem Club—Rheinhart Kleiner, Samuel Loveman, James F. Morton, Arthur Leeds, and especially Frank Belknap Long, the ostensible narrator of the tale—become involved in an adventure that takes them to dubious speakeasies, spiritualist sessions, and finally to the tunnels riddling the underside of Red Hook where swarms of rat-faced aliens carry out their nefarious practices to the lapping of oily subterranean rivers....

If the plot sounds not a little like "The Horror at Red Hook," it is no accident; for one of Cannon's (tongue-in-cheek) goals in this tale is to provide the supposed genesis for that story: it was, we learn, nothing more than a slightly fictionalised version of this "real" adventure into which Lovecraft and his friends were drawn by the great British detective—although, at Holmes's own suggestion, he himself was left out of the finished version. Cannon perhaps contrives rather too many correspondences between his tale and "Red Hook," and there are times when *Pulptime* reads like an affectionate parody of Lovecraft's story.

Indeed, what we have here is not a story but a vast "in-joke": the events of the tale, exciting and skilfully told as they are, serve merely as excuses for introducing as many "tips of the hat" to knowledgeable Lovecraftians as possible; nearly every utterance by Lovecraft in this story is derived from his tales or letters, or from memoirs about him. There is, certainly, no question of Cannon's thorough research into the "historicity" of his tale: when he casually notes that Lovecraft was cheerful because he had "found earlier that day a volume of Bulwer Lytton in a second-hand bin for just 10¢," he knows that only a few readers will remember the passage in Lovecraft's letter to his aunt (20 May 1925; *Selected Letters* 2.7–8) where he announces this exact fact. Such an example could be multiplied on almost every page; it is as if Cannon has written a sort of quiz for Lovecraftians, challenging them to identify as many recondite allusions of this sort as they can. Lovecraft's associates, too, are described, although briefly, with a wealth of accurate detail, both as to their occupations and as to their personal characteristics.

But, again, an in-joke is not a story. However entertaining these references are to learned Lovecraftians, one misses the sheer narrative skill that Cannon displayed so well in "The Madness out of Space": the nearest analogy to *Pulptime* is if "The Battle That Ended the Century" had been written out to novel length. It is almost as if *Pulptime* preceded "The Madness out of Space" in date of composition; for the former is much more derivative and much less independent a work than the latter.

But perhaps comparison of these two works is unjust, for their purposes are clearly distinct: "The Madness out of Space" is a "serious" pastiche, while the very premise of *Pulptime*—the collaboration of Sherlock Holmes and H. P. Lovecraft—relegates it to the borderland of parody. And as a parody—or, shall we say, a *jeu d'esprit*—it succeeds supremely well: there is something an every page to elicit a smile or chuckle, and the concluding portion of the narrative does succeed in raising tension somewhat; while the multiple twists of the climax confirm the final utterance put into Holmes's mouth: "It is usual that the audience comes away all the more satisfied for having been so thoroughly mystified." In sum, this book can easily provide a few hours of harmless entertainment to the Lovecraft fan, while it will keep the wheels of the Lovecraft scholar's mind turning rapidly and pleasurably. And since Cannon clearly had no loftier aims than this for his delightful tale, we can uphesitatingly pronounce it a success.

Scream for Jeeves (Wodecraft Press, 1994) may not actually involve Lovecraft as a character, but it is so delightful that I cannot pass up the chance to discuss it. In this slim book Cannon presents three stories simultaneously parodying Lovecraft and P. G. Wodehouse, along with a lengthy and substantial, if a trifle chatty and informal, rumination on the tenuous interrelations between Lovecraft, Wodehouse, and Sir Arthur Conan Doyle (Doyle has been thrown in on the rather slim excuse that a "Mr Altamont"—the pseudonym used by Sherlock Holmes in "His Last Bow"—appears in the third story). There are not many individuals who have expertise in all three of these authors; in particular, I suspect that the Lovecraftian community is woefully ignorant of Wodehouse. If so, the loss is entirely theirs; for there is no more wholesome humourist in literary history. As a result, in spite (or perhaps because) of the lack of scholarly rigour in this concluding essay, almost everyone is likely to learn something about one or the other of these authors.

But it is the stories themselves—the first two of which appeared previously in *Crypt of Cthulhu* under the pseudonym "H. P. G. Wodecraft"—that are the centrepiece of this perfectly delightful book. All three of them—"Cats, Rats, and Bertie Wooster," "Something Foetid," and "The Rummy Affair of Young Charlie"—are written in accordance with the same framework or methodology: Cannon has retold a given Lovecraft story in the first-person voice of Wodehouse's rather dim-witted but engaging man-about-town, Bertie Wooster, and his "gentleman's gentleman," the imperturbable Jeeves. The result is screamingly funny. The "Rummy Affair" begins "Life is a hideous thingummy," and proceeds to retell a portion of *The Case of Charles Dexter Ward* (with a little of "The Music of Erich Zann" thrown in); the other two tales present fractured versions of "The Rats in the Walls" and "Cool Air" (with a more than cameo appearance by Randolph Carter).

It is difficult to analyse humour—a point made by Cannon in his afterword when he notes the appalling dearth of academic criticism on Wodehouse, who is surely one of the great writers of our time—but after having read these stories twice through I believe I am finally getting an inkling of the surprisingly complex feat Cannon has performed here: he is simultaneously parodying Lovecraft *à la* Wodehouse and parodying Wodehouse *à la* Lovecraft. Only those relatively few readers who know both authors can possibly "get" all the jokes, especially as so many of them go by so fast. There are more laughs per square inch in these stories than in any humorous material I have ever read in my life. My feeling is, however, that Wodehouseans may be left a little in the dark at some of the humour, which depends on a fairly detailed and sophisticated knowledge of Lovecraft. Perhaps not even many Lovecraftians would catch this reference, as Bertie's Aunt Agatha chides him for his failure to settle down and marry: "It is celibate bachelors like you, Bertie, who make a person realise why the human race will have to give way to the hardy coleopterous species." And Wodehouseans will surely be puzzled at some of the dishes Bertie orders at dinner with Charlie Ward—*ris de Dhole à la Financière* and *velouté aux fleurs de Tcho-tcho*.

If many of the best "lines" in these stories are taken directly from Lovecraft (the trick being to insert them in ludicrous contexts), Cannon has nevertheless managed a breathtakingly skilful pastiche of Wodehouse in the general narration. Wodehouse is so difficult an author to imitate that few have even made the attempt; but Cannon has plunged boldly in and performed the feat. (Lovecraft is also difficult to imitate, but many would-be pastichists have failed to realise it.) In a sense, of course, Cannon is aided by the fact that there is a sly undercurrent of the comic running through even the most chillingly horrific of Lovecraft's tales; in such a work as "Cool Air" the comic ("More—more!") rises pretty close to the surface.

By all means rush out and pick up *Scream for Jeeves*, but be prepared to suffer acute pain in the head, throat, stomach, or whatever other part of the body is affected by excess laughter. Like the best of Wodehouse (and unlike most other examples of Lovecraftian humour), these tales can be read over and over again with increasing enjoyment. Jason Eckhardt's piquant illustrations provide the finishing touch to the most wholesomely entertaining book to appear on the Lovecraftian horizon in many years.

In the ten years following the appearance of L. Sprague de Camp's *Lovecraft: A Biography* and Willis Conover's *Lovecraft at Last* (both 1975) little advance was made in the probing of Lovecraft's life. His surviving friends seem to have told us all they know, and it is left to independent scholars to ferret out what secrets they can from extant written sources. It is just this sort of research that Richard A. Lupoff, in *Lovecraft's Book* (Arkham House, 1985), has conducted in unearthing a spectacular but hitherto completely unknown series of events in which Lovecraft became involved in 1927. The Freedom of Information Act allowed Lupoff to have access to now declassified papers concerning Lovecraft's embroilment with a Nazi plan for the overthrow, both moral and military, of the United States.

This plan, masterminded by Kurt Lüdecke, a close associate of Hitler, would have involved Lovecraft's writing a treatise, *New America and the Coming World Order*, expounding Lovecraft's views on Aryan supremacy and the need to preserve the racial purity of the nation. But the writing of this book—which, coming from one of untainted old American ancestry, would carry much greater weight than if written by a German-American or, worse still, some member of an alien stock—would be only the intellectual patina of a much more nefarious plot to invade the United States by means of secret underwater stations from which thousands of German soldiers would flood the American coastline, Atlantic and Pacific.

It is not remarkable that this whole bizarre affair has been kept out of most of Lovecraft's correspondence: Lovecraft alluded to it only briefly in random letters to Clark Ashton Smith and Robert E. Howard when he asked them to pursue some leads in the matter; while certain letters to Vincent Starrett—who was of some importance in ultimately freeing Lovecraft from the clutches of the Germans—seem not to have been preserved. This volume, however, contains a key letter by Starrett that Lupoff has discovered. No doubt Lovecraft was debriefed by the U.S. government after the whole incident was over, and was asked not to mention it to anyone; and yet, as Lupoff notes in conclusion, it is clear that the affair provided the nucleus for "The Shadow over Innsmouth," where the purely political and military events here recorded were transformed by Lovecraft's literary alchemy into a tale of cosmic horror.

Certain details in the narrative, however, might raise suspicions as to its reliability. I will require considerable documentation before believing that the teetotaler Lovecraft, purely upon Starrett's insistence, had wine, brandy, and two martinis in the course of one evening. Lovecraft imbibes frequently in this book, and there is also a considerable amount of mastication going on—as Lovecraft once remarked, "how these birds do *eat!*" More seriously, why is it that Lovecraft, although at the end of the events he discovers the evils of Nazism, begins praising Hitler unabashedly in the 1930s?

Still, these questions aside, *Lovecraft's Book* is a major contribution to Lovecraft biography. Parts of it read as excitingly as a novel, and the photographs gracing the volume call for high praise in themselves—each has been selected to illustrate the events of the chapter which it heads, and we find rare and lovely snapshots of Providence, Marblehead, and the leading characters of this drama. This work is bound to cause controversy—for, in spite of an impressive bibliography at the rear of the volume, there is no documentation for the specific incidents related here—but we are confident that an important and mysterious episode in Lovecraft's life, and in the political and social history of his time, has been elucidated.

[P.S. (2008): This review was written at the urging of James Turner, editorial director of Arkham House, who wished me to foster the illusion that Lupoff's book was a true account of a secret chapter in Lovecraft's life. I have considerable reservations about the overall thrust and quality of the book, as I outlined to Lupoff himself in a long letter I wrote to him when he let me read the unabridged ms. of the book, about twice as long as the version published by Arkham House. This unabridged version has now been published under its original title, *Marblehead* (2007).]

Informed readers know Kenneth W. Faig, Jr, as perhaps the most distinguished—and certainly the most unassuming—of Lovecraft's biographers; a man who brings not only the highest scholarly standards but empathy and psychological insight to the study of Lovecraft the man. Very few, however—only those shrinking members of the Esoteric Order of Dagon amateur press association, where *Tales of the Lovecraft Collectors* (Moshassuck Press, 1989; Necronomicon Press, 1995) appeared serially from 1979 to 1988—know of Faig as a fiction writer. It is remarkable how many leading Lovecraft scholars have tried their hand—successfully—at fiction: the list begins with Donald R. Burleson, Will Murray, Peter Cannon, Robert M. Price, and Jason C. Eckhardt, and could be extended further. Even Marc A. Michaud and I have been known to pen a few tales. I do not know why I found it surprising that Faig should be of this number; but this made my delight all the more pronounced as I read this slim but substantial volume.

Tales of the Lovecraft Collectors fits a little anomalously into that already anomalous subgenre where Lovecraft himself is featured as a character. Faig's contribution is anomalous because Lovecraft himself never actually appears except via the letters or accounts of those who have met him. *Tales of the Lovecraft Collectors* is a complex series of four tales unified by the narrative voice of one David Parkes Boynton, a wealthy Fall River industrialist who knew Lovecraft slightly and in fact turns out to be a cousin of Lovecraft's. His diary—"edited" by Faig—tells of his encounter with several Lovecraft collectors, and carries us from Mexico to England to Providence, and along the way we learn several curious tidbits of information: the whereabouts of the ms. of "The Shadow out of Time"; the originals of Lovecraft's Juan Romero and Nyarlathotep; the Druidic leanings of Lovecraft's father; and, most surprising of all, the daughter Lovecraft begat from a pretty Italian girl he met at age nineteen. It is all good fun, made all the more so by Faig's richly textured style—interlaced by many documents and cameo appearances by August Derleth, R. H. Barlow, and other real people—and keen insight into Lovecraft's character and motives. One passage in particular I found deeply moving, where Lovecraft tells of a pestiferous occultist who is maintaining the esoteric "truth" of his work:

> "Remember, cousin, the dreams of dreamers leave their property once they have been set down on paper. They can easily become the common stock of charlatans who pretend that dreams are real. But life is real, not dreams. My parents are both dead and my wife and I, I fear, have permanently separated. She wanted a divorce, but a gentleman does not divorce his wife without cause. My dreams and the literary friends who share them are to a large extent my life today. Otherwise, I have only these familiar scenes, my home, and my aunt to relieve my loneliness. So, cousin, grant me liberty of my dreams. If lesser minds abuse them, pay no heed. It will always be so."

All students of Lovecraft will derive both pleasure and edification from this work. In the final analysis, one character's description of Boynton's diary could apply to the work as a whole: "I think a Lovecraftian who read it through would thoroughly enjoy it. It has a ring of authenticity to it. Of course I realize that it's fiction, but I think this fellow . . . must have had a special background to write it."

Proceeding from Faig's sensitively and intelligently written work to *Shadows Bend*, by David Barbour and Richard Raleigh (Ace, 2000), is a prototypical descent from the sublime to the ridiculous. This novel recounts how, in the summer of 1935, Lovecraft receives from his friend Samuel Loveman a Kachina doll representing one of the gods of the Hopi or Navajo tribes, and finds that the object plagues him with nightmares—in particular, a part that falls out of the doll's head, which Lovecraft dubs the Artifact. Believing that he is being stalked by unseen enemies, Lovecraft feels he has no choice but to take a long bus ride down to Cross Plains, Texas, to team up with his epistolary friend Robert E. Howard, to put down whatever horror has been unleashed by the Artifact. The two writers take a long drive to Auburn, California, to meet Clark Ashton Smith (who, conveniently enough, has picked up a copy of the *Necronomicon* "in Latin cipher" [!]), picking up along the way a whore (!!) named Glory McKenna. All along they are pursued by "odd men" in a black sedan (shoggoths, evidently) who cause a certain amount of annoying trouble, and in the end, after visiting Smith (who characteristically seduces Glory, much to Howard's outrage), our three voyagers enter a subterranean cave in New Mexico and put an end to some nameless terror that (naturally) is about to overwhelm mankind.

This does not sound like a very prepossessing theme for a novel, and it isn't. It is never made clear what exactly is the threat that is hanging over Lovecraft or humanity, nor how exactly our valiant writers manage to suppress it. What is more, for large parts of this windy book nothing much happens: we are evidently to be enthralled merely by witnessing the revered Lovecraft and Howard engaging in mundane activities, like eating at a restaurant, driving in a car (there's lots of this), or preparing a meal at Smith's house.

As for the portrayal of Lovecraft, it can only be called fabulously inept. Within the first 40 pages we find that Lovecraft wears a bow tie (which he never wore), uses a cane (which he never used), confesses to "an irrational fear of insects" (which he never had), and admits to being in Providence in early August 1935 (he was in fact in Florida). We then see Lovecraft repeatedly eating cans of pork and beans (purchased in a grocery store in Texas) *in a restaurant*, causing Howard great mortification. This is all too silly. Lovecraft was entirely capable of purchasing a humble meal in a restaurant, especially as it cost little more than a quarter in 1935. More grotesquely, Lovecraft eats pork and beans *for breakfast*, when I thought everyone knew that his breakfasts invariably consisted of doughnuts (or, in a pinch, vanilla wafers) and cheese. Much later, Lovecraft announces his weight as 160 pounds, when in fact his weight during the last ten years of his life never exceeded 144.

All these things may seem picayune, but they lend increasing weight to the supposition that Messrs. Barbour and Raleigh have no idea what they are talking about. The authors effusively praise L. Sprague de Camp for his biographical work on both Lovecraft and Howard, but even de Camp did not make errors like these, or the more serious ones about Lovecraft's character and attitudes that follow. Almost the very first words out of Lovecraft's mouth, when he meets Howard, is: "I am a man of semi-invalid constitution." This description may have applied to the first thirty years of his life, but Lovecraft admitted frequently in letters that "My health improved vastly and rapidly . . . about 1920–21," so that in the last fifteen years of his life he was full of nervous energy, capable of outwalking any of his friends during treks through the ancient colonial cities he loved. We later see Lovecraft entering the meagre public library at Las Vegas and urging the librarian to subscribe to *Weird Tales* because, in his words, "you would find some fine examples of popular writing." Can Barbour and Raleigh really be unaware that Lovecraft despised *Weird Tales* exactly because it contained a dreary abundance of "popular writing" by such luminaries as Seabury Quinn and Nictzin Dyalhis, in which the genuinely meritorious contributions of Smith, Howard, Whitehead, and a very few others appeared like scattered pearls in a mass of ordure?

Our esteemed authors try to show off their learning by having Glory (who spent three years at Vassar) attempt a derivation of the word *Necronomicon*: "If I remember my Latin, it means something like 'The Book of the Names of the Dead.'" Too bad the word *Necronomicon* is Greek. What is more, Glory's etymology is widely divergent both from Lovecraft's own (erroneous) etymology ("Image [or Picture] of the Laws of the Dead") and from the real etymology that I established more than two decades ago: "An Examination [or Classification] of the Dead." How many times does one have to repeat that the *nom* in *Necronomicon* has nothing to do either with *onoma* (name) or with *nomos* (law)?

Even aside from all these absurd mistakes, the characterisation of Lovecraft, Howard, and Smith is so superficial, wooden, and hackneyed as to seem a caricature. We are treated only to their external mannerisms, and the authors seem to have no clue as to their inner mentalities. Lovecraft is made to speak in the most pompous, orotund manner imaginable, while Howard's speech is full of slang and oaths (usually of the "What in the Sam Hill!" nature). Smith is not on the scene long enough to say anything of consequence. All these figures—and Glory McKenna as well—are mere marionettes, stick figures made to blunder clumsily through a series of adventures utterly lacking in sense, inner logic, or even interest.

Shadows Bend ranks high among the most stupid, pointless, ridiculous, inept, bungling, preposterous, silly, boring, shoddy, and moronic novels I have ever had the misfortune to read. We are informed that it is the authors' first novel; one can only hope against hope that it will be their last. And one can also hope that Nyarlathotep will cause all copies of it to be sucked up into merited oblivion in the audient void.*

Peter Cannon's *The Lovecraft Chronicles* (Mythos Books, 2004) is not merely a fictionalised biography. It is what I believe is termed "alternate history": that what-if brand of science fantasy that conjectures the state of the world if, say, Hitler had won World War II, or the telephone had never been invented, or George W. Bush had not stolen the election of 2000. In this case, Cannon wonders: what if, in 1933, the prestigious New York firm of Alfred A. Knopf had actually accepted, instead of rejecting, a collection of tales by Lovecraft? Would Lovecraft's life have changed? Would subsequent history—literary, political, social—have changed? Cannon provides an emphatic yes to the first query, but is a bit more reserved as to the second. Nevertheless, his conclusion that Lovecraft would have gone far beyond his forty-six and a half years and lived to a normal life span of seventy years, dying only in 1960, is unexceptionable.

But the charm of *The Lovecraft Chronicles* is in seeing exactly how Lovecraft's life and career change—and change, generally, for the better—with that Knopf acceptance. The book is structured in three parts, each narrated by a different person. Each of these persons—the vivacious teenager Clarissa Stone, the somewhat older Englishwoman Leonora Lathbury, and the first-year Brown University graduate student Bobby Pratt—happens to be Lovecraft's secretary, a position he can now afford given his new-found literary success. The novel, I will admit, takes a little while gathering steam, but with the Knopf deal things pick up quickly. One of the stories in the book, "Herbert West—Reanimator," becomes a movie from the studio of Hal Roach; and, still more surprisingly, when Lovecraft goes to Hollywood to be a possible screenwriter, his stiff and vaguely corpselike features make him the perfect candidate for a bit part as a reanimated corpse! So begins Lovecraft's brief career as a Hollywood actor.

It is all good fun, but the experienced Lovecraftian will derive the greatest pleasure in seeing exactly what liberties Cannon does or does not take with the historical record. Consider this passage:

> During this period [the fall of 1933] H. P. produced two new stories, one a recasting in prose of some of his "Fungi from Yuggoth" sonnets, the other an elaboration of a dream about an evil clergyman in a garret full of forbidden books. . . . H. P. did not send these new tales on the rounds of his literary cir-

---

*In this instance I am gratified to note that my prediction appears to have come true: neither David Barbour nor Richard Raleigh (whose name, by a malign accident, is that of a pseudonym Lovecraft himself used on one occasion) have as yet written another novel. Perhaps reviews have some minimal influence after all . . .

cle, but instead submitted them, along with "The Thing on the Doorstep," directly to the editor of *Weird Tales*. [Farnsworth] Wright . . . snapped up these three new tales immediately.

There is such an exquisite mixture of fact and fiction here that untangling them is nearly impossible. The first sentence is strictly factual, although Cannon deliberately obscures the fact that that rewriting of the *Fungi* sonnets ("The Book") is a fragment, not a completed story. Moreover, the second story—"The Evil Clergyman"—was merely an account of a dream included in a letter to Bernard Austin Dwyer, and it was Dwyer who submitted the "story" to *Weird Tales* after Lovecraft's death. Finally, "The Thing on the Doorstep," although written in August 1933, was not submitted to *Weird Tales* until the fall of 1936. Cannon, I repeat, is fully aware of all these facts, and his manipulation of them is in strict accord with his contention that Lovecraft's career would have flowered rather than petered out as the 1930s advanced.

The second part of the book, set mostly in 1936, is to my mind the most successful. Lovecraft, with his new-found success (he is by no means a bestselling writer, but now has sufficient means for his own comfort), fulfils a lifelong dream by travelling to England—where, surprisingly (or perhaps not so surprisingly, given his later political views), he becomes friends with George Orwell and actually participates briefly if somewhat ignominiously in the Spanish Civil War against Franco. But the real heart of this section is his halting romance with Leonora Lathbury. In part one Lovecraft had managed to dodge the young Clarissa's schoolgirl crush on him, but he is not so successful with the more mature Leonora. If readers think it implausible for Lovecraft to be the protagonist of a love story, they should read how Cannon handles this segment of the novel. It is delicate, true to character, and entirely without sentimentality. There is a wistful poignancy throughout this section: not only is it heart-warming to see Lovecraft finally attain his goal of reaching Mother England, socialising jovially with Arthur Machen among others, but in his involvement with Leonora he seems to be ripening emotionally just as his work is ripening intellectually. How his impending marriage to Leonora is shattered at the last moment is too good to reveal here.

The third section of the book is the skimpiest both in length and in substance. One gets the suspicion that Cannon is getting a bit tired. The narrative skips abruptly to 1960, at which point the ageing Lovecraft has managed to repurchase his birthplace, 454 Angell Street in Providence, and decorate it in the manner he remembered as a boy. He has written almost no fiction since the 1940s, when Edmund Wilson harshly reviewed several of his books in the *New Yorker,* but additional film adaptations and the generosity of August Derleth's Arkham House allow him continued comfort, if not luxury. Frank Long and his actual wife, the late lamented Lyda, make a rather buffoonish appearance. Without giving away the ending, I will simply remark that the conclusion left me with a bit of a bad taste in my mouth.

My keenest regret is that *The Lovecraft Chronicles* was not twice or three times as long as it is. Cannon's literary gifts are of such a high order—skill at character depiction, an unfailing ability to keep the narrative moving, a penchant both for dry humour and for pathos—that we would like to see him exercise them to their fullest extent. Instead of hastily and sketchily summarising the events of the twenty-four years between parts two and three, why not elaborate them in detail? Cannon's portrayal of Lovecraft—nearly all his utterances are cleverly extracted or adapted from statements in his letters—rings so true that we would like to see him put Lovecraft on stage at other key moments in history. What, for example, would Lovecraft have made of World War II, and in particular the appalling revelations of the Holocaust, which definitively made the abstract racism of his earlier years morally indefensible? How would Lovecraft have adapted to the outwardly staid but inwardly seething 1950s? What would he have had to say of (or to) James Dean, Joe McCarthy, Elvis Presley? Or is it possible that Cannon is saving all these matters for a sequel?

But whatever one may think of the ending, *The Lovecraft Chronicles* is a book to enchant and captivate everyone who has the least interest in the dreamer from Providence. How many of us have wished that he had not been so poor, not eaten so badly, and not been so discouraged at the rejection of his best work? By all rights, Lovecraft should have lived to 1960 or even 1970, and enjoyed at least a modicum of the fame that came to him only after death. Kenneth W. Faig, Jr, once wrote: "We would surely all wish for him a better share of life were he to be given a second round; he surely never lacked the ability to do hard, careful work and perhaps only his disinclination toward self-promotion denied him greater material success." *The Lovecraft Chronicles* gives Lovecraft that second round, and shows that, with only a minimal augmentation of self-promotion, he might indeed have had the material success that would have made such a difference in his life. It is that air of "what if"—that sense that Lovecraft was so close, and yet so far, from reaching the goals he had set for himself as man and writer—that makes *The Lovecraft Chronicles* the poignant human document that it is.

Some Lovecraft Scholarship

The history of scholarly work on Lovecraft is, in some ways, as enthralling a narrative as the history of Lovecraft's slow, uncertain, but now definitive ascent into the canon of American literature. From the admiring (or, at times, hostile) surveys of his work in the amateur press, to enthusiastic (or hostile) letters in

Weird Tales and other pulp magazines, to the halting, occasionally amateurish studies in the burgeoning fantasy fandom movement of the 1930s and 1940s, where such pioneers as George T. Wetzel, Matthew H. Onderdonk, and Fritz Leiber began laying the groundwork for the sound analysis of Lovecraft's work and thought—all these elements led to the unexpected flowering of genuine criticism in the 1970s, led by Dirk W. Mosig, Donald R. Burleson, and other scholars. It was just at this time that I myself, as a shy and diffident teenager, began making my own tentative investigations into Lovecraft, and so I was in a position to gain an eyewitness view of the ascent of Lovecraft studies from the domain of well-meaning but frequently blundering fans to that of genuine scholars, both independent and academic, who have revealed the nearly inexhaustible depths and complexities of Lovecraft's literary work. During these last thirty years I have had occasion to assess the work of some of the leading figures in Lovecraft scholarship, and I present some of the results below.

Barton L. St Armand

H. P. Lovecraft: New England Decadent (Silver Scarab Press, 1979) is a revision—very slight, so far as I can tell—of an essay published in 1975 in the French journal Caliban and typifies those qualities that have made Prof. St Armand one of the most brilliant of modern Lovecraft scholars: a smooth and elegant style (if at times tainted with overly glib academic rhetoric), a wide erudition in all the fields (Puritanism, Symbolism, Poe, and Lovecraft's own life and thought) discussed, and a thesis—that Lovecraft was a "peculiar conjunction of Aestheticism and Puritanism"—whose provocativeness is matched by its formidable presentation. The essay, however, also reveals certain flaws characteristic of its author, and perhaps more generally characteristic of standard literary scholarship: a tendency to overemphasise and exaggerate (with a corresponding ignorance—deliberate in some cases—of evidence contrary to the theory being advanced), a tendency to engage in abstractions instead of concrete realities, and a tendency toward the display of erudition for its own sake.

That Lovecraft adopted certain of the aesthetic theories of the Decadents can perhaps not be denied; and that Lovecraft, in some of his ethical or behavioural attitudes, brings Puritanism to mind can also (although with much greater reservation) be accepted. But whether these two traits alone formed what we know as the complex personality of H. P. Lovecraft can rightly be questioned. Indeed, Ben P. Indick, in a brief rebuttal to St Armand's original article, asserted precisely this point—that Puritanism and Decadence were only two of the many influences working upon Lovecraft's mind. Such things as the influence of classical antiquity, of modern science, of philosophers from the pre-Socratics through Bertrand Russell (St Armand mentions in passing the "cosmic pessimism of Schopenhauer and Nietzsche," ignoring the fact that Nietzsche's thought is in many ways a repudiation of Schopenhauer's and that it presents a vigorously positive outlook—a "saying 'yes' to life," as he frequently expressed it), and countless other minor influences are ignored or glossed over by St Armand. Admittedly, the author was not attempting a comprehensive analysis of Lovecraft's thought; but such statements as "In sum Lovecraft remained . . . a Providence Aesthete, a New England Decadent, and a Cosmic Puritan" come dangerously close to limiting and trivialising the scope and breadth of Lovecraft's achievements both in his philosophy and in his literary work.

How much of a Decadent was Lovecraft, in any case? Did he not write, so early as 1927, that "I delight[ed] [in youth] to echo Continental iconoclasm and to experiment in the literary sophistication, ennui, and decadent symbolism which those around me exalted and practiced . . . [but] this phase . . . was exceedingly brief with me" (*Selected Letters* 2.138)? Indeed, we can trace almost exactly the period of Lovecraft's "Decadent" pose as spanning roughly the years 1921 to 1926—a conclusion that St Armand unconsciously acknowledges when he finds Decadent thought most purely expressed in the three Lovecraft tales concerning artists: "The Music of Erich Zann" (1921), "The Horror at Red Hook" (1925), and "Pickman's Model" (1926). (Ironically, the tale of Lovecraft's that is most emphatically Decadent—"The Hound" [1922]—is one of his poorest works.) What of Decadence is there in *At the Mountains of Madness* (1931) or "The Shadow out of Time" (1934-35)? Indeed, Lovecraft's Decadent phase must surely have been "exceedingly brief."

That the Decadents found a peculiar thrill in the witnessing of civilisation's collapse may be true; but that Lovecraft felt similarly is greatly open to question. St Armand actually quotes a letter by Lovecraft (*Selected Letters* 3.41) where he states that "There may be some—such as the 19th century decadents in France—who can derive a sort of pleasurable tragic exaltation from the picture of themselves as the crew of a sinking ship. There is quite a kick in the idea for those who like that kind of thing." But surely the implication here is that Lovecraft was *not* one of those who liked that kind of thing? This is only one of many instances where St Armand reveals a singular—almost perverse—inability to gauge the tone of Lovecraft's remarks, or to distinguish between his serious and his playful utterances (note St Armand's sober citation of Lovecraft's joking comment: "Give me a drink of hot blood with a Celtic foe's skull as a beaker!" [*Selected Letters* 1.156]). In any case, Lovecraft has made another utterance about the decline of civilisation that seems far more typical of his thought: "Personally, we can do all in our power to stave off the calamity [of civilisation's collapse], and then step aside with the resignation of a dying man, or of a 6th century Roman confronted by the Dark Ages" (*Selected Letters* 3.59). That this perfectly rational (St Armand consistently underemphasies Lovecraft's rationalism) attitude has anything to do with the Decadents may well be doubted. The Decadents, in any case, certainly had no monopoly on the "fascination with decadence," since we can find it throughout Western thought from Thucydides and Tacitus to Oswald Spengler and Arnold Toynbee.

It is in such distortions of Lovecraft's views that St Armand reveals that exaggeration which ultimately weakens his thesis. He is merely *trying too hard* to get his point across, and ignores much evidence contrary to his views. The exaggeration can be seen in St Armand's remarking of Lovecraft's "delight in tracing his family tree (with a pride which nearly amounted to primitive ancestor-worship)." Actually Lovecraft wrote (*Selected Letters* 2.213) that "My researches [into genealogy] have so far been confined wholly to pre-digested data dug up and formulated by earlier and better family archivists than myself"; it was largely W. B. Talman who egged Lovecraft on in his efforts. Similarly, St Armand speaks of Lovecraft's "almost idolatrous admiration for Machen, Dunsany, . . . Algernon Blackwood, and Montague Rhodes James" (later adding Clark Ashton Smith to the list). This does not quite accord with Lovecraft's blandly dismissing Machen's imagination as "not cosmic" (*Selected Letters* 4.4), his regretting Dunsany's lessening of power in his later work, his branding M. R. James as the "earthiest member of the 'big four'" (*Selected Letters* 4.15), and his speaking of Blackwood's "vast unevenness and poor prose style" (*Selected Letters* 5.384). Here again Lovecraft shows himself to be more rational and objective than St Armand would like—perhaps precisely because the Decadents did not show such rationalism and objectivity.

St Armand also makes the claim that "It was from Poe . . . that Lovecraft ultimately derived his philosophy of cosmic decline, basing it on . . . *Eureka*." Aside from the fact that Lovecraft may never have read *Eureka* (it is not mentioned, so far as I know, in anything Lovecraft ever wrote, and St Armand cites no source) and probably would have laughed at its outmoded science and pompous philosophy if he had, his ideas on the decline of civilisation (if indeed he had such pronounced ideas on the matter as St Armand claims) stemmed more likely from his absorption of classical culture ("The illusion of steady collective 'progress' toward any desirable end is of relatively recent origin, & becomes absurd when we reflect that Periclean Greece lies some 2400 years behind our own essentially mediocre age" [*Selected Letters* 3.42]) and of that eighteenth-century English (not Continental, as St Armand implies when he calls Lovecraft a *philosophe*) culture which Lovecraft felt to be the "final phase of that perfectly unmechanised aera which as a whole gave us our most satisfying life" (*Selected Letters* 3.50). Lovecraft gained much from Poe's aesthetics; but that he gained anything from *Eureka* is a question requiring much independent proof outside of any "internal evidence."

The matter of Lovecraft's ties with Puritan ethics is perhaps even easier to demolish than his connexions with the Decadents; for St Armand quotes many relevant passages himself, but fails to follow out their conclusions. Lovecraft held "the pompous & theocratic philosophy of the Puritans in the most abysmal contempt, [but] I believe in an honour & fastidiousness of conduct which *makes me act like* [my emphasis] a Puritan & earn the name of Puritan from all that are not of that dull breed of cattle themselves" (*Selected Letters* 1.298). We may add another similar passage: "Whilst I do share the basic New-England respect for an orderly life & social organisation (as did also Plato, John Locke, and many other non-Yankees), I have no belief in religion. . . . I likewise oppose the Puritan concept of ethics in art & literature" (*Selected Letters* 5.361-62). St Armand actually cites a passage (*Selected Letters* 1.229) where Lovecraft states that "I despise Bohemians, who think it essential to art to lead wild lives," but fails to quote the rest of it: "My loathing is not from the standpoint of Puritan morality, but from that of aesthetic independence." Whether Lovecraft is rationalising here or not is beside the point; a critic is bound to quote the entire passage—not just the part that seems to confirm his thesis—so that the reader has the tools to decide the matter for himself. In any event, it seems to me that much of Lovecraft's ethics is derived from ancient thought, notably Epicureanism (cf. *Selected Letters* 1.111, where Epicurus is called "the leading ethical philosopher of the world"); and in view of Lovecraft's atheistic stance it becomes vaguely absurd to call him a "Cosmic Puritan." St Armand, of course, tries to bolster his doctrine in a rather ingenious way, by sprinkling the *word* "Puritan" into various concepts where it cannot conceivably belong: hence we read of "Lovecraft's taste in art [as] polariz[ing] into the warm and the cold, the soft and the hard, the Decadent and the Puritan"; we find Lovecraft's cosmicism related to "the Puritan consciousness" and are presented with quotations from a sermon by Jonathan Edwards which are wholly irrelevant given Lovecraft's atheism; we read of "Lovecraft's conception of the imminence of [an] unspeakable, a Puritan terror," whatever that may be; and finally we read even of a "Puritan reality."

There are some rather more trivial errors that may be worth correction. On the first page of St Armand's essay we are introduced to "Robert E. Barlow" instead of Robert H. Barlow; we find the common mistake that Erich Zann played a violin instead of the Renaissance viol; we are given the implication that "The Music of Erich Zann" was influenced by E. T. A. Hoffmann, when Lovecraft had in fact not read Hoffmann when he wrote the tale (cf. *Selected Letters* 1.214); and St Armand should know better than to repeat the exploded myth (created by W. Paul Cook and fostered by Vincent Starrett) that Lovecraft cultivated a spectral pallor—a myth at which anyone who reads of Lovecraft's basking in the sun of St Augustine would smile.

I have tended here to dwell upon the possible flaws and extravagances of St Armand's work largely because its virtues hardly need citation. St Armand's thesis is, in any case, sound enough if, as I have suggested, pressed a little too hard; his ability to marshal evidence and his manner of presenting it are formidable; and his little book is at once an entertainment and a feast for the mind—something that cannot be said for the bulk of dry literary scholarship that is produced in such deplorably massive quantities in our age. Moreover, we find some particularly valuable insights here: we are given much information on the painter Nicholas Roerich; we find some splendid illustrations of works by Fuseli, Goya, Clark Ashton Smith, John Martin, Beardsley, S. H. Sime, and Doré, some of which surely inspired Lovecraft; and we find a fascinatingly detailed and illuminating analysis of "The Horror at Red Hook" (the studies of "Pickman's Model" and "The Music of Erich Zann" are less comprehensive). In sum, one wishes that St Armand had taken the time to expand his essay into a full-length study, and to discuss in far greater detail all the points at hand; but the work as we have it will, as with anything this author writes, remain a standard work of Lovecraft criticism with which all subsequent scholars, whether agreeing or disagreeing, will have to deal.

Donald R. Burleson

Throughout the 1970s we were bombarded with valiant but inept attempts at Lovecraft criticism by self-appointed critics who in reality knew not the first thing about criticism: with the happy exception of Maurice Lévy's fine *Lovecraft ou du fantastique* (1972), it is painful to recall such things as Lin Carter's *Look Behind the "Cthulhu Mythos"* (1972), John Taylor Gatto's Monarch Note on Lovecraft (1977), Philip A. Shreffler's *H. P. Lovecraft Companion* (1977), and, perhaps the worst of them all, Darrell Schweitzer's *Dream Quest of H. P. Lovecraft* (1978). Hence one's first reaction after finishing Donald R. Burleson's *H. P. Lovecraft: A Critical Study* (Greenwood Press, 1983) is simply relief: here at last is a competent scholar who knows Lovecraft, knows literary criticism, and can unite the two into a penetrating study that will certainly rival Lévy's book as the finest single treatment of Lovecraft.

There are so many good things about this book that one hardly knows where to start listing them. Perhaps the most important is simply Burleson's (generally) sane and level-headed approach: he lets Lovecraft speak for himself, instead of arrogantly assuming that Lovecraft really meant *this* when he says *that* (something I find with annoying frequency in the work of the otherwise brilliant Barton L. St Armand). The result is that Burleson understands the cosmic scope of Lovecraft's work, and indeed expresses it as well as I've ever heard it:

> The horror, ultimately, in a Lovecraft tale is not some gelatinous lurker in dark places, but rather the realisation, by the characters involved, of their helplessness and their insignificance in the scheme of things—their terribly ironic predicament of being sufficiently well-developed organisms to perceive

and feel the poignancy of their own motelike unimportance in a blind and chaotic universe which neither loves them nor even finds them worthy of notice, let alone hatred or hostility.

This seems to me exactly right, and it leads Burleson to the following important conclusion: "This ironic capability to sense one's own vanishingly small place in the universe is the central feature of the Lovecraft Mythos and constitutes an effect virtually unprecedented in literature." With this general overview of Lovecraft's work, it is rare that Burleson goes astray in the interpretation of individual tales and poems.

Burleson's thorough training in academic literary criticism leads him to make further breakthroughs that should have been made long ago: the notion of "ironic impressionism" as central to Lovecraft's approach; the frequent Lovecraftian use of the unreliable narrator whose words we are compelled to disbelieve, with the result that extraordinary tension is created; the failure of several of Lovecraft's early satiric tales ("The Terrible Old Man," "In the Vault") because of a heavy-handed irony and excessive authorial editorialising by which "Lovecraft unwittingly emulates the . . . nineteenth-century novels that he so disliked"; the striking influence of Milton upon the opening of "The Colour out of Space"; and, perhaps most brilliant of all, the employment of myth criticism to produce a revised interpretation of "The Dunwich Horror," whereby the Whateley twins are seen as the real "heroes" of the tale and Dr Armitage a mere buffoon. I am not, however, entirely convinced that Lovecraft openly intended satire on *Weird Tales* stories using the naive "good vs. evil" dichotomy that the surface reading of the tale appears to embody, but nevertheless Burleson's analysis is, I find, even more convincing than that presented in his *Lovecraft Studies* article of 1980.

Any faults detectable in this book can only be faults of detail. My only general complaint is the amount of space spent upon plot description—which oftentimes has nothing to do with the analysis of the tale, and which any reader well versed in Lovecraft's work will find a little tedious. Indeed, there is a certain ambiguity in the assumed audience for this book: surely it cannot have been intended for those who have no knowledge whatever of Lovecraft, since the very technical discussions of certain points would be incomprehensible to such persons; and we all wish for a critic of Burleson's acuteness more space for real analysis of the works in question. There moreover seems to be a certain lack of coherent structure in the book: the chronological approach adopted by Burleson is eminently sensible, but there is the danger of the book's becoming a mere *vade mecum* to Lovecraft—a description of one work after the other without any space devoted to unification and general analysis. Burleson's "Epilogue" is eloquent in stating Lovecraft's value as an artist, but perhaps more space could have been given to tying together the various themes running through Lovecraft's work. Finally, the bibliography is unusually brief—there is nothing at all by Dirk W. Mosig or Robert M. Price, although some of Mosig's works are cited in the notes, and it is cluttered with references to books by Poe, Machen, Dunsany, etc., which really need not have been included. There is much more valuable Lovecraft criticism than is listed here. A corollary to this is Burleson's intermittent failure to acknowledge other scholars' contributions: the most startling is his omitting to note St Armand's discovery of the passage in Jung's *Man and His Symbols* describing a dream by Jung that oddly parallels "The Rats in the Walls"; and in his analysis of "The Thing on the Doorstep" Burleson fails to note that the possibility of Edward Derby's being an amalgam of Lovecraft and Alfred Galpin was derived from my article "Autobiography in Lovecraft." Burleson is elsewhere profuse in his acknowledgement of my assistance to him, hence I must attribute these lapses to oversight.

A very quick rundown of other minor errors: Lovecraft did not meet Donald or Howard Wandrei during his initial New York period of 1924-26. Lovecraft did more than write "a certain amount of poetry"—it fills well over 500 pages. "Nemesis" dates to late 1917 (cf. *Selected Letters* 1.51), not June 1918 (I confess that this was an error I initially made in my chronology of Lovecraft's works). Lovecraft did not actually consult Pigafetta's *Regnum Congo*, but got information on it through an essay by T. H. Huxley. Lovecraft was surely not familiar with the theories of Jung when he wrote "The Rats in the Walls," as Burleson seems to imply—his knowledge came only in the late 1920s. It is unlikely that Walter de la Poer's name was derived from Walter de la Mare, since Lovecraft had not read any of de la Mare's works by 1923 (cf. *Selected Letters* 2.53). The Latin phrase *ex oblivione* more probably means "from oblivion," rather than "out of oblivion" (i.e., of life), hence probably refers to the narrator's telling his account when he is already in oblivion. "Herbert West—Reanimator" was only Lovecraft's first professionally published *story*, as he had published some poems professionally in the late 1910s. I suspect that what Edward Derby, in "The Thing on the Doorstep," is trying to say over the telephone at the end is simply his own name, "Ed-ward": the ms. reading is actually "glub-glub," not "glub . . . glub," making it unlikely that Derby is trying to imitate his old three-and-two knock, a strange thing to do over the phone anyway. A much closer model for Zadok Allen in "The Shadow over Innsmouth" than the old Civil War veteran whom Lovecraft knew in his youth is a character in Herbert S. Gorman's novel *The Place Called Dagon* (1927), which clearly influenced Lovecraft. Finally, it is surely not "virtually certain" that Lovecraft derived the idea of the *Necronomicon* from Hawthorne, although this is one likely source: in all probability this complex idea was drawn from many diverse sources.

The above criticisms clearly show how solid is Burleson's achievement: there may be chinks here and there, but the armour overall stands firm.

Nearly every page contains some enlightening note on a tale or poem (indeed, Burleson's study of several key Lovecraft poems is one of the great virtues of his book); and throughout we feel the hand of a master critic who has thoroughly grasped his subject and strives to convey the excitement and admiration he feels for it. The very simple title of this book is fitting for a work that shall take its place as a landmark in the critical analysis of Lovecraft, and a standard for all future scholarship in the field.

I must announce at the outset that Burleson's *Lovecraft: Disturbing the Universe* (University Press of Kentucky, 1990) is dedicated to me. This gesture by the acutest critic in Lovecraft studies is, of course, enormously gratifying, and is a testament to the mutual benefit that Don Burleson and I have derived over the many years of our association. I make this announcement only to fend off accusations of churlishness in my following remarks: I am certain that Burleson would wish me to write an honest evaluation of his much-awaited new book, an evaluation that is no more than one person's judgment—albeit a fairly well-reasoned one, I trust—of a very difficult book and a very difficult critical methodology.

What all these laborious preliminaries amount to is that I do not agree with the premises and approach of this book. It is a forthright and highly stimulating attempt to "deconstruct" Lovecraft, and is the summation of Burleson's shorter work in this regard. Now I am not a deconstructionist, although I do not imagine that I have escaped the influence of this school any more than other critics have. If I belong to any school, it is a sort of amalgam of the philosophical or ethical criticism pioneered by Leslie Stephen and practised today (in highly variable ways) by Wayne C. Booth, Tzvetan Todorov,* and others, and the political or cultural criticism represented by such diverse critics as Raymond Williams, Terry Eagleton, and Edward W. Said. This latter school (as with its more formal and dogmatic offshoot, Marxist criticism) has its affinities with deconstruction and poststructuralism generally, but in many of their fundamental premises the two are antipodally opposed.

Deconstruction rests upon the belief that language is so fluid as to be infinitely variable: there is no "stable" or "univocal" meaning to any word, much

---

*For Booth see *The Company We Keep: An Ethics of Fiction* (1988). Todorov's *Literature and Its Theorists* (1984) seems to make a fairly pronounced break with his original structuralist stance, so that he now affirms that "It is time to come (back) to the self-evident facts that we should never have forgotten: literature has to do with human existence. It is a discourse oriented toward—let us not be intimidated by the ponderous words—truth and morality.... Literature would be nothing at all if it did not allow us to reach a better understanding of life." See also Tobin Siebers, *The Ethics of Criticism* (1989).

less a text that comprises many words. Deconstruction, therefore, sets about to "subvert" such standard interpretations of a text—to show that it may mean something other than what its surface meaning seems to suggest. There are already several troubling things about this formulation. First, such a conception really does in the end make language meaningless—or, rather, it suggests that any given word can mean anything (or be made to mean anything) if it is deconstructed long enough. Deconstructionists, including Burleson, try to avoid this conclusion, but it cannot be done: no other result is possible from the claim of language's *infinite* mutability. (Burleson himself, in discussing "The Nameless City," writes: ". . . one may say that unrestricted naming is tantamount—after all—to no naming—that to be known by too many names is not to be known by any.") Second, the deconstructionists seem guilty of setting up a straw man in claiming that prior critical approaches somehow claimed that texts do have a "univocal" significance. What critical school, at least in this century, ever maintained such a thing? Has there not always been a plurality of interpretations of almost any text one can name? We have such a plurality even in the humble field of Lovecraft studies, and even with so slight a tale as "The Terrible Old Man" (is it a racist story? is it a satire? if so, who is the target of satire?). Burleson says coyly, "We must of course abandon the quaint notion that a literary text has a fixed, single 'meaning'"; but this notion was abandoned long ago, if it was in fact ever held.

The curious thing with all this is that the deconstructionists themselves are seemingly given to categorical and dogmatic assertions of their own theory while ridiculing such things in others. When Burleson says, "Language *is* playful, and its playfulness can be readily observed," he gives the impression of uttering an incontrovertible and self-evident truth. One wonders what the deconstructionists would do if someone were to deconstruct the pillars of their own critical theory.

The general problem with much of this sort of criticism is that its utterances are continually and confusingly wavering between literal and metaphorical levels of signification. Hence when Burleson says, "Texts, in my view, continue to write themselves by being read," he cannot possibly be meaning this literally (for that would be nonsense); he is really uttering a metaphor for the rather commonplace notion that different readers respond differently to the same text. The metaphorical version is certainly more piquant and vivid, but it is really saying nothing especially new or provocative. Now there is nothing wrong, even in critical discourse, with writing metaphorically; but there *is* something wrong if those metaphors are meant to be interpreted literally and if they are really masking a poverty of original thinking.

In fact, the not so hidden agenda of Burleson's book is to elevate Lovecraft in the academic community by demonstrating that his deconstructibility is a sign of the depth and profundity of his work. Even this goal, laudable as it is, cannot stand up to scrutiny. Since deconstruction is primarily a theory of *language* and not of *literature,* it cannot possibly make value judgments on the merits of a given work of literature. Here again the notion of the *infinite* or endless play of language causes trouble. There can be no degrees of infinity, so that the deconstruction of a single word—say, the "stop" on a stop sign—can in theory progress exactly as far as the deconstruction of *Finnegans Wake.* One supposes even a single letter could be so deconstructed: if I wanted to be waggish, I could assert that *The Scarlet Letter* is simply a grandiose deconstruction of the letter "A"; but this would confer no literary value on the letter "A." Burleson mentions the possibility of deconstructing a Harlequin romance only to dismiss it, even though such a procedure might be highly illuminating (not to mention amusing). But the fact that deconstructionists have turned more frequently to such old mossbacks of the Canon as Yeats, Joyce, and Shelley than to Harlequin romances may have much more to do with academic stodginess, elitism, and ideology* than with anything else. And the whole conception is in danger of being circular. Burleson says that "the potential for such a reading is a measure of how substantial or 'literary' a text is"; but what *is* a literary text but a text that literary critics have chosen to examine? And why is it that such murky writers as Donne, Hopkins, and Stevens are deconstructed (and, indeed, studied generally) far more than such paragons of clarity and rationalism as Addison, Johnson, Gray, and Macaulay? There are such obvious historical and cultural factors at work here that to ignore them, and to assert that some writers are studied merely because they are "better" or "more profound" than others, is simply not to see the whole picture. Indeed, the deconstructionists' perennial hunt for paradox and aporia is an interesting cultural phenomenon in itself, not only in that it is surprisingly similar to the much-maligned New Critics' nose for irony, tension, and paradox but in that it is the pinnacle of the entire twentieth century's disdain for clear statement and clear thinking (I need hardly note the exceptions of Russell, Ayer, and a few other stalwarts—among them Lovecraft).

There is also a problem of what one does after one has deconstructed a text. Burleson certainly asserts that deconstruction can never be completed, that it is always possible to continue the process *ad infinitum.* This may be true in theory, but in practice I would imagine it to be both increasingly difficult and increasingly sterile. Terry Eagleton, specifically discussing deconstruction, wryly looked forward to the day when blank pages would be presented as examples of scholarship;† but is this suggestion so horribly off the mark?

---

*Burleson makes the sanguine announcement that with deconstruction "we pass beyond ideology"; but Eagleton and others have pointedly noted the ideological biases of even the most abstract deconstructionist methodology.

†"Since no deconstructive critical text will be quite purged of some particles of

The final argument that deconstructionists make when all others fail is to assert that the distinction between literature and criticism has now been destroyed. Harold Bloom—who in every other regard is emphatically not a deconstructionist or even a poststructuralist, as he has made abundantly clear to me—is rather big on this: since in his view all texts are merely responses to other texts, then critical texts are just as "literary" as those customarily thought to be so. And while in his case (and in Burleson's as well) there may be some truth to the remark—at least in the sense that Bloom's lush and vibrant writing, and Burleson's lean elegance and precision, can classify as literature—one wonders whether this whole notion has simply been invented by dusty academics increasingly irked at the attention paid to legitimate writers as opposed to themselves. Can these critics really maintain with a straight face that their arcane disquisitions are somehow literarily valuable? It must be a very comforting notion.

Let me at last turn to some specifics of Burleson's book. The deconstructionist methodology he uses most frequently is that of etymology. The thinking is that tracing the etymological roots of a word will reveal resonances that may complement but also "subvert" the surface meaning of the word and the sentence in which it resides. In a few instances Burleson makes some slight but demonstrable errors (the Latin *ille* does not mean "yonder"; *Cthulhu* cannot be derived from the Greek *chthonos*) or highly suspect conjectures (I question the derivation of *Ulthar* from the Latin *ultimus*); but even at its best the procedure seems to be merely a symptom (or allegory, to use deconstructionist terminology) of the deconstructionists' predisposition to look only for those things that confirm their theory. They claim that they do not wish to "privilege" either side of a binary opposition, but it certainly seems as if, when given the opposition between ambiguity and clarity, they "privilege" the former. Hence Burleson finds that the "*-side-*" of "Outsider" "suggests" *sidle*—"to move sideways, indirectly, furtively, deviously"; but why could it not just as plausibly suggest *side*, as in the side of a house, thereby denoting rootedness and fixity? This sort of thing occurs on nearly every page. Indeed, Burleson's whole book, I regret to say, strikes me as a somewhat mechanical application of standardised deconstructionist methodology: on one side we have the theory, on the other side the text, so let's see what the outcome is. That outcome is rarely a surprise.

As a result, it becomes obvious that what Burleson is really doing is not deconstructing Lovecraft so much as using Lovecraft as an excuse to "prove"

---

positivity, a further text will always be needed to dissolve these away, and that in turn be vulnerable to another, for so long as blank pages are unacceptable as scholarly publications." Terry Eagleton, *The Function of Criticism* (London: Verso, 1984), p. 105.

the truth of deconstruction. It is uncanny how everything in Lovecraft, on Burleson's analysis, points in this direction—to such a degree that Burleson is obliged to anticipate the common complaint that deconstruction makes all texts sound the same. But let the reader judge:

On "The Statement of Randolph Carter": ". . . the reader's . . . desire to press for definite meanings and settled results . . . is always fruitless, problematic, destined to face built-in undecidabilities."

On "The Terrible Old Man": "The text is open to the free play of signification and interpretation, closed to any possibility of final or settled understanding: closed to closure."

On "The Cats of Ulthar": ". . . the cats symbolize the free-flowing and uncontrollable workings of language . . ."

On "The Nameless City": "The text is a sand dance of necessary indeterminacy."

On "The Outsider": "Here again the text's supplementarities are self-subverting with regard to privileged terms."

On "The Strange High House in the Mist": "The text is a dance of mists and dreams of mists, its web of language labyrinthine and as dizzying as the crag, its energies given over to allegorization of unsettled reading."

All this makes doubly problematical Burleson's attempt to glorify Lovecraft on account of his deconstructibility, since any text might well have sufficed for the purpose. Burleson seeks to deflect this criticism by asserting, in his conclusion, that "The themes . . . that pervade Lovecraft's tales conceptually suggest the deconstructive spirit"; but I remain unconvinced of this. Relatively few of the discussions in this book seem to me specific to *Lovecraft*. Lovecraft's texts (or, in some cases, individual words from them) are often used as the springboard for linguistic analyses that do not or need not apply to the stories in any concrete or compelling way.

But it would be unfair to conclude this review with nothing but negative judgments. *Lovecraft: Disturbing the Universe* is the most challenging book ever written on Lovecraft; on every page one can sense Burleson's keenness of insight and subtlety of approach. His opening chapter on deconstructionist theory is about as clear and lucid an account as I have ever read; its problematical aspects are inherent in the theory and not in Burleson's exposition of it. Individual passages in the book are uncommonly fine: Burleson's careful dissection of the titles of Lovecraft's stories is highly stimulating, and more work should be done in this regard; his chapter on "The Terrible Old Man" (an elaboration of his groundbreaking 1984 article, his first deconstructionist piece) is very illuminating; and the brief paragraph on the mythic hero archetype in "The Colour out of Space" left me wanting much more of this sort of criticism, however conventional it may be to Burleson. In any case, it is entirely conceivable that Burleson will not find much force in any of my criticisms: they may either stem from a lack of complete understanding of deconstruction or (even though I have attempted to direct my criticisms from within the logic of his methodology) be a product of my disagreement with his whole approach. It may simply be a matter of his going his way and I going mine; and my way is encapsulated most succinctly by Edward W. Said: "My position is that texts are worldly, to some degree they are events, and, even when they appear to deny it, they are nevertheless part of the social world, human life, and of course the historical moments in which they are located."* Burleson is free to deconstruct this if he likes, but I doubt whether that would change my view appreciably, just as I doubt whether my comments here will affect his.

In the end I am certainly not one of those who would wish to stifle deconstruction and somehow banish it from the realm of critical discourse: I have occasionally found it highly suggestive, especially in the writings of Burleson. Nor am I one who wrings his hands and laments that deconstruction is somehow the harbinger of (pardon me) the decline of the West. But I believe that deconstruction must come to terms with what appear to be serious contradictions and deficiencies in its premises and its practice. It is certainly too early to pass a verdict on deconstruction; my own view is that other critical approaches simply produce better results. But the matter is open.

Peter Cannon

Peter Cannon's *The Chronology out of Time: Dates in the Fiction of H. P. Lovecraft* (Necronomicon Press, 1986) is a book I would very much like to have written. Even the most casual reader of Lovecraft must have sensed the unprecedented *precision* of his work—a precision not only of diction, construction, and philosophical orientation, but a precision of setting. Aside from the Dunsanian fantasies and the earlier Poe-esque tales (where such precision would in fact be detrimental), Lovecraft's fiction is unquestionably rooted in a very real time (the period of Lovecraft's own life) and place (the New England he knew so well). There are not many authors in all literature—Dickens, Hardy, and Faulkner are the ones that immediately come to mind—for whom Peter Cannon could have done what he has done here: make a chronology of events in Lovecraft's stories from the early Middle Ages to 1935. It is amazing how much there is to list: from the Renaissance to the twentieth century things *happen* in Lovecraft, whether it be the various translations of the *Necronomicon* or the destruction of Dunwich. In horror fiction only M. R. James can even

---

*Edward W. Said, *The World, the Text, and the Critic* (Cambridge, MA: Harvard University Press, 1983), p. 13.

approach the fanatical exactitude with which Lovecraft established this mythical chronology, this bold rewriting of history.

The parameters of Cannon's chronology might initially seem arbitrary, but they ultimately justify themselves. Why limit the chronology to no earlier than 700 (the *floruit* of Abdul Alhazred) and no later than 1935 (the death of Robert Blake)? It is because the events before and after these dates—as far back as the heyday of the Great Race 150,000,000 years ago and as far forward as the death of the sun—can all be found in At the Mountains of Madness and "The Shadow out of Time," and then only on the assumption (now questioned by Robert M. Price) that the occasional inconsistencies between the two stories can be harmonised. Why include dates only from the two revisions "The Mound" and "Out of the Aeons"? Well, the other revisions don't actually offer much in terms of dating anyhow.

We can learn much from this listing. One wonders, for example, why Lovecraft set "The Picture in the House" in 1896, when he wrote the story in 1920. The plot does not depend on this date, for the supernatural premise of the story—that the old man has outlived his normal span through cannibalism—could certainly have allowed the cheerful carnivore to live a few more decades, closer to the time of the story's composition. This story—as well, perhaps, as "Beyond the Wall of Sleep," set in 1901 but written in 1919—may represent a transition from the never-never-land of "The Tomb" to the contemporaneousness of "The Rats in the Walls."

Again, Cannon remarks that the sparseness of events in the nineteenth century—indeed, if we remove the events uncovered by the newspaper reporter in "The Haunter of the Dark," almost nothing remains between the death of Joseph Curwen in 1771 and the fall of the meteorite in 1882, aside from the endless cycle of births and deaths in "The Shunned House"—is a result of Lovecraft's "antipathy to the Victorian age." There may be more to it than that. Certainly Lovecraft had no fondness for the hypocrisy and shallowness of Victorian society, but more than that the whole nineteenth century represented a sort of limbo—separate alike from the hallowed eighteenth century and the grinding reality of the twentieth. It had for Lovecraft not yet become history—and therefore he could not write about it as he did the eighteenth century in The Case of Charles Dexter Ward—and it did not have the immediacy of his own day.

All this makes me wonder why Lovecraft went to such trouble to refashion history in this way. To be more precise, it was not that he was rewriting history; rather, he was simply *filling in the gaps*. Just as his whole aesthetic of weird fiction required that he create "*supplements* rather than *contradictions*" of the "real" universe, so Lovecraft felt compelled to insert nameless events into the interstices of history. The past is not as bland and straightforward as the history books tell us; *other things* have happened that make our existence on this earth infinitely more precarious. This is the secret of Lovecraft's horrific effectiveness: it is not merely that we must be on guard for things that *will* occur; it is that we are rendered totally helpless because certain things have *already* occurred. R'lyeh will rise again because it rose before; the Old Ones will rule once more because they ruled long ago. It is this historical determinism that makes Lovecraft's world so profoundly dispiriting.

The history of Cannon's *H. P. Lovecraft* (Twayne, 1989) is extremely bizarre. Dirk W. Mosig, the father of modern Lovecraft studies, was assigned the task of writing it in 1975; but, after dawdling for years under the burden of too many other commitments, he abandoned the project. He wished Donald R. Burleson to take over the work (just as Mosig recommended that I write the lesser *Reader's Guide to H. P. Lovecraft* for Starmont House), but G. K. Hall passed Burleson over and assigned it instead to Barton L. St Armand—no doubt on the questionable belief that St Armand, a more conventionally acceptable academic, could carry out the task more satisfactorily. St Armand, himself withdrawing from the field, gave up the assignment around 1984, and eventually it devolved upon Peter Cannon.

In the end we can say, without offence to anyone, that no better candidate could have been chosen. Mosig, although vastly learned, would probably have written an effusively praiseworthy work making dubious claims as to Lovecraft's merits as writer and thinker. Burleson had already written his *H. P. Lovecraft: A Critical Study* (1983) for Greenwood Press, and it would have been a squandering of his talents had he been compelled to write another handbook for students. I myself lost all interest in writing another book analogous to my *Reader's Guide* (1982) and worked instead on a lengthy philosophical study, *H. P. Lovecraft: The Decline of the West* (Starmont House, 1990). There are several other scholars in the field—David E. Schultz and Steven J. Mariconda are only two—who could have written this book; but only Cannon occupies the unique position of being both in the field and outside it. A look at any page of Cannon's notes to this book will show how thoroughly he has absorbed current Lovecraft scholarship (as, for example, St Armand has not), citing things so obscure as amateur press fanzines. But Cannon, who has a strong academic and publishing background, is no mere devotee or uncritical admirer; and his knowledge of the wider world of literature allows him to give Lovecraft his rightful, perhaps somewhat humble, place in American and world literature. When Cannon writes that "Lovecraft needs to gain a wider audience outside the genre," he may be referring subconsciously, but entirely aptly, to readers like himself.

Everything in this book—from the chronology to the bibliography—is sane, balanced, accurate, and comprehensive. No better introduction to Lovecraft has ever been written, and perhaps ever will be written. The opening biographical chapter is the most concentrated and succinct thing of its kind I have ever read, and—aside from a curious silence on Lovecraft's marriage, never dealt with thoroughly anywhere in this book—brings Lovecraft to life in a few pages more vividly than L. Sprague de Camp did in his entire biography.

Cannon has adopted some unconventional structural methods in his book, notably the arrangement of Lovecraft's work not so much chronologically as "geographically." This method has much to recommend it, but also results in some anomalies. Cannon's categorisation of Lovecraft's early work under the thematic rubrics of "The Past," "The Sea," "Below," "Beyond," "Dreamland," and "Decadence" is ingenious and brings to light significant patterns in the early tales, but the gradual development of Lovecraft's mastery of technique is somewhat obscured. We read about "The Lurking Fear" (1922) before we read about "Herbert West—Reanimator" (1921-22), and Lovecraft's considerable advance in plotting is not made evident. Moreover, Cannon later discusses *The Case of Charles Dexter Ward* before *The Dream-Quest of Unknown Kadath*, evidently unaware that the latter's repudiation of the dream-world led directly to the paean to the realities of New England life and history in the former.

A more serious flaw in this book is that Cannon does not seem to have any overall view of the purpose or direction of Lovecraft's work. In criticising Burleson's critical study (perhaps rightly) for excessive plot synopses, Cannon ignores the fact that much of his own book is open to the same charge. The book gets so bogged down in summarising and analysing each and every story Lovecraft wrote—something Cannon does, admittedly, with great adeptness, quoting just those portions of the tales that highlight their important features—that we have trouble ascertaining what Lovecraft's work is really adding up to. Cannon in fact does not seem to have an especially lofty view of Lovecraft; there is nothing intrinsically wrong with this, but to call Lovecraft merely "one of America's greatest literary eccentrics" seems a little shabby. Cannon tries to bolster Lovecraft's standing by comparing him with recognised authors, including Hawthorne, Melville, Faulkner, O'Neill, and others; but this sort of thing—especially a somewhat grotesque comparison of "Out of the Aeons" with Evelyn Waugh—may backfire by appearing unintentionally comic. This is not the way to exalt Lovecraft's status. Cannon's very brief concluding chapter does not encapsulate Lovecraft's achievement—as we might have expected and wanted—but cursorily studies the vicissitudes of his critical acceptance. Here Lovecraft is compared implausibly to Conan Doyle as an author appealing to "juvenile" tastes—something that completely overlooks the fact that Lovecraft's work has a philosophical depth and richness entirely absent in that of Sherlock Holmes's creator.

There is a further want of proportion in the relative amount of space given to Lovecraft's early and late work. No one would deny that Lovecraft's stories up to 1926 are on the whole undistinguished (Cannon himself calls them "apprentice" work); but Cannon devotes some 40 pages to these tales, and only 60 to the later, longer narratives. His study of nearly all the later tales is unsatisfactory, and the analysis stops just when we are expecting it to begin. There is so much more to be said about these tales, and Cannon surely has so many valuable insights to offer, that we cannot but wish he had compressed the early chapters and lengthened the later ones.

Cannon is curiously insensitive to some of Lovecraft's intentions. In particular he fails to note the self-parodic humour of "Herbert West— Reanimator" and "The Hound," and also the double-edged satire in "The Terrible Old Man," which is no hostile snarl at aliens (as Cannon, echoing de Camp, believes) but is as much a send-up of "the charmed circle of New England life and traditions" as it is an attack on foreigners. Cannon's own predilections are not hidden in this book, either: he has always been fond of "The Dunwich Horror"; but, without adopting Burleson's notion that it is a satire, he can only conclude lamely that "the tale . . . ranks among his strongest, by virtue of its high level of excitement and suspense." Well, on such criteria we must give Robert Ludlum and Sidney Sheldon high marks as literary artists. Similarly, Cannon's somewhat embarrassing fondness for the confused "Medusa's Coil" makes him remark soberly that it "merits more critical scrutiny than it has hitherto received." Perhaps "Ashes" does also.

And yet, aside from being a valuable guide to the undergraduate, graduate student, or even professor interested in commencing a study of Lovecraft, this book offers some new insights. Cannon is undoubtedly right in detecting the narrator's friend in "Hypnos" as a thinly disguised Edgar Allan Poe (although what we are to make of this, neither Cannon nor I can imagine); he remarks with great acuity that the "three members [of the Whateley family in "The Dunwich Horror"] may be viewed as grotesque parodies of his grandfather, his mother, and himself"; and he points out a number of obvious parallels between *The Case of Charles Dexter Ward* and *The Picture of Dorian Gray*, something that at any rate never penetrated my thick wits before. A footnote studying examples of "latch" imagery in Lovecraft could be the nucleus of an article similar to Cannon's own "Sunset Terrace Imagery."

Cannon is almost excessively generous in acknowledging his fellow scholars in the field. This is useful in alerting the novice to how much has been written on Lovecraft in non-academic sources, but it leads Cannon to cite even the dubious work of John Taylor Gatto and Darrell Schweitzer. And there are some slips: he credits James Egan's undistinguished *Extrapolation* article of 1982 for the view that "The Dunwich Horror" is an obvious parody of the Immaculate Conception, but Maurice Lévy had made the point more cogently a decade before; and Cannon states that Joel Manton in "The Unnamable" may be a disguised version of Maurice W. Moe, forgetting that I first made this identification in my old "Autobiography in Lovecraft." (This is no doubt an oversight, as Cannon otherwise cites my work far more often than he should have, and does not cite his own previous writing to the degree it deserves.)

The majority of the above remarks are of the nature of quibbles; any book would be open to them. I cannot reiterate strongly enough how thoroughly professional in every sense is this work; it is a credit to Twayne, to Lovecraft, and to Peter Cannon. This book was the first important contribution to the great celebration of Lovecraft's centennial, and it can take its place as a thorough, challenging work that cannot be ignored. There is more meat in this book than in anything of comparable size in the field.

Cannon's collected essays—gathered in *"Sunset Terrace Imagery in Lovecraft" and Other Essays* (Necronomicon Press, 1990)—comprise a surprisingly slight volume; but his major work has been embodied in his Twayne study and in *The Chronology out of Time*, so perhaps it would not be fair to expect his occasional pieces to have the solidity of these works. Still, to refer to these essays as "slight" is sadly on the mark: they do not add up to more than the sum of their parts.

The fundamental problem with Cannon's whole methodology (and this is evident even in his Twayne book) is his apparent belief that paraphrase and quotation are valid substitutes for analysis; or, rather, that they in themselves constitute analysis. "Lovecraft's Old Men" does little more than cite passages from Lovecraft's stories in which old men are described. What is the real significance of these figures? This is never truly discussed. To say of the Terrible Old Man that he "comes off as an unpleasant creature, not really human" is to say nothing. Even Will Murray's bizarre but suggestive conjecture that the Terrible Old Man is a sort of cat is more interesting than Cannon's discussion of this tale; for at least Murray is trying to dig a little below the surface, whereas Cannon is seemingly concerned only with making deft quotations from Lovecraft's stories. This sort of failing dogs even Cannon's well-known piece on "Sunset Terrace Imagery in Lovecraft." Here we are simply presented with a sheaf of quotations from Lovecraft's letters and stories pertaining to sunsets. What then? What are we to make of this recurring image? The article, like many in this book, ends just where it ought to begin.

One of my complaints of Cannon's Twayne book is that his opinion of Lovecraft did not seem to be especially high. I do not mean to suggest that everyone who writes about Lovecraft should think him a great writer; but occasionally Cannon takes what seem to me some cheap shots. In attempting to place Lovecraft within the mainstream of American literature, Cannon compares him to William Faulkner, referring to both writers' creation of a fictional world and their concern with the themes of miscegenation and the omnipotence of the past. But then Cannon adds: "Where Lovecraft fundamentally departs of course from Faulkner, and thereby disqualifies himself from serious consideration by the critics and academics who determine what is worthy of immortality in our literature, is in supplying a supernatural basis for his fiction." It is not clear that Cannon actually endorses this outrageous statement; but the fact that he makes no further comment on it suggests that he does. It contains, of course, two serious fallacies: (1) critics and academics do not determine what is worthy of immortality, readers do; (2) there is no earthly reason why the supernatural should disqualify a work from serious consideration; it is simply that most mainstream critics, ignorant of the rhetoric of the weird tale, are unable to interpret the symbolism of the supernatural in a given story. Later Cannon, in vaunting the Inklings over Lovecraft, says that "Lovecraft . . . never engaged in any work apart from his writing that demanded anywhere near a full use of his mental powers." What on earth does this mean? Did the Inklings ever do so? And since Lovecraft spent the majority of his time writing, surely he was using his full mental powers most of the time. Finally, Cannon states superciliously that, "almost in spite of himself, Lovecraft does imbue his work with complexity and meaning." "Almost in spite of himself"? Lovecraft strikes me as one of the most conscious writers I have ever read—he knew exactly what he was doing, and he is almost always a better analyst of his work and thought than any of his critics. And Cannon's subsequent analysis of Lovecraft's "complexity and meaning" rests entirely upon conceptions found in Lovecraft's letters, particularly in the matters of his "cosmic" perspective and his elimination of the "human element" in his tales. There is no "in spite of himself" here.

As it is, Cannon's best work may be in that anomalous subgenre we know as Lovecraftian humour. "HPL and JFK" is quite amusing, a send-up of those countless comparisons of Lovecraft with the most improbable figures in literature and history; but even *Pulptime*, the greatest work ever written featuring Lovecraft as a character, could not have prepared us for "Asceticism and Lust: The Greatest Lovecraft Revision." This is the best Lovecraftian parody ever written. It is in such works that Cannon's wide reading and urbane humour come to the fore; and however frivolous they may appear, it is clear that these pieces could only have been written by someone with a thorough knowledge of Lovecraft as well as a sophisticated wit that Lovecraft would have envied. (I should note that Cannon has long been fond of parodying me, but this is something I take with all the good humour intended; and perhaps it has helped deflate some of my own pomposity and seriousness.)

I do not by any means wish to condemn Cannon's Lovecraft scholarship; rather, my remarks are of the nature of a plea—a plea for Cannon to apply more emphatically that critical sensibility which he has in such abundance, to dig a little deeper into Lovecraft's work and thought, and not to be content with writing *New Yorker*-style pieces that fall unsatisfyingly between true scholarship and popular ephemera. The sort of belletristic criticism Cannon writes has long been scorned by critics, for the simple reason that it really does not say very much: we don't learn much more than we knew before. I mean no disrespect when I say that "In Search of Lovecraft's Newburyport" may be the best piece in this book because it seems to be the only one that embodies genuinely original research. Cannon's moving tribute to Frank Belknap Long would have much value if Long were a more significant figure than he is; perhaps in the end the piece will be remembered most for its elucidation of the writing of Cannon's own *Pulptime*.

Robert M. Price

Robert M. Price's *H. P. Lovecraft and the Cthulhu Mythos* (Starmont House, 1990) consists largely of his best essays from *Crypt of Cthulhu*, the legendary fanzine he began in 1981. If the essays have any unity, it is through the insights they provide on Lovecraft's myth-cycle, insights derived from Price's formidable knowledge of religious studies. Price seems virtually alone in making the "Cthulhu Mythos" the prime focus of his scholarship, but he has certainly shed much interesting light on the subject from his unique and authoritative perspective.

I have, however, both some minor quibbles and some major disagreements with Price's conclusions. "Lovecraft's Concept of Blasphemy" (1981), among his first major pieces, seems slightly flawed in not considering the undercurrent of humour and parody that accompanies Lovecraft's use of the term "blasphemy" and its derivatives in his work. As a complete secularist, Lovecraft could not possibly have taken this notion seriously, however much he might rob the word of explicitly religious connotation; I maintain, indeed, that every single usage of the term in his fiction is potentially if not actually parodic. Without this perspective Price presents some very strange impressions of Lovecraft's characters. Is Randolph Carter "one of Machen's 'great sinners'" (whatever Machen meant by that phrase) for daring to challenge Nyarlathotep in *The Dream-Quest of Unknown Kadath*? How could he be, since in the end he succeeds in his quest? Is it the case that "Charles Dexter Ward came to a bad end because of his occult researches"? Surely the matter is much more complicated than that, and surely the true "blasphemer" in *The Case of Charles Dexter Ward* is Joseph Curwen, not Ward, who is ultimately accorded considerable sympathy.

There are two essays in Price's book that will provoke great controversy— "The Lovecraft-Derleth Connection" and "H. P. Lovecraft and the Cthulhu Mythos." The first is part of what seems to be a systematic (and, to my mind, somewhat insidious) attempt by Price to show that Lovecraft's and Derleth's visions are not as far apart as was thought by Richard L. Tierney and Dirk W. Mosig, who first exposed Derleth's perversions of the myth-cycle. When I published this essay in *Lovecraft Studies*, I added an editorial postscript disputing or qualifying Price's interpretations. Price later remarked to me that he thought my comments somewhat unjust, in that they seemed to present a caricature of his piece; but I stand by my remarks, since to my mind Price presents a caricature of the relationship of Lovecraft and Derleth. In claiming that Lovecraft foreshadows Derleth's opposition of "good" Elder Gods and "evil" Old Ones in his various depictions of cosmic battles between races in *At the Mountains of Madness* and "The Shadow out of Time," Price is very much in error; for, firstly, no apocalyptic significance is implied by Lovecraft in these battles (we are dealing here, as Price has himself shown, with extraterrestrials and not gods), and secondly, there is no legitimate "good vs. evil" struggle. When the Old Ones of *At the Mountains of Madness* battle the Great Race, who are "good" or "evil" here? This moral element is entirely lacking in Lovecraft. Price also maintains that Lovecraft anticipates Derlethian notions of divine intervention in human affairs when Nodens saves Randolph Carter from Nyarlathotep in *Dream-Quest*. But Nodens does not seem to have any actual role in Carter's foiling of Nyarlathotep: this is something Carter appears to effect on his own (indeed, the logic of the story requires it), and Nodens does little more than cheerlead from the grandstand. In any case, one does not know how seriously to take all this in Lovecraft; who or what is Nodens, anyway? To conclude from all this that, "for some important points in Derleth's schema, Lovecraft did provide smaller or larger precedents" is highly misleading; and it becomes even more disingenuous when Price concludes that he is really in "full agreement" with Tierney's and Mosig's views!

Price's overall view of the Mythos is encapsulated in "H. P. Lovecraft and the Cthulhu Mythos," which appears to be his rebuttal to those who downplay the importance of the Mythos as an element or facet of Lovecraft's work. Here some mighty strange things are going on. Price first admits that to divide Lovecraft's stories arbitrarily into such categories as "Cthulhu Mythos," "Dunsanian," and "New England Horror" is a serious perversion of the unity of Lovecraft's work, but he then reintroduces these distinctions backhandedly by dividing Lovecraft's work into the "Dunsanian canon," the "Cthulhu cycle," and the "Arkham cycle"; Price thinks that to brand these as bodies of lore rather than individual stories somehow lends them validity, but some serious difficulties result. Lovecraft almost never used these "bodies of lore" separately in his stories, so that to distinguish them is to fly in the face of what Lovecraft was actually doing. Price applies the term "Cthulhu cycle" to the lore about Lovecraft's extraterrestrial deities—Cthulhu, Yog-Sothoth, etc.; but surely we learn more about Yog-Sothoth in "The Dunwich Horror" than in any other tale, and it was that story that Lovecraft referred to explicitly as part of the "Arkham cycle"! Price (like modern deconstructionists) is forced into the desperate expedient of ignoring or contravening Lovecraft's own testimony in order to preserve a distinction in Lovecraft's stories that is no less artificial than the one he is discarding. He gives the game away, of course, by remarking casually "that Lovecraft drew a distinction, *or at least that we ought to draw one,* between the separate myth-cycles"!

Another component of Price's agenda is the reintroduction of Mythos contributions by other writers, which have been summarily banished to the purgatory of mediocrity where they belong by scholars who wish to preserve the purity of Lovecraft's vision. Here again Price tips his hand by stating that "several of the early additions to the Cthulhu Mythos . . . were fully as enjoyable as Lovecraft's own creations." I shall not dispute Price on what he finds enjoyable, but I must simply remark that nearly all Cthulhu Mythos tales by writers other than Lovecraft strike me as rubbish. In referring to Lovecraft's welcoming of additions to the Mythos by other writers, Price says that "Lovecraft . . . adopted Kuttner's *Book of Iod* . . . and Willis Conover's *Ghorl Nigral* into the Cthulhu Mythos." Come again? Does Lovecraft mention these anywhere save in letters? Lovecraft went on about both these titles in letters to Kuttner and Conover simply in order to be kind to those youths. I did not know it was so easy to make additions to the Mythos. I hereby come up with an occult work, *Liber Nincompoopus,* by the German mystic Augustus von Plagiarius. Presto! I'm in the Mythos!

But Price's misguided zealotry on this matter ought not to blind us to the real advances he has made in Lovecraft studies, even though this book by no means contains them all. "Demythologizing Cthulhu" is, I maintain, a landmark in the interpretation of Lovecraft, even though Price has now modified its conclusions somewhat; "Lovecraft's Use of of Theosophy" makes an ironclad case for the influence of theosophy on "The Call of Cthulhu" and "The Shadow out of Time"; "The Revision Mythos" (an article, I may add with some arrogance, whose nucleus was mine, and which I myself was supposed to write, although Price has done it far better than I could) conclusively establishes the existence of a separate sub-Mythos in Lovecraft's revisions; "Genres in the Lovecraftian Library" draws important distinctions between Lovecraft's mythical books, some being grimoires, others demonologies, scriptures, or works of other types. In all the twenty-eight articles in this volume illuminating insights are made, provocative views offered, and a touch of humour added to leaven what might otherwise seem ponderous and academic. I wish Price were a little more rigorous in his citations (bibliographical information for works is often not supplied, and it is not always clear whether he is referring to the old or the corrected texts of Lovecraft's work) and in his revisions of some of these articles. Some pieces seem a little frivolous or negligible, but on the whole we have here a solid volume that gives a fine sampling of Price's nine-year campaign to popularise and elucidate the Cthulhu Mythos.

Kenneth W. Faig, Jr

Kenneth W. Faig, Jr, is in some ways an even more pioneering Lovecraft scholar than Dirk W. Mosig. Having begun his researches on Lovecraft's life and early writings around 1970, when he was a graduate student at Brown University, he made some remarkable discoveries and effectively initiated serious biographical study of Lovecraft. He produced a 400-page manuscript, "Lovecraftian Voyages," that contains a wealth of information that every biographer (including L. Sprague de Camp and myself) has drawn upon. Faig was, in some senses, almost too far ahead of his time; his work, published and unpublished, fell upon stony ground because the Lovecraft fan community was not prepared for it. Faig's own modesty and lack of self-promotion has also caused him to be unjustly overlooked; but if the history of Lovecraft studies is ever written, he will occupy a central and indispensable place.

When we turn to Faig's *The Parents of Howard Phillips Lovecraft* (Necronomicon Press, 1990), we find a work that is satisfying in almost every way. Here we have a real advance in our knowledge of Lovecraft: Faig has not only gathered together nearly everything that is known about Lovecraft's parents (much of which he has unearthed himself), but has interpreted this somewhat sparse material with a care, subtlety, and penetration that allows startling new insights to be revealed. Consider the matter of the confinement of Lovecraft's father in 1893. Lovecraft was apparently led to believe that his father had suffered some sort of stroke that left him paralysed and comatose; but Faig, studying the family anecdote (first reported by Arthur S. Koki) that Lovecraft's father had to be returned from Chicago to Providence under restraint (presumably in a straitjacket), shows clearly that he could not have been stricken with paralysis at that time, and was probably never in a true coma during his five years' interment. This is a conclusion anyone could have reached—the information was available to all—but it was Faig who actually took the trouble to analyse the evidence and note its discrepancies.

Faig's long account of Lovecraft's mother is the most fully realised portrait we have ever had, and again new insights emerge. Lovecraft's mother did not approve of his involvement in amateur journalism; she was horrified at his attempted enlistment in 1917; and in 1918 the last remaining adult male of the family—her brother Edwin E. Phillips—died: all these facts are clearly relevant to Sarah Susan Lovecraft's gradual mental deterioration through the 1910s until her final breakdown in 1919, and Faig has narrated the account ably.

Faig has also reprinted Clara Hess's remarks about Lovecraft and his mother, which contain some of the most poignant reflections I have ever read. This neighbour of the Lovecrafts never saw the two of them together—an anomaly Faig is right to emphasise. And how can we not be moved by Hess's simple account of Lovecraft's lonely childhood?

> Howard used to go out into the fields in back of my home to study the stars. One early fall evening several of the children in the vicinity assembled to watch him from a distance. Feeling sorry for his loneliness I went up to him and asked him about his telescope and was permitted to look through it. But his language was so technical that I could not understand it and I returned to my group and left him to his lonely study of the heavens.

Faig's work is a model of biographical research, and he is a master in the analysis of evidence, in cautious conjectures on Lovecraft's psychological state, and in the smooth flow of narrative. In subsequent works he continues to make a sound, thorough, comprehensive biography possible by the invaluable ancillary research he is supplying. The two books he has issued from his Moshassuck Press—*Some of the Descendants of Asaph Phillips and Esther Whipple of Foster, Rhode Island* (1993) and Charles C. Beaman and Casey B. Tyler's *Early Historical Accounts of Foster, Rhode Island* (1993)—are, as he himself acknowledges, only of indirect interest to Lovecraftians, but they contain information that simply cannot be found elsewhere.

Lovecraft's own genealogical researches were at best casual and secondhand: he derived much of the knowledge of his paternal line from notes left by his paternal grandmother, while his friend Wilfred B. Talman (a true genealogist) would occasionally prod him into doing work of his own. The genealogical information contained in Lovecraft's letters is frequently suspect, and Faig has devoted the last several years to correcting and augmenting it. He presents a titanic quantity of data in *Some of the Descendants of Asaph Phillips and Esther Whipple,* which lists nearly every known biographical fact about Lovecraft's maternal line beginning with his great-great-grandfather and proceeding down to still-living descendants. Lovecraft's grandfather, mother, father, aunts, and cousins are all included here, and Faig draws upon census records, obituaries, and other evidence to paint biographical portraits of 211 individuals.

In *Early Historical Accounts of Foster, Rhode Island,* Faig has reprinted two treatises from the middle to late 1800s on the town where Lovecraft's maternal line originated. Here again the relation to Lovecraft is tangential, but it should now be obvious that even the most indirect light that can be shed on Lovecraft is of some value. Both these volumes contain material not likely to have been issued by any other publisher, and Faig's unambitious small press should be supported by all Lovecraftians.

Edward W. O'Brien, Jr

Edward W. O'Brien, Jr's strange and charming booklet *Insidious Garden: A Look at Horror Fiction* (Moshassuck Press, 1988) reprints an essay first appearing in the *Wanderer*, a national Catholic weekly. In this article O'Brien finds nearly all writers of horror fiction—especially Lovecraft, "the most dangerous of the macabre authors"—morally questionable because of their emphasis on death, decay, and the lack of salvation. Prefacing this short essay is a lengthy publisher's note by Kenneth W. Faig, Jr, and since this actually takes up the majority of the booklet, it is fitting to comment on it.

In Faig's meandering preface—focussing principally upon the two other important negative views of Lovecraft, those by Edmund Wilson and Colin Wilson—we perhaps do not learn much that is new, but the uninitiated reader will be treated to a wealth of interesting material, both biographical and critical. For me, some of the most charming parts of this long piece are the occasional ventures into unaffected autobiography: it is strangely fitting that we should know something of the man who has shed so much light on the man Lovecraft. There are certain peculiar errors here—Faig follows Colin Wilson in dating "The Picture in the House" by its publication date of 1924 rather than its date of composition (1920); and Lovecraft did not submit handwritten fair copies of his tales to Edwin Baird of *Weird Tales* in 1923, but single-spaced typescripts (still extant in the John Hay Library)—but on the whole his rambling, almost free-associationist style is as delightful a contrast to plodding academic scholarship as can be imagined.

As an atheist I shall try not to be unfair or unkind to O'Brien, although I confess I found his tract irksomely naive. Focusing upon "The Picture in the House," he concludes that Lovecraft wrote the story "to exploit our weaknesses for violence, horror, and depravity." This is nonsense. What Lovecraft was trying to do in this and all his other stories was to express a world-view. O'Brien vaguely realises this but doesn't want to admit it; or, rather, cannot bring himself to admit that that world-view—which has no place for God, and which depicts man as an insignificant atom lost in the vast vortices of space and time—has just as much validity as (indeed, to most intelligent persons nowadays, more validity than) his own Christian viewpoint. He concludes by calling the story "horrifying and *untrue*" (my emphasis)—but this is simply a rhetorical ploy by one who has already assumed the self-evident truth of the Christian world-view. Yes, Lovecraft did see the world as a pretty awful place, with justice an illusion, religion a cheerful opiate, and nothing waiting for us after death save the bliss of utter oblivion. But perhaps this is in fact how things are—certainly all the evidence we can gather points to it. Given this view of life, Lovecraft was (if I may borrow the religionist's terminology) morally obligated to express it in his work. To have done otherwise would have been a sham and a pretence.

O'Brien is also somewhat naive in seeing any direct relationship between the reading of horror literature and pessimism, loss of faith, or antisocial behaviour. This is analogous to the right-wing view that watching pornography will automatically incite someone to rape and violence. Psychologists would have a much easier time of things if the relation of thought to action were as simple as that.

But what is important about O'Brien's work is that he sees Lovecraft as a powerful force not because of all the nasty horrors lurking in his work but precisely because he expresses a world-view effectively and emphatically. I am constantly amazed at the many Christians of my acquaintance who can read Lovecraft with complete insouciance, unaware of how systematically he is dismantling their whole conception of the universe. O'Brien is at least consistent and perceptive enough to see beyond Lovecraft's liquescent horrors to the real horror—humanity's spiritual loneliness, helplessness, and purposelessness—at the core of his work.

Robert H. Waugh

Robert H. Waugh is a remarkable phenomenon in Lovecraft studies. No one could have predicted, when he published his first, relatively brief essay, "The Hands of H. P. Lovecraft" (*Lovecraft Studies*, Fall 1988), that he would evolve into one of the most dynamic and challenging critics of the Providence dreamer in recent years. At a time when, perhaps through a kind of exhaustion or surfeit, some of our leading critics—Barton L. St. Armand, Donald R. Burleson, Robert M. Price, David E. Schultz, even the indefatigable S. T. Joshi—appear to have finished saying what they have to say on Lovecraft, Waugh has written article after substantial article breaking new ground, not so much in the accumulation of facts (most of these have by now already been unearthed), but in the advancement of bold new interpretations of Lovecraft's work. These articles have now been gathered in a splendid volume, *The Monster in the Mirror: Looking for H. P. Lovecraft* (Hippocampus Press, 2006).

In a sense, Waugh's career mirrors that of Lovecraft himself. Just as the Providence writer proceeded from rather nebulous, adjective-laden sketches and prose-poems to immense, richly complex novellas, so have Waugh's essays have become increasingly longer and denser, with an exponential increase in their substance and their suggestiveness. The radical revision of that first essay, now titled "Lovecraft's Hands," would be sufficient to prove it—it has been rewritten so exhaustively as to constitute a new piece. I will be honest and say that I am not always clear on the overall thrust and direction of some of Waugh's essays, but every one of them contains flashes of insight, sometimes tossed off almost incidentally, that make their reading a rewarding experience. At times Waugh seems almost to be free-associating, leading the reader from one topic to another as a bee flits from one flower to the next; but he does so with such intellectual rigour that each point is illuminated before the next is approached. No scholar has read Lovecraft's work (fiction, poetry, essays, letters) more sensitively; no one has absorbed the best Lovecraft scholarship with a due understanding of both its virtues and its shortcomings; and no one has placed Lovecraft in a broader aesthetic and philosophical spectrum that brings the entire history of Western literature and thought into play.

There are two original essays in *The Monster in the Mirror*, and they constitute the final two essays in the book. The first, "Lovecraft and Leopardi: Sunsets and Moonsets," compares the writings and thought of Lovecraft and the great Italian poet, essayist, and thinker. This kind of "compare and contrast" essay could easily have become sophomoric, for of course there is no reason to think that Lovecraft was in any way familiar with Leopardi; one is reminded of Peter Cannon's whimsical essay comparing Lovecraft and John F. Kennedy. But Waugh's analysis is written with such panache and sensitivity that at times it seems as if Lovecraft and Leopardi are speaking to each other, discussing their respective views on cosmicism, fantasy, and human morality in a dialogue that spans the centuries and their differing languages. Waugh had done the same in an earlier essay, "Lovecraft and Keats Confront the 'Awful Rainbow,'" but here it is managed with still greater verve and subtlety.

The other original essay, one of the longest in the book, is "Lovecraft Born Again: An Essay in Apologetic Criticism." The aim of this essay is not merely to show that some of Lovecraft's conceptions are harmonious with Christian thought but that Lovecraft's stories make some "kind of sense . . . to a Christian." I suspect that the great majority of Christians do not read Lovecraft's stories with the kind of care that Waugh himself does, and therefore they are not particularly disturbed with the manifestly atheistic subtext found in them—they read them as entertaining stories, and that is the end of it. A few readers take Lovecraft's work much more seriously: two decades ago Edward W. O'Brien actually maintained that Lovecraft's tales were "evil" and should be avoided by the devout—perhaps an extreme reaction, but one that at least perceives that there is more going on in those tales than merely the exhibition of bug-eyed monsters.

In putting forth this partial and tentative reconciliation of Lovecraft with Christianity, Waugh resurrects the notion (first propounded by Barton L. St Armand) that Lovecraft is a kind of aesthetic or philosophic schizophrenic: that he maintains one thing in his letters (the expression of his philosophical views) and another thing in his fiction. In this formulation Waugh is not nearly so crude as St Armand, who went to the extent of maintaining that Lovecraft was "at once a defender and upholder of a strict universe of natural law as well as its secret subverter"; but his general tendency is in this direction.

I believe, however, that both Waugh and St Armand have failed to grasp the complex rhetoric of Lovecraft's fiction. How is that fiction an expression of his mechanistic materialist stance? Is it, in fact, an expression of it? Great care must be taken in interpreting Lovecraft's statements regarding the nature and purpose of weird fiction. Lovecraft well knew that he could not possibly induce fear in others if he did not induce fear in himself. What, to a materialist like Lovecraft, would constitute the most fearful conception he could imagine? Would it not be the revelation (convincingly expressed in a work of fiction) of the inadequacy of materialism? In "Notes on Writing Weird Fiction" Lovecraft writes: "I choose weird stories because they suit my inclination best—one of my strongest and most persistent wishes being to achieve, momentarily, the illusion of some strange suspension or violation of the galling limitations of time, space, and natural law which for ever imprison us and frustrate our curiosity about the infinite cosmic spaces beyond the radius of our sight and analysis" (*Collected Essays* 2.175-76). Waugh quotes this remark but does not seem to grasp its full implications. If Lovecraft were not, in actual fact, convinced that the universe is materialistic, then he could not possibly find any kind of imaginative release in the "illusion" of its subversion or violation; and that violation occurs only "momentarily" because it takes place only within the context of a work of fiction.

In a sense, Waugh seems guilty of regarding Lovecraft's tales as mimetic—as reflections of events that could conceivably happen in the real world. But Lovecraft's brand of weird fiction posits events that *"could not possibly happen"* (*Selected Letters* 3.434). It is not sufficient to say that Lovecraft did not believe (philosophically) in the literal reality of Cthulhu; it is that he *knew* that an entity like Cthulhu could not possibly exist in our cosmos. It was only the convincing exhibition (through all the aesthetic means available to him) of the *possibility* of a Cthulhu that gave him the imaginative liberation he sought. Consider this passage from a letter of 1930:

> I get no kick at all from *postulating what isn't so*, as religionists and idealists do. That leaves me cold—in fact, I have to stop dreaming about an unknown realm (such as Antarctica or Arabia Deserta) as soon as the explorers enter it and discover a set of real conditions which dreams would be forced to contradict. My big kick comes from *taking reality just as it is*—accepting all the limitations of the most orthodox science—and then permitting my symbolising faculty to *build outward* from the existing facts; rearing a structure of *indefinite promise and possibility* whose topless towers are in no cosmos or dimension penetrable by the contradicting-power of the tyrannous and inexorable intellect. But the whole secret of the kick is *that I know damn well it isn't so.* (*Selected Letters* 3.140)

I am not sure that this does not express the sum total of Lovecraft's aesthetic of weird fiction—and that final sentence is the key that unlocks the riddle of Lovecraft's apparent "schizophrenia" in seeming to postulate non-materialistic or super-materialistic phenomena in his stories. *He knew damn well it wasn't so.*

This is why it is highly dangerous to appeal to the stories when attempting to ascertain what Lovecraft "believed." Waugh occasionally falls into this error. When Waugh writes that Lovecraft "does believe in the existence of physical law, its coherence, rationality, and uniformity—but breaking with Haeckel he also entertains the idea that the universe is so large that areas might exist where the universality of law breaks down," his evidence for this astonishing assertion is . . . the opening paragraph of "The Call of Cthulhu." But that utterance is made precisely for the purpose of laying down the foundation for the tale's ultimate (fictional and fictitious) subversion of materialism—something Lovecraft knew damn well wasn't so. Consider a passage in a 1929 letter where he is coming to terms with the theory of relativity and maintaining (in contrast to a wide array of mystics and religionists who were attempting to maintain that relativity had suddenly justified all kinds of outmoded thoughts regarding the existence of God): "We *know* these [natural] laws work *here,* because we have applied them in countless ways and have *never* found them to fail. . . . [F]or many trillion and quadrillion miles outward from us the conditions of space are sufficiently like our own to be comparatively unaffected by relativity. That is, these surrounding stellar regions may be taken as part of our illusion-island in infinity, since the laws that work on earth work scarcely less well some distance beyond it" (*Selected Letters* 2.264-65). Similarly, Waugh asserts (from the evidence of the fiction) that "For Lovecraft dreams represent a remarkable evasion of the appearance of things," but they do nothing of the sort.

In other instances where Waugh attempts to establish that "the philosophic dregs of religion tainted Lovecraft," he comes mighty close to special pleading. No one is likely to think that Lovecraft is the more religious simply because he uses names taken from the Bible, since of course these names are bestowed mostly upon New England characters whose nomenclature, derived largely from the Old Testament, Lovecraft is echoing merely for the sake of verisimilitude. And when Waugh maintains that the Gardner family in "The Colour out of Space" suffers "damnation," he seems guilty of a misuse of the word—for the notion of damnation cannot possibly be separated from the notion of some kind of post-mortem punishment, something entirely absent in the story. The Gardners simply die—horribly and grotesquely, to be sure, but that is all there is to it. Waugh quotes a line from the story in which the Gardners "walked half in another world between lines of nameless guards to a certain and familiar doom"—but a doom is very different from damnation.

I trust the above remarks sufficiently suggest that, even when one differs with Waugh's analyses and conclusions, they nonetheless stimulate thought to an exceptional degree and compel one to come to terms with one's own understanding of the Providence writer. Substantial as *The Monster in the Mirror* is, it by no means embodies Waugh's final words on Lovecraft. Several previously published essays do not appear in the book, and so Waugh already has the nucleus of a second volume of essays. It is to be hoped that some of our leading scholars absorb the variegated intellectual nourishment this book has to offer, so that they may be reminded that the work of interpreting Lovecraft is far from over.

Index

Abner, Kenneth 17
Ackroyd, Peter 87
Acolytes of Cthulhu (Price) 21
"Action" (Schow) 53
Acts of Love (Gullette) 44
Adams, Benjamin 224-25
Adrian, Jack 76
Adventures of Opal and Cupid, The (Tryon) 103, 104
"Agatha's Ghost" (Campbell) 116
"Age of Desire, The" (Campbell) 131
Aickman, Robert 33, 34, 35, 102, 107, 114, 133, 136, 180
Aiken, Conrad 143
Aiken, Joan 76, 79-80
Albert, Walter 179
"Alchemist, The" (Lovecraft) 202
Aldiss, Brian 47
Algernon Blackwood: A Bio-Bibliography (Ashley) 68-69
Algernon Blackwood: An Extraordinary Life (Ashley) 65-68
"All Dracula's Children" (Simmons) 47
"All for Sale" (Campbell) 117
"'All She Said Was "Yes"'" (Jackson) 92
All That Glitters (Tryon) 103, 104
Allingham, Margery 108
Alone with the Horrors (Campbell) 15, 109-14
"Alternative, The" (Campbell) 115
Always Comes Evening (Howard) 39
Ambrose Bierce and the Queen of Spades (Hall) 167-68
Ambrosia 44
American Psycho (Ellis) 50
Amory, Mark 183
Anatomy of Horror (Barclay) 178

Anatomy of Wonder (Barron) 173, 177
"Ancestral Footstep, The" (Hawthorne) 174
Ancient Exhumations (Sargent) 221
Ancient Images (Campbell) 119
Ancient Track, The (Lovecraft) 38
"'And No Bird Sings'" (Benson) 79
"'And the Dead Spake'" (Benson) 79
Anderson, Kevin J. 48
"Angels' Moon" (Koja) 49
"Animal Fair, The" (Bloch) 101
Aniolowski, David Scott 220
Anne Rice (Roberts) 195-96
Another Eucharist (Gullette) 44
Anthony, Craig 220
Antieau, Kim 48
Arbor House Celebrity Book of Horror Stories, The 100
"Are You Loathsome Tonight?" (Brite) 225
Argosy 18
Arkham House 15-16, 17, 21-27, 39, 43, 60, 191, 201, 203, 204, 205, 211, 230, 235
Arkham's Masters of Horror (Ruber) 23-27
Arroyo (Burleson) 146-49
Arthur, John 17
Arthur Machen: Apostle of Wonder (Valentine-Dobson) 70-71, 74
Ash-Tree Press 16, 17, 80, 83
"Ashes" (Lovecraft-Eddy) 253
Ashley, Mike 65-70, 176, 178, 179
Asimov, Isaac 46
Asimov, Janet 47
Asquith, Cynthia 34
Astounding Science Fiction 205
Astounding Stories 18, 205

At the Mountains of Madness (Lovecraft) 160, 203, 205, 206, 238, 250, 257
At the Mountains of Madness and Other Tales of Terror (Lovecraft) 201
Austin, Sherry 165–66
"Autoepitaphy" (Caldecott) 88
"Autumn Cricket" (Dunsany) 34

"Babel's Children" (Barker) 136
"Baby" (Campbell) 111
"Back for Christmas" (Collier) 33
Bacon, Sir Francis 188
"Bad Guy Hats" (Schow) 140
Baird, Edwin 261
Baldwin, Louisa 29
Ballantine Books 201–5
Ballard, J. G. 133–34
Balzac, Honoré de 176
Banks, Iain 102
Barbaric Triumph, The (Herron) 186
Barbauld, Anna Letitia 28
Barbour, David 232–34
Barclay, Glen St John 178
Barker, Clive 16, 56, 57, 102, 111, 114, 131–37, 139, 141, 146, 165, 206, 231
Barlow, R. H. 19, 39
"Barrens, The" (Wilson) 215
Barrett, Neal, Jr 53
Barron, Neil 173, 176–79
"Bars on Satan's Jailhouse, The" (Partridge) 151
"Battle That Ended the Century, The" (Lovecraft-Barlow) 227
Baudelaire, Charles 39, 41, 176
"Be Yourself" (Bloch) 22
Beaman, Charles C. 260
Bear, Greg 15
"Beast in the Cave, The" (Lovecraft) 202
"Beast with Five Fingers, The" (Harvey) 33
"Beckoning Fair One, The" (Onions) 33

Beckwith, Henry L. P. 183
"Becoming Visible" (Campbell) 116
"Behold, I Stand at the Door and Knock" (Price) 220
Bell, Ian 74–76
Benson, E. F. 76–80, 178
Benson, Frank 72
Berglund, E. P. 221
Best of H. P. Lovecraft, The (Lovecraft) 203–4, 205
Best Supernatural Stories (Lovecraft) 24
"Between the Lights" (Benson) 79
Between the Minute and the Hour (Burrage) 81
Beyond the Lamplight (Burleson) 143–44
"Beyond the Threshold" (Derleth) 210
"Beyond the Wall of Sleep" (Lovecraft) 176, 202, 216, 250
Beyond the Wall of Sleep (Lovecraft) 202, 216
"Beyond Words" (Campbell) 111
Bierce, Ambrose 9, 32, 33, 34, 36–37, 41, 43, 50, 166–68, 173, 175, 176, 178, 193, 196, 217–18
Bierstadt, E. H. 184
"Big 'C,' The" (Lumley) 214
"Bight of Sonic Blasters" (Daniels) 41–42
Billson, Anne 136
"Biography of a Story" (Jackson) 194
Biography of Lord Dunsany (Amory) 183
Bishop, Michael 15, 48
Bishop, Zealia 219
"Black Bargain" (Bloch) 22
"Black Brat of Dunwich, The" (Sargent) 221
Black Castle, The (Daniels) 95
Black Leather Required (Schow) 61, 138–42
"Black Man with a Horn" (Klein) 219
Black Spirits and White (Cram) 30

Black Sunday (Harris) 152
"Black Vulture, The" (Sterling) 37
Black Wine (Campbell-Grant) 111
Blackwood, Algernon 9, 27, 34, 35, 65-70, 88, 114, 117, 137, 159, 173, 175, 178, 194, 195, 196, 239
"Blade and the Claw, The" (Cave) 215
"Blagdaross" (Dunsany) 165
Blake, William 135
Blatty, William Peter 180
Bleiler, E. F. 182-83
Blessing of Pan, The (Dunsany) 185
Blish, James 218-19
Bloch, Robert 15, 21, 22, 29, 50-52, 101, 150, 152, 196, 203-4, 207, 210, 211, 216, 218
Blood Kiss, The (Etchison) 98
Bloom, Harold 247
"Body Politic, The" (Barker) 136
Boerem, R. 108
Book of Dreams, A (Gullette) 45
Books of Blood (Barker) 135, 136
Booth, Wayne C. 244
Borden, Lizzie 68
Boston, Bruce 40
Bowen, Elizabeth 34, 35
"Bowmen, The" (Machen) 70
Bradbury, Ray 25, 27, 100, 141, 143, 150, 166
Brahms, Johannes 104
Brandner, Gary 213, 215
Brandt & Brandt 89
Brangham, Godfrey 73
Breach, Arthur William Lloyd 220
Breiding, G. Sutton 40
Brennan, Joseph Payne 39
Bride of Frankenstein (film) 179
Bright Messenger, The (Blackwood) 67
Brite, Poppy Z. 225
"Broadcast" (Campbell) 111
Brontës, the 32, 33
Brown, Charles Brockden 49, 50
Bryan, William Jennings 191

Bryant, Edward 57, 60, 142
Budrys, Algis 101
"Buffalo Hunter, The" (Straub) 107
"Bulletin" (Jackson) 91
Bulwer-Lytton, Edward 28, 227
Burke, Rusty 192
Burks, Arthur J. 26-27
Buranelli, Vincent 196
Burleson, Donald R. 142-49, 186, 213, 231, 237, 241-49, 251, 252, 262
Burnham, Crispin 220
Burning Court, The (Carr) 95
Burrage, A. M. 16, 80-83
Burrell, Christopher 180
By the Waters of Babylon (Tryon) 103, 104
Byatt, A. S. 35

Cabal (Barker) 135, 136
Cabell, James Branch 70, 175
"Cabin in the Woods, The" (Laymon) 224-25
Cadnum, Michael 87
Caldecott, Andrew 87-89
Caliban 237
California Gothic (Etchison) 98
"Call Home" (Etchison) 52, 98
"Call of Cthulhu, The" (Lovecraft) 207, 211, 214, 225, 258, 265
Campbell, John W. 18, 26, 205
Campbell, Joseph 188
Campbell, Ramsey 15, 26, 27, 29, 30, 34, 35, 52, 53, 55, 59, 61, 65, 82, 95, 98, 101, 106, 107, 109-31, 134, 135, 136, 143, 144, 150, 156, 159, 164, 173, 178, 180, 192, 208, 210, 213, 215, 219
"Cancer Causes Rats" (Hodge) 54
Canning Wonder, The (Machen) 70
Cannon, Peter 22, 186, 196, 219, 226-29, 231, 234-36, 249-56, 263
Cardin, Matt 225
Carpenter, Lynette 192

Carr, John Dickson 95, 108
Carroll, Noël 173, 180
Carter, Lin 40, 75, 202, 218, 219, 241
Case, David 15
Case of Charles Dexter Ward, The (Lovecraft) 160, 201, 202, 205, 228, 250, 252, 253, 256
"Case of Mr Ryalstone, The" (Burrage) 82
"Casting the Runes" (James) 31
Castle, Mort 213, 215
"Castle of the Honda Monsters" (Partridge) 151
Castro, Adam-Troy 138
"Caterpillars" (Benson) 79
Cather, Willa 32
"Cats of Ulthar, The" (Lovecraft) 248
Catullus (C. Valerius Catullus) 36
Cave, Hugh B. 21, 101, 213, 215, 220
"Celephaïs" (Lovecraft) 205
"Cellars, The" (Campbell) 110, 112
"Cement Surroundings" (Lumley) 210
Centaur, The (Blackwood) 65, 67, 69
Cervantes, Miguel de 145
Chamberlain, Houston Stewart 182
Chambers, Robert W. 163, 217-18
Chandler, Raymond 20
"Chaos into Time, The" (Cisco) 163
Chaosium 216
Chappell, Fred 59-60, 219
Charwoman's Shadow, The (Dunsany) 185
Cheever, John 34, 35
Cheryn, Jerome 48
Children of Cthulhu, The (Pelan-Adams) 224-25
"Children of the Kingdom, The" (Klein) 133
"Children of the Night" (Rusch) 46
"Chimney, The" (Campbell) 126
Chizmar, Richard 53-55

Christie, Agatha 108, 191
"Christmas Carrion" (Burleson) 144
Chronology out of Time, The (Cannon) 249-51, 254
"Chui Chai" (Somtow) 48
Cisco, Michael 162-64
Citizen Vampire (Daniels) 95
Citro, Joseph A. 183, 213, 215
Clark, Alan M. 58
Clarke, Arthur C. 26
Clemm, Maria 169
Cline, Leonard 87
Clive Barker's Shadows in Eden (Jones) 131-37
"Clock, The" (Harvey) 33
Close to the Bone (Taylor) 56
Clute, John 187
Cold Blood (Chizmar) 53-55
Cold Hand in Mine (Aickman) 114
Cold Harbour (Young) 87
"Cold Print" (Campbell) 110, 113, 208
Cold Print (Campbell) 111, 219
Coleridge, Samuel Taylor 36, 162-63
Collected Ghost Stories of E. F. Benson, The (Benson) 76-80
Collected Ghost Stories of M. R. James, The (James) 32
Collected Poems (Wandrei) 39
Collected Poems: Nightmares and Visions (Tierney) 40-41
Collected Works (Bierce) 37
Collier, John 33, 102, 178
Collins, Nancy A. 48, 54
"Colossus" (Wandrei) 17, 18
Colossus (Wandrei) 17, 19
"Colossus Eternal" (Wandrei) 17, 18
"Colour out of Space, The" (Lovecraft) 35, 202, 203, 214, 242, 248, 265
Colour out of Space, The (Lovecraft) 202
Come Along with Me (Jackson) 33, 89, 90, 91, 193

"Come, Go Home with Me" (Austin) 165
Complete Masters of Darkness, The (Etchison) 99-103
"Concussion" (Campbell) 110
"Confession of Charles Linkworth, The" (Benson) 77
Connoisseur and Other Stories, The (de la Mare) 33
Connolly, Cyril 71
Connors, Scott 186, 187, 191
Conover, Willis 229, 258
Conrad, Joseph 74, 75
"Contagion, The" (Asimov) 47
"Conversations in a Dead Language" (Ligotti) 158
Cook, W. Paul 240
"Cool Air" (Lovecraft) 228, 229
Copper, Basil 16, 21, 28-29, 219
"Cottage Tenant" (Long) 102
"Count Magnus" (James) 31
Count of Eleven, The (Campbell) 113, 117, 121, 125, 128, 131
Countess of Lowndes Square, The (Benson) 76
"Coup de Grâce, The" (Bierce) 50
"Coyotes" (Partridge) 151
Cram, Ralph Adams 28, 30
Crane, Hart 38, 60
Crawford, Gary William 175-76, 179
Crawford, William L. 182
"Crawling Chaos, The" (Lovecraft-Jackson) 206
Crawling Chaos (Lovecraft) 205-7
"Creature on the Couch, The" (Bishop) 48
Crispin, A. C. 49
Crockett, Davy 170
Crofts, Anna Helen 202
"Crouch End" (King) 221
Crow, The (film) 142
Crowley, Aleister 177
Crowned Heads (Tryon) 103, 104

Crypt of Cthulhu 9, 228, 258
Cthulhu Mythos 24, 83, 110, 162, 201, 207-25, 256-58
Cthulhu Mythos Bibliography and Concordance, A (Jarocha-Ernst) 208
Cthulhu 2000 (Turner) 15
Cthulhu's Heirs (Stratman) 219-21
Cujo (King) 106
Cullen, John 104
Culture Publications 20
Curse of the Wise Woman, The (Dunsany) 185
Cutting Edge (Etchison) 99

"Dagon" (Lovecraft) 83
Dagon (Chappell) 59, 219
Dagon 160
Dagon and Other Macabre Tales (Lovecraft) 176
Dahl, Roald 175
Dahmer, Jeffrey 55
Dalby, Richard 74, 76-80, 100
Damnation Game, The (Barker) 131-32, 133, 136, 139
Daniels, Keith Allen 41-42
Daniels, Les 95-98, 102, 181
Dark at Heart (Lansdale) 52-53
Dark Barbarian, The (Herron) 186, 187
Dark Chamber, The (Cline) 87
Dark Companions (Campbell) 101, 110-11, 116
Dark Country, The (Etchison) 98
Dark Feasts (Campbell) 109
Dark Gods (Klein) 101
"Dark Isle, The" (Bloch) 22
Dark Odyssey (Wandrei) 39
Dark of the Moon (Derleth) 19, 36
Dark Things (Derleth) 19, 211
Darker Passions (Bryant) 57
Darkling, The (Kesterton) 16
Darkling Tide, The (Long) 39
Darkside (Etchison) 98
Datlow, Ellen 10

Davidson, Avram 101
Davies, L. P. 175
de Camp, L. Sprague 25, 101, 102, 182, 185, 229, 233, 252, 259
de la Mare, Walter 32, 33, 50, 76, 80, 177, 243
"De Mortuis" (Collier) 33
De Vermis Mysteriis (Prinn) 22
"Dead Giveaway" (Shea) 211
"Dead Man, The" (Bradbury) 100
Dead Reckonings 10
Dead Titans, Waken! (Wandrei) 19
"Deadtime Story" (Etchison) 99
"Daemon Lover, The" (Jackson) 193
Death Artist, The (Etchison) 98-99
"Death of Edgar Allan Poe, The" (Cisco) 163
"Death of Halpin Frayser, The" (Bierce) 33
Death Stalks the Night (Cave) 21
"Death Watch" (Cave) 220
Decoded Mirrors (Tem) 58
"Decodings" (Tem) 58
"Deep Ones, The" (Wade) 211
"Deepnet" (Langford) 59
Dehan, Richard 29
Delderfield, R. F. 105
Demons by Daylight (Campbell) 59, 101, 110, 113, 115, 219
"Depths, The" (Campbell) 111-12
Derleth, August 15, 16, 17, 19, 21, 23-24, 25, 26, 27, 36, 39, 43, 50, 51, 191, 201, 202, 203, 206, 207-8, 209-12, 214, 216-17, 218, 222, 231, 235, 256-57
Descartes, René 188, 189
"Descent into Egypt, A" (Blackwood) 69
"Descent into the Maelström, A" (Poe) 74
Desirable Residences and Other Stories (Benson) 76-77
"Detailer, The" (Etchison) 99
"Devil of a Tale" (Jackson) 90

Dialhys, Nictzin 233
Dickens, Charles 32, 169, 249
Dickinson, Emily 36
Dictionary of National Biography 87
"Dinner for a Gentleman" (Jackson) 90
"Dirty Work" (Shiner) 53
Discoverie of Witchcraft, The (Scot) 169
Divinity Student, The (Cisco) 162
"Do Not Hasten to Bid Me Adieu" (Partridge) 150
Dobson, Roger 70-71, 73, 75
"Documents in the Case of Elizabeth Akeley" (Lupoff) 218
"Dog Park, The" (Etchison) 99
Dolores Claiborne (King) 106
Don't Dream (Wandrei) 17, 18
Doom That Came to Sarnath, The (Lovecraft) 201, 202
Door Below, The (Cave) 21
"Down in the Mouth" (Burleson) 143-44
"Down There" (Campbell) 112
Doyle, Sir Arthur Conan 211, 226-27, 228, 252
"Dr. Bondi's Methods" (Cisco) 163
Dr Grimshawe's Secret (Hawthorne) 174
Dr Jekyll and Mr Hyde (Stevenson) 82
Dr Stiggins (Machen) 70, 71
Dracula (Stoker) 46, 195
Dracula (film) 45, 46
"Dracula 1944" (Hoch) 47
Dragonfly (Durbin) 22-23
Drake, David 219
Dream-Cycle of H. P. Lovecraft, The (Lovecraft) 204-5
Dream quest of H. P. Lovecraft, The (Schweitzer) 241
Dream-Quest of Unknown Kadath, The (Lovecraft) 201, 202, 205, 220, 252, 256, 257
Dreamer's Tales, A (Dunsany) 165

"Dreams in the Witch House, The" (Lovecraft) 83
Dreams of Dark and Light (Lee) 15
Dreams of Lovecraftian Horror (Pugmire) 221
"Dressmaker's Mannequin, The" (Austin) 165
Dryden, John 169
"Duc de L'Omelette, The" (Poe) 169
Dumas, Alexandre 84
Dunn, Katherine 48
Dunsany, Lord 9, 27, 34, 35, 36, 65, 67, 69, 74, 117, 134, 157, 165, 176, 183–85, 194, 195, 196, 197, 207, 225, 239, 249
Dunsany the Dramatist (Bierstadt) 184
"Dunwich Horror, The" (Lovecraft) 26, 108, 202, 203, 204, 220, 242, 253, 257
Dunwich Horror, The (Lovecraft) 202
Dunwich Horror and Others, The (Lovecraft) 203, 204
Durbin, Frederic S. 22–23
"Dust-Cloud, The" (Benson) 77, 78
"Dweller in Darkness, The" (Derleth) 211
Dziemianowicz, Stefan 9, 24, 58, 87–89, 142

Eagleton, Terry 244, 246
Early Historical Accounts of Foster, Rhode Island (Beaman-Tyler) 260
Ebony and Crystal (Smith) 39
Eckhardt, Jason C. 231
Ecstasy and Other Poems (Wandrei) 39
Eddison, E. R. 41, 97
Eddy, C. M., Jr. 26
Edelman, Scott 59
Edkins, Ernest A. 190
Education of Uncle Paul, The (Blackwood) 65, 68, 69
Effinger, George Alec 101
Egan, James 193, 253
Eldritch Tales 220, 226

"Elegie" (Burrell) 180
Elgar, Edward 68
Eliot, T. S. 38
Ellis, Bret Easton 50
Ellison, Harlan 45, 46
Emperor of Dreams (Sidney-Fryer) 43
Encyclopedia of Fantasy (Clute) 187
Encyclopedia of Philosophy, The 188
Encyclopédie (d'Alembert et al.) 188
"End of a Summer's Day, The" (Campbell) 113
"End of the Line" (Campbell) 113
Eng, Steve 176
"Entertainment, The" (Campbell) 117
Epicurus 240
Episodes Before Thirty (Blackwood) 66, 67
Esoteric Order of Dagon 231
Esquire 18
Estleman, Loren D. 47
Etchison, Dennis 52, 61, 98–103, 135, 144, 180
Eureka (Poe) 239
Euripides 36
"Evening with Aldous Huxley, An" (Daniels) 42
"Events Concerning a Nude Fold-Out Found in a Harlequin Romance, The" (Lansdale) 53
Everts, R. Alain 74
"Evil Clergyman, The" (Lovecraft) 235
Exorcisms and Ecstasies (Wagner) 21
Exorcist, The (Blatty) 180, 196
"Experience and Fiction" (Jackson) 194
Extra Day, The (Blackwood) 68
Extrapolation 253
"Eye and the Finger, The" (Wandrei) 18
Eye and the Finger, The (Wandrei) 17

Face That Must Die, The (Campbell) 55, 111, 116, 118, 121, 125, 126, 131
Faig, Kenneth W., Jr 73, 230–32, 236, 259–60, 261
"Falco Ossifracus" (Miniter) 226
"Fall of the House of Usher, The" (Poe) 28, 35
"Family" (Oates) 102
Fantastic 91
Fantastic Poetry (Lovecraft) 38
Fantasy: The Literature of Subversion (Jackson) 173, 180
Fantasy Literature (Barron) 177
Farmer, Philip José 46, 47, 48, 210
Farris, John 138, 178
Faulkner, William 175, 249, 254
"Feaster from the Stars, The" (Berglund) 221
Fedogan & Bremer 17–21, 58
"Feet Foremost" (Hartley) 29
Ferris, Henry 16–17
"Festival, The" (Lovecraft) 202
"Fête" (Rutherford) 42–43
Fiedler, Leslie A. 181
Fifty-one Tales (Dunsany) 158
Final Edition (Benson) 77, 78
Finch, Paul 225
Finn, Mark 188, 191
Finney, Charles G. 175
"Firebrand Symphony, The" (Hodge) 225
"Firebrands of Torment, The" (Cisco) 163
Fires Burn Blue (Caldecott) 87, 89
Fish Dinner in Memison, A (Eddison) 97
Fisher, Benjamin Franklin, IV 174, 177, 179
Flaubert, Gustave 176
Flesh Artist, The (Taylor) 56–57
Fleurs du mal, Les (Baudelaire) 41
Flint Knife, The (Benson) 76

Flowers from the Moon and Other Lunacies (Bloch) 22
Flute Song (Burleson) 144–46
"Fog Horn, The" (Bradbury) 100
49 Pieces (Gullette) 45
Four Shadowings (Burleson) 142, 143
Fowles, John 134
Fox, Randy 58
Fragment of Life, A (Machen) 70, 72
Frank, Frederick S. 174, 177
Frankenstein (Shelley) 46, 174
Frankenstein (film) 45, 46
"Franklyn Paragraphs, The" (Campbell) 110, 219–20
Fraser, Phyllis 174
Freeman, Mary Eleanor Wilkins 30, 165
Freisner, Esther M. 48
Friedman, Lenemaja 178, 192, 197
"Friends of the Friends, The" (James) 32
From a Safe Distance (Gullette) 45
"From Beyond" (Lovecraft) 159, 202, 206
"From the Papers of Helmut Hecker" (Williamson) 214
"Frosty" (Burleson) 143
Fruit Stoners, The (Blackwood) 68
Fuentes, Carlos 167
"Fulfillment" (Tierney) 41
Fungi from Yuggoth (Lovecraft) 17, 40, 223, 234

Gaiman, Neil 135, 205
Galpin, Alfred 191, 243
"Garden of Blackred Roses, A" (Grant) 102
Gardiner, Patrick 188
Gardner, Erle Stanley 191
Garth, Samuel 169
Garton, Ray 213, 215
Gaskell, Elizabeth 32
Gatto, John Taylor 241, 253
"General's Wife, The" (Straub) 102

Gerald's Game (King) 106
"Ghost Hunter, The" (Herbert) 29
"Ghost of the Valley, The" (Dunsany) 34
Ghost Pirates, The (Hodgson) 75
Ghost-Stories of an Antiquary (James) 32
Ghost Story (Straub) 109
Ghostly Tales (Campbell) 110, 111
Ghostly Tales of Henry James, The (James) 32
"Ghosts, The" (Dunsany) 34
Ghosts and Grisly Things (Campbell) 114-15
"Giantess" (Baudelaire) 41
Gilden, Mel 48
Girl Who Loved Tom Gordon, The (King) 106-7
"Glimmer, Glimmer" (Effinger) 101
Goblin Tower, The (Long) 39
Gods of Pegāna, The (Dunsany) 184
"Going Under" (Campbell) 115
Gold by Gold (Gorman) 84
Golden Gryphon Press 21
Goldstone, Adrian 70
Gordon, Tom 106-7
Gorman, Ed 54, 213, 215
Gorman, Herbert S. 83-87, 243
Goss, Michael 74, 75
Gothic Tales of Terror (Haining) 28, 30
Goya y Lucientes, Francisco José de 135
Graham, Heather 46
Grant, Charles L. 102, 136, 178
Grant, Donald M. 95
Graves, Clotilde Mary 29
Grayson, Perry M. 39
Great and Secret Show, The (Barker) 133, 135, 136
Great Tales of Terror and the Supernatural (Wise-Fraser) 174
Green Round, The (Machen) 71, 73
"Green Tea" (Le Fanu) 33
Green Transfer, The (Gullette) 45

Greenberg, Martin H. 51, 100, 212-16
Greenwood Press 187
Grenander, M. E. 176, 196
"Grey Brothers" (Caldecott) 88
"Grey House, The" (Copper) 28-29
Grimscribe (Ligotti) 156
Grin, Leo 188, 189-91
Grisham, John 191
Guillaud, Lauric 187
Gullette, Alan 44-45
"Gums" (Burleson) 143
Gurdjieff, George Ivanovich 67

"H. P. L." (Wilson) 214
H. P. Lovecraft (Cannon) 251-54
H. P. Lovecraft: A Critical Study (Burleson) 241-44, 251
H. P. Lovecraft: A Life (Joshi) 24, 189
H. P. Lovecraft: New England Decadent (St Armand) 237-41
H. P. Lovecraft: The Decline of the West (Joshi) 189, 251
H. P. Lovecraft and the Cthulhu Mythos (Price) 256-58
H. P. Lovecraft Companion, The (Shreffler) 241
Haber, Karen 47
Haeckel, Ernst 265
Haggard, H. Rider 207
Haining, Peter 27-30, 173, 176
"Hair of the Dog" (Burleson) 143
Hall, Joan Wylie 89, 92, 192-95, 197
Hall, Oakley 167-68
Hamlet (Shakespeare) 37
Hammett, Dashiell 100
"Hand in Glove" (Bowen) 34
"Hand of the O'Mecca, The" (Wandrei) 19
Hannibal (Harris) 152-53
Hannibal Rising (Harris) 153-56
"Happy Hour" (Watson) 29
Hardy, Thomas 32, 36, 174, 249
Haringa, Jack M. 10

Harris, Thomas 50, 152–56
Hartley, L. P. 29, 33, 34, 80, 178
Harvest Home (Tryon) 86, 103, 104, 106
Harvey, W. F. 33
Hashish-Eater, The (Smith) 27
Hastur Cycle, The (Price) 216–18
"Hate" (Tierney) 41
Haunted (Herbert) 29
"Haunted and the Haunters, The" (Bulwer-Lytton) 28
"Haunted House, The" (Woolf) 29
"Haunter of the Dark, The" (Lovecraft) 207, 250
"Haunter of the Graveyard, The" (Shea) 211
Haunting of Hill House, The (Jackson) 30, 90, 121, 192, 193, 194
Hautala, Rick 54, 183
Havoc, James 205–7
Hawthorne, Nathaniel 70, 84, 113, 174, 243
"*He* Will Be There" (Cisco) 163
Heald, Hazel 219
Hearn, Lafcadio 178
"Heart of Darkness" (Conrad) 88
Height of the Scream, The (Campbell) 110
Hellfire Club, The (Straub) 108
"Hell's Event" (Barker) 136
Hemingway, Ernest 57
Herbert, James 29, 178
"Herbert West—Reanimator" (Lovecraft) 163, 206, 234, 243, 252, 253
Hero with a Thousand Faces, The (Campbell) 188
Herrera, Philip 201
Herron, Don 186–92
"He's Going to Kill Me Tonight" (Rutherford) 43
Hess, Clara 259–60
Hichens, Robert 177
Hieroglyphics (Machen) 73
Highsmith, Patricia 55

Hill of Dreams, The (Machen) 71, 72, 73, 74
Hillyer, Robert 71
Hippocampus Press 87
"His Last Bow" (Doyle) 228
"Hit" (Barrett) 53
Hitchcock, Alfred 50, 100
Hitler, Adolf 230
Hoch, Edward D. 47, 52
Hodge, Brian 54, 225
Hodgson, William Hope 58, 74–76, 136
Hoffman, Barry 54
Hoffman, Charles 188, 191
Hoffman, Nina Kiriki 49
Hoffmann, E. T. A. 240
Hoffmann, Roald 41
Hogg, James 36
"Hollow Man, The" (Partridge) 151
Hoppenstand, Gary 135
"Horror at Red Hook, The" (Lovecraft) 226–27, 238, 241
"Horror-Horn, The" (Benson) 79
"Horror House of Blood" (Campbell) 109, 110
"Horror in the Museum, The" (Lovecraft-Heald) 206, 207
Horror in the Museum and Other Revisions, The (Lovecraft et al.) 175–76
Horror Literature (Barron) 176–79
Horror Literature (Tymn) 173–76
"Hound, The" (Lovecraft) 206, 238, 253
"Hounds of Tindalos, The" (Long) 163
House of Souls, The (Machen) 114
"House of the Hatchet" (Bloch) 29
House of the Seven Gables, The (Hawthorne) 174
House of the Toad, The (Tierney) 21
"House of Unrest, The" (Burrage) 81
House on Nazareth Hill, The (Campbell) 30, 117, 120–23, 126

House on the Borderland, The (Hodgson) 75
Houses Without Doors (Straub) 107
Howard, Elizabeth Jane 34
Howard, John 73
Howard, Nic 71
Howard, Robert E. 15, 22, 25, 39, 58, 68, 73, 186-92, 196, 206, 207, 230, 232-33
Hughes, Rhys 16
Human Chord, The (Blackwood) 65, 67
Hume, David 188
"Hunger, an Introduction" (Straub) 108
Huntington, Collis P. 168
Huxley, Thomas Henry 243
Huysmans, J.-K. 176
Hyman, Laurence Jackson 89
Hyman, Stanley Edgar 89, 91
"Hypnos" (Lovecraft) 253

"I Have a Special Plan for This World" (Ligotti) 161
I, Said the Fly (Shea) 57
"I Will Teach You" (Cisco) 163
"Ice Age of Dreams" (Cisco) 163, 164
"Imprisoned with the Pharaohs" (Lovecraft-Houdini) 202
"In Beauty, Like the Night" (Partridge) 150, 151
In Mayan Splendor (Long) 39
"In Memoriam: Robert Ervin Howard" (Lovecraft) 191
"In the Bag" (Campbell) 111
In the Fire of Spring (Tryon) 104
"In the Night, in the Dark" (Ligotti) 157
"In the Trees" (Campbell) 111
"In the Tube" (Benson) 77
"In the Vault" (Lovecraft) 203, 206, 242
"In the Walls of Eryx" (Lovecraft-Sterling) 202

Incarnate (Campbell) 112, 117
Incredible Adventures (Blackwood) 67, 114
Indick, Ben P. 237
Inhabitant of the Lake, The (Campbell) 110, 115
"Inn of the Flying Dragon, The" (Le Fanu) 50
Innsmouth Heritage, The (Stableford) 58
"Inside the Cackle Factory" (Etchison) 99
Insidious Garden (O'Brien) 261-62
Interview with the Vampire (Rice) 47
"Intoxicated, The" (Jackson) 92
Intruders (Burrage) 80
"Invisible Empire, The" (Van Pelt) 225
Invisible Sun (Wandrei) 19
Irrational Numbers (Langford) 59

Jackson, Barry 89
Jackson, Marylou 89
Jackson, Rosemary 173, 180
Jackson, Shirley 9, 30, 33, 50, 89-92, 102, 106, 114, 121, 136, 178, 183, 192-95, 197
Jacobi, Carl 21, 27
"Jacqueline Ess: Her Last Will and Testament" (Barker) 131
James, Henry 31, 32, 33, 34, 50
James, M. R. 29, 31-32, 33, 34, 35, 76, 77, 80, 88, 112, 117, 133, 165, 175, 195, 196, 239, 249
James, P. D. 108
James Joyce: His First Forty Years (Gorman) 84
Jarocha-Ernst, Chris 208
Jerome, Jerome K. 71
"Jerusalem's Lot" (King) 211
"Jesse" (Tem) 52
Jewett, Sarah Orne 165
Jimbo (Blackwood) 67, 68, 69

"Jody and Annie on TV" (Shirley) 54–55
John Silence–Physician Extraordinary (Blackwood) 67
Johnson, George Clayton 101
Jones, Stephen 21, 58, 131–37
Joshi, S. T. 189–90, 262
Joyce, James 84
"Judgment Day" (de Camp) 102
Julius LeVallon (Blackwood) 67, 69
Jung, C. G. 243
Just an Ordinary Day (Jackson) 89–92, 193
Juvenal (D. Junius Juvenalis) 183

"Kadath" (Winter-Damon) 220
"Kamikaze Butterflies" (Schow) 141, 142
Kaminsky, Stuart A. 48
Keats, John 36, 38
Keller, David H. 27
Kelly, Ronald 54
Kendrick, Walter 179–81, 197
Kesterton, David 15–16
Kiernan, Caitlín R. 225
Kill Riff, The (Schow) 138
King in Yellow, The (Chambers) 163, 217, 218
King of Elfland's Daughter, The (Dunsany) 185
Kingdom of Fear (Underwood-Miller) 135
King, Stephen 15, 16, 26, 56, 95, 103, 106–7, 133, 134, 135, 136, 146, 165, 180, 183, 191, 196, 197, 204, 211, 215, 221
Kirk, Russell 16
Kisner, James 54
"Kit-Bag, The" (Blackwood) 69
Klein, T. E. D. 52, 53, 61, 95, 101, 111, 133, 135, 136, 150, 163, 164, 178, 180, 219
Kleiner, Rheinhart 226
Klossner, Michael 179

Kneale, Nigel 102
Knight, Damon 101
Knight, George 191
Knopf, Alfred A. 234
Koja, Kathe 49
Koki, Arthur S. 259
Koko (Straub) 107, 108
"Kokopelli" (Burleson) 144
Koontz, Dean R. 56, 103
Kosenko, Peter 194
Kuttner, Henry 258

La Motte Fouqué, Friedrich Heinrich Karl, baron de 176
"Ladder" (Klein) 101
Lady (Tryon) 103, 104
Lady Who Came to Stay, The (Spencer) 87
Lamb, Hugh 100
Lamia (Keats) 36
Langford, David 59
Lansdale, Joe R. 52–53, 54
Lansdale, Karen 52–53
Laski, Marghanita 34
"Last Call for the Sons of Shock" (Schow) 48, 140
Last Celt, The (Lord) 192
"Last Feast of Harlequin, The" (Ligotti) 159
"Last Kiss" (Partridge) 151
Last Pin, The (Wandrei) 19, 20, 21
"Last Reel, The" (Etchison) 98
Last Voice They Hear, The (Campbell) 123–24
Laymon, Richard 54, 224–25
Lazzari, Marie 159
Le Fanu, Joseph Sheridan 33, 34, 35, 50, 144, 159, 174, 178, 180, 195
Le Guin, Ursula K. 183
"League of Bald Men" (Wandrei) 20
Lebbon, Tim 225
Lee, Brandon 142
Lee, Edward 56, 57
Lee, Tanith 15

Leeds, Arthur 226
"Leftovers" (Burleson) 143
Leiber, Fritz 44, 101, 144, 187, 190, 197, 210, 211, 213, 219, 237
Leithauser, Brad 30-35
Lejeune, Anthony 71
Lemon Drops and Other Horrors (Burleson) 142-43
Leopardi, Giacomo 263
Level, Maurice 50
Levin, Ira 196
Lévy, Maurice 241, 253
Lewis, C. S. 22
Lewis, D. F. 56, 220
Lewis, M. G. ("Monk") 28, 195
Life among the Savages (Jackson) 192, 193
Ligotti, Thomas 52, 53, 61, 101, 135, 150, 156-62, 164, 173, 180
"Likeness, The" (Perez) 221
Linaweaver, Brad 48
Linzner, Gordon 220
Lion, the Witch and the Wardrobe, The (Lewis) 22
Little, Bentley 54
"Little Bride-of-a-Day" (Burrage) 81
"Little Ones" (Campbell) 116
"Little Place Off Elm Street, A" (Burleson) 143
"Little Voice, The" (Campbell) 111
Littlefield, Hazel 183
Living in Fear (Daniels) 181
Locke, John 188
Lodger, The (Chappell) 59-60
Lofts, Norah 29
Long, Frank Belknap 39, 102, 163, 207, 209, 211, 213, 226, 235, 256
Long Lost, The (Campbell) 117, 125
"Long Meg and Her Daughters" (Finch) 225
"Long Way Home, The" (Wilson) 53
Longfellow, Henry Wadsworth 84
Look Out He's Got a Knife 140
Lord, Glenn 192

Lord Dunsany: King of Dreams (Littlefield) 183
Lord Dunsany: Master of the Anglo-Irish Imagination (Joshi) 197
"Lord of the Castle" (Jackson) 90
"Lord of the Land" (Wilson) 215
Lost Angels (Schow) 137, 138, 139
"Lost Hearts" (James) 29
"Lost Soul" (Austin) 165
Lost Souls (Sullivan) 100
Lost Valley, The (Blackwood) 67
"Lottery, The" (Jackson) 192, 194
Lottery, The (Jackson) 89, 92, 114, 193
"Love Letters" (Monteleone) 54
Lovecraft, H. P. 34, 41, 65, 66, 68, 72, 88, 117, 126, 134, 157, 166; as character in fiction, 214, 226-36; and August Derleth, 23-24; editions of, 15, 24, 201-7; on films, 46; on William Hope Hodgson, 74, 75; and Robert E. Howard, 189-91; imitations of, 58-60, 83, 108, 110, 142-43, 144, 147-48, 150, 162-63, 207-25; letters of, 19, 21; on literature, 101, 111, 155; on Arthur Machen, 70, 71; his place in weird fiction, 25, 26, 27, 114, 135, 136, 137, 175, 192, 195; poetry of, 17, 38, 39, 40, 185; scholarship on, 9, 10, 25-26, 73, 173, 182-83, 186, 187, 196, 236-66; on weird fiction, 31, 50, 55, 83, 113, 141, 159, 174, 176, 178, 180
Lovecraft, Sarah Susan (Phillips) 259-60
Lovecraft, Winfield Scott 259
Lovecraft: A Biography (de Camp) 229
Lovecraft: A Look Behind the "Cthulhu Mythos" (Carter) 241
Lovecraft: Disturbing the Universe (Burleson) 244-49
Lovecraft Annual 10

Lovecraft at Last (Lovecraft-Conover) 229
Lovecraft Chronicles, The (Cannon) 234–36
Lovecraft ou du fantastique (Lévy) 241
Lovecraft Remembered (Cannon) 22
Lovecraft Studies 9, 10, 242, 257, 262
"Lovecraftian Voyages" (Faig) 259
Lovecraft's Book (Lupoff) 229–30
Lovecraft's Legacy (Weinberg-Greenberg) 212–16
"Loved Dead, The" (Lovecraft-Eddy) 26, 175, 180, 206, 207
"Lovely House, The" (Jackson) 33, 90, 192, 193
Loveman, Samuel 226, 232
"Loveman's Comeback" (Campbell) 113
"Lovers Meeting" (Jackson) 90
Lumley, Brian 15, 47, 210–11, 213, 214, 215, 221
Lupoff, Richard A. 210, 218, 229–30
"Lurking Fear, The" (Lovecraft) 252
Lurking Fear and Other Stories, The (Lovecraft) 201, 202
Lutz, John 46

McCammon, Robert R. 102
Machen, Arthur 9, 16, 34, 35, 66, 69, 70–74, 88, 113, 114, 126, 134, 137, 163, 173, 178, 195, 196, 218, 235, 239, 256
Machen, Janet 72
Machenalia (Russell) 16, 73
Mack, John 181
McKenna, Richard 102
"Mackintosh Willy" (Campbell) 112, 117
McLaughlin, Mark 223–24
McNail, Stanley 39, 44
McNaughton, Brian 17, 213, 214–15
McWilliams, Carey 176
"Mad at the Academy" (Freisner) 48

"Mad Night of Atonement" (Ligotti) 158
"Madness out of Space, The" (Cannon) 226, 227
Magazine of Fantasy and Science Fiction 91, 142
"Magic Mirror, The" (Blackwood) 69
Magic Mirror, The (Blackwood) 69–70
Magic of Shirley Jackson, The (Jackson) 89
Magic Terror (Straub) 108–9
Magistrale, Tony 197
Malleus Maleficarum (Sprenger-Kramer) 169
Malzberg, Barry N. 101
Mammoth Book of Haunted House Stories, The (Haining) 27–30
"Man-Eater, The" (Blackwood) 69
Man from Genoa, A (Long) 39
"Man in the Underpass, The" (Campbell) 112
Man Who Ate the Phoenix, The (Dunsany) 184
"Man Who Went Too Far, The" (Benson) 79
"Man Whom the Trees Loved, The" (Blackwood) 69
Man with the Barbed-Wire Fists, The (Partridge) 150–51
"Man with the Molten Face, The" (Wandrei) 20
Mankowitz, Wolf 176
Marble Faun, The (Hawthorne) 174
Marchers of Valhalla (Leiber) 187
Mariah of the Spirits and Other Southern Ghost Stories (Austin) 165–66
Mariconda, Steven J. 251
Martin, George R. R. 102
Martin, Valerie 104
Mary Queen of Scots 84
Mary Reilly (Martin) 104
Massie, Elizabeth 56
"Master of Rampling Gate, The" (Rice) 47

"Master of the Hounds, The" (Budrys) 101
Masterton, Graham 213-14, 215
Matheson, Richard 101, 143
Maturin, Charles Robert 28, 174, 195
"Maud-Evelyn" (James) 32
Maupassant, Guy de 176
Mayhar, Ardath 54
Maynard, L. H. 225
Medea (Euripides) 36
"Medusa, The" (Ligotti) 157
"Medusa's Coil" (Lovecraft-Bishop) 253
"Meet Me on the Other Side" (Navarro) 225
Melmoth the Wanderer (Maturin) 28, 97, 174, 195
Melville, Herman 75
"Memory of Beauty, The" (Blackwood) 69
Mencken, H. L. 191
Merritt, A. 197
"Meryphillia" (McNaughton) 214-15
MetaHorror (Etchison) 99, 144
Metamorphoses (Ovid) 169
Metcalfe, John 88
"Metzengerstein" (Poe) 28
Michaud, Marc A. 58, 231
Michener, James 134
"Midnight Meat Train, The" (Barker) 133
Midnight Sun (Campbell) 117, 136
Miéville, China 225
"Mikey Joe" (Burleson) 143
Milán, Victor 221
"Milk" (Burleson) 143
Mill, John Stuart 188
Millar, Margaret 55
Miller, Rex 54
Mind Parasites, The (Wilson) 59, 208, 218, 219
Miniter, Edith 226
Minnesota Quarterly 17

"Minutes" (Partridge) 151
Misery (King) 215
Moby-Dick (Melville) 132
Modern Weird Tale, The (Joshi) 9, 89, 103, 132, 195
Monk, The (Lewis) 28
"Monkey Treatment, The" (Martin) 102
Monster in the Mirror, The (Waugh) 262-66
"Monsters Are Due on Maple Street, The" (Serling) 115
"Monsters of the Midway" (Resnick) 47
Monteleone, Thomas F. 54, 101
Moore, Thomas 36
More Ghost Stories of an Antiquary (James) 35
More Shapes Than One (Chappell) 59
More Spook Stories (Benson) 76, 77
Morrell, David 52, 53, 54
Morris, Harry O. 162
Morrison, Michael A. 9, 135-36, 178
Morton, James F. 226
Morton, Thomas 86
Mosig, Dirk W. 217, 237, 243, 251, 256, 257, 259
Moskowitz, Sam 74
"Mound, The" (Lovecraft-Bishop) 148, 250
"Mr. Clubb and Mr. Cuff" (Straub) 108-9
"Mr Edward" (Lofts) 29
Mr. Fox and Other Feral Tales (Partridge) 58, 149
"Mr. Humphreys and His Inheritance" (James) 32
"Mr. Lucrada" (Lutz) 46
"Mr. Skin" (Milán) 221
"Mr Tilly's Séance" (Benson) 79
Mr. X (Straub) 108
"Mrs Amworth" (Benson) 79
"Mrs. God" (Straub) 107
"Mrs. Rinaldi's Angel" (Ligotti) 158

Munn, H. Warner 44
Murphy, Joe 220
Murphy, Pat 48
Murray, Will 186, 231, 254
"Music of Erich Zann, The" (Lovecraft) 228, 238, 240, 241
"Music Teacher, The" (Cheever) 34
"My Work Is Not Yet Done" (Ligotti) 159-61
My Work Is Not Yet Done (Ligotti) 159-62
Mysteries of the Worm (Bloch) 216, 218-19
Mysteries of Udolpho, The (Radcliffe) 28
Mystery (Straub) 108, 109
Mythos Books 162
"N" (Machen) 73
"Nameless City, The" (Lovecraft) 245, 248
"Napier Court" (Campbell) 29, 111
Narrative of Arthur Gordon Pym, The (Poe) 158
"Nathicana" (Lovecraft) 202
Navarro, Yvonne 225
"Near-Flesh" (Dunn) 48
Nebeker, Helen 194
Necrofile 9-10, 80, 157
Necronomicon Press 58-60
Necropsy 10
Needing Ghosts (Campbell) 127, 136, 159
Neilson, Keith 177-78
"Neither Brute Nor Human" (Wagner) 101
Nelson, Dale J. 73
"Nemesis" (Lovecraft) 243
Nevermore (Schechter) 168-70
New England's Gothic Literature (Ringel) 181-83
New Horizons: Yesterday's Portraits of Tomorrow (Derleth/Wrzos) 21
New Lovecraft Circle, The (Price) 21

New York Review of Books 9
New York Times 56, 87, 104, 149
New York Times Book Review 90
New Yorker 235, 255
Newman, Kim 135
Nietzsche, Friedrich 237-38
"Night Gallery, The" 215
Night Land, The (Hodgson) 75
Night Magic (Tryon et al.) 103-6
Night of the Living Dead, The (film) 150
Night of the Moonbow, The (Tryon) 103, 104
Night Shift (King) 103
Night Visions 3 (Campbell et al.) 111, 114
Night Visions 4 (Koontz et al.) 134
Night with Mephistopheles, A (Ferris) 17
"Nightmare" (Jackson) 90
"Nightmare Network, The" (Ligotti) 161
Nightmare's Disciple (Pulver) 221, 222-23
"1968 RPI" (Murphy) 220
Niven, Larry 48
No Blood Spilled (Daniels) 96-98
"No Love Lost" (Williamson) 52
"No One You Know" (Etchison) 98
"No Strings" (Campbell) 116
"No. 252 Rue M. le Prince" (Cram) 28
"Nobody's Perfect" (Farmer) 46
Noctuary (Ligotti) 156-59
Nolan, William F. 54, 100-101
Norton Book of Ghost Stories, The (Leithauser) 30-35
Not Broken, Not Belonging (Fox) 57-58
Not Exactly Ghosts (Caldecott) 87-89
"Notebook Found in a Deserted House" (Bloch) 210
"Notes for a Young Writer" (Jackson) 194

"Notes on Writing Weird Fiction" (Lovecraft) 264
"Novel of the Black Seal" (Machen) 218

Oates, Joyce Carol 90, 102
"Oberon Road" (Burrage) 81–82
O'Brien, Edward W., Jr 261-62, 263
Occult Files of Francis Chard, The (Burrage) 80
Ochse, Weston 225
O'Connor, Richard 176
Odyssey (Homer) 36
Oedipus Rex (Sophocles) 36
Oehlshlaeger, Fritz 194
"'Oh, Whistle, and I'll Come to You, My Lad'" (James) 31, 35
"Old Clothes" (Campbell) 111
Old Gringo, The (Fuentes) 167
"Old House in Vauxhall Walk, The" (Riddell) 28
Olivier, Sir Laurence 68
Olson, D. H. 20, 21
Olson, Michael 17
Olson, Paul F. 54
O'Malley, Kathleen 49
Onderdonk, Matthew H. 175, 237
"One-Night Strand" (Burleson) 143
"One Ordinary Day, with Peanuts" (Jackson) 91
One Safe Place, The (Campbell) 117–20
Onions, Oliver 33, 50, 76, 80, 178
"Open Window, The" (Saki) 33
Oppenheimer, Judy 91, 92, 192
"Order of Things Unknown, The" (Gorman) 215
Ornaments in Jade (Machen) 16, 73
Orwell, George 235
Other, The (Tryon) 103, 104, 106, 180, 196
"Other Bed, The" (Benson) 78
"Other Man, The" (Garton) 215
"Other Woman, The" (Austin) 165

"Out of the Aeons" (Lovecraft-Heald) 250, 252
"Outside the Door" (Benson) 78
"Outsider, The" (Lovecraft) 203, 247, 248
Outsider and Others, The (Lovecraft) 24, 114, 201, 211
Overnight, The (Campbell) 126–28
Ovid (P. Ovidius Naso) 169

"Pack, The" (Partridge) 150
Pact of the Fathers (Campbell) 125–26
Pan's Garden (Blackwood) 67
Parents of Howard Phillips Lovecraft, The (Faig) 259-60
"Partners" (Randisi) 48
Pathways to Elfland (Schweitzer) 183–85
Patridge, Norman 57, 58, 61, 149–51
"Patter of Tiny Feet, The" (Kneale) 102
"Pattern, The" (Campbell) 111
Patterson, Meredith L. 225
Pelan, John 224–25
Penzoldt, Peter 180
Perez, Dan 221
Peter Pan (Barrie) 135
Phillips, Edwin E. 259
Philosopher's Stone, The (Wilson) 212
Philosophy of Horror, The (Carroll) 173, 180
"Pick Me Up" (Schow) 52
"Pickman's Legacy" (Linzner) 220
"Pickman's Model" (Lovecraft) 163, 203, 238, 241
"Picture in the House, The" (Lovecraft) 204, 250, 261
Picture of Dorian Gray, The (Wilde) 253
"Pillar of Salt" (Jackson) 193
"Pirates" (Benson) 79
"Pitt Night at the Lewistone Boneyard" (Schow) 140

Place Called Dagon, The (Gorman) 83–87, 243
Plays for Earth and Air (Dunsany) 185
Poe, Edgar Allan 26, 34, 36, 41, 54, 65, 70, 74, 88, 113, 145, 157, 158, 160, 166, 169–70, 173, 174, 176, 177, 180, 195, 196, 206, 213, 215, 217, 239, 249, 253
Poems for Midnight (Wandrei) 39
Poe's Fiction: Romantic Irony in the Gothic Tales (Thompson) 176
"Poetry and the Gods" (Lovecraft-Crofts) 202
Pollin, Burton R. 176
"Poor Girl" (Taylor) 34
Portrait of a Man with Red Hair (Walpole) 30
"Possibility of Evil, The" (Jackson) 91–92
Potter, J. K. 114
Pound, Ezra 38
Preiss, Byron 45–49
"Preparations for the Game" (Tem) 102
"Previous Tenant, The" (Campbell) 34, 111, 115–16
Price, E. Hoffmann 25, 27
Price, Robert M. 21, 22, 162, 163, 186, 216–19, 220, 231, 243, 250, 256–58, 262
"Prince Alcouz and the Magician" (Smith) 27
"Principles and Parameters" (Patterson) 225
Prisoner in Fairyland, A (Blackwood) 67–68
Pritchett, V. S. 34, 35
"Prodigy of Dreams, The" (Ligotti) 158
Pronzini, Bill 48
"Property of the Ring" (Campbell) 27
Psycho (Bloch) 50, 152
Psycho-Paths (Bloch-Greenberg) 51–52
Pugmire, W. H. 221, 222, 225

Pulptime (Cannon) 226–27, 255, 256
Pulver, Joseph S., Sr. 221
Punter, David 173
"Pure Silver" (Crispin-O'Malley) 49
Purple Cloud, The (Shiel) 75

Quest for Sex, Truth and Reality (Lee) 56
Quinn, Seabury 15, 25, 27, 176, 233

Radcliffe, Ann 28, 49, 88, 195
Rahman, Philip J. 17
Raising Demons (Jackson) 192, 193
Raleigh, Richard 232–34
"Ramsey Campbell: An Appreciation" (Barker) 134–35
Ramsland, Katherine 195
Randisi, Robert J. 48
Ranieri, Roman A. 54
"Rats in the Walls, The" (Lovecraft) 175, 201, 203, 228, 243, 250
"Ra*e" (Campbell) 115
Reader's Guide to H. P. Lovecraft (Joshi) 251
"Real and the Counterfeit, The" (Baldwin) 29
"Recluse, A" (de la Mare) 33
"Recurring Doom, The" (Joshi) 208
"Red Brain, The" (Wandrei) 18
Red Dragon (Harris) 152
Red Dreams (Etchison) 98
"Red Light" (Schow) 139
"Red Light Hand" (Partridge) 151
Redbook 45
Reino, Joseph 197
Relling, William, Jr 54
"Remains to Be Seen" (Morrell) 52
Rendezvous in Averoigne, A (Smith) 15
"Renegade, The" (Jackson) 193
"Requiem for Mankind" (Wandrei) 19
Resnick, Mike 47
"Return Journey" (Campbell) 115
"Return of Hastur, The" (Derleth) 218

"Return of the Lloigor, The" (Wilson) 211-12
"Return of the Sorcerer, The" (Smith) 210
"Return of the White Ship, The" (Breach) 220
Rice, Anne 16, 45, 47, 56, 146, 195-96
Richards, I. A. 31
Riddell, Charlotte 28
Riddle and Other Stories, The (de la Mare) 33
Rime of the Ancient Mariner, The (Coleridge) 36
Ringel, Faye 181-83
"Rising with Surtsey" (Lumley) 210, 211
Ritual and Other Stories (Machen) 16
Ritual in the Dark (Wilson) 206
Roadkill Press 57-58
Robards, Karen 47
Robbins, Harold 153
Roberts, Bette B. 195-96
Roerich, Nicholas 241
"Roman Remains" (Blackwood) 69
"Romance of Certain Old Clothes, The" (James) 32, 34
"Room in the Castle, The" (Campbell) 110
Room in the Tower, The (Benson) 76, 77
"Root of Evil" (Jackson) 91
Rosemary's Baby (Levin) 196
Roth, Phyllis A. 196
Ruber, Peter 21, 23-27
Rusch, Kristine Kathryn 46, 47
Russ, Joanna 210
Russell, Bertrand 66, 188, 237
Russell, R. B. 16-17
Rutherford, Brett 41, 42-43, 45

Said, Edward W. 244, 249
St Armand, Barton L. 175, 237-41, 243, 251, 262, 263-64

Saki (H. H. Munro) 33
Sallee, Wayne Allen 56
Sammon, Paul 137, 142
San Veneficio Canon, The (Cisco) 162
Sanctity and Sin (Wandrei) 39
"Sand" (Blackwood) 69
"Sand Sculpture" (Schow) 139
Sandalwood (Smith) 37
Sands, Mirella 220
Sargent, Stanley C. 221
Satan Is a Mathematician (Daniels) 41-42
Sawyer, Andy 71, 74, 75
Sayers, Dorothy L. 100, 108
"Scar, The" (Campbell) 110, 112
Scared Stiff (Campbell) 111, 114
Scarf, The (Bloch) 50
Scarlet Letter, The (Hawthorne) 246
Schechter, Harold 168-70
Schoolgirl Murder Case, The (Wilson) 206
Schopenhauer, Arthur 237-38
Schorer, Mark 27
Schow, David J. 48, 52, 53, 55, 61, 137-42, 151
Schultz, David E. 39, 40, 186, 192, 210, 251, 262
Schumann, Clara 104
Schutz, Benjamin M. 47, 48
Schwader, Ann K. 223
Schwartz, Julius 205
Schweitzer, Darrell 9, 80, 81, 183-85, 220, 241, 253
Scientific Romance in Britain 1890-1950 (Stableford) 74
"Sciomancy Nights" (Daniels) 42
"Scoop Makes a Swirly" (Schow) 140
Scot, Reginald 169
Scott, Sir Walter 32, 33
Scream for Jeeves (Cannon) 219, 228-29
Scribner's 24
"Sea Change" (Johnson) 101
Second Ghost Book, The (Asquith) 34

Secret Glory, The (Machen) 71–72
Secret Glory: Chapters Five and Six, The (Machen) 72
Secret Hours (Cisco) 162–63
"Secret of the Heart, A" (Castle) 215
Secret of the Sangraal and Other Writings, The (Machen) 16
Secret Stories (Campbell) 128–31
"Sedalia" (Schow) 141
Seeing Red (Schow) 138, 139, 142
"Seeing the World" (Campbell) 113
Selected Letters (Lovecraft) 19, 21
Selected Poems (Smith) 37, 39
"Serenade of Starlight, The" (Pugmire) 225
Serling, Rod 47, 102, 175
Seven Modern Comedies (Dunsany) 185
"Seven Types of Ambiguity" (Jackson) 193
Sexual Chemistry (Stableford) 58
"Shadow from the Steeple, The" (Bloch) 210, 211
Shadow on the Blind, The (Baldwin) 29
"Shadow out of Time, The" (Lovecraft) 27, 148, 159, 201, 205, 206, 207, 211, 231, 238, 250, 257, 258
"Shadow over Innsmouth, The" (Lovecraft) 58, 83, 147, 203, 220, 225, 230, 243
Shadow over Innsmouth, The (Lovecraft) 182
Shadowland (Straub) 105
Shadowman (Etchison) 98
Shadows Bend (Barbour-Raleigh) 232–34
Shadows of Death (Lovecraft) 205
Shadows over Innsmouth (Jones) 21
"Shaft, The" (Schow) 138, 139–40
Shaft, The (Schow) 138, 139–40, 142
"Shaft No. 247" (Copper) 219
Shakespeare, William 90, 176, 213–14
"Shambler from the Stars, The" (Bloch) 211

Shards of Darkness (Berglund) 221
"She's Got the Look" (McLaughlin) 224
Shea, J. Vernon 211
Shea, Michael 57
Shelley, Mary 46, 47, 48, 174
Shelley, Percy Bysshe 38
Shepard, Lucius 15
Shiel, M. P. 71, 74, 75, 159, 197
Shiner, Lewis 53
Shirley, John 54–55, 142
Shirley Jackson: A Study of the Short Fiction (Hall) 89, 192–95
Shoggoth Cacciatoare and Other Eldritch Entrees (McLaughlin) 223–24
"Shootings of Achnaleish, The" (Benson) 77–78
Shreffler, Philip A. 241
"Shrine, The" (Morrell) 53
"Shunned House, The" (Lovecraft) 182–83, 250
Sidney-Fryer, Donald 37, 39–40, 43–44, 45, 187
Silence of the Lambs, The (Harris) 152
Silent Children (Campbell) 123, 124–25
"Silent Snow, Secret Snow" (Aiken) 143
"Silver Key, The" (Lovecraft) 203
Silver Salamander Press 56–57
Silver Scream (Schow) 138, 142
Silver Skull, The (Daniels) 95
Silverberg, Robert 45, 48
Simmons, Dan 47, 48, 57, 102
Simms, William Gilmore 174
Sims, M. P. N. 225
"Singular Death of Morton, The" (Blackwood) 69
"Sir Bertrand" (Barbauld) 28
"Sir Edmund Orme" (James) 32
"Sister City, The" (Lumley) 210–11
Sixty Selected Poems (Brennan) 39
Sixty Years of Arkham House (Joshi) 21
"Skeleton" (Bradbury) 100

Skene, Anthony 81
Skipp, John 138, 139
Skull-Face and Others (Howard) 191
Slippin' into Darkness (Partridge) 149–50, 151
"Slow" (Campbell) 117
"Small Assassin, The" (Bradbury) 27
Smith, Clark Ashton 15, 25, 26, 37, 38, 39, 40, 41, 42, 43, 44, 58, 68, 74, 147, 158, 184, 191, 197, 207, 209, 214, 230, 232–33
"Smoking Room, The" (Jackson) 90
"Sneering, The" (Campbell) 115
Snow, C. P. 41
"Snow Cancellations" (Burleson) 144
"Soldier's Visitor, The" (Blackwood) 69
Some Ghost Stories (Burrage) 80
Some of the Descendants of Asaph Phillips and Esther Whipple of Foster, Rhode Island (Faig) 260
Someone in the Room (Burrage) 80–83
Something Breathing (McNail) 39
Somtow, S. P. 48
Songs and Sonnets Atlantean (Sidney-Fryer) 40, 43
Songs and Sonnets Atlantean: The Second Series (Sidney-Fryer) 43–44
Songs of a Dead Dreamer (Ligotti) 101, 156
Sophocles 36
Sorcerer's Apprentice, The (Ewers) 105
"Soul Keeper" (Citro) 215
"Sound of Thunder, A" (Bradbury) 141
"Space-Eaters, The" (Long) 211
Spark, Muriel 35
"Spectacle of a Man, A" (Ochse) 225
Spector, Craig 138, 139
"Spectral Estate, The" (Ligotti) 158–59
Spencer, Herbert 189
Spencer, R. E. 87
Spenser, Edmund 176

Spicy Mystery Stories 20
Spinoza, Benedict de 188
Splatterpunks (Sammon) 137, 142
Spook Stories (Benson) 76, 77
Squires, Roy A. 42, 202
Stableford, Brian 58, 59, 74, 75, 177–78
Star-Treader and Other Poems, The (Smith) 37
Starlight Express, The (Blackwood) 67–68
Starrett, Vincent 70, 71, 226, 230, 240
"State versus Adam Shelley, The" (Schutz) 48
"Statement of Randolph Carter, The" (Lovecraft) 203, 248
Steel, Danielle 56, 134, 191
Stephen, Leslie 244
Sterling, Bruce 15
Sterling, George 36–37, 38, 40, 44
Sterling, Kenneth 202
Stern, Philip Van Doren 175
Stevenson, Robert Louis 195
Stewart, Sarah Hyman 89
"Sticks" (Wagner) 211
Stoker, Bram 195, 196
"Story of Duan Juan, A" (Pritchett) 34
Story of Mona Sheehy, The (Dunsany) 184
"Story We Used to Tell, The" (Jackson) 90
Stout, Rex 167
"Strange Adventures of a Private Secretary in New York, The" (Blackwood) 67
Strange Harvest (Wandrei) 17
"Strange High House in the Mist, The" (Lovecraft) 202, 248
Strange Journeys of Colonel Polders, The (Dunsany) 184, 185
Strange Things and Stranger Places (Campbell) 114

Stratman, Thomas M. K. 219–21
Straub, Peter 16, 56, 95, 102, 105, 107–9
"Street Was Chosen, A" (Campbell) 115
Strength to Dream, The (Wilson) 206
Strickland, Brad 48
Strieber, Whitley 148, 181
"Student of Geometry, A" (Burleson) 143
Studies in Weird Fiction 9, 10, 193
"Stuff of the Stars, Leaking, The" (Lebbon) 225
Styron, William 108
Subtler Magick, A (Joshi) 189
"Sugar and Spice and . . ." (Robards) 47
Suicide Artist, The (Edelman) 59
Sullivan, Jack 100, 174–75, 177
"Summer Afternoon" (Jackson) 90
"Summer People, The" (Jackson) 192
"Sunset Terrace Imagery in Lovecraft" and Other Essays (Cannon) 254–56
"Supernatural Horror in Literature" (Lovecraft) 50, 74, 83, 113, 176, 180, 225
Supernatural in Fiction, The (Penzoldt) 180
Swain, E. G. 16
Sweetser, Wesley 70, 196
Swinburne, Algernon Charles 38
Symons, Julian 176

TAL Publications 56, 57, 60
Tale of the Body Thief, The (Rice) 196
Tales of the Cthulhu Mythos (Derleth-Turner) 209–12
Tales of the Lovecraft Collectors (Faig) 231–32
"Tale of the Ragged Mountains, The" (Poe) 170
Tales from Tartarus (Russell) 16
Tales of the Cthulhu Mythos (Derleth) 15

Tales of the Lovecraft Mythos (Price) 21, 216
Talman, Wilfred B. 239, 260
Tartarus Press 16–17
Taylor, Elizabeth 34
Taylor, Lucy 56–57, 60, 138
"Teeth" (Cardin) 225
Tem, Melanie 48
Tem, Steve Rasnic 48, 52, 58, 102
Terminal Fright Publications 17
"Terrible Old Man, The" (Lovecraft) 144, 206, 242, 245, 248, 253, 254
"Terror from the Depths, The" (Leiber) 210, 211, 219
Tessier, Thomas 102
Testimony of the Suns, The (Sterling) 37
"That's the Story of My Life" (Pelan-Adams) 225
"Them Breaks" (Wilson) 52
"Thing in the Moonlight, The" 205
"Thing on the Doorstep, The" (Lovecraft) 201–2, 235, 243
Third Ghost Book, The (Asquith) 34
Third Grave, The (Case) 15
Thirty Years of Arkham House (Derleth) 21, 24, 209
"This Icy Region My Heart Encircles" (Tem) 48
Thompson, C. Hall 215
Thompson, G. R. 176
"Those of the Air" (Schweitzer-Van Hollander) 220
Three Impostors, The (Machen) 73
"Three Miles Up" (Howard) 34
Thrill of Fear, The (Kendrick) 179–81
Thrilling Mystery 69
Throat, The (Straub) 107, 108, 109
Throne of Bones, The (McNaughton) 17
Through the Crack (Blackwood) 68
"Through the Walls" (Campbell) 114–15
Tierney, Richard L. 17, 19, 21, 40–41, 256, 257

Time 201
Time Burial (Wandrei) 19, 20, 21
Todorov, Tzvetan 244
Told by the Dead (Campbell) 115–17
Tolkien, J. R. R. 73, 97
"Tomb, The" (Lovecraft) 202, 250
Tomb and Other Tales, The (Lovecraft) 201, 202
Tomb-Herd and Others, The (Campbell) 111
Tompkins, Steven 187, 191
"Tooth, The" (Jackson) 33
"Torch Song" (Cheever) 34
"Torture by Hope (Villiers de l'Isle Adam) 50
"Tower, The" (Laski) 34
Traitor, The (Cisco) 164
Transition of H. P. Lovecraft, The (Lovecraft) 205
"Translations" (Cisco) 163, 164
"Treasure of Abbot Thomas, The" (James) 112
"Tree, The" (de la Mare) 33
"Tree-Men of M'bwa, The" (Wandrei) 18
"Trees" (Gullette) 44–45
Tremayne, Peter 74
Trojan Publishing Corporation 20, 21
Trout, Steven R. 187, 188, 191
Tryon, Thomas 9, 86, 103–6, 180, 196
"Tsalal, The" (Ligotti) 158
Turn of the Screw, The (James) 50
Turner, James 15–16, 21, 60–61, 114, 209–12, 230
Tuttle, Lisa 114, 135
Twayne Publishers 195–97
Twelfth Night (Shakespeare) 90
Twenty-seven Liqueurs (Gullette) 45
"Twilight of the Dawn, The" (Koontz) 103
"Twilight of Time, The" (Wandrei) 18

"Twilight Zone, The" 101, 115
Two Cultures, The (Snow) 41
"Two Fragments" (Cisco) 163
Two Obscure Tales (Campbell) 59
Two Towers, The (Tolkien) 97
Tyler, Casey B. 260
Tymn, Marshall 173–76, 177, 178, 179
Tyrant, The (Cisco) 162

"Ugly" (Brandner) 215
Ultimate Dracula, The (Preiss et al.) 45–47, 48
Ultimate Frankenstein, The (Preiss et al.) 45, 47–48
Ultimate Werewolf, The (Preiss et al.) 45, 48–49
Ulysses (Joyce) 134
"Unleashed" (Hoffman) 49
"Unnamable, The" (Lovecraft) 205, 253
Unnatural Acts (Taylor) 56
Updike, John 108

Valentine, Mark 70–71, 74, 75
"Vampire in His Closet, The" (Graham) 46
Van Hollander, Jason 220
Van Pelt, James 225
Van Vechten, Carl 70
Varney the Vampire (Rymer) 96
"Vengeance of Earth, The" (Tierney) 40
Ventre, Gregory 73
"Victorian Pot Dresser, A" (Maynard-Sims) 225
Vidal, Gore 134
Villiers de l'Isle Adam, Philippe-Auguste 50
Visible and Invisible (Benson) 76, 77
Vision of a Castle Deep in Averonne, A (Sidney-Fryer) 44
Vision of Doom, A (Bierce) 37
"Vision on a Midsummer Night, A" (Tierney) 41

"Visit, A" (Jackson) 90, 193
"Voice, The" (Blackwood) 69
"Voice in the Bones, The" (Ligotti) 158
"Voice of the Beach, The" (Campbell) 113
Vonnegut, Kurt 45
Wade, James 211, 218
Wagner, Karl Edward 21, 101, 117, 210, 211, 218
Wakefield, H. Russell 16, 27
Waking Nightmares (Campbell) 111, 116
"Walkie-Talkie" (Burleson) 144
Walpole, Horace 195
Walpole, Hugh 30
Wanderer 261
Wandrei, Donald 15, 17–19, 20, 26, 36, 39, 40, 207, 243
Wandrei, Howard 19–21, 243
Washington Post 149
Wasp 167, 168
"Watching Me, Watching You" (Weldon) 29
"Water Nymphs, The" (Cisco) 163
Waterman, Edward 188–89
Watson, Ian 29
Waugh, Evelyn 114, 161, 252
Waugh, Robert H. 262–66
"Waxworks" (Burrage) 82–83
Weaveworld (Barker) 132, 133, 136
Web of Easter Island, The (Wandrei) 19
"Week in the Unlife, A" (Schow) 140
Weiler, Dennis E. 17
Weinberg, Robert E. 48, 176, 212–16
Weird Shadows over Innsmouth (Jones) 21
Weird Tale, The (Joshi) 9, 190, 194
"Weird Tales" (Chappell) 60

Weird Tales 9, 18, 20, 26, 69, 137, 141, 176, 207, 233, 235, 237, 242, 261
Weldon, Fay 29
Wellman, Manly Wade 213
Wells, H. G. 32
"Wendigo, The" (Blackwood) 65, 67
Wetzel, George T. 237
Wharton, Edith 35
"What He Chanced to Mould in Play" (Cisco) 163
What Rough Book (Daniels) 41
"What the Moon Brings" (Lovecraft) 202, 206
Wheatley, Dennis 178
Whelan, Michael 201, 203
"When They Gave Us Memory" (Etchison) 99
"Where the Tides Ebb and Flow" (Dunsany) 185
Where the Woodbine Twines (Austin) 166
"While She Was Out" (Bryant) 142
"Whining, The" (Campbell) 109
Whippoorwill Road (Rutherford) 41, 42–43
"Whisperer in Darkness, The" (Lovecraft) 201, 203, 207, 211, 217–18
White, Ted 203
"White People, The" (Machen) 73
"White Ship, The" (Lovecraft) 202, 220
Whitehead, Henry S. 233
Whitman, Walt 38
Wieland (Brown) 50
Wilde, Oscar 175
Wildside Press 187
Wilhelm, Kate 101
"Will" (Masterton) 213–14
William Hope Hodgson: Voyages and Visions (Bell) 74–76
Williams, Raymond 244
Williams, V. 73
Williams, William Carlos 38

Williamson, Chet 55, 80, 213, 214
Williamson, J. N. 52, 54
"Willows, The" (Blackwood) 65, 67
Wilson, Colin 59, 205, 206-7, 208, 210, 211-12, 218, 219, 261
Wilson, Edmund 235
Wilson, F. Paul 47, 53, 54, 55, 213, 215
Wilson, Gahan 52, 213, 214, 216
"Wine of Wizardry, A" (Sterling) 37
Wings of the Morning, The (Tryon) 103, 104
Winter, Douglas E. 54, 135
Winter-Damon, t. 220
Wise, Herbert A. 174
"Witch, The" (Jackson) 193
Wodehouse, P. G. 128, 228-29
Wolf, Leonard 46
Wolf Man, The (film) 45, 46
Wolfe, Gene 213, 215
"Woman in the Room, The" (King) 103
"Woman's Ghost Story, The" (Blackwood) 34
Wood, Jonathan 73

Woolf, Virginia 29
"Word, The" (Campbell) 116-17
"Words That Count, The" (Campbell) 101, 109
World Publishing Co. 24
Worming the Harpy and Other Bitter Pills (Hughes) 16
Worms Remember, The (Schwader) 223
"Worst Fog of the Year, The" (Campbell) 117
Wright, Farnsworth 235
Wrzos, Joseph 21
Wuthering Heights (Brontë) 33
Wynn, David 162

"Xélucha" (Shiel) 159

Yarbro, Chelsea Quinn 47, 52, 101
Year's Best Horror Stories, The (Wagner) 117
Yellow Fog (Daniels) 95-96, 97, 98
Young, Francis Brett 87

Zeising, Mark V. 60, 61
"Ziggles" (Burleson) 144

Acknowledgements

This volume contains a generous sampling of my book reviews, from as early as 1980 to 2007. Some of the reviews have been rewritten, and in some cases I have combined two or more reviews on related subjects into a single article; but for the most part, they have been printed largely as originally published. The sources of the reviews are as follows:

"Arkham House and Its Legacy" (*Weird Tales*, Fall 1998, Summer 2000). "The Haunted House" (*Necropsy*, Fall 2001). "Professionals and Amateurs" (*Necrofile*, Winter 1995). "Some Thoughts on Weird Poetry" (*Weird Tales*, Summer 1999; *Crypt of Cthulhu*, St. John's Eve 1983; *Necropsy*, Fall 2003); "Bram and Mary and Bela and Boris" (*Necrofile*, Winter 1992). "What the Hell Is Dark Suspense?" (*Necrofile*, Summer 1992). "The Small Press" (*Worlds of Fantasy and Horror*, Spring 1995).

"Algernon Blackwood: The Starlight Man" (*Weird Tales*, Summer 2002; *Studies in Weird Fiction*, Fall 1989; Fall 1988). "Arthur Machen: A Minor Classic" (*Studies in Weird Fiction*, Spring 1992; *Necrofile*, Winter 1998; *Studies in Weird Fiction*, Summer 1986). "William Hope Hodgson: Writer on the Borderland" (*Studies in Weird Fiction*, Summer 1987); "E. F. Benson: Spooks and More Spooks" (*Necrofile*, Winter 1994). "A. M. Burrage: The Ghost Man" (*Necrofile*, Summer 1998). "Herbert S. Gorman: Where Is the Place Called Dagon?" (*Necrofile*, Fall 1994). "Andrew Caldecott: The Well-Crafted Ghost" (*Studies in Weird Fiction*, Summer 2003). "Rescuing Shirley Jackson" (*Necrofile*, Summer 1997).

"Les Daniels: The Sardonic Vampire" (*Studies in Weird Fiction*, Spring 1989, Spring 1991). "Dennis Etchison and His Masters" (*Weird Tales*, Winter 2000/2001; *Necrofile*, Summer 1991). "Thomas Tryon: The Return of the Posthumous Collaboration" (*Necrofile*, Fall 1995). "Stephen King and God" (*Weird Tales*, Winter 1999/2000). "Peter Straub and the Blue Pencil" (*Weird Tales*, Winter 2000/2001). "Ramsey Campbell: Alone with a Master" (*Necrofile*, Spring 1993, Winter 1997; *Weird Tales*, Winter 1999/2000, Winter 2000/2001, Winter 2001-02; *Studies in Weird Fiction*, Spring 2005; *Dead Reckonings*, Spring 2007). "Clive Barker: Weird Fiction as Subversion" (*Necrofile*, Fall 1991). "David J. Schow: Zombies, Tapeworms, and Kamikaze Butterflies" (*Necrofile*, Summer 1994). "Donald R. Burleson: Enmeshed in the Bizarre" (*Necrofile*, Winter 1996, Spring 1997, Winter 1999). "Norman Partridge: Here to Stay" (*Worlds of Fantasy and Horror*, Spring 1995; *Weird Tales*, Winter 2001-02). "Thomas Harris: Lecter as Albatross" (*Weird Tales*, Winter 1999/2000). "Thomas Ligotti: The Long and the Short of It" (*Necrofile*, Spring 1994; *Studies in Weird Fiction*, Summer 2003). "Michael Cisco: Ligotti Redivivus?" (*Dead*

Reckonings, Fall 2007). "Sherry Austin: The Southern Ghost Story" (*Studies in Weird Fiction*, Summer 2003; *Dead Reckonings*, Spring 2007). "Shades of Edgar and Ambrose" (unpublished).

"The Charting of Horror Literature" (*Lovecraft Studies*, Fall 1981; *Necrofile*, Summer 1991; *Washington Post Book World*, 27 October 1991; *Studies in Weird Fiction*, Summer 1995). "Classics and Contemporaries" (*Studies in Weird Fiction*, Fall 1989; *Dark Man*, Winter 2004; *Necrofile*, Summer 1993, Fall 1995).

"Some Lovecraft Editions" (*Lovecraft Studies*, Spring 1982; *Crypt of Cthulhu*, Candlemas 1983; *Necrofile*, Fall 1995; *Lovecraft Studies*, Fall 1994). "The Cthulhu Mythos" (*Lovecraft Studies*, Spring 1990, Spring 1991; *Weird Tales*, Summer 2001; *Lovecraft Studies*, Spring 1994; *Weird Tales*, Summer 2002). "Lovecraft as a Character in Fiction" (*Crypt of Cthulhu*, Michaelmas 1984; *Lovecraft Studies*, Spring 1994, Fall 1985, Fall 1989; *Lovecraft Annual*, 2007; *Weird Tales*, Summer 2001). "Some Lovecraft Scholarship" (*Lovecraft Studies*, Fall 1980, Fall 1984, Fall 1990, Spring 1987, Fall 1993, Fall 1988; *Lovecraft Annual*, 2007).